The Philadelphia Negro

THE OXFORD W. E. B. DU BOIS

Henry Louis Gates, Jr., Editor

The Suppression of the African Slave-Trade to the United States of
America: 1638–1870
    Introduction: Saidiya Hartman

The Philadelphia Negro: A Social Study
    Introduction: Lawrence Bobo

The Souls of Black Folk
    Introduction: Arnold Rampersad

John Brown
    Introduction: Paul Finkelman

Africa, Its Geography, People and Products
Africa—Its Place in Modern History
    Introductions: Emmanuel Akyeampong

Black Reconstruction in America
    Introduction: David Levering Lewis

Black Folk: Then and Now
    Introduction: Wilson J. Moses

Dusk of Dawn
    Introduction: Kwame Anthony Appiah

The World and Africa
Color and Democracy: Colonies and Peace
    Introductions: Mahmood Mamdani and *Gerald Horne*

In Battle for Peace: The Story of My Eighty-third Birthday
    Introduction: Manning Marable

The Black Flame Trilogy: Book One
The Ordeal of Mansart
    Introduction: Brent Edwards
    Afterword: Mark Sanders

The Black Flame Trilogy: Book Two
Mansart Builds a School
Introduction: Brent Edwards
Afterword: Mark Sanders

The Black Flame Trilogy: Book Three
Worlds of Color
Introduction: Brent Edwards
Afterword: Mark Sanders

Autobiography of W. E. B. Du Bois
Introduction: Werner Sollors

The Quest of the Silver Fleece
Introduction: William L. Andrews

The Negro
Introduction: John K. Thornton

Darkwater: Voices from Within the Veil
Introduction: Evelyn Brooks Higginbotham

Gift of Black Folk: The Negroes in the Making of America
Introduction: Glenda Carpio

Dark Princess: A Romance
Introduction: Homi K. Bhabha

THE PHILADELPHIA NEGRO

A Social Study

W. E. B. Du Bois

Series Editor, Henry Louis Gates, Jr.

Introduction by Lawrence Bobo

OXFORD

UNIVERSITY PRESS

For Cornel West

OXFORD
UNIVERSITY PRESS

Oxford University Press, Inc., publishes works that further
Oxford University's objective of excellence in research,
scholarship, and education.

Oxford   New York
Auckland   Cape Town   Dar es Salaam   Hong Kong   Karachi
Kuala Lumpur   Madrid   Melbourne   Mexico City   Nairobi
New Delhi   Shanghai   Taipei   Toronto

With offices in
Argentina   Austria   Brazil   Chile   Czech Republic   France   Greece
Guatemala   Hungary   Italy   Japan   Poland   Portugal   Singapore
South Korea   Switzerland   Thailand   Turkey   Ukraine   Vietnam

Copyright © 2007 by Oxford University Press

Published by Oxford University Press, Inc.
198 Madison Avenue, New York, NY 10016
www.oup.com

Library of Congress Cataloging-in-Publication Data is available.

ISBN: 978-0-19-938370-2

Contents

MAPS

The Black Letters on the Sign: W. E. B. Du Bois and the Canon

"... the slave master had a direct interest in discrediting the personality of those he held as property. Every man who had a thousand dollars so invested had a thousand reasons for painting the black man as fit only for slavery. Having made him the companion of horses and mules, he naturally sought to justify himself by assuming that the negro was not much better than a mule. The holders of twenty hundred million dollars' worth of property in human chattels procured the means of influencing press, pulpit, and politician, and through these instrumentalities they belittled our virtues and magnified our vices, and have made us odious in the eyes of the world. Slavery had the power at one time to make and unmake Presidents, to construe the law, and dictate the policy, set the fashion in national manners and customs, interpret the Bible, and control the church; and, naturally enough, the old masters set themselves up as much too high as they set the manhood of the negro too low. Out of the depths of slavery has come this prejudice and this color line. It is broad enough and black enough to explain all the malign influences which assail the newly emancipated millions to-day.... The office of color in the color line is a very plain and subordinate one. It simply advertises the objects of oppression, insult, and persecution. It is not the maddening liquor, but the black letters on the sign telling the world where it may be had ... Slavery, stupidity, servility, poverty, dependence, are undesirable conditions. When these shall cease to be coupled with color, there will be no color line drawn."

—FREDERICK DOUGLASS, "The Color Line," 1881.

William Edward Burghardt Du Bois (1868–1963) was the most prolific and, arguably, the most influential African American writer of his generation. The novelist and poet James Weldon Johnson (1871–1938) once noted the no single work had informed the shape of the African American literary tradition, except perhaps *Uncle Tom's Cabin*, than had Du Bois's seminal collection of essays *The Souls of Black Folk* (1903). While trained as a sociologist at Berlin and as a historian at Harvard, Du Bois was fearless in the face of genre—even when some of the genres that he sought to embrace did not fully embrace him in return. Du Bois published twenty-two single-author works, twenty-one in his lifetime (his *Autobiography*, edited by his friend and literary executor, Herbert Aptheker, would not be published until

1968). A selection of his greatest works, *An ABC of Color: Selections from over a Half Century of the Writings of W. E. B. Du Bois*, appeared in 1963, the year he died. And while these books reflect a wide variety of genres—including three widely heralded and magisterial books of essays published in 1903, 1920, and 1940 (*The Souls of Black Folk, Darkwater: Voices from within the Veil*, and *Dusk of Dawn: An Essay toward an Autobiography of a Race Concept*), one biography, five novels, a pioneering sociological study of a black community, five books devoted to the history of Africa, three historical studies of African American people, among others—Du Bois was, in the end, an essayist, an essayist of the first order, one of the masters of that protean form that so attracted Du Bois's only true antecedent, Frederick Douglass (1818–1895) as well as Du Bois's heir in the history of the form, James Baldwin (1924–1987). (Baldwin, like Du Bois, would turn repeatedly to fiction, only to render the form as an essay.)

Du Bois, clearly, saw himself as a man of action, but a man of action who luxuriated within a verdant and fecund tropical rainforest of words. It is not Du Bois's intoxication with words that marks his place in the history of great black public intellectuals—persons of letters for whom words are a vehicle for political action and their own participation in political movements. After all, one need only recall Du Bois's predecessor, Frederick Douglass, or another of his disciples, Martin Luther King Jr. for models in the African American tradition of leaders for whom acting and speaking were so inextricably intertwined as to be virtually coterminous; no, the novelty of Du Bois's place in the black tradition is that he wrote himself to a power, rather than spoke himself to power. Both Douglass and King, for all their considerable literary talents, will be remembered always for the power of their oratory, a breathtaking power exhibited by both. Du Bois, on the other hand, was not a great orator; he wrote like he talked, and he talked like an extraordinarily well-educated late Anglo-American Victorian, just as James Weldon Johnson did; no deep "black" stentorian resonances are to be found in the public speaking voices of either of these two marvelous writers. Booker T. Washington (1856–1915) spoke in a similar public voice.

First and last, W. E. B. Du Bois was a writer, a writer deeply concerned and involved with politics, just as James Baldwin was; as much as they loved to write, Douglass and King were orators, figures fundamentally endowed with a genius for the spoken word. Even Du Bois's colleague, William Ferris, commented upon this anomaly in Du Bois's place in the tradition, at a time (1913) when he had published only five books: "Du Bois," Ferris wrote, "is one of the few men in history who was hurled on the throne of leadership by the dynamic force of the written word. He is one of the few writers who leaped to the front as a leader and became the head of a popular movement through impressing his personality upon men by means of a book" ("The African Abroad," 1913). Despite the fact that Du Bois by this time had published his Harvard doctoral dissertation in history, *The Suppression of the African Slave-Trade* (1896), his sociological study, *The Philadelphia Negro* (1899), *The Souls of Black Folk* (1903), the sole biography that he would publish, *John Brown* (1909), and his first of five novels, *The Quest of the Silver Fleece* (1911), Ferris attributed Du Bois's catapult to leadership to one book and one book alone, *The Souls of Black Folk*. Indeed, it is probably true that had Du Bois published this book alone, his place in the canon of African American literature would have been secure, if perhaps not as fascinating!

The Souls of Black Folk, in other words, is the one book that Du Bois wrote which most of us have read in its entirety. It is through *The Souls of Black Folk* that we center Du Bois's place in the literary canon; it is through *Souls* that we structure the arc of his seven decade career as a man of letters. There are many good reasons for the centrality of this magical book to Du Bois's literary career, but it is also the case that the other works that comprise Du Bois's canon deserve fresh attention as a whole. And it is for this reason that my colleagues and I have embarked upon this project with Oxford University Press to reprint Du Bois's single-authored texts, and make them available to a new generation of readers in a uniform edition. The only other attempt to do so—Herbert Aptheker's pioneering edition of Du Bois's complete works, published in 1973—is, unfortunately, long out of print.

The Souls of Black Folk is such a brilliant work that it merits all of the attention that it has been given in the century since it was published. In April 1903, a thirty-five-year-old scholar and budding political activist published a 265 page book subtitled "Essays and Sketches," consisting of thirteen essays and one short story, addressing a wide range of topics, including the story of the freed slaves during Reconstruction, the political ascendancy of Booker T. Washington, the sublimity of the spirituals, the death of Du Bois's only son Burghardt, and lynching. Hailed as a classic even by his contemporaries, the book has been republished in no fewer than 120 editions since 1903. In fact, it is something of a rite of passage for younger scholars and writers to publish their take on Du Bois's book in new editions aimed at the book's considerable classroom market.

Despite its fragmentary structure, the book's disparate parts contribute to the sense of a whole, like movements in a symphony. Each chapter is pointedly "bicultural," prefaced by both an excerpt from a white poet and a bar of what Du Bois names "The Sorrow Songs" ("some echo of haunting melody from the only American music which welled up from black souls in the dark past.") Du Bois's subject was, in no small part, the largely unarticulated beliefs and practices of American Negroes, who were impatient to burst out of the cotton fields and take their rightful place as Americans. As he saw it, African American culture in 1903 was at once vibrant and disjointed, rooted in an almost medieval agrarian past and yet fiercely restive. Born in the chaos of slavery, the culture had begun to generate a richly variegated body of plots, stories, melodies, and rhythms. In *The Souls of Black Folk*, Du Bois peered closely at the culture of his kind, and saw the face of black America. Actually, he saw two faces. "One ever feels his two-ness—an American, a Negro," Du Bois wrote. "Two souls, two thoughts, two unreconciled strivings; two warring ideals in one dark body, whose dogged strength alone keeps it from being torn asunder." He described this condition as "double consciousness," and his emphasis on a fractured psyche made *Souls* a harbinger of the modernist movement that would begin to flower a decade or so later in Europe and in America.

Scholars, including Arnold Rampersad, Werner Sollors, Dickson Bruce, and David Levering Lewis, have debated the origins of Du Bois's use of the concept of "double consciousness," but what's clear is that its roots are multiple, which is appropriate enough, just as it is clear that the source of one of Du Bois's other signal metaphors—"the problem of the twentieth-century is the problem of the color line"—came to him directly from Frederick Douglass's essay of that title. Du Bois had studied in Berlin during a Hegel revival, and Hegel, famously, had written on the relationship between master and bondsman, whereby each defines himself through the recognition of the other. But the concept comes up, too, in Emerson, who wrote in 1842 of the split between our reflective self, which wanders through the realm of ideas, and the active self, which dwells in the here and how, a tension that recurs throughout the Du Bois oeuvre: "The worst feature of this double consciousness is that the two lives, of the understanding and of the soul, which we lead, really show very little relation to each other."

Even closer to hand was the term's appearance in late-nineteenth-century psychology. The French psychologist, Alfred Binet, writing in his 1896 book, *On Double Consciousness*, discusses what he calls "bipartititon," or "the duplication of consciousness": "Each of the consciousnesses occupies a more narrow and more limited field than if there existed one single consciousness containing all the ideas of the subject." William James, who taught Du Bois at Harvard, talked about a "second personality" that characterized "the hypnotic trance." When Du Bois transposed this concept from the realm of the psyche to the social predicament of the American Negro, he did not leave it unchanged. But he shared with the psychologists the notion that double consciousness was essentially an affliction. "This American world," he complained, yields the Negro "no true self-consciousness, but only lets him see himself through the revelation of the other world. It is a peculiar sensation, this double-consciousness, this sense of always looking at one's self through the eyes of others, of measuring one's soul by the tape of a world that looks on in amused contempt and pity." Sadly, "the double life every American Negro must live, as a Negro and as an American," leads inevitably to "a painful self-consciousness, an almost morbid sense of personality and a moral hesitancy which is fatal to self-confidence." The result is "a double life, with double thoughts, double duties and double social classes," and worse, "double words and double ideas," which "tempt the mind to pretense or revolt, hypocrisy or to radicalism." Accordingly, Du Bois wanted to make the American Negro whole; and he believed that only desegregation and full equality could make this psychic integration possible.

And yet for subsequent generations of writers, what Du Bois cast as a problem was taken to be the defining condition of modernity itself. The diagnosis, one might say, outlasted the disease. Although Du Bois would publish twenty-two books, and thousands of essays and reviews, no work of his has done more to shape an African American literary history than *The Souls of Black Folk*, and no metaphor in this intricately layered book has proved more enduring than that of double consciousness, including Du Bois's other powerfully resonating metaphors, that of "the veil" that separates black America from white America, and his poignant revision of Frederick Douglass's metaphor of "the color line," which Du Bois employed in that oft-repeated sentence, "The problem of the twentieth-century is the problem of the color line"—certainly his most prophetic utterance of many.

Like all powerful metaphors, Du Bois's metaphor of double consciousness came to have a life of its own. For Carl Jung, who visited the United States in the heyday of the "separate but equal" doctrine, the shocking thing wasn't that black culture was not equal, the shocking thing was that is was not separate! "The naïve European," Jung wrote, "thinks of America as a white nation. It is not wholly white, if you please; it is partly colored," and this explained, Jung continued, "the slightly Negroid mannerisms of the American." "Since the Negro lives within your cities and even within your houses," Jung continued, "he also lives within your skin, subconsciously." It wasn't just that the Negro was an American, as Du Bois would note, again and again, but that the American was, inevitably and inescapably, a Negro. The bondsman and the slave find their identity in each other's gaze: "two-ness" wasn't just a black thing any longer. As James Baldwin would put it, "Each of us, helplessly and forever, contains the other—male in female, female in male, white in black, black in white."

Today, talk about the fragmentation of culture and consciousness is a commonplace. We know all about the vigorous intermixing of black culture and white, high culture and low—from the Jazz Age freneticism of what the scholar Ann Douglass calls "mongrel Manhattan" to Hip Hop's hegemony over American youth in the late-twentieth and early-twenty-first centuries. Du Bois yearned to make the American Negro one, and lamented that he was two. Today, the ideal of wholeness has largely been retired. And cultural multiplicity is no longer seen as the problem, but as a solution—a solution to the confines of identity itself. Double consciousness, once a disorder, is now the cure. Indeed, the only complaint we moderns have is that Du Bois was too cautious in his accounting. He'd conjured "two souls, two thoughts two unreconciled strivings." Just two, Dr. Du Bois, we are forced to ask today? Keep counting.

And, in a manner of speaking, Du Bois did keep counting, throughout the twenty two books that comprise the formal canon of his most cogent thinking. The hallmark of Du Bois's literary career is that he coined the metaphors of double-consciousness and the veil—reappropriating Frederick Douglass's seminal definition of the semi-permeable barrier that separates and defines black-white racial relations in America as "the color line"—to define the place of the African American within modernity. The paradox of his career, however, is that the older Du Bois became, the more deeply he immersed himself in the struggle for Pan-Africanism and decolonization against the European colonial powers, and an emergent postcolonial "African" or "Pan-Negro" social and political identity—culminating in his own life in his assumption of Ghanaian citizenship in 1963. And the "blacker" that his stand against colonialism became, the less "black," in a very real sense, his analysis of what he famously called "The Negro Problem" simultaneously became. The more "African" Du Bois became, in other words, the more cosmopolitan his analysis of the root causes of anti-black and -brown and -yellow racism and colonialism became, seeing the status of the American Negro as part and parcel of a larger problem of international economic domination, precisely in the same way that Frederick Douglass rightly saw the construction of the American color line as a function of, and a metaphor for, deeper, structural, economic relations—"not the maddening liquor, but the black letters on the sign telling the world where it may be had," as Douglass so thoughtfully put it. The Negro's being-in-the-world, we might say, became ever more complex for Du Bois the older he grew, especially as the Cold War heated up and the anti-colonial movement took root throughout Africa and the Third World.

Ironically, Du Bois himself foretold this trajectory in a letter he wrote in 1896, reflecting on the import of his years as a graduate student at Friedrich Wilhelm University in Berlin: "Of the greatest importance was the opportunity which my *Wanderjahre* [wander years] in Europe gave of looking at the world as a man and not simply from a narrow racial and provincial outlook." How does the greatest black intellectual in the twentieth century—"America's most conspicuously educated Negro," as Werner Sollors puts it in his introduction to Du Bois's *Autobiography* in this series—make the rhetorical turn from defining the Negro American as a metaphor for modernity, at the turn of the century, to defining the Negro—at mid-century—as a metonym of a much larger historical pattern of social deviance and social dominance that had long been central to the fabric of world order, to the fabric of European and American domination of such a vast portion of the world of color? If, in other words, the Negro is America's metaphor for Du Bois in 1903, how does America's history of black-white relations become the metaphor of a nefarious pattern of economic exploitation and dominance by the end of Du Bois's life, in 1963? Make no mistake about it: either through hubris or an uncanny degree of empathy, or a mixture of both, throughout his life, W. E. B. Du Bois saw his most naked and public ambitions as well as his most private and intimate anxieties as representative of those of his countrymen, the American Negro people. Nevertheless, as he grew older, the closer he approached the end of his life, Du Bois saw the American Negro as a metaphor for class relations within the wider world order.

In order to help a new generation of readers to understand the arc of this trajectory in Du Bois's thinking, and because such a large part of this major thinker's oeuvre remains unread, Oxford University Press and I decided to publish in a uniform edition the twenty-one books that make up Du Bois's canon and invited a group of scholars to reconsider their importance as works of literature, history, sociology, and political philosophy. With the publication of this series, Du Bois's books are once again in print, with new introductions that analyze the shape of his career as a writer, scholar, and activist.

Reading the canon of Du Bois's work in chronological order, a certain allegorical pattern emerges, as Saidiya Hartman suggests in her introduction to *The Suppression of the African Slave-Trade*. Du Bois certainly responded immediately and directly to large historical events through fierce and biting essays that spoke adamantly and passionately to the occasion. But he also used the themes of his books to speak to the larger import of those events in sometimes highly mediated ways. His first book, for example, proffers as its thesis, as Hartman puts it, a certain paradox: "the slave trade flourished under the guise of its suppression," functioning legally for twenty years following the Compromise of the Federal Convention of 1787 and "illegally for another half century." Moreover, Du Bois tackles this topic at precisely the point in American history when Jim Crow segregation is becoming formalized through American law in the 1890s, culminating in 1896 (the year of the publication of his first book) with the infamous *Plessy v. Ferguson* "separate but equal" decision of the Supreme Court—exactly twenty years following the end of Reconstruction. Three years later, as Lawrence Bobo shows, Du Bois publishes *The Philadelphia Negro* in part to detail the effects of the "separate but equal" doctrine on the black community.

Similarly, Du Bois's biography of John Brown appeared in the same year as a pioneering band of blacks and whites joined together to form the National Association for the Advancement of Colored People (NAACP), the organization that would plot the demise of legal segregation through what would come to be called the Civil Rights Movement, culminating in its victory over de jure segregation in the Supreme Court's *Brown v. Board of Education* decision, which effectively reversed the *Plessy* decision, and in the Civil Rights Act of 1964 and the Voting Rights Act of 1965. John Brown, for Du Bois, would remain the emblem of this movement.

Likewise, Du Bois's first novel, *The Quest of the Silver Fleece*, published just two years following his biography of John Brown, served as a subtle critique both of an unreflective assimilationist ideology of the early NAACP through its advocacy of "a black-owned farming cooperative in the heart of the deep South," as William Andrews puts it, just as it surely serves as a critique of Booker T. Washington's apparently radical notion that economic development for the newly freed slaves could very well insure political equality in a manner both irresistible and inevitable, an argument, mind you, frequently made today under vastly different circumstances about the role of capitalism in Du Bois's beloved Communist China.

Du Bois registers his critique of the primitivism of the Harlem Renaissance in *The Gift of Black Folk*, as Glenda Carpio cogently argues, by walking "a tightrope between a patriotic embrace of an America in which African American culture has become an inextricable part and an exhortation of the rebellion and struggle out of which that culture arose." In response to the voyeurism and faddishness of Renaissance Harlem, Du Bois harshly reminds us that culture is a form of labor, too, a commodity infinitely exploitable, and that the size of America's unprecedented middle class can be traced directly to its slave past: "It was black labor that established the modern world commerce which began first as a commerce in the bodies of the slaves themselves and was the primary cause of the prosperity of the first great commercial cities of our day"—cities such as New York, the heart of the cultural movement that some black intellectuals passionately argued could very well augur the end of racial segregation throughout American society, or at least segregation between equal classes across the color line.

Paul Finkelman, in his introduction to *John Brown*, quotes the book's first line: "The mystic spell of Africa is and ever was over all America." If that is true, it was also most certainly the case for Du Bois himself, as John Thornton, Emmanuel Akyeampong, Wilson J. Moses, and Mahmood Mamdani show us in their introductions to five books that Du Bois published about Africa, in 1915, 1930, 1939, and 1947. Africa, too, was a recurring metaphor in the Duboisian canon, serving variously as an allegory of the intellectual potential of persons of African descent; as John K. Thornton puts it, "What counted was that African history had movement and Africans were seen as historical actors and not simply as stolid recipients of foreign techniques and knowledge," carefully "integrating ancient Egypt into *The Negro* as part of that race's history, without having to go to the extreme measure of asserting that somehow the Egyptians were biologically identical to Africans from further south or west." The history of African civilization, in other words, was Du Bois's ultimate argument for the equality of Americans white and black.

Similarly, establishing his scholarly mastery of the literature of African history also served Du Bois well against ideological rivals such as Marcus Garvey, who attacked Du Bois for being "too assimilated," and "not black enough." Du Bois's various studies of African history also served as a collective text for the revolutions being formulated in the forties and fifties by Pan-African nationalists such as Kwame Nkrumah and Jomo Kenyatta, who would lead their nations to independence against the European colonial powers. Du Bois was writing for them, first as an exemplar of the American Negro, the supposed vanguard of the African peoples, and later, and more humbly, as a follower of the African's lead. As Wilson J. Moses notes, Du Bois once wrote that "American Negroes of former generations had always calculated that when Africa was ready for freedom, American Negroes would be ready to lead them. But the event was quite opposite." In fact, writing in 1925 in an essay entitled "Worlds of Color," an important essay reprinted as "The Negro Mind Reaches Out" in Alain Locke's germinal anthology *The New Negro* (as Brent Staples points out in his introduction to Du Bois's fifth novel, *Worlds of Color*, published just two years before he died), Du Bois had declared that "led by American Negroes, the Negroes of the world are reaching out hands toward each other to know, to sympathize, to inquire." And, indeed, Du Bois himself confessed at his ninety-first birthday celebration in Beijing, as Moses notes, that "once I thought of you Africans as children, whom we educated Afro-Americans would lead to liberty. I was wrong." Nevertheless, Du Bois's various books on Africa, as well as his role as an early theorist and organizer of the several Pan-African Congresses between 1900 and 1945, increasingly underscored his role throughout the first half of the century as the father of Pan-Africanism, precisely as his presence and authority within such civil rights organizations as the NAACP began to wane.

Du Bois's ultimate allegory, however, is to be found in *The Black Flame Trilogy*, the three novels that Du Bois published just before repatriating to Ghana, in 1957, 1959, and 1961. The trilogy is the ultimate allegory in Du Bois's canon because, as Brent Edwards shows us in his introductions to the novels, it is a fictional representation of the trajectory of Du Bois's career, complete with several characters who stand for aspects of Du Bois's personality and professional life, including Sebastian Doyle, who "not only studied the Negro problem, he embodied the Negro problem. It was bone of his bone and flesh of his flesh. It made his world and filled his thought," as well as Professor James Burghardt, trained as a historian at Yale and who taught, as Du Bois had, at Atlanta University, and who believed that "the Negro problem must no longer be regarded emotionally. It must be faced scientifically and solved by long, accurate and intense investigation. Moreover, it was not one problem, but a series of problems interrelated with the social problems of the world. He laid down a program of study covering a hundred years."

But even more important than these allegorical representations of himself, or early, emerging versions of himself, Du Bois used *The Black Flame* novels to underscore the economic foundation of anti-black racism. As Edwards notes, "The real villain," for Du Bois, "is not an individual Southern aristocrat or racist white laborer, but instead capitalism itself, especially in the corporate form that has dominated the economic and social landscape of the world for more than a century," which underscores Du Bois's ideological transformations from an integrationist of sorts to an emergent mode of African American, first, and then Pan-Africanist cultural nationalism, through socialism, landing squarely in the embrace of the Communist Party just two years before his death.

Despite this evolution in ideology, Mansart, Du Bois's protagonist in the triology, ends his series of intellectual transformations precisely where Du Bois himself began as he embarked upon his career as a professor just a year after receiving his Harvard PhD in 1895. In language strikingly familiar to his statement that the time he spent in Berlin enabled him to look "at the world as a man and not simply from a narrow racial and provincial outlook," Du Bois tells us in the final volume of the trilogy that Mansart "began to have a conception of the world as one unified dwelling place. He was escaping from his racial provincialism. He began to think of himself as part of humanity and not simply as an American Negro over against a white world." For all of his ideological permutations and combinations, in other words, W. E. B. Du Bois—formidable and intimidating ideologue and ferocious foe of racism and colonialism—quite probably never veered very far from the path that he charted for himself as a student, when he fell so deeply in love with the written word that he found himself, inevitably and inescapably, drawn into a life-long love affair with language, an affair of the heart to which he remained faithful throughout an eighty-year career as a student and scholar, from the time he entered Fisk University in 1885 to his death as the Editor of "The Encyclopedia Africana" in 1963. And now, with the publication of the Oxford W. E. B. Du Bois, a new generation of readers can experience his passion for words, Du Bois's love of language purely for its own sake, as well as a conduit for advocacy and debate about the topic that consumed him his entire professional life, the freedom and the dignity of the Negro.

✦ ✦ ✦

The first volume in the series is Du Bois's revised dissertation, and his first publication, entitled *The Suppression of the African Slave-Trade to the United States of America*. A model of contemporary historiography that favored empiricism over universal proclamation, *Suppression* reveals the government's slow movement toward abolition as what the literary scholar Saidiya Hartman calls in her introduction "a litany of failures, missed opportunities, and belated acts," in which a market sensibility took precedence over moral outrage, the combination of which led to the continuation of the Atlantic slave trade to the United States until it was no longer economically beneficial.

Lawrence D. Bobo, one of the foremost urban sociologists working today, argues in his introduction to *The Philadelphia Negro: A Social Study* (1899), that Du Bois was not only an innovative historian, as Hartman properly identifies him, but also a groundbreaking social scientist whose study of Philadelphia displays "the most rigorous and sophisticated social science of its era by employing a systematic community social survey method." Although it was well reviewed at its publication—which coincided with the advent of the field of urban sociology—*The Philadelphia Negro* did not become the subject of significant scholarly attention until the 1940s, and has become, since then, a model for the study of black communities.

The distinguished scholar of black literature and culture, Arnold Rampersad, calls *The Souls of Black Folk* "possibly the most important book ever penned by a black American"—an assertion with which I heartily agree. A composite of various essays, subjects, and tones, *Souls* is both very much of its time, and timeless. It contributed to the American lexicon two terms that have been crucial for more than a century in understanding the African American experience: the "color line" and "double consciousness." For Rampersad, that we have learned so much about both issues since Du Bois first wrote, but have not made either irrelevant to our twenty-first century experience is, in a real way, our scholarly blessing and burden.

Abandoning the scholarly and empirical prowess so vividly on display in *Suppression* and *Philadelphia Negro*, Du Bois meant his biography of John Brown to be not a work of scholarship but rather one "about activism, social consciousness, and the politics of race," argues the legal historian Paul Finkelman in his introduction to *John Brown* (1909). The only biography in Du Bois's vast oeuvre, the book grew out of his participation in the Niagara Movement's meeting at Harpers Ferry in 1906 (an event the centenary of which I had the good fortune to celebrate), and—with the myth of John Brown taking precedence at times over the facts of his life—marks Du Bois's transition from professional academic to full-time activist.

There was not a genre that Du Bois did not attempt in his long career as a writer. After the John Brown biography, Du Bois turned to the novel. In his introduction to *The Quest of the Silver Fleece* (1911), Du Bois's first novel, the literary historian William Andrews looks beyond the Victorian diction and sometimes purple prose to see a work that is the "most noteworthy Great *African* American Novel of its time." *Quest* is a "Southern problem" novel writ large on a national and even mythic canvas, and one that is ultimately radical in its endorsement of strong black womanhood, equality and comradeship between the sexes, and, in Du Bois's words, "a bold regeneration of the land," which for Andrews means a hitherto-unheard-of proposed economic alliance between poor blacks and poor whites in the rural South.

Moving from a national to an international canvas, Du Bois published *The Negro* (1915), more than half of which is devoted to African history. In this way, John K. Thornton argues in his introduction, Du Bois firmly grounded for an educated lay readership the history of African Americans in the history of Africa. Drawing on the emergent disciplines of anthropology and linguistics and including, even sketchily, accounts of what would now be called Diaspora communities in the Caribbean and Latin America, *The Negro* is important in that it presents, in Thornton's words, "African history [as having] movement and Africans . . . as historical actors and not simply as stolid recipients of foreign techniques and knowledge."

Dismissed by some critics and lauded by others as the "militant sequel" to *The Souls of Black Folk*, *Darkwater: Voices from Within the Veil* (1920) appeared in a world radically transformed by the ravages of World War I. In addition to these international upheavals, and to the "crossing and re-crossing" of the color line engendered by the war, the historian Evelyn Brooks Higginbotham tells us in her magisterial introduction to this volume that blacks at home in the U.S. faced major changes and relocations. The Great Migration was in full swing when Du Bois wrote *Darkwater*, and the change in the center of black life is reflected in the change of scene to the North, a far, urban cry from the rural setting of most of *Souls*. If *Souls* saw the American landscape in black and white, Higginbotham finds that *Darkwater* is like chiaroscuro, the painting technique developed by artists of the Italian Renaissance: "Du Bois, like these Renaissance painters, moves beyond the contouring line of the two-dimensional and introduces depth and volume through his representation of color—through his contrast and shading of white and various darker peoples." Higginbotham goes on to say that "Du Bois continually undermines the fixedness of racial boundaries and subverts the visual coherence of racial identities to an extent that cannot be accidental." The Du Bois who emerges in *Darkwater* is increasingly a citizen of the world, whose gaze may be fixed on his native land but whose understanding of that land is inextricably bound to the larger world around him.

The Gift of Black Folk (1924) had an odd genesis as part of the Knights of Columbus's series on "Racial Contributions to the United States." In her introduction, Glenda Carpio notes that Du Bois's celebration of black accomplishments did not turn away from the bitter history of slavery that spawned them: these were not gifts always rendered freely, Carpio points out. Though less substantial than many of his other works, and primarily a catalog of black accomplishments across different fields, *Gift* is notable for the complex ways Du Bois links African American contributions in the arenas of labor, war, church and social life, fraternal organizations, and especially the arts, by both women and men, to the bitter history of slavery.

Homi Bhabha sees *The Dark Princess* (1928) as another odd work, a "Bollywood-style Bildungsroman," in which the race-man Mathew Towns teams with Kautilya, the "dark Princess of the Tibetan Kingdom of Bwodpur," to combat international colonialism in the struggle for global emancipation. But in this somewhat messy novel, which renders the international scenes with a Zolaesque precision, Bhabha detects a serious philosophical purpose: to elaborate on the "rule of juxtaposition" (first defined in *Darkwater*), which "creat[es] an enforced intimacy, an antagonistic proximity, that defines the color-line as it runs across the uncivil society of the nation."

Du Bois moved from the esoteric exercise of *The Dark Princess* to a more accessible form for his next publications, *Africa, Its Geography, People and Products*, and

Africa—Its Place in Modern History (1930). Published as Blue Books for the educated lay reader by E. Haldeman-Julius of Girard, Kansas, the two volumes are,
for the African historian and African Emmanuel Akyeampong, remarkably useful and trenchant. The first volume is a relatively straightforward analysis of
Africa's geography, climate, and environment, and the impact these physical factors have had on the development of African civilization. The second volume,
which seeks "to place the continent at the very center of ancient and modern history," is more polemical, with economics cited as the central motivating factor
behind modern colonialism and the slave trade.

The anger that was evident in the second of the two Blue Books came to full
flower in *Black Reconstruction* (1935), a sweeping corrective to contemporary his-
tories of the Reconstruction era, which (white) historians had shaped with the
view of blacks as inadequate to the task of capitalizing on the freedom that emancipation had given them, and black history as "separate, unequal, and irrelevant,"
in the words of Du Bois's Pulitzer Prize-winning biographer, David Levering
Lewis. Inspired by *The Gift of Black Folk* and from Du Bois's own withdrawal of his
article on the Negro in the *Encyclopedia Britannica*, which demanded an excision of
"a paragraph on the positive Reconstruction role of black people," *Black Reconstruction* provided original interpretations of black labor's relation to industrial
wealth and, most radically, of the *agency* of black people in determining their lives
after the Civil War. In his introduction, Lewis contends, rightly, that the books
marks a progression in Du Bois's thought, from his early faith in academic knowledge and empiricism as a cure-all for the nation's problems, to the "more effective
strategy of militant journalism informed by uncompromising principles and vital
social science."

Wilson J. Moses presents *Black Folk Then and Now* (1939) as a midway point
between *The Negro* (1915) and *The World and Africa* (1946). While all three volumes
sought to address the entire span of black history, the special mandate of *Black
Folk* was to "correct the omissions, misinterpretations, and deliberate lies that
[Du Bois] detected in previous depictions of the Negro's past." In this volume, he
went back to the original Herodotus and provided his own translation, which led
him to affirm, with other black writers, that the Egyptians were, indeed, black (a
conclusion he had resisted earlier in his career). But even in this work, with such
evidence of his intellectual background on display, Du Bois is less interested in
intellectual history than in social history. Even as he tracks developments in the
United States, the Caribbean, Latin America, Du Bois neglects the Pan-African
movement and his own involvement in it.

Du Bois's autobiography, on the other hand, shows a man far more interested
in writing about his intellectual journey than his personal or social life. The
philosopher Anthony Appiah, in his subtle introduction to *Dusk of Dawn*, tells us
that Du Bois was famous for nothing so much as his accomplishments as an intellectual and a writer; his institutional affiliations (with the NAACP, with the Pan-
African Congress) were fleeting, and his internal contradictions were vexing (he
was both a committed Socialist and a committed elitist). The aim of this account,
like so much of Du Bois's other work, was to address the problem of the color line,
and he presents his distinguished, singular life as emblematic of that problem,
and himself as hopeful for its solution.

At the time he rejoined the NAACP to oversee its global programming in 1944, Du Bois was prepared to dedicate himself completely to the abolition of colonialism, which he saw as the driving force behind all global conflicts. What was remarkable about his anti-colonialism was, as Gerald Horne rightly points out in his introduction to *Color and Democracy* (1946), Du Bois's inclusion of Asia, and particularly Japan, in the discussion. As fertile ground for colonial enterprises, Asia yielded still more evidence of the "inviolate link between color and democracy."

Color continued to preoccupy Du Bois, and in *The World and Africa*, he attempted to correct the ways in which color (black) had affected history. Mahmood Mamdani tells us in his introduction that Du Bois's motivation in writing this somewhat hasty volume was to tell the story of "those left out of recorded history" and to challenge, in effect, "an entire tradition of history-writing . . . modern European historiography." Du Bois was aware that this was just a beginning to a much larger project, to connect the history of Europe that dominated the academic discipline of history to events and progress in the world at large, including Africa.

In Battle for Peace: The Story of My 83rd Birthday features an embattled Du Bois enduring prosecution by (and eventually winning acquittal from) the federal government whose indictment of him as an unregistered agent for the Soviet Union was, according to Manning Marable, a trumped-up means by which to discredit the great black leader and frighten his fellow supporters of international peace into silence. It worked, at least in part: while Du Bois drew support from many international associations, the NAACP essentially abandoned him. Ten years later, in 1961, Du Bois would permanently leave the United States for Ghana.

Brent Hayes Edwards in his introduction calls the *Black Flame* trilogy of novels Du Bois's most neglected work. Written in the last few years of life, *The Ordeal of Mansart* (1957), *Mansart Builds a School* (1959), and *Worlds of Color* (1961) follow the life of Manuel Mansart from his birth in 1876 (the last year of Reconstruction) to his death in 1956, a period which spans his rise from a noted but provincial Southern educator to a self-educating citizen of the world of color. With its alternating apocalyptic and utopian tone, its depiction of real historical figures and events, and its thoughtful "animation of economic history and especially labor history," the *Black Flame* trilogy offers, according to Edwards, "the clearest articulation of Du Bois's perspective at the end of his life, and his reflections on an unparalleled career that had stretched from Reconstruction through the Cold War."

Du Bois was a largely marginalized figure in the last decade of his life, and his work published at that time, most notably the *Black Flame* trilogy, went into the critical and cultural abyss. Mark Sanders suggests that the "invisibility" of the trilogy, then and now, can be explained by an evolution in literary "taste" in the 1950s, wrought by new trends in literary criticism and magazine culture, the emergence of the Civil Rights Movement, and Du Bois's own development. Even if we have rejected in many real ways the ethos of the 1950s, for Sanders, our prescriptions for taste still owe a great deal to that decade.

Werner Sollors finds "four major narrative strains" in the posthumously published *Autobiography of W. E. B. Du Bois* (1968): the personal (including "startling" sexual revelations from the famously staid Du Bois); the academic, editorial, and organizational, in which his work is fully explored, and the political is always personal even while science and reason are held to be the solution to the race problem; the Communist, first as interested onlooker and then as Party member; and the elderly, in which an old man takes stock of contemporary youth culture with something of a jaundiced eye. Sollors suggests that far from being disjointed, the various strands of the *Autobiography* are united by Du Bois's ongoing quest for recognition. I would argue that there is nothing pathetic in this quest; it is simply the desire for respect from the society (black and white) that Du Bois spent his long life trying to understand.

Henry Louis Gates, Jr.
Cambridge, Massachusetts
December 7, 2006

Introduction

Lawrence Bobo, Stanford University

The Philadelphia Negro: A Social Study, first published by W. E. B. Du Bois in 1899, was then and remains to this day a magnificent scholarly achievement. It documents in systematic and meticulous detail the living circumstances at the close of the nineteenth century of the largest black population outside the South. In its use of a systematic method of community social survey, it shows the most rigorous and sophisticated empirical social science of its era. In an understated but ultimately clear and convincing manner, *The Philadelphia Negro* advances both a framework for studying the black community and a powerful sociological—not biological, nor psychological, nor otherwise victim-blaming account— of the factors causing black disadvantage. And it shows how careful social research might be linked fruitfully to the ambition of reform and advocacy for social justice on behalf of a stigmatized people.

These many qualities notwithstanding, Du Bois's work waited many years before rising to a place of serious and enduring recognition among that of other social scientists. To be sure, the popular press initially reacted favorably to the work, with positive reviews appearing in such publications as *The Nation* and *The Literary Digest*. Some academic outlets also praised his work at the time. For example, the *Yale Review* opined that *The Philadelphia Negro* was "not merely a credit to its author and to the race of which he is a member; it is a credit to American scholarship, and a distinct and valuable addition to the world's stock of knowledge concerning an important and obscure theme. It is the sort of book of which we have too few, and of which it is impossible that one should have too many." Likewise, black outlets responded favorably, with the *A.M.E. Church Review* writing: "At last we have a volume of the highest scientific value on a sociological subject and written by a Negro."[1]

With the clarity of hindsight, one can now comfortably say that by any objective assessment the book constitutes a landmark in sociological research. The research for and writing of *The Philadelphia Negro* was undertaken and completed at a point when the fledgling discipline of sociology was just taking shape. The first sociology department in the United States was established at the University of Chicago in 1892, followed in 1894 by Columbia University. Émile Durkheim (1858–1917), considered the creator of sociology, published his best-known work, *Suicide*, in 1897. Thus the publication of an ambitious, carefully crafted, and meticulously documented study of urban social life should arguably have drawn significant scholarly attention and made a lasting imprint on the young discipline. Despite being a major sociological work written at the very dawn of the discipline, Du Bois's work was not reviewed in the *American Journal of Sociology*, founded at the University of Chicago in 1895. And even though many of those who came to found the leading sociology departments were aware of Du Bois's work and sometimes cited it, in no way was *The Philadelphia Negro* given proper recognition by social scientists of the day.[2]

Today, scholars spanning the fields of sociology, history, political science, anthropology, education, urban studies, and even philosophy are bringing *The Philadelphia Negro* to a place of prominence that it should have garnered long ago. The resurrection of Du Bois began, in many respects, with the training at the University of Chicago of black sociologists such as Charles S. Johnson and E. Franklin Frazier. Then with the publication of two other landmark investigations, the Swedish economist Gunnar Myrdal's massive two-volume *An American Dilemma: The Negro Problem and Modern Democracy* in 1944 and St. Clair Drake and Horace Cayton's *Black Metropolis* in 1945, a trend began to usher back into view the type of work at which Du Bois had been the pioneer. Myrdal, for example, applauded Du Bois's interpretive and analytic framework, writing that it "stands out even today as a most valuable contribution" for its seeing the conditions of blacks as rooted in systematic social sources. Such a perspective was quite at odds with prevailing modes of thinking when Du Bois wrote. Myrdal also suggested that *The Philadelphia Negro* was the best model for the study of black communities, though he bemoaned that it "is now all but forgotten." It is rare to find a sociological study that has grown markedly in influence a century after its initial publication. But this is precisely the case for W. E. B. Du Bois's magisterial community survey *The Philadelphia Negro*.

In June 1896, Du Bois received an invitation for a one-year appointment from Charles C. Harrison, then the acting provost of the University of Pennsylvania. Harrison's invitation had come at the behest of Susan Wharton, a member of the powerful Wharton family and an activist social reformer deeply involved with the College Settlement Association. Like many progressive elite Philadelphians of the time, Harrison and Wharton were concerned about the growing black presence in Philadelphia and about the array of ills that blacks were seen as bringing with them. Hence the charge to Du Bois from Harrison was to "know precisely how this class of people live; what occupations they follow; from what occupations they are excluded; how many of their children go to school; and to ascertain every fact which will throw light on this social problem."[3]

Du Bois entered the enterprise as a committed empirical social scientist. He was openly critical of the sweeping generalizations and the sort of grand theorizing then common in the emerging field of sociology. He preferred an inductive approach. He brought to the task a zeal for gathering facts and assembling data that had been cultivated during his years at Harvard under Albert Bushnell Hart and even move so during his studies in Berlin under the German political economist Gustav Schmoller. But he did not pursue science for science alone. Du Bois saw his scholarly work as intimately linked to the task of reform and social change so desperately needed by blacks in his time.

The young sociologist's ambition was to provide a comprehensive analysis of Philadelphia's Seventh Ward, then the largest concentration of blacks in the city. Du Bois and his wife lived in the Seventh Ward during Du Bois's fifteen months of research and writing. Du Bois developed six interview and enumeration protocols. He did so with enormous care and sophistication, almost certainly drawing on the model of Charles Booth's *Life and Labor of the People in London* (1889) and the *Hull House Maps and Papers* (1895), which focused on Chicago.[4] Du Bois conducted several thousand interviews himself, which he tabulated to produce numerous tables, counts, and figures reported in the book. When appropriate, he even systematically compared his own data to that from the London studies and other sources in order to bring real comparative authority to his work. Du Bois's topical range spanned from careful assessments of the work, pay, and regular expenditures of blacks to the charting of their health and well-being, and it reached all the way to considering matters of schooling, civic groups, community and family life, and social activities.

Contrary to the presumptions of his sponsors and to received wisdom of the time, Du Bois eschewed interpreting the hardship in which most black Philadelphians lived as a reflection of basic black capabilities.[5] Instead Du Bois crafted a historically grounded analysis of blacks, whose circumstances had clear social or environmental roots. His framework stresses the interplay of six factors: (1) a history of enslavement, servitude, and oppression; (2) demographic composition effects such as the disproportion of women to men; (3) the economic positioning and intensifying competition with free whites both native born and newly arrived from Europe; (4) racial prejudice and discrimination; (5) the resources, internal structure, dynamics, and leadership of the black community itself; and (6) the moral agency and capacity for black self-determination. Of these, Du Bois clearly placed the economy as a central factor shaping the circumstances and life chances of black Philadelphians.[6] And there in particular he documented how blacks were closed out of and sometimes consciously pushed out of various lines of work.

The Philadelphia Negro is a work of enduring importance for several reasons beyond the extraordinary detail of the conditions of the black community that Du Bois documented or the general sociological interpretation that he fashioned. Du Bois also identified a series of conditions and processes of enduring relevance to the evolving status of blacks in America. First, a signal feature of Du Bois's approach was to highlight the internal heterogeneity and complexity of the black population itself. He put forward what may be the first effort to describe empirically a class structure within the black community. He even identified a sort of "submerged tenth" that has similarities to more contemporary discussions of an "urban underclass" or new ghetto poverty. In time, that attention to class stratification within the black population only grew in relevance to social-scientific examinations of the black experience.

Second, in *The Philadelphia Negro* Du Bois provided an early focus on black families and the challenges they faced. Indeed, Du Bois pointed to "the early breaking up of family life" among blacks as a serious problem. Equally telling of the power of Du Bois's insight is the analytical stance that he took on this problem. He traced the fragility of black families (a) to the traumatic and oppressive slave experience, (b) to economic marginalization, and (c) to an at best indifferent and often deliberately unwelcoming social climate of opinion among whites. Consistent with the temper of the times and his own Victorian inclinations, Du Bois called upon blacks to establish stronger, healthier family ties and norms. Placing the family at the center of examinations of the status of black Americans is, of course, a thread that runs from Du Bois to E. Franklin Frazier to the controversial Moynihan Report in the 1960s to the more recent sociological scholarship of William Julius Wilson and his discussion of *The Truly Disadvantaged* (1987) and *When Work Disappears* (1996).[7]

Third, Du Bois focused much attention on the problem of black involvement with crime. After documenting disproportionate black involvement with crime, Du Bois wrote: "There is a widespread feeling that something is wrong with a race that is responsible for so much crime, and that strong remedies are called for ... Indeed, to the minds of many, this is the real Negro problem." He was the first scholar to venture the hypothesis that much black involvement in crime might be traceable to a reaction against patterns of exclusion, marginalization, and stigmatization facing African Americans.

Fourth, Du Bois compared the black condition to that of white European immigrants then also coming to Philadelphia in large numbers. The conditions that he documented heavily influenced later sociological examinations of the "immigrant analogy" hypothesis. Du Bois's attention to occupational exclusion, segregation, and prejudice influenced the work of the eminent sociologist Stanley Lieberson and his definitive work on the subject, *A Piece of the Pie: Blacks and White Immigrants since 1880* (1980).

Scholars today draw on *The Philadelphia Negro* for many purposes, and by doing so they acknowledge and reinforce the remarkable breadth and quality of the work that Du Bois did more than a century ago. Contemporary scholars look to Du Bois for his attention to and discussions of the role of the black middle class.[8] He was an early voice identifying the powerful role of the church in black social life and community affairs.[9] Du Bois put forward one of the most complete and holistic treatments of racial prejudice as a factor shaping the status of blacks in American society.[10] He had a posture of both sympathetic engagement and also strong normative judgment regarding the behavior of the poorest and most disadvantaged segments of the black population.[11] Du Bois's ideas in *The Philadelphia Negro* continue to influence how political scientists approach issues of black political discourse and involvement.[12] And of course, many of those who seek to develop new general theories of race and society owe a clear debt to *The Philadelphia Negro*.[13]

The Philadelphia Negro is an even more remarkable achievement when judged in the light of two other considerations. Du Bois carried out the research without the sort of financial resources, institutional support, or social standing that Charles Booth or Hull House researchers had. Moreover, Du Bois managed to craft an approach and an argument that rose above much of the worst of the racial ideology reigning at the time. It is important to recall that Du Bois wrote during a period when even the main currents of progressive elite white opinion saw blacks, on the whole, as a lesser race best suited to a limited range of roles in society.[14] Thus Du Bois did not garner an appointment at a major mainstream university after producing a scientific work of monumental scale and cutting-edge quality. Indeed, so powerful was the ideology of segregation in this era that the idea of getting an appointment at a mainstream university had scarcely occurred to Du Bois himself, who assumed instead that he would join one of the black universities. He did, however, hope and argue for support and collaboration with major white scholars and institutions in a future program of research on African Americans.[15] Though he himself did much important work from his subsequent perch at Atlanta University, Du Bois did so with little support from his white peers.

We should never forget that in addition to his achievements as an organizer and political activist, and in addition to his achievements of a more literary tilt, such as the immortal *The Souls of Black Folk* (1903), W. E. B. Du Bois spent many years as an empirical social scientist. He is, unambiguously, one of the pioneers of systematic survey research and community studies. He is thus a founding figure in the discipline of sociology. With *The Philadelphia Negro* in particular, Du Bois made a profoundly inspiring and lasting contribution to knowledge and to the way in which many scholars do their work.

NOTES

1. Michael B. Katz and Thomas J. Sugrue, "The Context of *The Philadelphia Negro*: The City, the Settlement House Movement, and the Rise of the Social Sciences," in *W. E. B. Du Bois, Race, and the City: "The Philadelphia Negro" and Its Legacy*, edited by Michael B. Katz and Thomas J. Sugrue (Philadelphia: University of Pennsylvania Press, 1998), p. 26.

2. Elliot Rudwick, "Note on a Forgotten Black Sociologist: W. E. B. Du Bois and the Sociological Profession," *American Sociologist* 4 (1969): 303–306; Dan S. Green and Edwin D. Driver, "W. E. B. Du Bois: A Case in the Sociology of Sociological Negation," *Phylon* 37 (1976): 308–333; and R. Charles Key, "Society and Sociology: The Dynamics of Black Sociological Negation," *Phylon* 39 (1978): 35–48.

3. Quoted in David Levering Lewis, *W. E. B. Du Bois: Biography of a Race, 1868–1919* (New York: Holt, 1993), p. 188.

4. Martin Bulmer, "W.E. B. Du Bois as a Social Investigator: *The Philadelphia Negro*, 1899," in *The Social Survey in Historical Perspective, 1880–1940*, edited by Martin Bulmer, Kevin Bales, and Kathryn Kish Sklar (New York: Cambridge University Press, 1991), pp. 170–188.

5. Mia Bay, "'The World Was Thinking Wrong about Race': *The Philadelphia Negro* and Nineteenth-Century Science," in *W. E. B. Du Bois, Race, and the City: "The Philadelphia Negro" and Its Legacy*, edited by Michael B. Katz and Thomas J. Sugrue (Philadelphia: University of Pennsylvania Press, 1998), pp. 41–60.

6. Jacqueline Jones, "'Lifework' and Its Limits: The Problem of Labor in *The Philadelphia Negro*," in *W. E. B. Du Bois, Race, and the City: "The Philadelphia Negro" and Its Legacy*, edited by Michael B. Katz and Thomas J. Sugrue (Philadelphia: University of Pennsylvania Press, 1998), and Alice O'Connor, *Poverty Knowledge: Social Science, Social Policy, and the Poor in Twentieth-Century U.S. History* (Princeton, N.J.: Princeton University Press, 2001).

7. See essays in Obie Clayton, Ronald B. Mincy, and David Blankenhorn, editors, *Black Fathers in Contemporary American Society: Strengths, Weaknesses, and Strategies for Change* (New York: Russell Sage Foundation, 2003).

8. Mary Patillo, "Black Middle Class Neighborhoods," *Annual Review of Sociology* 31 (2005): 305–329.
9. Omar M. McRoberts, *Streets of Glory: Church and Community in a Black Urban Neighborhood* (Chicago: University of Chicago Press, 2003).
10. Lawrence D. Bobo, "Reclaiming a Du Boisian Perspective on Racial Attitudes," *Annals of the American Academy of Political and Social Science* 568 (2000): 186–202.
11. Alford A. Young, *The Minds of Marginalized Black Men: Making Sense of Mobility, Opportunity, and Future Life Chances* (Princeton, N.J.: Princeton University Press, 2004).
12. Michael C. Dawson, *Black Visions: The Roots of Contemporary African-American Political Ideologies* (Chicago: University of Chicago Press, 2001); Melissa Victoria Harris-Lacewell, *Barbershops, Bibles, and BET: Everyday Talk and Black Political Thought* (Princeton, N.J.: Princeton University Press, 2004).
13. Howard Winant, "Race and Race Theory," *Annual Review of Sociology* 26 (2000): 169–185, and Tukufu Zuberi, *Thicker Than Blood: How Racial Statistics Lie* (Minneapolis: University of Minnesota Press, 2001).
14. George M. Fredrickson, *The Black Image in the White Mind: The Debate on Afro-American Character and Destiny, 1817–1914* (New York: Harper and Row, 1971), and Jonathan H. Turner and Royce Singleton, "A Theory of Ethnic Oppression: Toward a Reintegration of Cultural and Structural Concepts in Ethnic Relations Theory," *Social Forces* 56 (1978): 1001–1018.
15. W. E. B. Du Bois, "The Study of Negro Problems," *Annals of the American Academy of Political and Social Science* 11 (1898): 1–23.

The Philadelphia Negro

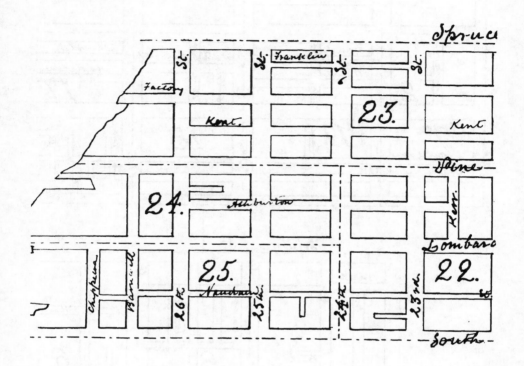

SEVENTH WARD

[*Taken from publications of the American Academy, No. 150, July 2, 1895.*
The large figures refer to voting precincts.]

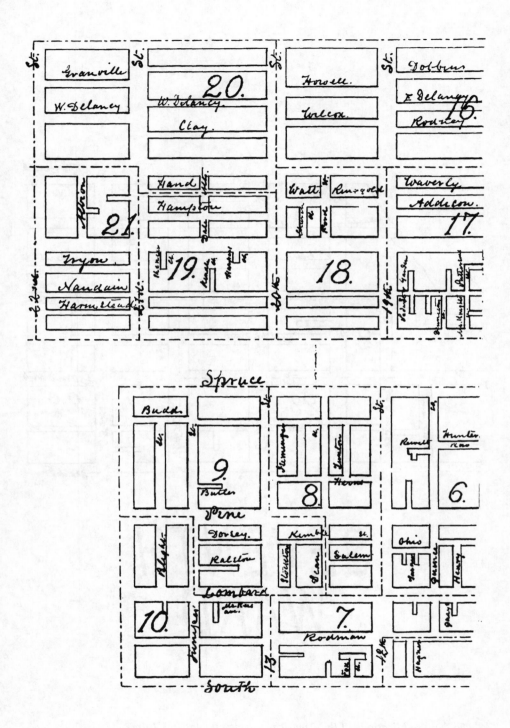

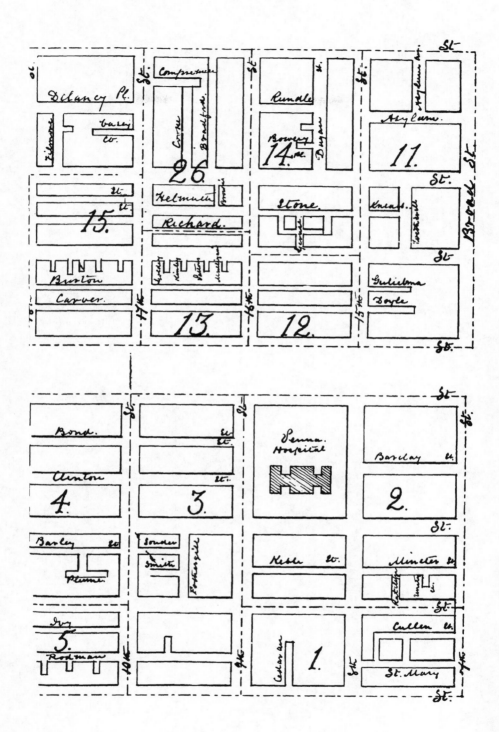

CHAPTER I

The Scope of This Study

1. General Aim—This study seeks to present the results of an inquiry undertaken by the University of Pennsylvania into the condition of the forty thousand or more people of Negro blood now living in the city of Philadelphia. This inquiry extended over a period of fifteen months and sought to ascertain something of the geographical distribution of this race, their occupations and daily life, their homes, their organizations, and, above all, their relation to their million white fellow-citizens. The final design of the work is to lay before the public such a body of information as may be a safe guide for all efforts toward the solution of the many Negro problems of a great American city.

2. The Methods of Inquiry—The investigation began August the first, 1896, and, saving two months, continued until December the thirty-first, 1897. The work commenced with a house-to-house canvass of the Seventh Ward. This long narrow ward, extending from South Seventh street to the Schuylkill River and from Spruce street to South street, is an historic centre of Negro population, and contains to-day a fifth of all the Negroes in this city.[1] It was therefore thought best to make an intensive study of conditions in this district, and afterward to supplement and correct this information by general observation and inquiry in other parts of the city.

Six schedules were used among the nine thousand Negroes of this ward; a family schedule with the usual questions as to the number of members, their age and sex, their conjugal condition and birthplace, their ability to read and write, their occupation and earnings, etc.; an individual schedule with similar inquiries; a home schedule with questions as to the number of rooms, the rent, the lodgers, the conveniences, etc.; a street schedule to collect data as to the various small streets and alleys, and an institution schedule for organizations and institutions; finally a slight variation of the individual schedule was used for house-servants living at their places of employment.[2]

This study of the central district of Negro settlement furnished a key to the situation in the city; in the other wards therefore a general survey was taken to note any striking differences of condition, to ascertain the general distribution of these people, and to collect information and statistics as to organizations, property, crime and pauperism, political activity, and the like. This general inquiry, while it lacked precise methods of measurement in most cases, served nevertheless to correct the errors and illustrate the meaning of the statistical material obtained in the house-to-house canvass.

Throughout the study such official statistics and historical matter as seemed reliable were used, and experienced persons, both white and colored, were freely consulted.

3. The Credibility of the Results—The best available methods of sociological research are at present so liable to inaccuracies that the careful student discloses the results of individual research with diffidence; he knows that they are liable to error from the seemingly ineradicable faults of the statistical method, to even greater error from the methods of general observation, and, above all, he must ever tremble lest some personal bias, some moral conviction or some unconscious trend of thought due to previous training, has to a degree distorted the picture in his view. Convictions on all great matters of human interest one must have to a greater or less degree, and they will enter to some extent into the most cold-blooded scientific research as a disturbing factor.

Nevertheless here are social problems before us demanding careful study, questions awaiting satisfactory answers. We must study, we must investigate, we must attempt to solve; and the utmost that the world can demand is, not lack of human interest and moral conviction, but rather the heart-quality of fairness, and an earnest desire for the truth despite its possible unpleasantness.

In a house-to-house investigation there are, outside the attitude of the investigator, many sources of error: misapprehension, vagueness and forgetfulness, and deliberate deception on the part of the persons questioned, greatly vitiate the value of the answers; on the other hand, conclusions formed by the best trained and most conscientious students on the basis of general observation and inquiry are really inductions from but a few of the multitudinous facts of social life, and these may easily fall far short of being essential or typical.

The use of both of these methods which has been attempted in this study may perhaps have corrected to some extent the errors of each. Again, whatever personal equation is to be allowed for in the whole study is one unvarying quantity, since the work was done by one investigator, and the varying judgments of a score of census-takers was thus avoided.[3]

Despite all drawbacks and difficulties, however, the main results of the inquiry seem credible. They agree, to a large extent, with general public opinion, and in other respects they seem either logically explicable or in accord with historical precedents. They are therefore presented to the public, not as complete and without error, but as possessing on the whole enough reliable matter to serve as the scientific basis of further study, and of practical reform.

NOTES

1. I shall throughout this study use the term "Negro," to designate all persons of Negro descent, although the appellation is to some extent illogical. I shall, moreover, capitalize the word, because I believe that eight million Americans are entitled to a capital letter.
2. See Appendix A for form of schedules used.
3. The appended study of domestic service was done by Miss Isabel Eaton, Fellow of the College Settlements Association. Outside of this the work was done by the one investigator.

CHAPTER II

◆

The Problem

4. The Negro Problems of Philadelphia—In Philadelphia, as elsewhere in the United States, the existence of certain peculiar social problems affecting the Negro people are plainly manifest. Here is a large group of people—perhaps forty-five thousand, a city within a city—who do not form an integral part of the larger social group. This in itself is not altogether unusual; there are other unassimilated groups: Jews, Italians, even Americans; and yet in the case of the Negroes the segregation is more conspicuous, more patent to the eye, and so intertwined with a long historic evolution, with peculiarly pressing social problems of poverty, ignorance, crime and labor, that the Negro problem far surpasses in scientific interest and social gravity most of the other race or class questions.

The student of these questions must first ask, What is the real condition of this group of human beings? Of whom is it composed, what sub-groups and classes exist, what sort of individuals are being considered? Further, the student must clearly recognize that a complete study must not confine itself to the group, but must specially notice the environment; the physical environment of city, sections and houses, the far mightier social environment—the surrounding world of custom, wish, whim, and thought which envelops this group and powerfully influences its social development.

Nor does the clear recognition of the field of investigation simplify the work of actual study; it rather increases it, by revealing lines of inquiry far broader in scope than first thought suggests. To the average Philadelphian the whole Negro question reduces itself to a study of certain slum districts. His mind reverts to Seventh and Lombard streets and to Twelfth and Kater streets of to-day, or to St. Mary's in the past. Continued and widely known charitable work in these sections makes the problem of poverty familiar to him; bold and daring crime too often traced to these centres has called his attention to a problem of crime, while the scores of loafers, idlers and prostitutes who crowd the sidewalks here night and day remind him of a problem of work.

All this is true—all these problems are there and of threatening intricacy; unfortunately, however, the interest of the ordinary man of affairs is apt to stop here. Crime, poverty and idleness affect his interests unfavorably and he would have them stopped; he looks upon these slums and slum characters as unpleasant things which should in some way be removed for the best interests of all. The social student agrees with him so far, but must point out that the removal of unpleasant features from our complicated modern life is a delicate operation requiring knowledge and skill; that a slum is not a simple fact, it is a symptom and that to know the removable causes of the Negro slums of Philadelphia requires a study that takes one far beyond the slum districts. For few Philadelphians realize how the Negro population has grown and spread. There was a time in the memory of living men when a small district near Sixth and Lombard streets comprehended the great mass of the Negro population of the city. This is no longer so. Very early the stream of the black population started northward, but the increased foreign immigration of 1830 and later turned it back. It started south also but was checked by poor houses and worse police protection. Finally with gathered momentum the emigration from the slums started west, rolling on slowly and surely, taking Lombard street as its main thoroughfare, gaining early foothold in West Philadelphia, and turning at the Schuylkill River north and south to the newer portions of the city.

Thus to-day the Negroes are scattered in every ward of the city, and the great mass of them live far from the whilom centre of colored settlement. What, then, of this great mass of the population? Manifestly they form a class with social problems of their own—the problems of the Thirtieth Ward differ from the problems of the Fifth, as the black inhabitants differ. In the former ward we have represented the rank and file of Negro working-people; laborers and servants, porters and waiters. This is at present the great middle class of Negroes feeding the slums on the one hand and the upper class on the other. Here are social questions and conditions which must receive the most careful attention and patient interpretation.

Not even here, however, can the social investigator stop. He knows that every group has its upper class; it may be numerically small and socially of little weight, and yet its study is necessary to the comprehension of the whole—it forms the realized ideal of the group, and as it is true that a nation must to some extent be measured by its slums, it is also true that it can only be understood and finally judged by its upper class.

The best class of Philadelphia Negroes, though sometimes forgotten or ignored in discussing the Negro problems, is nevertheless known to many Philadelphians. Scattered throughout the better parts of the Seventh Ward, and on Twelfth, lower Seventeenth and Nineteenth streets, and here and there in the residence wards of the northern, southern, and western sections of the city is a class of caterers, clerks, teachers, professional men, small merchants, etc., who constitute the aristocracy of the Negroes. Many are well-to-do, some are wealthy, all are fairly educated, and some liberally trained. Here too are social problems—differing from those of the other classes, and differing too from those of the whites of a corresponding grade, because of the peculiar social environment in which the whole race finds itself, which the whole race feels, but which touches this highest class at most points and tells upon them most decisively.

Many are the misapprehensions and misstatements as to the social environment of Negroes in a great Northern city. Sometimes it is said, here they are free; they have the same chance as the Irishman, the Italian, or the Swede; at other times it is said, the environment is such that it is really more oppressive than the situation in Southern cities. The student must ignore both of these extreme statements and seek to extract from a complicated mass of facts the tangible evidence of a social atmosphere surrounding Negroes, which differs from that surrounding most whites; of a different mental attitude, moral standard, and economic judgment shown toward Negroes than toward most other folk. That such a difference exists and can now and then plainly be seen, few deny; but just how far it goes and how large a factor it is in the Negro problems, nothing but careful study and measurement can reveal.

Such then are the phenomena of social condition and environment which this study proposes to describe, analyze, and, so far as possible, interpret.

5. Plan of Presentment—The study as taken up here divides itself roughly into four parts: the history of the Negro people in the city, their present condition considered as individuals, their condition as an organized social group, and their physical and social environment. To the history of the Negro but two chapters are devoted—a brief sketch—although the subject is worthy of more extended study than the character of this essay permitted.

Six chapters consider the general condition of the Negroes: their number, age and sex, conjugal condition, and birthplace; what degree of education they have obtained, and how they earn a living. All these subjects are treated usually for the Seventh Ward somewhat minutely, then more generally for the city, and finally such historical material is adduced as is available for comparison.

Three chapters are devoted to the group life of the Negro; this includes a study of the family, of property, and of organizations of all sorts. It also takes up such phenomena of social maladjustment and individual depravity as crime, pauperism and alcoholism.

One chapter is devoted to the difficult question of environment, both physical and social, one to certain results of the contact of the white and black races, one to Negro suffrage, and a word of general advice in the line of social reform is added.

CHAPTER III

◆

The Negro in Philadelphia, 1638–1820

6. General Survey—Few States present better opportunities for the continuous study of a group of Negroes than Pennsylvania. The Negroes were brought here early, were held as slaves along with many white serfs. They became the subjects of a protracted abolition controversy, and were finally emancipated by gradual process. Although, for the most part, in a low and degraded condition, and thrown upon their own resources in competition with white labor, they were nevertheless so inspired by their new freedom and so guided by able leaders that for something like forty years they made commendable progress. Meantime, however, the immigration of foreign laborers began, the new economic era of manufacturing was manifest in the land, and a national movement for the abolition of slavery had its inception. The lack of skilled Negro laborers for the factories, the continual stream of Southern fugitives and rural freedmen into the city, the intense race antipathy of the Irish and others, together with intensified prejudice of whites who did not approve of agitation against slavery—all this served to check the development of the Negro, to increase crime and pauperism, and at one period resulted in riot, violence, and bloodshed, which drove many Negroes from the city.

Economic adjustment and the enforcement of law finally allayed this excitement, and another period of material prosperity and advance among the Negroes followed. Then came the inpouring of the newly emancipated blacks from the South and the economic struggle of the artisans to maintain wages, which brought on a crisis in the city, manifested again by idleness, crime and pauperism.

Thus we see that twice the Philadelphia Negro has, with a fair measure of success, begun an interesting social development, and twice through the migration of barbarians a dark age has settled on his age of revival. These same phenomena would have marked the advance of many other elements of our population if they had been as definitely isolated into one indivisible group. No differences of social condition allowed any Negro to escape from the group, although such escape was continually the rule among Irish, Germans, and other whites.

7. The Transplanting of the Negro, 1638–1760—The Dutch, and possibly the Swedes, had already planted slavery on the Delaware when Penn and the Quakers arrived in 1682.[1] One of Penn's first acts was tacitly to recognize the serfdom of Negroes by a provision of the Free Society of Traders that they should serve fourteen years and then become serfs—a provision which he himself and all the others soon violated.[2]

Certain German settlers who came soon after Penn, and who may or may not have been active members of the Society of Friends, protested sturdily against slavery in 1688, but the Quakers found the matter too "weighty."[3] Five years later the radical seceders under Kieth made the existence of slavery a part of their attack on the society. Nevertheless the institution of slavery in the colony continued to grow, and the number of blacks in Philadelphia so increased that as early as 1693 we find an order of the Council against the "tumultuous gatherings of the negroes of the towne of philadelphia, on the first dayes of the weeke."[4]

In 1696 the Friends began a cautious dealing with the subject, which in the course of a century led to the abolition of slavery. This growth of moral sentiment was slow but unwaveringly progressive, and far in advance of contemporary thought in civilized lands. At first the Friends sought merely to regulate slavery in a general way and prevent its undue growth. They therefore suggested in the Yearly Meeting of 1696, and for some time thereafter, that since traders "have flocked in amongst us and . . . increased and multiplied negroes amongst us," members ought not to encourage the further importation of slaves, as there were enough for all purposes. In 1711 a more active discouragement of the slave trade was suggested, and in 1716 the Yearly Meeting intimated that even the buying of imported slaves might not be the best policy, although the Meeting hastened to call this "caution, not censure."

By 1719 the Meeting was certain that their members ought not to engage in the slave trade, and in 1730 they declared the buying of slaves imported by others to be "disagreeable." At this milestone they lingered thirty years for breath and courage, for the Meeting had evidently distanced many of its more conservative members. In 1743 the question of importing slaves, or buying imported slaves, was made a disciplinary query, and in 1754, spurred by the crusade of Say, Woolman and Benezet, offending members were disciplined. In the important gathering of 1758 the same golden rule was laid down as that with which the Germans, seventy years previous, had taunted them, and the institution of slavery was categorically condemned.[5] Here they rested until 1775, when, after a struggle of eighty-seven years, they decreed the exclusion of slaveholders from fellowship in the Society.

While in the councils of the State Church the freedom of Negroes was thus evolving, the legal status of Negroes of Pennsylvania was being laid. Four bills were introduced in 1700: one regulating slave marriages was lost; the other three were passed, but the Act for the Trial of Negroes—a harsh measure providing death, castration and whipping for punishments, and forbidding the meeting together of more than four Negroes—was afterward disallowed by the Queen in Council. The remaining acts became laws, and provided for a small duty on imported slaves and the regulation of trade with slaves and servants.[6]

In 1706 another act for the trial of Negroes was passed and allowed. It differed but slightly from the Act of 1700; it provided that Negroes should be tried for crimes by two justices of the peace and a jury of six freeholders; robbery and rape were punished by branding and exportation, homicide by death, and stealing by whipping;[7] the meeting of Negroes without permission was prohibited. Between this time and 1760 statutes were passed regulating the sale of liquor to slaves and the use of firearms by them; and also the general regulative Act of 1726, "for the Better Regulation of Negroes in this Province." This act was especially for the punishment of crime, the suppression of pauperism, the prevention of intermarriage, and the like—that is, for regulating the social and economic status of Negroes, free and enslaved.[8]

Meantime the number of Negroes in the colony continued to increase; by 1720 there were between 2500 and 5000 Negroes in Pennsylvania; they rapidly increased until there were a large number by 1750—some say 11,000 or more—when they decreased by war and sale, so that the census of 1790 found 10,274 in the State.[9]

The slave duties form a pretty good indication of the increase of Negro population.[10] The duty in 1700 was from 6s. to 20s. This was increased, and in 1712, owing to the large importations and the turbulent actions of Negroes in neighboring States, a prohibitive duty of £20 was laid.[11] England, however, who was on the eve of signing the Assiento with Spain, soon disallowed this act and the duty was reduced to £5. The influx of Negroes after the English had signed the huge slave contract with Spain was so large that the Act of 1726 laid a restrictive duty of £10. For reasons not apparent, but possibly connected with fluctuations in the value of the currency, this duty was reduced to £2 in 1729, and seems to have remained at that figure until 1761.

The £10 duty was restored in 1761, and probably helped much to prevent importation, especially when we remember the work of the Quakers at this period. In 1773 a prohibitive duty of £20 was laid, and the Act of 1780 finally prohibited importation. After 1760 it is probable that the efforts of the Quakers to get rid of their slaves made the export slave trade much larger than the importation.

Very early in the history of the colony the presence of unpaid slaves for life greatly disturbed the economic condition of free laborers. While most of the white laborers were indentured servants the competition was not so much felt; when they became free laborers, however, and were joined by other laborers, the cry against slave competition was soon raised. The particular grievance was the hiring out of slave mechanics by masters; in 1708 the free white mechanics protested to the Legislature against this custom,[12] and this was one of the causes of the Act of 1712 in all probability. When by 1722 the number of slaves had further increased, the whites again protested against the "employment of blacks," apparently including both free and slave. The Legislature endorsed this protest and declared that the custom of employing black laborers and mechanics was "dangerous and injurious to the republic."[13] Consequently the Act of 1726 declared the hiring of their time by Negro slaves to be illegal, and sought to restrict emancipation on the ground that "free negroes are an idle and slothful people," and easily become public burdens.[14]

As to the condition of the Negroes themselves we catch only glimpses here and there. Considering the times, the system of slavery was not harsh and the slaves received fair attention. There appears, however, to have been much trouble with them on account of stealing, some drunkenness and general disorder. The preamble of the Act of 1726 declares that "it too often happens that Negroes commit felonies and other heinous crimes," and that much pauperism arises from emancipation. This act facilitated punishment of such crimes by providing indemnification for a master if his slave suffered capital punishment. They were declared to be often "tumultuous" in 1693, to be found "cursing, gaming, swearing, and committing many other disorders" in 1732; in 1738 and 1741 they were also called "disorderly" in city ordinances.[15]

In general, we see among the slaves at this time the low condition of morals which we should expect in a barbarous people forced to labor in a strange land.

8. Emancipation, 1760–1780—The years 1750–1760 mark the culmination of the slave system in Pennsylvania and the beginning of its decline. By that time most shrewd observers saw that the institution was an economic failure, and were consequently more disposed than formerly to listen to the earnest representations of the great antislavery agitators of that period. There were, to be sure, strong vested interests still to be fought. When the £10 duty act of 1761 was pending, the slave merchants of the city, including many respectable names, vigorously protested; "ever desirous to extend the Trade of this Province," they declared that they had "seen for some time past the many inconveniencys the Inhabitants have suffered for want of Labourers and Artificers," and had consequently "for some time encouraged the importation of Negroes." They prayed at the very least for delay in passing this restrictive measure. After debate and altercation with the governor the measure finally passed, indicating renewed strength and determination on the part of the abolition party.[16]

Meantime voluntary emancipation increased. Sandiford emancipated his slaves in 1733, and there were by 1790 in Philadelphia about one thousand black freedmen. A school for these and others was started in 1770 at the instance of Benezet, and had at first twenty-two children in attendance.[17] The war brought a broader and kindlier feeling toward the Negroes; before its end the Quakers had ordered manumission,[18] and several attempts were made to prohibit slavery by statute. Finally, in 1780, the Act for the Gradual Abolition of Slavery was passed.[19] This act, beginning with a strong condemnation of slavery, provided that no child thereafter born in Pennsylvania should be a slave. The children of slaves born after 1780 were to be bond-servants until twenty-eight years of age—that is, beginning with the year 1808 there was to be a series of emancipations. Side by side with this growth of emancipation sentiment went an increase in the custom of hiring out Negro slaves and servants, which increased the old competition with the whites. The slaves were owned in small lots, especially in Philadelphia, one or two to a family, and were used either as house servants or artisans. As a result they were encouraged to learn trades and seem to have had the larger share of the ordinary trades of the city in their hands. Many of the slaves in the better families became well-known characters—as Alice, who for forty years took the tolls at Dunk's Ferry; Virgil Warder, who once belonged to Thomas Penn, and Robert Venable, a man of some intelligence.[20]

9. The Rise of the Freedman, 1780–1820—A careful study of the process and effect of emancipation in the different States of the Union would throw much light on our national experiment and its ensuing problems. Especially is this true of the experiment in Pennsylvania; to be sure, emancipation here was gradual and the number emancipated small in comparison with the population, and yet the main facts are similar: the freeing of ignorant slaves and giving them a chance, almost unaided from without, to make a way in the world. The first result was wide-spread poverty and idleness. This was followed, as the number of freedmen increased, by a rush to the city. Between 1790 and 1800 the Negro population of Philadelphia County increased from 2489 to 6880, or 176 per cent, against an increase of 43 per cent among the whites. The first result of this contact with city life was to stimulate the talented and aspiring freedmen; and this was the easier because the freedman had in Philadelphia at that time a secure economic foothold; he performed all kinds of domestic service, all common labor and much of the skilled labor. The group being thus secure in its daily bread needed only leadership to make some advance in general culture and social effectiveness. Some sporadic cases of talent occur, as Derham, the Negro physician, whom Dr. Benjamin Rush, in 1788, found "very learned."[21] Especially, however, to be noted are Richard Allen,[22] a former slave of the Chew family, and Absalom Jones,[23] a Delaware Negro. These two were real leaders and actually succeeded to a remarkable degree in organizing the freedmen for group action. Both had bought their own freedom and that of their families by hiring their time—Allen being a blacksmith by trade, and Jones also having a trade. When, in 1792, the terrible epidemic drove Philadelphians away so quickly that many did not remain to bury the dead, Jones and Allen quietly took the work in hand, spending some of their own funds and doing so well that they were publicly commended by Mayor Clarkson in 1794.[24]

The great work of these men, however, lay among their own race and arose from religious difficulties. As in other colonies, the process by which the Negro slaves learned the English tongue and were converted to Christianity is not clear. The subject of the moral instruction of slaves had early troubled Penn and he had urged Friends to provide meetings for them.[25] The newly organized Methodists soon attracted a number of the more intelligent, though the masses seem at the end of the last century not to have been church-goers or Christians to any considerable extent. The small number that went to church were wont to worship at St. George's, Fourth and Vine; for years both free Negroes and slaves worshiped here and were made welcome. Soon, however, the church began to be alarmed at the increase in its black communicants which the immigration from the country was bringing, and attempted to force them into the gallery. The crisis came one Sunday morning during prayer when Jones and Allen, with a crowd of followers, refused to worship except in their accustomed places, and finally left the church in a body.[26]

This band immediately met together and on April 12, 1787, formed a curious sort of ethical and beneficial brotherhood called the Free African Society. How great a step this was, we of to-day scarcely realize; we must remind ourselves that it was the first wavering step of a people toward organized social life. This society was more than a mere club: Jones and Allen were its leaders and recognized chief officers; a certain parental discipline was exercised over its members and mutual financial aid given. The preamble of the articles of association says: "Whereas, Absalom Jones and Richard Allen, two men of the African Race, who for their religious life and conversation, have obtained a good report among men, these persons from a love to the people of their own complexion whom they beheld with sorrow, because of their irreligious and uncivilized state, often communed together upon this painful and important subject in order to form some kind of religious body; but there being too few to be found under the like concern, and those who were, differed in their religious sentiments; with these circumstances they labored for some time, till it was proposed after a serious communication of sentiments that a society should be formed without regard to religious tenets, provided the persons lived an orderly and sober life, in order to support one another in sickness, and for the benefit of their widows and fatherless children."[27]

The society met first at private houses, then at the Friends' Negro school house. For a time they leaned toward Quakerism; each month three monitors were appointed to have oversight over the members; loose marriage customs were attacked by condemning cohabitation, expelling offenders and providing a simple Quaker-like marriage ceremony. A fifteen-minute pause for silent prayer opened the meetings. As the representative body of the free Negroes of the city, this society opened communication with free Negroes in Boston, Newport and other places. The Negro Union of Newport, R. I., proposed in 1788 a general exodus to Africa, but the Free African Society soberly replied: "With regard to the emigration to Africa you mention we have at present but little to communicate on that head, apprehending every pious man is a good citizen of the whole world." The society co-operated with the Abolition Society in studying the condition of the free blacks in 1790. At all times they seem to have taken good care of their sick and dead and helped the widows and orphans to some extent. Their methods of relief were simple: they agreed "for the benefit of each other to advance one-shilling in silver Pennsylvania currency a month; and after one year's subscription, from the dole hereof then to hand forth to the needy of the Society if any should require, the sum of three shillings and nine pence per week of the said money; provided the necessity is not brought on them by their own imprudence." In 1790 the society had £42 9s. 1d. on deposit in the Bank of North America, and had applied for a grant of the Potter's Field to be set aside as a burial ground for them, in a petition signed by Dr. Rush, Tench Coxe and others.

It was, however, becoming clearer and clearer to the leaders that only a strong religious bond could keep this untrained group together. They would probably have become a sort of institutional church at first if the question of religious denomination had been settled among them; but it had not been, and for about six years the question was still pending. The tentative experiment in Quakerism had failed, being ill suited to the low condition of the rank and file of the society. Both Jones and Allen believed that Methodism was best suited to the needs of the Negro, but the majority of the society, still nursing the memory of St. George's, inclined toward the Episcopal church. Here came the parting of the ways: Jones was a slow introspective man, with a thirst for knowledge, with high aspirations for his people; Allen was a shrewd, quick, popular leader, positive and dogged and yet far-seeing in his knowledge of Negro character. Jones therefore acquiesced in the judgment of the majority, served and led them conscientiously and worthily, and eventually became the first Negro rector in the Episcopal church of America. About 1790 Allen and a few followers withdrew from the Free African Society, formed an independent Methodist church which first worshiped in his blacksmith's shop on Sixth near Lombard. Eventually this leader became the founder and first bishop of the African Methodist Episcopal Church of America—an organization which now has 500,000 members, and is by long odds the vastest and most remarkable product of American Negro civilization.[28]

Jones and the Free African Society took immediate steps to secure a church; a lot was bought at the corner of Fifth and Adelphi streets in February, 1792, and by strenuous effort a church was erected and dedicated on the seventeenth of July, 1794. This was the first Negro church in America, and known as the First African Church of St. Thomas; in the vestibule of the church was written: "The people that walked in darkness have seen a great light." Bethel Church was erected by Allen and his followers in 1796, the same year that a similar movement in New York established the Zion Methodist Church. In 1794, too, the Methodists of St. George's, viewing with some chagrin the widespread withdrawal of Negroes from their body, established a mission at Camperdown, in the northeastern part of the city, which eventually became the present Zoar Church.

The general outlook for the Negroes at this period was encouraging, notwithstanding the low condition of the masses of the race. In 1788 Pennsylvania amended the Act of 1780, so as to prevent the internal and foreign slave trade, and correct kidnapping and other abuses that had arisen.[29] The convention which adopted the Constitution of 1790 had, in spite of opposition in the convention, refused to insert the word "white" in the qualifications for voters, and thus gave the right of suffrage to free Negro property holders; a right which they held, and, in most counties of the State, exercised until 1837.[30] The general conference of Abolition Societies, held in Philadelphia in 1794, started an agitation which, when reinforced by the news of the Haytian revolt, resulted in the national statute of 1794, forbidding the export slave trade.[31] In 1799 and 1800 Absalom Jones led the Negroes to address a petition to the Legislature, praying for immediate abolition of slavery, and to Congress against the fugitive slave law, and asking prospective emancipation for all Negroes. This latter petition was presented by Congressman Waln, and created an uproar in the House of Representatives; it was charged that the petition was instigated by the Haytian revolutionists and finally the Negroes were censured for certain parts of the petition.[32]

The condition of the Negroes of the city in the last decade of the eighteenth and the first two decades of the nineteenth century, although without doubt bad, slowly improved; an insurance society, in 1796, took the beneficial features of the old Free African Society. Some small essays were made in business, mostly in small street stands, near the wharves; and many were in the trades of all kinds. Between 1800 and 1810 the city Negro population continued to increase, so that at the latter date there were 100,688 whites and 10,522 blacks in the city, the Negroes thus forming the largest per cent of the population of the city that they have ever attained. The free Negroes also began to increase from the effect of the abolition law. The school established in 1770 continued, and was endowed by bequests from whites and Negroes. It had 414 pupils by 1813. In this same year there were six Negro churches and eleven benevolent societies. When the war broke out many Philadelphia Negroes were engaged on land and sea. Among these was James Forten—a fine character, expressive of the best Negro development of the time. Born in 1766, and educated by Benezet, he "was a gentleman by nature, easy in manner and able in intercourse; popular as a man of trade or gentleman of the pave, and well received by the gentry of lighter shade."[33] For years he conducted a sail-making trade, employing both whites and Negroes. In 1814 he, Jones, Allen and others were asked, in the midst of the alarm felt at the approach of the British, to raise colored troops. A meeting was called and 2500 volunteers secured, or three-fourths of the adult male population; they marched to Gray's Ferry and threw up fortifications. A battalion for service in the field was formed, but the war closed before they reached the front.[34]

The Negroes at this time held about $250,000 of city property, and on the whole showed great progress since 1780. At the same time there were many evidences of the effects of slavery. The first set of men emancipated by law were freed in 1808, and probably many entitled to freedom were held longer than the law allowed or sold out of the State. As late as 1794 some Quakers still held slaves, and the papers of the day commonly contain such advertisements, as:

"To be Sold for want of Employ, For a term of years, a smart active Negro boy, fifteen years of age. Enquire at Robert McGee's board yard, Vine street wharf."[35]

NOTES

1. Cf. Scharf-Westcott's "History of Philadelphia," I, 65, 76. DuBois' "Slave Trade," p. 24.
2. Hazard's "Annals," 553. Thomas' "Attitude of Friends Toward Slavery," 266.
3. There is some controversy as to whether these Germans were actually Friends or not; the weight of testimony seems to be that they were. See, however, Thomas as above, p. 267, and Appendix. "Pennsylvania Magazine," IV, 28–31; The *Critic*, August 27, 1897. DuBois' "Slave Trade," p. 20, 203. For copy of protest, see published fac-simile and Appendix of Thomas. For further proceedings of Quakers, see Thomas and DuBois, *passim*.
4. "Colonial Records," I, 380–81.
5. Thomas, 276; Whittier Intro. to Woolman, 16.
6. See Appendix B.
7. "Statutes-at-Large," Ch. 143, 881. See Appendix B.
8. "Statutes-at-Large," III, pp. 250, 254; IV, 59 ff. See Appendix B.
9. DuBois' "Slave Trade," p. 23, note. U. S. Census.
10. See Appendix B. Cf. DuBois' "Slave Trade," *passim*.
11. DuBois' "Slave Trade," p. 206.
12. Scharf-Westcott's "History of Philadelphia," 1, 200.
13. Watson's "Annals," (Ed. 1850) 1, 98.
14. See Appendix B.
15. Cf. Chapter XIII.
16. "Colonial Records," VIII, 576; DuBois' "Slave Trade," p. 23.
17. Cf. Pamphlet: "Sketch of the Schools for Blacks," also Chapter VIII.
18. Cf. Thomas' "Attitude of Friends," etc., p. 272.
19. Dallas' "Laws," 1, 838, Ch. 881; DuBois' "Slave Trade," p. 225.
20. Cf. Watson's "Annals" (Ed. 1850), 1, 557, 101–103, 601, 602, 515.
21. The *American Museum*, 1789, pp. 61–62.
22. For life of Allen, see his "Autobiography," and Payne's "History of the A. M. E. Church."

23. For life of Jones, see Douglass' "Episcopal Church of St. Thomas."

24. The testimonial was dated January 23, 1794, and was as follows: "Having, during the prevalence of the late malignant disorder, had almost daily opportunities of seeing the conduct of Absalom Jones and Richard Allen, and the people employed by them to bury the dead, I, with cheerfulness give this testimony of my approbation of their proceedings as far as the same came under my notice. Their diligence, attention and decency of deportment, afforded me at the time much satisfaction.   WILLIAM CLARKSON, Mayor."
    From Douglass' "St. Thomas' Church."

25. See Thomas, p. 266.

26. See Allen's "Autobiography," and Douglass' "St. Thomas.'"

27. Douglass' "St. Thomas.'"

28. There is on the part of the A. M. E. Church a disposition to ignore Allen's withdrawal from the Free African Society, and to date the A. M. E. Church from the founding of that society, making it older than St. Thomas. This, however, is contrary to Allen's own statement in his "Autobiography." The point, however, is of little real consequence.

29. Carey & Bioren, Ch. 394. DuBois' "Slave Trade," p. 231.

30. The constitution, as reported, had the word "white," but this was struck out at the instance of Gallatin. Cf. Ch. XVII.

31. Cf. DuBois' "Slave Trade," Chapter VII.

32. "Annals of Congress," 6 Cong., I Sess., pp. 229–45. DuBois' "Slave Trade," pp. 81–83.

33. Quoted by W. C. Bolivar in Philadelphia *Tribune*.

34. Delany's "Colored People," p. 74.

35. Dunlap's *American Daily Advertiser*, July 4, 1791. William White had a large commission-house on the wharves about this time. Considerable praise is given the Insurance Society of 1796 for its good management. Cf. "History of the Insurance Companies of North America." In 1817 the first convention of Free Negroes was held here, through the efforts of Jones and Forten.

CHAPTER IV

◆

The Negro in Philadelphia, 1820–1896

10. Fugitives and Foreigners, 1820–1840—Five social developments made the decades from 1820 to 1840 critical for the nation and for the Philadelphia Negroes; first, the impulse of the industrial revolution of the nineteenth century; second, the reaction and recovery succeeding the War of 1812; third, the rapid increase of foreign immigration; fourth, the increase of free Negroes and fugitive slaves, especially in Philadelphia; fifth, the rise of the Abolitionists and the slavery controversy.

Philadelphia was the natural gateway between the North and the South, and for a long time there passed through it a stream of free Negroes and fugitive slaves toward the North, and of recaptured Negroes and kidnapped colored persons toward the South. By 1820 the northward stream increased, occasioning bitterness on the part of the South, and leading to the Fugitive Slave Act of 1820, and the counter acts of Pennsylvania in 1826 and 1827.[1] During this time new installments of Pennsylvania freedmen, and especially their children, began to flock to Philadelphia. At the same time the stream of foreign immigration to this country began to swell, and by 1830 aggregated half a million souls annually. The result of these movements proved disastrous to the Philadelphia Negro; the better classes of them—the Joneses, Allens and Fortens—could not escape into the mass of white population and leave the new Negroes to fight out their battles with the foreigners. No distinction was drawn between Negroes, least of all by the new Southern families who now made Philadelphia their home and were not unnaturally stirred to unreasoning prejudice by the slavery agitation.

To this was added a fierce economic struggle, a renewal of the fight of the eighteenth century against Negro workmen. The new industries attracted the Irish, Germans and other immigrants; Americans, too, were flocking to the city, and soon to natural race antipathies was added a determined effort to displace Negro labor—an effort which had the aroused prejudice of many of the better classes, and the poor quality of the new black immigrants to give it aid and comfort. To all this was soon added a problem of crime and poverty. Numerous complaints of petty thefts, house-breaking, and assaults on peaceable citizens

15

were traced to certain classes of Negroes. In vain did the better class, led by men like Forten, protest by public meetings their condemnation of such crime;[2] the tide had set against the Negro strongly, and the whole period from 1820 to 1840 became a time of retrogression for the mass of the race, and of discountenance and repression from the whites.

By 1830 the black population of the city and districts had increased to 15,624, an increase of 27 per cent for the decade 1820 to 1830, and of 48 per cent since 1810. Nevertheless, the growth of the city had far outstripped this; by 1830 the county had nearly 175,000 whites, among whom was a rapidly increasing contingent of 5000 foreigners. So intense was the race antipathy among the lower classes, and so much countenance did it receive from the middle and upper class, that there began, in 1829, a series of riots directed chiefly against Negroes, which recurred frequently until about 1840, and did not wholly cease until after the war. These riots were occasioned by various incidents, but the underlying cause was the same: the simultaneous influx of freedmen, fugitives and foreigners into a large city, and the resulting prejudice, lawlessness, crime and poverty. The agitation of the Abolitionists was the match that lighted this fuel. In June and July, 1829, Mrs. Fanny Wright Darusmont, a Scotch woman, gave a number of addresses in Philadelphia, in which she boldly advocated the emancipation of the Negroes and something very like social equality of the races. This created great excitement throughout the city, and late in the fall the first riot against the Negroes broke out, occasioned by some personal quarrel.[3]

The Legislature had proposed to stop the further influx of Southern Negroes by making free Negroes carry passes and excluding all others; the arrival of fugitives from the Southampton massacre was the occasion of this attempt, and it was with difficulty that the friends of the Negro prevented its passage.[4] Quakers hastened to advise against the sending of fugitives to the State, "as the effects of such a measure would probably be disastrous to the peace and comfort of the whole colored population of Pennsylvania." Edward Bettle declared in 1832: "The public mind here is more aroused even among respectable persons than it has been for several years," and he feared that the laws of 1826 and 1827 would be repealed, "thus leaving kidnappers free scope for their nefarious labors."[5]

In 1833 a demonstration took place against the Abolitionists, and in 1834 serious riots occurred. One night in August a crowd of several hundred boys and men, armed with clubs, marched down Seventh street to the Pennsylvania Hospital. They were joined by others, and all proceeded to some places of amusement where many Negroes were congregated, on South street, near Eighth. Here the rioting began, and four or five hundred people engaged in a free street fight. Buildings were torn down and inmates assaulted on Bedford and St. Mary streets and neighboring alleys, until at last the policemen and constables succeeded in quieting the tumult. The respite, however, was but temporary. The very next night the mob assembled again at Seventh and Bainbridge; they first wrecked a Negro church and a neighboring house, then attacked some twenty Negro dwellings; "great excesses are represented as having been committed by the mob, and one or two scenes of a most revolting character are said to have taken place." That the riots occurred by prearranged plan was shown by the signals—lights in windows—by which the houses of the whites were distinguished and those of the Negroes attacked and their inmates assaulted and beaten. Several persons were severely injured in this night's work and one Negro killed, before the mayor and authorities dispersed the rioters.

The next night the mob again assembled in another part of the city and tore down another Negro church. By this time the Negroes began to gather for self-defence, and about one hundred of them barricaded themselves in a building on Seventh street, below Lombard, where a howling mob of whites soon collected. The mayor induced the Negroes to withdraw, and the riot ended. In this three days' uprising thirty-one houses and two churches were destroyed and Stephen James "an honest, industrious colored man" killed.[6]

The town meeting of September 15 condemned the riots and voted to reimburse the sufferers, but also took occasion to condemn the impeding of justice by Negroes when any of their number was arrested, and also the noise made in Negro churches. The fires smouldered for about a year, but burst forth again on the occasion of the murder of his master by a Cuban slave, Juan. The lower classes were aroused and a mob quickly assembled at the corners of Sixth and Seventh and Lombard streets, and began the work of destruction and assault, until finally it ended by setting fire to a row of houses on Eighth street, and fighting off the firemen. The following night the mob met again and attacked a house on St. Mary street, where an armed body of Negroes had barricaded themselves. The mayor and recorder finally arrived here and after severely lecturing the Negroes (!) induced them to depart. The whole of the afternoon of that day black women and children fled from the city.[7]

Three years now passed without serious disturbance, although the lawless elements which had gained such a foothold were still troublesome. In 1838 two murders were committed by Negroes—one of whom was acknowledged to be a lunatic. At the burial of this one's victim, rioting again began, the mob assembling on Passyunk avenue and Fifth street and marching up Fifth. The same scenes were re-enacted but finally the mob was broken up.[8] Later the same year, on the dedication of Pennsylvania Hall, which was designed to be a centre of anti-slavery agitation, the mob, encouraged by the refusal of the mayor to furnish adequate police protection, burned the hall to the ground and the next night burned the Shelter for Colored Orphans at Thirteenth and Callowhill streets, and damaged Bethel Church, on Sixth street.[9]

The last riot of this series took place in 1842 when a mob devastated the district between Fifth and Eighth streets, near Lombard street, assaulted and beat Negroes and looted their homes, burned down a Negro hall and a church; the following day the rioting extended to the section between South and Fitzwater streets and was finally quelled by calling out the militia with artillery.[10]

While these riots were taking place a successful effort was made to deprive free Negroes of the right of suffrage which they had enjoyed nearly fifty years. In 1836 a case came before the court of a Negro who had been denied the right of voting. The court decided in a peculiar decision that free Negroes were not "freemen" in the language of the constitution and, therefore that Negroes could not vote.[11] The reform convention settled the matter by inserting the word "white" in the qualifications for election in the Constitution of 1837.[12] The Negroes protested earnestly by meetings and appeals. "We appeal to you" said they, "from the decision of the 'Reform Convention,' which has stripped us of a right peaceably enjoyed during forty-seven years under the constitution of this commonwealth. We honor Pennsylvania and her noble institutions too much to part with our birthright, as her free citizens, without a struggle. To all her citizens the right of suffrage is valuable in proportion as she is free; but surely there are none who can so ill afford to spare it as ourselves." Nevertheless the right was lost, for the appeal fell on deaf ears.[13]

A curious comment on human nature is this change of public opinion in Philadelphia between 1790 and 1837. No one thing explains it—it arose from a combination of circumstances. If, as in 1790, the new freedmen had been given peace and quiet and abundant work to develop sensible and aspiring leaders, the end would have been different; but a mass of poverty-stricken, ignorant fugitives and ill-trained freedmen had rushed to the city, swarmed in the vile slums which the rapidly growing city furnished, and met in social and economic competition equally ignorant but more vigorous foreigners. These foreigners outbid them at work, beat them on the streets, and were enabled to do this by the prejudice which Negro crime and the anti-slavery sentiment had aroused in the city.

Notwithstanding this the better class of Negroes never gave up. Their school increased in attendance; their churches and benevolent societies increased; they held public meetings of protest and sympathy. And twice, in 1831 and 1833, there assembled in the city a general convention of the free Negroes of the country, representing five to eight States, which, among other things, sought to interest philanthropists of the city in the establishment of a Negro industrial school.[14] When the Legislature showed a disposition in 1832 to curtail the liberties of Negroes, the Negroes held a mass meeting and memorialized the lawmaking body and endeavored to show that all Negroes were not criminals and paupers; they declared that while the Negroes formed eight per cent of the population they furnished but four per cent of the paupers; that by actually produced tax receipts they could show that Negroes held at least $350,000 of taxable property in the city. Moreover, they said, "Notwithstanding the difficulty of getting places for our sons to learn mechanical trades, owing to the prejudices with which we have to contend, there are between four and five hundred people of color who follow mechanical employments."[15] In 1837 the census of the Abolition Society claimed for the Negroes 1724 children in school, $309,626 of unencumbered property, 16 churches and 100 benevolent societies.

11. The Guild of the Caterers, 1840–1870—The outlook for the Negro in Philadelphia about 1840 was not encouraging. The last of the first series of riots took place in 1842, and has been mentioned. The authorities were wakened to their duty by this last outbreak of barbarism, and for several years the spirit of lawlessness, which now extended far beyond the race question and seriously threatened the good name of the city, was kept within control. However, in 1849, a mob set upon a mulatto who had a white wife, at the corner of Sixth street and St. Mary's, and there ensued a pitched battle for a night and a day; firemen fought with firemen; the blacks, goaded to desperation, fought furiously; houses were burned and firearms used, with the result that three white men and one Negro were killed and twenty-five wounded persons taken to the hospital. The militia was twice called before the disturbance was quelled. These riots and the tide of prejudice and economic proscription drove so many Negroes from the city that the black population actually showed a decrease in the decade 1840–50. Worse than this, the good name of the Negroes in the city had been lost through the increased crime and the undeniably frightful condition of the Negro slums. The foreign element gained all the new employments which the growing industries of the State opened, and competed for the trades and common vocations. The outlook was certainly dark.

It was at this time that there arose to prominence and power as remarkable a trade guild as ever ruled in a mediæval city. It took complete leadership of the bewildered group of Negroes, and led them steadily on to a degree of affluence, culture and respect such as has probably never been surpassed in the history of the Negro in America. This was the guild of the caterers, and its masters include names which have been household words in the city for fifty years: Bogle, Augustin, Prosser, Dorsey, Jones and Minton. To realize just the character of this new economic development we must not forget the economic history of the slaves. At first they were wholly house servants or field hands. As city life in the colony became more important, some of the slaves acquired trades, and thus there arose a class of Negro artisans. So long as the pecuniary interests of a slaveholding class stood back of these artisans the protests of white mechanics had little effect; indeed it is probable that between 1790 and 1820 a very large portion, and perhaps most, of the artisans of Philadelphia were Negroes. Thereafter, however, the sharp competition of the foreigners and the demand for new sorts of skilled labor of which the Negro was ignorant, and was not allowed to learn, pushed the black artisans more and more to the wall. In 1837 only about 350 men out of a city population of 10,500 Negroes, pursued trades, or about one in every twenty adults.

The question, therefore, of obtaining a decent livelihood was a pressing one for the better class of Negroes. The masses of the race continued to depend upon domestic service, where they still had a practical monopoly, and upon common labor, where they had some competition from the Irish. To the more pushing and energetic Negroes only two courses were open: to enter into commercial life in some small way, or to develop certain lines of home service into a more independent and lucrative employment. In this latter way was the most striking advance made; the whole catering business, arising from an evolution shrewdly, persistently and tastefully directed, transformed the Negro cook and waiter into the public caterer and restaurateur, and raised a crowd of underpaid menials to become a set of self-reliant, original business men, who amassed fortunes for themselves and won general respect for their people.

The first prominent Negro caterer was Robert Bogle, who, early in the century, conducted an establishment on Eighth street, near Sansom. In his day he was one of the best known characters of Philadelphia, and virtually created the business of catering in the city.[16] As the butler or waiter in a private family arranged the meals and attended the family on ordinary occasions, so the public waiter came to serve different families in the same capacity at larger and more elaborate functions; he was the butler of the smart set, and his taste of hand and eye and palate set the fashion of the day. This functionary filled a unique place in a time when social circles were very exclusive, and the millionaire and the French cook had not yet arrived. Bogle's place was eventually taken by Peter Augustin, a West Indian immigrant, who started a business in 1818 which is still carried on. It was the Augustin establishment that made Philadelphia catering famous all over the country. The best families of the city, and the most distinguished foreign guests, were served by this caterer. Other Negroes soon began to crowd into the field thus opened. The Prossers, father and son, were prominent among these, perfecting restaurant catering and making many famous dishes. Finally came the triumvirate Jones, Dorsey and Minton, who ruled the fashionable world from 1845–1875. Of these Dorsey was the most unique character; with little education but great refinement of manner, he became a man of real weight in the community, and associated with many eminent men. "He had the sway of an imperial dictator. When a Democrat asked his menial service he refused, because 'he could not wait on a party of persons who were disloyal to the government, and Lincoln'—pointing to the picture in his reception rooms—'was the government.' "[17] Jones was Virginia born, and a man of great care and faithfulness. He catered to families in Philadelphia, New Jersey and New York.[18] Minton, the younger of the three, long had a restaurant at Fourth and Chestnut, and became, as the others did, moderately wealthy.[19]

Such men wielded great personal influence, aided the Abolition cause to no little degree, and made Philadelphia noted for its cultivated and well-to-do Negro citizens. Their conspicuous success opened opportunities for Negroes in other lines. It was at this time that Stephen Smith amassed a very large fortune as a lumber merchant, with which he afterward handsomely endowed a home for aged and infirm Negroes. Whipper, Vidal and Purnell were associated with Smith at different times. Still and Bowers were coal merchants and Adger was in the furniture business. There were also some artists of ability: Bowser, who painted a portrait of Lincoln, and Douglass and Burr; Johnson, the leader of a famous colored band and a composer.[20]

During this time of effort, advance and assimilation the Negro population increased but slowly, for the economic struggle was too earnest for young and indiscriminate marriages, and immigrants had been frightened away by the riots. In 1840 there were 19,833 Negroes in the county, and ten years later, as has been noted, there were only 19,761. For the next decade there was a moderate increase to 22,185, when the war brought a slight decrease, leaving the Negro population 22,147 in 1870. Meantime the white population had increased by leaps and bounds:

POPULATION OF PHILADELPHIA COUNTY, 1840–1870

Date	Whites	Negroes
1840	238,204	19,833
1850	389,001	19,761
1860	543,344	22,185
1870	651,854	22,147

In 1810 the Negroes had formed nearly one-tenth of the total population of the city, but in 1870 they formed but little over one thirty-third, the lowest proportion ever reached in the history of Philadelphia.

The general social condition showed some signs of improvement from 1840 on. In 1847 there were 1940 Negro children in school; the Negroes held, it was said, about $400,000 in real estate and had 19 churches and 106 benevolent societies. The mass of the race were still domestic servants—about 4000 of the 11,000 in the city proper being thus employed, a figure which probably meant a considerable majority of the adults. The remainder were chiefly employed as laborers, artisans, coachmen, expressmen and barbers.

The habitat of the Negro population changed somewhat in this period. About 1790 one-fourth of the Negroes lived between Vine and Market and east of Ninth; one-half between Market and South, mostly in the alleys bounded by Lombard, Fifth, Eighth and South; one-eighth lived below South, and one-eighth in the Northern Liberties. Many of these, of course, lived in white families. In 1837 a quarter of the Negroes were in white families, a little less than one-half were in the city limits centring at Sixth and Lombard or thereabouts; a tenth lived in Moyamensing, a twentieth in the Northern Liberties, and the remaining part in Kensington and Spring Garden districts. The riots concentrated this population somewhat, and in 1847, of the 20,000 Negroes in the county, only 1300 lived north of Vine and east of Sixth. The rest were in the city proper, in Moyamensing and in Southwark. Moyamensing was the worst slum district: between South and Fitzwater and Fifth and Eighth there were crowded 302 families in narrow, filthy alleys. Here was concentrated the worst sort of depravity, poverty, crime and disease. The present slums at Seventh and Lombard are bad and dangerous, but they are decent compared with those of a half century ago. The Negroes furnished one-third of all the commitments for crime in 1837, and one-half in 1847.

Beginning with 1850 the improvement of the Negro was more rapid. The value of real estate held was estimated to have doubled between 1847 and 1856. The proportion of men in the trades remained stationary; there were 2321 children in school. Toward the time of the outbreak of war the feeling toward the Negro in certain classes softened somewhat, and his staunch friends were enabled to open many benevolent institutions; in many ways a disposition to help them was manifested: the newspapers treated them with more respect, and they were not subject so frequently to personal insult on the street.

They were still kept off the street cars in spite of energetic protest. Indeed, not until 1867 was a law passed prohibiting this discrimination. Judicial decisions upheld the railways for a long time, and newspapers and public opinion supported them. When by Judge Allison's decision the attitude of the courts was changed, and damages granted an evicted Negro, the railway companies often side-tracked and left cars which colored passengers had entered. Separate cars were run for them on some lines, and in 1865 a public ballot on the cars was taken to decide the admission of Negroes. Naturally the conductors returned a large majority against any change. Finally, after public meetings, pamphlets and repeated agitation, the prospective enfranchisement of the freedmen gained what decency and common sense had long refused.[21]

Steps toward raising Negro troops in the city were taken in 1863, as soon as the efficiency of the Negro soldier had been proven. Several hundred prominent citizens petitioned the Secretary of War and were given permission to raise Negro regiments. The troops were to receive no bounties, but were to have $10 a month and rations. They were to rendezvous at Camp William Penn, Chelten Hills. A mass meeting was soon held attended by the prominent caterers, teachers and merchants, together with white citizens, at which Frederick Douglass, W. D. Kelley and Anna Dickinson spoke. Over $30,000 was raised in the city by subscription, and the first squad of soldiers went into camp June 26, 1863. By December, three regiments were full, and by the next February, five. The first three regiments, known as the Third, Sixth and Eighth United States Regiments of Colored Troops, went promptly to the front, the Third being before Fort Wagner when it fell. The other regiments followed as called, leaving still other Negroes anxious to enlist.[22]

After the war and emancipation great hopes were entertained by the Negroes for rapid advancement, and nowhere did they seem better founded than in Philadelphia. The generation then in its prime had lived down a most intense and bitter race feud and had gained the respect of the better class of whites. They started with renewed zeal, therefore, to hasten their social development.

12. The Influx of the Freedmen, 1870–1896—The period opened stormily, on account of the political rights newly conferred on black voters. Philadelphia city politics have ever had a shady side, but when it seemed manifest that one political party, by the aid of Negro votes, was soon to oust the time-honored incumbents, all the lawless elements which bad city government for a half-century had nurtured naturally fought for the old régime. They found this the easier since the city toughs were largely Irish and hereditary enemies of the blacks. In the spring elections of 1871 there was so much disorder, and such poor police protection, that the United States marines were called on to preserve order.[23]

In the fall elections street disorders resulted in the cold-blooded assassination of several Negroes, among whom was an estimable young teacher, Octavius V. Catto. The murder of Catto came at a critical moment; to the Negroes it seemed a revival of the old slavery-time riots in the day when they were first tasting freedom; to the better classes of Philadelphia it revealed a serious state of barbarism and lawlessness in the second city of the land; to the politicians it furnished a text and example which was strikingly effective and which they did not hesitate to use. The result of all this was an outburst of indignation and sorrow, which was remarkable, and which showed a determined stand for law and order. The outward expression of this was a great mass meeting, attended by some of the best citizens, and a funeral for Catto which was perhaps the most imposing ever given to an American Negro.[24]

This incident, and the general expression of opinion after the war, showed a growing liberal spirit toward the Negro in Philadelphia. There was a disposition to grant him, within limits, a man's chance to make his way in the world; he had apparently vindicated his right to this in war, and his ability for it in peace. Slowly, but surely, therefore, the community was disposed to throw off the trammels, brush away petty hindrances and to soften the harshness of race prejudice, at least enough to furnish the new citizen the legal safeguards of a citizen and the personal privileges of a man. By degrees the restrictions on personal liberty were relaxed; the street cars, which for many years had sought by every species of proscription to get rid of colored passengers or carry them on the platform, were finally compelled by law to cancel such rules; the railways and theatres rather tardily followed, and finally even the schools were thrown open to all.[25] A deep-rooted and determined prejudice still remained, but it showed signs of yielding.

It cannot be denied that the main results of the development of the Philadelphia Negro since the war have on the whole disappointed his well-wishers. They do not pretend that he has not made great advance in certain lines, or even that in general he is not better off to-day than formerly. They do not even profess to know just what his condition to-day is, and yet there is a widespread feeling that more might reasonably have been expected in the line of social and moral development than apparently has been accomplished. Not only do they feel that there is a lack of positive results, but the relative advance compared with the period just before the war is slow, if not an actual retrogression; an abnormal and growing amount of crime and poverty can justly be charged to the Negro; he is not a large taxpayer, holds no conspicuous place in the business world or the world of letters, and even as a working man seems to be losing ground. For these reasons those who, for one purpose and another, are anxiously watching the development of the American Negro desire to know first how far these general impressions are true, what the real condition of the Negro is and what movements would best be undertaken to improve the present situation. And this local problem is after all but a small manifestation of the larger and similar Negro problems throughout the land.

For such ends the investigation, the results of which are here presented, was undertaken. This is not the first time such a study has been attempted. In 1837, 1847 and 1856 studies were made by the Abolition Society and the Friends and much valuable data procured.[26] The United States censuses have also added to our general knowledge, and newspapers have often interested themselves in the matter. Unfortunately, however, the Friends' investigations are not altogether free from a suspicion of bias in favor of the Negro, the census reports are very general and newspaper articles necessarily hurried and inaccurate. This study seeks to cull judiciously from all these sources and others, and to add to them specially collected data for the years 1896 and 1897.

Before, however, we enter upon the consideration of this matter, we must bring to mind four characteristics of the period we are considering: (1) The growth of Philadelphia; (2) the increase of the foreign population in the city; (3) the development of the large industry and increase of wealth, and (4) the coming in of the Southern freedmen's sons and daughters. Even Philadelphians hardly realize that the population of their staid old city has nearly doubled since the war, and that consequently it is not the same place, has not the same spirit, as formerly; new men, new ideas, new ways of thinking and acting have gained some entrance; life is larger, competition fiercer, and conditions of economic and social survival harder than formerly. Again, while there were perhaps 125,000 foreign born persons in the city in 1860, there are 260,000 now, not to mention the children of the former born here. These foreigners have come in to divide with native Americans the industrial opportunities of the city, and have thereby intensified competition. Thirdly, new methods of conducting business and industry are now rife: the little shop, the small trader, the house industry have given way to the department store, the organized company and the factory. Manufacturing of all kinds has increased by leaps and bounds in the city, and to-day employs three times as many men as in 1860, paying three hundred millions annually in wages; hacks and expressmen have turned into vast inter-urban businesses: restaurants have become palatial hotels—the whole face of business is being gradually transformed. Finally, into this rapid development have precipitated themselves during the last twenty years fifteen thousand immigrants, mostly from Maryland, Virginia and Carolina—untrained and poorly educated countrymen, rushing from the hovels of the country or the cottages of country towns, suddenly into the new, strange life of a great city to mingle with 25,000 of their race already there. What has been the result?

[NOTE—There was a small riot in 1843 during the time of Mayor Swift. In 1832 began a series of literary societies—the Library Company, the Banneker Society, etc., —which did much good for many years. The first Negro newspaper of the city, the "Demosthenian Shield," appeared in 1840. Among men not already mentioned in this period should be noted the Rev. C. W. Gardner, Dr. J. Bias, the dentist, James McCrummell, and Sarah M. Douglass. All these were prominent Negroes of the day and had much influence. The artist, Robert Douglass, is the painter of a portrait of Fannie Kemble, which its Philadelphia owner to-day prefers to attribute to Thomas Dudley.]

NOTES

1. These laws were especially directed against kidnapping, and were designed to protect free Negroes. See Appendix B. The law of 1826 was declared unconstitutional in 1842 by the U. S. Supreme Court. See 16 Peters, 500 ff.
2. A meeting of Negroes held in 1822, at the A. M. E. Church, denounced crime and Negro criminals.
3. Scharf-Westcott's "History of Philadelphia," I, 824. There was at this time much lawlessness in the city which had no connection with the presence of Negroes, and which led to rioting and disorder in general. Cf. Price's "History of Consolidation."
4. Southampton was the scene of the celebrated Nat Turner insurrection of Negroes.
5. Letter to Nathan Mendelhall, of North Carolina.
6. Hazard's "Register," XIV, 126–28, 200–203.
7. *Ibid.*, XVI. 35–38.
8. Scharf-Westcott's "Philadelphia," I, 654–55.
9. Price, "History of Consolidation," etc., Ch. VII. The county eventually paid $22,658.27, with interest and costs, for the destruction of the hall.
10. Scharf-Westcott, I, 660–61.
11. Case of Fogg *vs.* Hobbs, 6 Watts, 553–560. See Chapter XII.
12. See Chapter XII and Appendix B.
13. Appeal of 40,000 citizens, etc., Philadelphia, 1838. Written chiefly by the late Robert Purvis, son-in-law of James Forten.

14. See Minutes of Conventions; the school was to be situated in New Haven, but the New Haven authorities, by town meeting, protested so vehemently that the project had to be given up. Cf. also Hazard, V, 143.

15. Hazard's "Register," IX, 361–62.

16. Biddle's "Ode to Bogle," is a well-known squib; Bogle himself is credited with considerable wit. "You are of the people who walk in darkness," said a prominent clergyman to him once in a dimly lighted hall. "But," replied Bogle, bowing to the distinguished gentleman, "I have seen a great light."

17. See in Philadelphia *Times,* October 17, 1896, the following notes by "Megargee:" Dorsey was one of the triumvirate of colored caterers—the other two being Henry Jones and Henry Minton—who some years ago might have been said to rule the social world of Philadelphia through its stomach. Time was when lobster salad, chicken croquettes, deviled crabs and terrapin composed the edible display at every big Philadelphia gathering, and none of those dishes were thought to be perfectly prepared unless they came from the hands of one of the three men named. Without making any invidious comparisons between those who were such masters of the gastronomic art, it can fairly be said that outside of his kitchen, Thomas J. Dorsey outranked the others. Although without schooling, he possessed a naturally refined instinct that led him to surround himself with both men and things of an elevating character. It was his proudest boast that at his table, in his Locust street residence, there had sat Charles Sumner, William Lloyd Garrison, John W. Forney, William D. Kelley and Fred Douglass. . . . Yet Thomas Dorsey had been a slave; had been held in bondage by a Maryland planter. Nor did he escape from his fetters until he had reached a man's estate. He fled to this city, but was apprehended and returned to his master. During his brief stay in Philadelphia, however, he made friends, and these raised a fund of sufficient proportion to purchase his freedom. As a caterer he quickly achieved both fame and fortune. His experience of the horrors of slavery had instilled him with an undying reverence for those champions of his down-trodden race, the old-time Abolitionists. He took a prominent part in all efforts to elevate his people, and in that way he came in close contact with Sumner, Garrison, Forney and others.

18. Henry Jones was in the catering business thirty years, and died September 24, 1875, leaving a considerable estate.

19. Henry Minton came from Nansemond County, Virginia, at the age of nineteen, arriving in Philadelphia in 1830. He was first apprenticed to a shoemaker, then went into a hotel as waiter. Finally he opened dining rooms at Fourth and Chestnut. He died March 20, 1883.

20. This band was in great demand at social functions, and its leader received a trumpet from Queen Victoria.

21. See Spiers' "Street Railway System of Philadelphia," pp. 23–27; also unpublished MS. of Mr. Bernheimer, on file among the senior theses in the Wharton School of Finance and Economy, University of Pennsylvania.

22. Pamphlet on "Enlistment of Negro Troops," Philadelphia Library.

23. Cf. Scharf-Westcott, I, 837.

24. The following account of an eye-witness, Mr. W. C. Bolivar, is from the Philadelphia *Tribune,* a Negro paper: "In the spring election preceding the murder of Octavius V. Catto, there was a good deal of rioting. It was at this election that the United States Marines were brought into play under the command of Col. James Forney. Their very presence had the salutary effect of preserving order. The handwriting of political disaster to the Democratic party was plainly noticed. This galled 'the unterrified,' and much of the rancor was owing to the fact that the Negro vote would guarantee Republican supremacy beyond a doubt. Even then Catto had a narrow escape through a bullet shot at Michael Maher, an ardent Republican, whose place of business was at Eighth and Lombard streets. This assault was instigated by Dr. Gilbert, whose paid or coerced hirelings did his bidding. The Mayor, D. M. Fox, was a mild, easygoing Democrat, who seemed a puppet in the hands of astute conscienceless men. The night prior to the day in question, October 10, 1871, a colored man named Gordon was shot down in cold blood on Eighth street. The spirit of mobocracy filled the air, and the object of its spleen seemed to have been the colored men. A cigar store kept by Morris Brown, Jr., was the resort of the Pythian and Banneker members, and it was at this place on the night prior to the murder that

Catto appeared among his old friends for the last time. When the hour arrived for home going, Catto went the near and dangerous way to his residence, 814 South street, and said as he left, 'I would not stultify my manhood by going to my home in a roundabout way.' When he reached his residence he found one of its dwellers had his hat taken from him at a point around the corner. He went out and into one of the worst places in the Fourth Ward and secured it.

"Intimidation and assault began with the opening of the polls. The first victim was Levi Bolden, a playfellow, as a boy, with the chronicler of these notes. Whenever they could conveniently catch a colored man they forthwith proceeded to assail him. Later in the day a crowd forced itself into Emeline street and battered in the brains of Isaac Chase, going into his home, wreaking their spite on this defenceless man, in the presence of his family. The police force was Democratic, and not only stood idly by, but gave practical support. They took pains to keep that part of the city not in the bailiwick of the rioters from knowing anything of what was transpiring. Catto voted and went to school, but dismissed it after realizing the danger of keeping it open during the usual hours. Somewhere near 3 o'clock as he neared his dwelling, two or three men were seen to approach him from the rear, and one of them, supposed to have been either Frank Kelly or Reddy Dever, pulled out a pistol and pointed it at Catto. The aim of the man was sure, and Catto barely got around a street car before he fell. This occurred directly in front of a police station, into which he was carried. The news spread in every direction. The wildest excitement prevailed, and not only colored men, but those with the spirit of fair play, realized the gravity of the situation, with a divided sentiment as to whether they ought to make an assault on the Fourth Ward or take steps to preserve the peace. The latter prevailed, and the scenes of carnage, but a few hours back, when turbulence was supreme, settled down to an opposite state of almost painful calmness. The rioting during that day was in parts of the Fifth, Seventh and Fourth wards, whose boundary lines met. It must not be supposed that the colored people were passive when attacked, because the records show 'an eye for an eye and a tooth for a tooth,' in every instance. No pen is graphic enough to detail the horrors of that day. Each home was in sorrow, and strong men wept like children, when they realized how much had been lost in the untimely death of the gifted Catto.

"Men who had sat quietly unmindful of things not directly concerning themselves, were aroused to the gravity of the situation, wrought by the spirit of a mob, came out of their seclusion and took a stand for law and order. It was a righteous public sentiment that brought brute force to bay. The journals not only here, but the country over, with one voice condemned the lawless acts of October 10, 1871. Sympathetic public gatherings were held in many cities, with the keynote of condemnation as the only true one. Here in Philadelphia a meeting of citizens was held, from which grew the greater, held in National Hall, on Market street, below Thirteenth. The importance of this gathering is shown by a list its promoters. Samuel Perkins, Esq., called it to order, and the eminent Hon. Henry C. Carey presided. Among some of those in the list of vice-presidents were Hon. William M. Meredith, Gustavus S. Benson, Alex. Biddle, Joseph Harrison, George H. Stuart, J. Effingham Fell, George H. Boker, Morton McMichael, James L. Claghorn, F. C. and Benjamin H. Brewster, Thomas H. Powers, Hamilton Disston, William B. Mann, John W. Forney, John Price Wetherill, R. L. Ashhurst, William H. Kemble, William S. Stokley, Judge Mitchell, Generals Collis and Sickel, Congressmen Kelley, Harmer, Myers, Creely, O'Neill, Samuel H. Bell and hundreds more. These names represented the wealth, brains and moral excellence of this community. John Goforth, the eminent lawyer, read the resolutions, which were seconded in speeches by Hon. William B. Mann, Robert Purvis, Isaiah C. Weirs, Rev. J. Walker Jackson, Gen. C. H. T. Collis and Hon. Alex. K. McClure. These all breathed the same spirit, the condemnation of mob law and a demand for equal and exact justice to all. The speech of Col. McClure stands out boldly among the greatest forensic efforts ever known to our city. His central thought was 'the unwritten law,' which made an impression beyond my power to convey. In the meanwhile, smaller meetings were held in all parts of the city to record their earnest protest against the brute force of the day before. That was the end of disorder in a large scale here. On the sixteenth of October the funeral occurred. The body lay in state at the armory of the First Regiment, Broad and Race streets, and was guarded by the military. Not since the funeral cortege of President Lincoln had there been one as large or as imposing in Philadelphia. Outside of the Third Brigade, N. G. P., detached commands from the First Division, and the military from New Jersey, there were civic organizations by the hundreds from Philadelphia, to say nothing of various bodies from Washington, Baltimore, Wilmington, New York and adjacent places. All the city offices were closed, beside many schools. City Councils attended in a body, the State Legislature was present, all the city employees marched in line, and personal friends came from far and near to testify their practical sympathy. The military was under the command of General Louis Wagner, and the civic bodies marshaled by Robert M. Adger. The pall-bearers were Lieutenant Colonel Ira D. Cliff, Majors John W. Simpson and James H. Grocker, Captains J. F. Needham and R. J. Burr, Lieutenants J. W. Diton, W. W. Morris and Dr. E. C. Howard, Major and Surgeon of the Twelfth Regiment. This is but a mere glance backward at the trying days of October, 1871, and is written to refresh the minds of men and women of that day, as well as to chronicle a bit of sad history that this generation may be informed. And so closed the career of a man of splendid equipment, rare force of character, whose life was so interwoven with all that was good about us, as to make it stand out in bold relief, as a pattern for those who have followed after."

25. Cf. Appendix B.
26. See Appendix C. The inquiry of 1838 was by the Philadelphia Society for Promoting the Abolition of Slavery, and the report was in two parts, one a register of trades and one a general report of forty pages. The Society of Friends, or the Abolition Society, undertook the inquiry of 1849, and published a pamphlet of forty-four pages. There was also the same year a report on the health of colored convicts. A pamphlet by Edward Needles was also published in 1849, comparing the Negroes in 1837 and 1848. Benjamin C. Bacon, at the instance of the Abolition Society, made the inquiry in 1856, which was published that year. In 1859, a second edition was issued with criminal statistics. All these pamphlets may be consulted at the Library Company of Philadelphia, or the Ridgway branch.

CHAPTER V

◆

The Size, Age and Sex of the Negro Population

13. The City for a Century—The population of the county[1] of Philadelphia increased about twenty-fold from 1790 to 1890; starting with 50,000 whites and 2500 Negroes at the first census, it had at the time of the eleventh census, a million whites and 40,000 Negroes. Comparing the rate of increase of these two elements of the population we have:

RATES OF INCREASE OF NEGROES AND WHITES

Decade from	Negroes	Whites	Decade from	Negroes	Whites
1790–1800	176.42%	42.92%	1840–1850* . .	.36%	63.30%
1800–1810	52.93	35.55	1850–1860 . .	12.26	39.67
1810–1820	13.00	22.80	1860–1870* . .	.17	19.96
1820–1830	31.39	39.94	1870–1880 . .	43.13	25.08
1830–1840	27.07	37.54	1880–1890 . .	24.20	23.42

*Decrease for Negroes.

The first two decades were years of rapid increase for the Negroes, their number rising from 2489 in 1790 to 10,552 in 1810. This was due to the incoming of the new freedmen and of servants with masters, all to some extent attracted by the social and industrial opportunities of the city. The white population during this period also increased largely, though not so rapidly as the Negroes, rising from 51,902 in 1790 to 100, 688 in 1810. During the next decade the war had its influence on both races although it naturally had its greatest effect on the lower which increased only 13 per cent against an increase of 28.6 per cent among the Negroes of the country at large. This brought the Negro population of the county to 11,891, while the white population stood at 123,746. During the next two decades, 1820 to 1840, the Negro population rose to 19,833, by natural increase and immigration, while the white population, feeling the first effects of foreign immigration, increased to 238,204. For the next thirty years the continued foreign arrivals, added to natural growth, caused the white population to increase nearly three-fold, while the same cause combined with others allowed an increase of little more than 2000 persons among the Negroes, bringing the black population up to 22,147. In the last two decades the rush to cities on the part of both white and black has increased the former to 1,006,590 souls and the latter to 39,371. The following table gives the exact figures for each decade:

POPULATION OF PHILADELPHIA, 1790–1890

	WHITES		NEGROES		TOTAL	
DATE	CITY	COUNTY	CITY	COUNTY	CITY	COUNTY
1790	. . .	51,902	. . .	2,489	23,552	54,391
1800	. . .	74,129	. . .	6,880	41,220	81,009
1810	. . .	100,688	. . .	10,552	53,722	111,240
1820	56,220	123,746	7,582	11,891	63,802	135,637
1830	. . .	173,173	. . .	15,624	80,462	188,797
1838	. . .	. . .	. . .	17,500	. . .	. . .
1840	83,158	238,204	10,507	19,833	93,665	258,037
1847	. . .	. . .	11,000?	20,240	. . .	. . .
1850	110,640	389,001	10,736	19,761	121,376	408,762
1856	. . .	. . .	. . .	. . .	. . .	. . .
1860		543,344		22,185		565,529
1870		651,854		22,147		674,022*
1880		815,362		31,699		847,170*
1890		1,006,590		39,371		1,046,946*

*These totals include Chinese, Indians, etc.

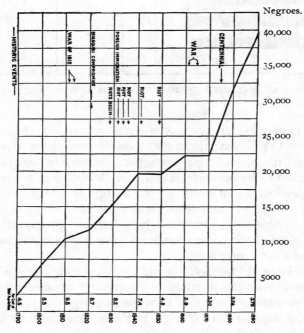

INCREASE OF THE NEGRO POPULATION IN PHILA-
DELPHIA FOR A CENTURY.

[NOTE.—Each horizontal line represents an increment of 2500 persons in population; the upright lines represent the decades. The broken diagonal shows the course of Negro population, and the arrows above recall historic events previously referred to as influencing the increase of the Negroes. At the base of the upright lines is a figure giving the percentage which the Negro population formed of the total population.]

The Negro has never formed a very large percent of the population of the city, as this diagram shows:

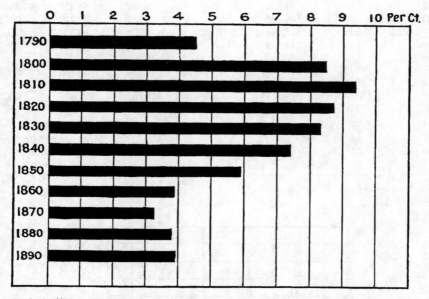

PROPORTION OF NEGROES IN TOTAL POPULATION OF PHILADELPHIA.

A glance at these tables shows how much more sensitive the lower classes of a population are to great social changes than the rest of the group; prosperity brings abnormal increase, adversity, abnormal decrease in mere numbers, not to speak of other less easily measurable changes. Doubtless if we could divide the white population into social strata, we would find some classes whose characteristics corresponded in many respects to those of the Negro. Or to view the matter from the opposite standpoint we have here an opportunity of tracing the history and condition of a social class which peculiar circumstances have kept segregated and apart from the mass.

If we glance beyond Philadelphia and compare conditions as to increase of Negro population with the situation in the country at large we can make two interesting comparisons: the rate of increase in a large city compared with that in the country at large; and the changes in the proportion of Negro inhabitants in the city and the United States.

INCREASE OF NEGROES IN THE UNITED STATES AND IN THE CITY
OF PHILADELPHIA COMPARED

| | INCREASE IN | | | PERCENTAGE OF NEGROES IN TOTAL POPULATION IN | |
DECADE	PHILADELPHIA %	UNITED STATES %	CENSUS YEAR	PHILADELPHIA %	UNITED STATES %
1790–1800	176.42	32.33	1790	4.57	19.27
1800–1810	52.93	37.50	1800	8.49	18.88
1810–1820	13.00	28.59	1810	9.45	19.03
1820–1830	31.39	31.44	1820	8.76	18.39
1830–1840	27.07	23.40	1830	8.27	18.10
1840–1850	.36*	26.63	1840	7.39	16.84
1850–1860	12.26	22.07	1850	4.83	15.69
1860–1870	.17*	9.86	1860	3.92	14.13
1870–1880	43.13	34.85	1870	3.28	12.66
1880–1890	24.20	13.51	1880	3.74	13.12
			1890	3.76	11.93

*Decrease.

A glance at the proportion of Negroes in Philadelphia and in the United States shows how largely the Negro problems are still problems of the country. (See diagram of the proportion of Negroes in the total population of Philadelphia and of the United States on next page.)

This is even more striking if we remember that Philadelphia ranks high in the absolute and relative number of its Negro inhabitants. For the ten largest cities in the United States we have:

TEN LARGEST CITIES IN THE UNITED STATES ARRANGED ACCORDING
TO NEGRO POPULATION

CITIES	NEGRO POPULATION	CITIES	PROPORTION OF NEGROES TO TOTAL POPULATION
1. Baltimore	67,104	1. Baltimore	15.49%
2. Philadelphia . . .	39,371	2. St. Louis	5.94
3. St. Louis	26,865	3. Philadelphia	3.76
4. New York	23,601	4. Cincinnati	3.72
5. Chicago	14,271	5. Boston	1.76
6. Cincinnati	11,655	6. New York	1.55
7. Brooklyn	10,287	7. Chicago	1.29
8. Boston	8,125	8. Brooklyn	1.27
9. Cleveland	2,989	9. Cleveland	1.14
10. San Francisco . .	1,847	10. San Francisco	.61

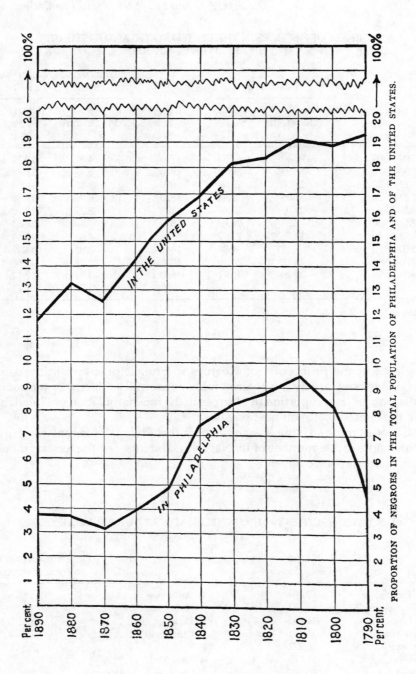

PROPORTION OF NEGROES IN THE TOTAL POPULATION OF PHILADELPHIA AND OF THE UNITED STATES.

Total population of *Boston*, 1820, **43,298.**

Norfolk, Va., Total population, 1890, **34,871.**

New York, Total population, 1790, **33,131.**

Harrisburg, Pa., Total population, 1890, **39,385.**

Total population of *Philadelphia*, 1800, **41,220.**

Chicago, Total population, 1850, **29,963.**

Negroes of *Philadelphia*, 1890, **39,371.**

Washington, Total population, 1850, **40,001.**

Of all the large cities in the United States, only three have a larger absolute Negro population than Philadelphia: Washington, New Orleans and Baltimore. We seldom realize that none of the great Southern cities, except the three mentioned, have a colored population approaching that of Philadelphia:

COLORED* POPULATION OF LARGE SOUTHERN CITIES

CITIES	COLORED INHABITANTS	CITIES	COLORED INHABITANTS
Washington, D. C.	75,697	Nashville, Tenn.	29,395
New Orleans, La.	64,663	Memphis, Tenn.	28,729
Philadelphia, Pa.	40,374*	Louisville, Ky.	28,672
Richmond, Va.	32,354	Atlanta, Ga.	28,117
Charleston, S. C.	31,036	Savannah, Ga.	22,978

*Includes Chinese, Japanese and civilized Indians, an insignificant number in these cases.

Taken by itself, the Negro population of Philadelphia is no insignificant group of men, as the foregoing diagrams show. (See page 33.)

In other words, we are studying a group of people the size of the capital of Pennsylvania in 1890, and as large as Philadelphia itself in 1800.

Scanning this population more carefully, the first thing that strikes one is the unusual excess of females. This fact, which is true of all Negro urban populations, has not often been noticed, and has not been given its true weight as a social phenomenon.[2] If we take the ten cities having the greatest Negro populations, we have this table:[3]

COLORED* POPULATION OF TEN CITIES BY SEX

CITIES	MALES	FEMALES
Washington	33,831	41,866
New Orleans	28,936	35,727
Baltimore	29,165	38,131
Philadelphia	18,960	21,414
Richmond, Va.	14,216	18,138
Nashville	13,334	16,061
Memphis	13,333	15,396
Charleston, S. C.	14,187	16,849
St. Louis	13,247	13,819
Louisville, Ky.	13,348	15,324
Total	192,557	232,725
Proportion	1,000	1208.5

*Includes Chinese, Japanese and civilized Indians—an element that can be ignored, being small.

This is a very marked excess and has far-reaching effects. In Philadelphia this excess can be traced back some years:

PHILADELPHIA NEGROES BY SEX[4]

	County of Philadelphia				City of Philadelphia		
Year	Males	Females	Number Females to 1000 Males	Year	Males	Females	Number Females to 1000 Males
1820 . .	5,220	6,671	1,091	1820 . .	3,156	4,426	1,383
1838 . .	6,896	9,146	1,326	1838 . .	3,772	5,304	1,395
1840 . .	8,316	11,515	1,387	1840 . .	3,986	6,521	1,630
1850 . .				1850 . .	8,435	11,326	1,348
1890 . .				1890 . .	18,960	21,414	1,127

The cause of this excess is easy to explain. From the beginning the industrial opportunities of Negro women in cities have been far greater than those of men, through their large employment in domestic service. At the same time the restriction of employments open to Negroes, which perhaps reached a climax in 1830–1840, and which still plays a great part, has served to limit the number of men. The proportion, therefore, of men to women is a rough index of the industrial opportunities of the Negro. At first there was a large amount of work for all, and the Negro servants and laborers and artisans poured into the city. This lasted up until about 1820, and at that time we find the number of the sexes approaching equality in the county, although naturally more unequal in the city proper. In the next two decades the opportunities for work were greatly restricted for the men, while at the same time, through the growth of the city, the demand for female servants increased, so that in 1840 we have about seven women to every five men in the county, and sixteen to every five in the city. Industrial opportunities for men then gradually increased largely through the growth of the city, the development of new callings for Negroes and the increased demand for male servants in public and private. Nevertheless the disproportion still indicates an unhealthy condition, and its effects are seen in a large percent of illegitimate births, and an unhealthy tone in much of the social intercourse among the middle class of the Negro population.[5]

Looking now at the age structure of the Negroes, we notice the disproportionate number of young persons, that is, women between eighteen and thirty and men between twenty and thirty-five. The colored population of Philadelphia contains an abnormal number of young untrained persons at the most impressionable age; at the age when, as statistics of the world show, the most crime is committed, when sexual excess is more frequent, and when there has not been developed fully the feeling of responsibility and personal worth. This excess is more striking in recent years than formerly, although full statistics are not available:

PROPORTION OF POPULATION	1848	1880	1890*
Under 5 years	14.7	9.8	7.8
Under 15 years	33.6	. . .	22.5
15 to 50 years	41.8	. . .	63.6†
Over 50 years	9.9	. . .	6.1‡

* Including Chinese, Japanese and Indians.
†15 to 55.
‡Over 55.

This table is too meager to be conclusive, but it is probable that while the age structure of the Negro urban population in 1848 was about normal, it has greatly changed in recent years. Detailed statistics for 1890 make this plainer:

NEGROES * OF PHILADELPHIA BY SEX AND AGE, 1890

AGES	MALES	PER CENT	FEMALES	PER CENT	TOTAL
Under 1	400	2.1	369	1.7	769
1 to 4	1,121	5.9	1,264	5.9	2,385
5 to 9	1,458	7.7	1,515	7.1	2,973
10 to 14	1,409	7.5	1,567	7.4	2,976
15 to 19	2,455	7.7	2,123	9.9	3,578
20 to 24	2,408	12.9	3,133	14.8	5,541
25 to 29	1,521	13.5	2,774	13.1	5,295
30 to 34	2,034	10.9	2,046	9.6	4,080
35 to 44	3,375	18.0	3,139	14.8	6,514
45 to 54	1,645	8.7	1,783	8.4	3,428
55 to 64	581	3.1	799	3.9	1,380
65 and over	376	2.0	726	3.4	1,102
Unknown	177	. .	176	. .	353
Total	18,960	100.0	21,414	100.0	40,374

* Includes 1003 Chinese, Japanese and Indians.

Comparing this with the age structure of other groups we have this table:[6]

AGE	NEGROES OF PHILADELPHIA	NEGROES U. S.	ENGLAND	FRANCE	GERMANY	UNITED STATES
Under 10	15.31	28.22	23.9	17.5	24.2	24.29
10 to 20	16.37	25.19	21.3	17.4	20.7	21.70
20 to 30	27.08	17.40	17.02	16.3	16.2	18.24
30 and over ..	41.24	29.19	37.6	48.8	38.9	35.77

In few large cities does the age structure approach the abnormal condition here presented; the most obvious comparison would be with the age structure of the whites of Philadelphia, for 1890, which may be thus represented:

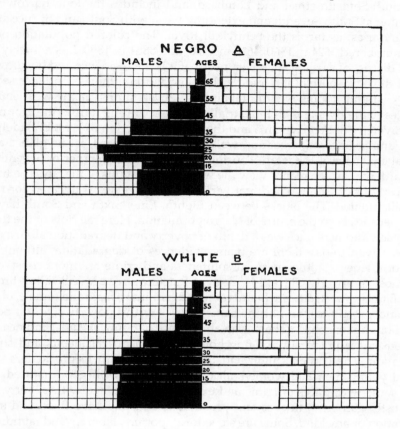

We find then in Philadelphia a steadily and, in recent years, rapidly growing Negro population, in itself as large as a good-sized city, and characterized by an excessive number of females and of young persons.

14. The Seventh Ward, 1896—We shall now make a more intensive study of the Negro population, confining ourselves to one typical ward for the year 1896. Of the nearly forty thousand Negroes in Philadelphia in 1890, a little less than a fourth lived in the Seventh Ward, and over half in this and the adjoining Fourth, Fifth and Eighth Wards:

WARD	NEGROES	WHITES
Seventh	8,861	21,177
Eighth	3,011	13,940
Fourth	2,573	17,792
Fifth	2,335	14,619

The distribution of Negroes in the other wards may be seen by the accompanying map. (See opposite page.)

The Seventh Ward starts from the historic centre of Negro settlement in the city, South Seventh street and Lombard, and includes the long narrow strip, beginning at South Seventh and extending west, with South and Spruce streets as boundaries, as far as the Schuylkill River. The colored population of this ward numbered 3621 in 1860, 4616 in 1870, and 8861 in 1890. It is a thickly populated district of varying character; north of it is the residence and business section of the city; south of it a middle class and workingmen's residence section; at the east end it joins Negro, Italian and Jewish slums; at the west end, the wharves of the river and an industrial section separating it from the grounds of the University of Pennsylvania and the residence section of West Philadelphia.

Starting at Seventh street and walking along Lombard, let us glance at the general character of the ward. Pausing a moment at the corner of Seventh and Lombard, we can at a glance view the worst Negro slums of the city. The houses are mostly brick, some wood, not very old, and in general uncared for rather than dilapidated. The blocks between Eighth, Pine, Sixth and South have for many decades been the centre of Negro population. Here the riots of the thirties took place, and here once was a depth of poverty and degradation almost unbelievable. Even to-day there are many evidences of degradation, although the signs of idleness, shiftlessness, dissoluteness and crime are more conspicuous than those of poverty. The alleys[7] near, as Ratcliffe street, Middle alley, Brown's court, Barclay street, etc., are haunts of noted criminals, male and female, of gamblers and prostitutes, and at the same time of many poverty-stricken people, decent but not energetic. There is an abundance of political clubs, and nearly all the houses are practically lodging houses, with a miscellaneous and shifting population. The corners, night and day, are filled with Negro loafers—ablebodied young men and women, all cheerful, some with good-natured, open faces, some with traces of crime and excess, a few pinched with poverty. They are mostly gamblers, thieves and prostitutes, and few have fixed and steady occupation of any kind. Some are stevedores, porters, laborers and laundresses. On its face this slum is noisy and dissipated, but not brutal, although now and then highway robberies and murderous assaults in other parts of the city are traced to its denizens. Nevertheless the stranger can usually walk about here day and night with little fear of being molested, if he be not too inquisitive.[8]

Passing up Lombard, beyond Eighth, the atmosphere suddenly changes, because these next two blocks have few alleys and the residences are good-sized and pleasant. Here some of the best Negro families of the ward live. Some are wealthy in a small way, nearly all are Philadelphia born, and they represent an early wave of emigration from the old slum section.[9] To the south, on Rodman street, are families of the same character. North of Pine and below Eleventh there are practically no Negro residences. Beyond Tenth street, and as far as Broad street, the Negro population is large and varied in character. On small streets like Barclay and its extension below Tenth—Souder, on Ivy, Rodman, Salem, Heins, Iseminger, Ralston, etc., is a curious mingling of respectable working people and some of a better class, with recent immigrations of the semi-criminal class from the slums.

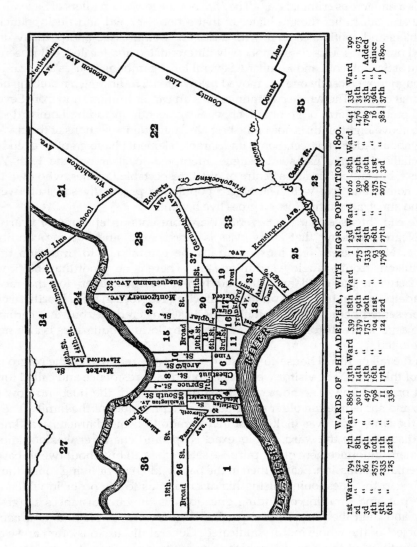

WARDS OF PHILADELPHIA, WITH NEGRO POPULATION, 1890.

1st Ward	794	7th Ward	886	13th Ward	539	18th Ward	1	23d Ward	275	28th Ward	1026	33d Ward	641	33d Ward	190
2d "	522	8th "	301	14th "	1379	19th "	1333	24th "	930	29th "	1476	31th "	1073 Added
3d "	861	9th "	497	15th "	1751	20th "	1333	25th "	260	30th "	1789	35th "	" since
4th "	2573	10th "	798	16th "	104	21st "	93	26th "	1375	31st "	16	36th "	1890.
5th "	2335	11th "	11	17th "	124	22d "	1798	27th "	2077	32d "	382	37th "	
6th "	125	12th "	338											

39

On the larger streets, like Lombard and Juniper, there live many respectable colored families—native Philadelphians, Virginians and other Southerners, with a
fringe of more questionable families. Beyond Broad, as far as Sixteenth, the good
character of the Negro population is maintained except in one or two back
streets.[10] From Sixteenth to Eighteenth, intermingled with some estimable families, is a dangerous criminal class. They are not the low, open idlers of Seventh and
Lombard, but rather the graduates of that school: shrewd and sleek politicians,
gamblers and confidence men, with a class of well-dressed and partially unde-
tected prostitutes. This class is not easily differentiated and located, but it seems to
centre at Seventeenth and Lombard. Several large gambling houses are near here,
although more recently one has moved below Broad, indicating a reshifting of the
criminal centre. The whole community was an earlier immigration from Seventh
and Lombard. North of Lombard, above Seventeenth, including Lombard street
itself, above Eighteenth, is one of the best Negro residence sections of the city, centring about Addison street. Some undesirable elements have crept in even here,
especially since the Christian League attempted to clear out the Fifth Ward
slums,[11] but still it remains a centre of quiet, respectable families, who own their
own homes and live well. The Negro population practically stops at Twenty-
second street, although a few Negroes live beyond.

We can thus see that the Seventh Ward presents an epitome of nearly all
the Negro problems; that every class is represented, and varying conditions
of life. Nevertheless one must naturally be careful not to draw too broad
conclusions from a single ward in one city. There is no proof that the proportion between the good and the bad here is normal, even for the race in
Philadelphia; that the social problems affecting Negroes in large Northern cities
are presented here in most of their aspects seems credible, but that certain of
those aspects are distorted and exaggerated by local peculiarities is also not to
be doubted.

In the fall of 1896 a house-to-house visitation was made to all the Negro families of this ward. The visitor went in person to each residence and called for the
head of the family. The housewife usually responded, the husband now and
then, and sometimes an older daughter or other member of the family. The fact
that the University was making an investigation of this character was known
and discussed in the ward, but its exact scope and character was not known.
The mere announcement of the purpose secured, in all but about twelve cases,[12]
immediate admission. Seated then in the parlor, kitchen, or living room, the visitor began the questioning, using his discretion as to the order in which they
were put, and omitting or adding questions as the circumstances suggested.
Now and then the purpose of a particular query was explained, and usually
the object of the whole inquiry indicated. General discussions often arose as to
the condition of the Negroes, which were instructive. From ten minutes to an
hour was spent in each home, the average time being fifteen to twenty-five
minutes.

Usually the answers were prompt and candid, and gave no suspicion of previous preparation. In some cases there was evident falsification or evasion. In
some cases there was evident falsification or evasion. In such cases the visitor

The Seventh Ward of Philadelphia

The Distribution of Negro Inhabitants Throughout the Ward, and their social condition

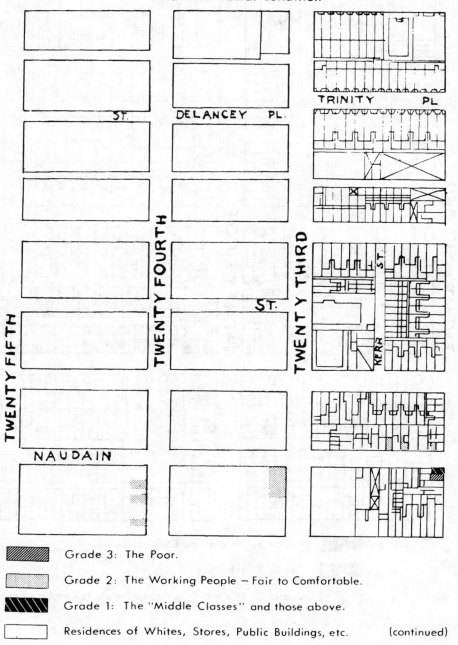

Grade 3: The Poor.

Grade 2: The Working People — Fair to Comfortable.

Grade 1: The "Middle Classes" and those above.

Residences of Whites, Stores, Public Buildings, etc.

(continued)

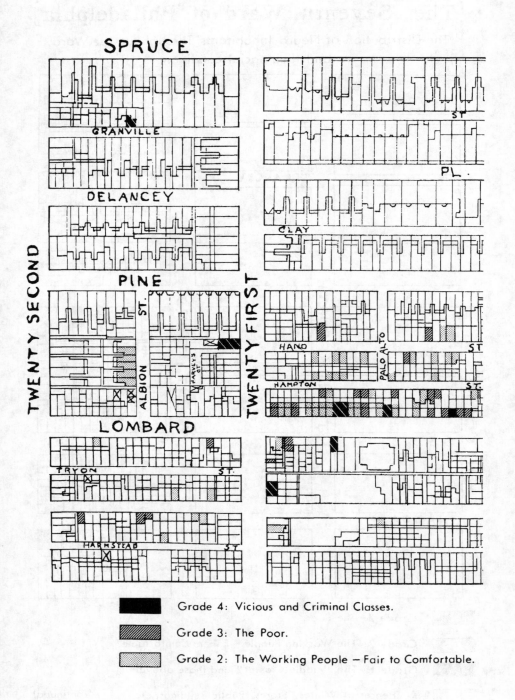

SPRUCE

GRANVILLE

DELANCEY

PINE

LOMBARD

TWENTY SECOND

TWENTY FIRST

ST

PL.

CLAY

HAND   ST

HAMPTON   ST.

PALO ALTO

ALBION

MARY ST

TRYON   ST.

HARMSTEAD   ST.

■ Grade 4: Vicious and Criminal Classes.

▨ Grade 3: The Poor.

▦ Grade 2: The Working People – Fair to Comfortable.

(For a more detailed explanation of the meaning of the different grades, see § 46, chap. xv.)

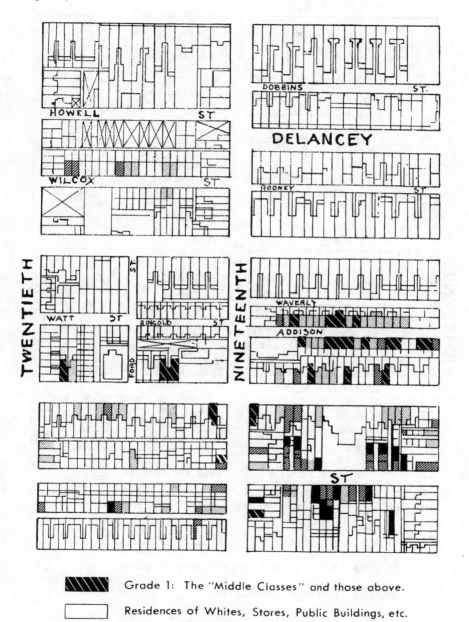

Grade 1: The "Middle Classes" and those above.

Residences of Whites, Stores, Public Buildings, etc.

(continued)

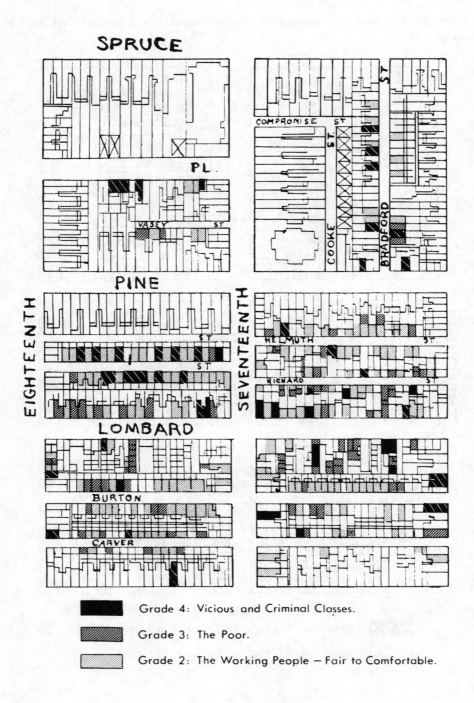

SPRUCE

COMPROMISE ST

PL.

VASEY ST

COOKE ST

BRADFORD

ST

PINE

ST

ST

HELMUTH ST

RICHARD ST

LOMBARD

BURTON

CARVER

Grade 4: Vicious and Criminal Classes.

Grade 3: The Poor.

Grade 2: The Working People — Fair to Comfortable.

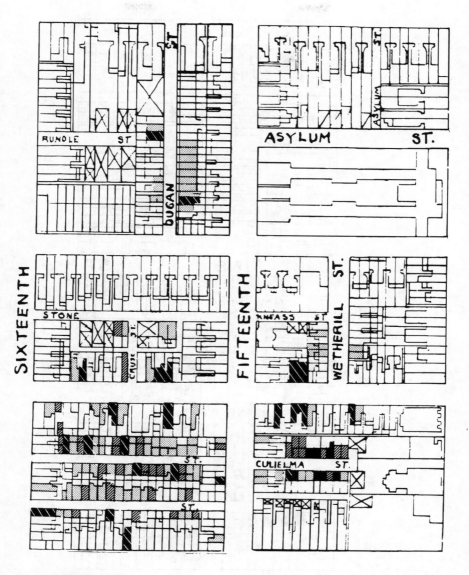

Grade 1: The "Middle Classes" and those above.

Residences of Whites, Stores, Public Buildings, etc.

(continued)

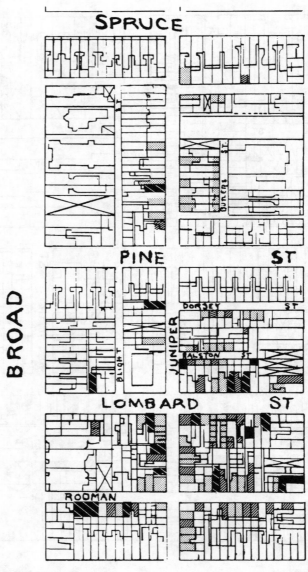

SPRUCE

BROAD

PINE ST

LOMBARD ST

ROOMAN

■ Grade 4: Vicious and Criminal Classes.

▨ Grade 3: The Poor.

▢ Grade 2: The Working People — Fair to Comfortable.

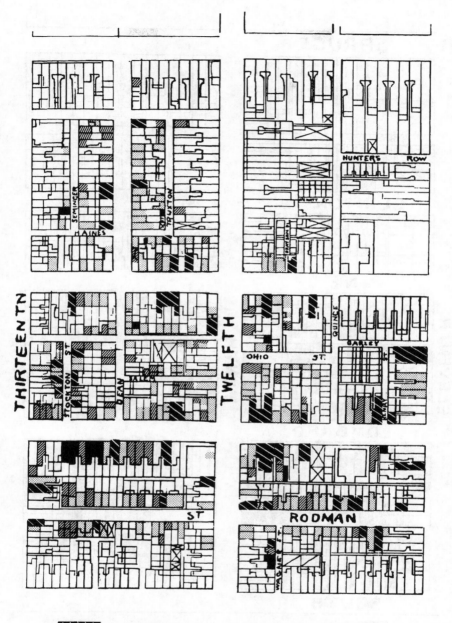

Grade 1: The "Middle Classes" and those above.

Residences of Whites, Stores, Public Buildings, etc.

(continued)

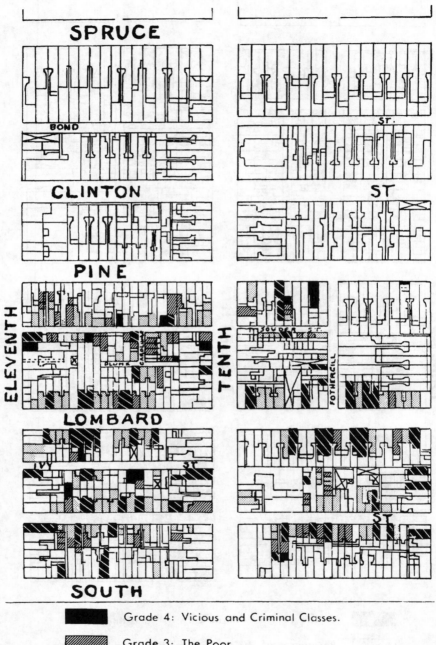

SPRUCE

BOND ST.

CLINTON ST

PINE

ELEVENTH

SOUDER ST.

PLUME

GASKILL

TENTH

FOTHERGILL

LOMBARD

IVY ST

ST

SOUTH

Grade 4: Vicious and Criminal Classes.

Grade 3: The Poor.

Grade 2: The Working People — Fair to Comfortable.

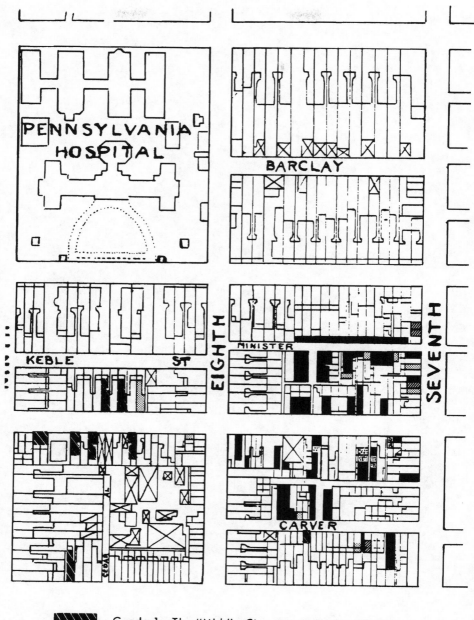

PENNSYLVANIA
HOSPITAL

BARCLAY

KEBLE   ST

MINISTER

EIGHTH

SEVENTH

CARVER

▨ Grade 1: The "Middle Classes" and those above.

☐ Residences of Whites, Stores, Public Buildings, etc.

made free use of his best judgment and either inserted no answer at all, or one which seemed approximately true. In some cases the families visited were not at home, and a second or third visit was paid. In other cases, and especially in the case of the large class of lodgers, the testimony of landlords and neighbors often had to be taken.

No one can make an inquiry of this sort and not be painfully conscious of a large margin of error from omissions, errors of judgment and deliberate deception. Of such errors this study has, without doubt, its full share. Only one fact was peculiarly favorable and that is the proverbial good nature and candor of the Negro. With a more cautious and suspicious people much less success could have been obtained. Naturally some questions were answered better than others; the chief difficulty arising in regard to the questions of age and income. The ages given for people forty and over have a large margin of error, owing to ignorance of the real birthday. The question of income was naturally a delicate one, and often had to be gotten at indirectly. The yearly income, as a round sum, was seldom asked for; rather the daily or weekly wages taken and the time employed during the year.

On December 1, 1896, there were in the Seventh Ward of Philadelphia 9675 Negroes; 4501 males and 5174 females. This total includes all persons of Negro descent, and thirty-three intermarried whites.[13] It does not include residents of the ward then in prisons or in almshouses. There were a considerable number of omissions among the loafers and criminals without homes, the class of lodgers and the club-house habitués. These were mostly males, and their inclusion would somewhat affect the division by sexes, although probably not to a great extent.[14] The increase of the Negro population in this ward for six and a half years is 814, or at the rate of 14.13 per cent per decade. This is perhaps somewhat smaller than that for the population of the city at large, for the Seventh Ward is crowded and overflowing into other wards. Possibly the present Negro population of the city is between 43,000 and 45,000. At all events it is probable that the crest of the tide of immigration is passed, and that the increase for the decade 1890–1900 will not be nearly as large as the 24 per cent of the decade 1880–1890.

NEGRO POPULATION OF SEVENTH WARD

AGE	MALE	FEMALE
Under 10	570	641
10 to 19	483	675
20 to 29	1,276	1,444
30 to 39	1,046	1,084
40 to 49	553	632
50 to 59	298	331
60 to 69	114	155
70 and over	41	96
Age unknown	120	116
Total	4,501	5,174
Grand total		9,675

The division by sex indicates still a very large and, it would seem, growing excess of women. The return shows 1150 females to every 1000 males. Possibly through the omission of men and the unavoidable duplication of some servants lodging away from their place of service, the disproportion of the sexes is exaggerated. At any rate it is great, and if growing, may be an indication of increased restriction in the employments open to Negro men since 1880 or even since 1890.

The age structure also presents abnormal features.[15] Comparing the age structure with that of the large cities of Germany, we have:

AGE	NEGROES OF PHILADELPHIA	LARGE CITIES OF GERMANY
Under 20	25.1	39.3
20 to 40	51.3	37.2
Over 40	23.6	23.5

Comparing it with the Whites and Negroes in the city in 1890, we have:

AGE	NEGROES OF PHILADELPHIA, 1896, SEVENTH WARD	NEGROES* OF PHILADELPHIA, 1890	NATIVE WHITES OF PHILADELPHIA, 1890
Under 10	12.8%	15.31%	24.6%
10 to 20	12.3	16.37	19.5
20 to 30	28.7	27.08	18.5
30 and over	46.2	41.24	37.4

*Includes 1003 Chinese, Japanese and Indians.

As was noticed in the whole city in 1890, so here is even more striking evidence of the preponderance of young people at an age when sudden introduction to city life is apt to be dangerous, and of an abnormal excess of females.

NOTES

1. The unit for study throughout this essay has been made the *county* of Philadelphia, and not the city, except where the city is especially mentioned. Since 1854, the city and county have been coterminous. Even before that the population of the "districts" was for our purposes an urban population, and a part of the group life of Philadelphia.

2. My attention was first called to this fact by Professor Kelly Miller, of Howard University; cf. "Publications of American Negro Academy," No. 1. There is probably, in taking censuses, a larger percentage of omissions among males than among females; such omissions would, however, go but a small way toward explaining this excess of females.

3. In a good many of the Eleventh Census tables, "Chinese, Japanese and civilized Indians," were very unwisely included in the total of the Colored, making an error to be allowed for when one

studies the Negro. In most cases the discrepancy can be ignored. In this case this fact but serves to decrease the excess of females, as these other groups have an excess of males. The city of Philadelphia has 1003 Chinese, Japanese and Indians. The figures for the whole United States show that this excess of females is probably confined to cities:

NEGROES ACCORDING TO SEX

Section	Males	Females
United States	3,725,561	3,744,479
North Atlantic	133,277	136,629
South Atlantic	1,613,769	1,648,921
North Central	222,384	208,728
South Central	1,739,565	1,739,686
Western	16,566	10,515

4. Figures for other years have not been found.
5. In social gatherings, in the churches, etc., men are always at a premium, and this very often leads to lowering the standard of admission to certain circles, and often gives one the impression that the social level of the women is higher than the level of the men.
6. The age groupings in these tables are necessarily unsatisfactory on account of the vagaries of the census.
7. "In the Fifth Ward only there are 171 small streets and courts; Fourth Ward, 88. Between Fifth and Sixth, South and Lombard streets, 15 courts and alleys." "First Annual Report College Settlement Kitchen." p. 6.
8. In a residence of eleven months in the centre of the slums, I never was once accosted or insulted. The ladies of the College Settlement report similar experience. I have seen, however, some strangers here roughly handled.
9. It is often asked why do so many Negroes persist in living in the slums. The answer is, they do not; the slum is continually scaling off emigrants for other sections, and receiving new accretions from without. Thus the efforts for social betterment put forth here have often their best results elsewhere, since the beneficiaries move away and others fill their places. There is, of course, a permanent nucleus of inhabitants, and these, in some cases, are really respectable and decent people. The forces that keep such a class in the slums are discussed further on.
10. Gulielma street, for instance, is a notorious nest for bad characters, with only one or two respectable families.
11. The almost universal and unsolicited testimony of better class Negroes was that the attempted clearing out of the slums of the Fifth Ward acted disastrously upon them; the prostitutes and gamblers emigrated to respectable Negro residence districts, and real estate agents, on the theory that all Negroes belong to the same general class, rented them houses. Streets like Rodman and Juniper were nearly ruined, and property which the thrifty Negroes had bought here greatly depreciated. It is not well to clean a cess-pool until one knows where the refuse can be disposed of without general harm.
12. The majority of these were brothels. A few, however, were homes of respectable people who resented the investigation as unwarranted and unnecessary.
13. Twenty-nine women and four men. The question of race intermarriage is discussed in Chapter XIV.
14. There may have been some duplication in the counting of servant girls who do not lodge where they work. Special pains was taken to count them only where they lodge, but there must have been some errors. Again, the Seventh Ward has a very large number of lodgers; some of these form a sort of floating population, and here were omissions; some were forgotten by landladies and others purposely omitted.

15. There is a wide margin of error in the matter of Negroes' ages, especially of those above fifty; even of those from thirty-five to fifty, the age is often unrecorded and is a matter of memory, and poor memory at that. Much pains was taken during the canvass to correct errors and to throw out obviously incorrect answers. The error in the ages under forty is probably not large enough to invalidate the general conclusions; those under thirty are as correct as is general in such statistics, although the ages of children under ten is liable to err a year or so from the truth. Many women have probably understated their ages and somewhat swelled the period of the thirties as against the forties. The ages over fifty have a large element of error.

CHAPTER VI

◆

Conjugal Condition

15. The Seventh Ward—The conjugal condition of the Negroes above fifteen years of age living in the Seventh Ward is as follows:[1]

Conjugal Condition	Males	Per Cent	Females	Per Cent
Single	1,482	41.4	1,240	30.5
Married	1,876	52.5	1,918	47.1
Widowed	200 ⎫	6.1	841 ⎫	22.4
Permanently separated	18 ⎭		66 ⎭	
Total	3,576	100.0	4,065	100.0
Unknown	125	. . .	179	. . .
Under 15	800	. . .	930	. . .
Total population	4,501	. . .	5,174	. . .

For a people comparatively low in the scale of civilization there is a large proportion of single men—more than in Great Britain, France or Germany; the number of married women, too, is small, while the large number of widowed and separated indicates widespread and early breaking up of family life.[2] The number of single women is probably lessened by unfortunate girls, and increased somewhat by deserted wives who report themselves as single. The number of deserted wives, however, allowing for false reports, is astoundingly large and presents many intricate problems. A very large part of charity given to Negroes is asked for this reason. The causes of desertion are partly laxity in morals and partly the difficulty of supporting a family.

The lax moral habits of the slave régime still show themselves in a large amount of cohabitation without marriage. In the slum districts there are many such families, which remain together years and are in effect common law marriages. Some of these connections are broken by whim or desire, although in many cases they are permanent unions.

The economic difficulties arise continually among young waiters and servant girls; away from home and oppressed by the peculiar lonesomeness of a great city, they form chance acquaintances here and there, thoughtlessly marry and soon find that the husband's income cannot alone support a family; then comes a struggle which generally results in the wife's turning laundress, but often results in desertion or voluntary separation.

The great number of widows is noticeable. The conditions of life for men are much harder than for women and they have consequently a much higher death rate. Unacknowledged desertion and separation also increases this total. Then, too, a large number of these widows are simply unmarried mothers and thus represent the unchastity of a large number of women.[3]

The result of this large number of homes without husbands is to increase the burden of charity and benevolence, and also on account of their poor home life to increase crime. Here is a wide field for social regeneration.

Separating the sexes by age periods according to conjugal condition we have these tables:

MALES

CONJUGAL CONDITION	15–19	20–29	30–39	40–49	50–59	60–69	70 AND OVER	UNK. AGE
Single	250	783	298	90	23	6	2	20
Married	2	474	681	396	212	79	17	15
Widowed ...	..	7	43	53	42	30	21	4
Separated ...	..	3	9	5	1	..	..	..

FEMALES

CONJUGAL CONDITION	15–19	20–29	30–39	40–49	50–59	60–69	70 AND OVER	UNK. AGE
Single	337	559	222	68	32	9	3	10
Married	35	754	633	326	110	34	4	22
Widowed ...	..	47	192	217	179	111	88	9
Separated ..	..	23	22	12	5	1	1	2

When we remember that in slavery-time slaves usually began to cohabit at an early age, these figures indicate the sudden and somewhat disastrous application of the preventive check to population through the economic stress of life in large cities. Negro girls no longer marry in their 'teens as their mothers and grandmothers did. Of those in the twenties over 40 per cent are still unmarried, and of those in the thirties 21 per cent. So sudden a change in marriage customs means grave dangers, as shown by the fact that forty-five of the married couples under forty were permanently separated and 239 women were widowed.

If we reduce the general conjugal condition to per cents, we have this table:

MEN

CONJUGAL CONDITION	15–40		40–60		OVER 60	
		%		%		%
Single	1,333	52.2	113	13.7	8	5.1
Married	1,157	45.3	608	73.9	96	62.0
Widowed	50 ⎱		95 ⎱		51	32.9
Separated	12 ⎰	2.5	6 ⎰	12.4		
Total	2,552	100	822	100	155	100

Here it is plain that although a large per cent of men under forty marry there is nevertheless a number who wait until they are settled in life and have a competence. With the mass of Negroes, however, the waiting past the fortieth year means simply increased caution about marriage; or, if they are widowers, about remarriage. Consequently while, for instance, in Germany 84.8 per cent of the men from forty to sixty are married, among the Negroes of this ward less than 74 per cent are married. At the same time there are indications of a large number of broken marriage ties. Of the men under forty the bulk marry late, that is in the thirties:

CONJUGAL CONDITION	20–29	30–39
Single	61.8%	29%
Married	37.4	66
Widowed .... ⎱		
Separated .... ⎰	.8	5
Total	100%	100%

Turning now to the women, we have a table in which the noticeable feature is the extraordinary number of widowed and separated persons, indicating

CONJUGAL CONDITION	15–40		40–60		OVER 60	
	NUMBER	PER CENT	NUMBER	PER CENT	NUMBER	PER CENT
Single	1,118	39.6	100	10.5	12	4.9
Married	1,422	50.3	436	46.0	38	15.0
Widowed	239 ⎱		396 ⎱		199 ⎱	
Separated	45 ⎰	10.1	17 ⎰	43.5	2 ⎰	80.1
Total	2,824	100	949	100	251	100

economic stress, a high death rate and lax morality. Such are the social results of a large excess of young women in a city where young men cannot afford to marry. Of the women below forty, we have this tabulation:

CONJUGAL CONDITION	15–19	20–29	30–39
Single	90.6%	40.4%	20.8
Married	9.4	54.5	59.2
Widowed	.0	5.1	20.0
Separated			

The comparatively large number of separations is here to be noticed, and the fact that over a fifth of the women between thirty and forty are unmarried and 40 per cent are without husbands.

From all these statistics, making some allowance for the small number of persons counted and the peculiar conditions of the ward, we may conclude:

1. That a tendency to much later marriage than under the slave system is revolutionizing the Negro family and incidentally leading to much irregularity.
2. There is nevertheless still the temptation for young men and women under forty to enter into matrimony before their economic condition warrants it.
3. Among persons over forty there is a marked tendency to single life.
4. The very large number of the widowed and separated points to grave physical, economic and moral disorder.

16. The City—The census of 1890 showed that the conjugal condition of Negroes in the city was as follows:

CONJUGAL CONDITION	MALES OVER 15		FEMALES OVER 15	
	NUMBER	PER CENT	NUMBER	PER CENT
Single	6,047	44.0	6,267	37.8
Married	7,042	51.3	7,154	42.5
Widowed	603	4.4	3,078	18.6
Divorced	15	.3	35	1.1
Total	13,707	100	16,534	100

Similar statistics for native whites with native parents for the city, are:

CONJUGAL CONDITION	MALES OVER 15	FEMALES OVER 15
Single	43.2%	38.0%
Married	52.0	49.0
Widowed	4.5	13.7
Divorced	.3	.3
Total	100%	100%

These figures, although six years earlier, for the most part confirm the statistics of the Seventh Ward, except in the statistics of separation. In this respect the returns for the Seventh Ward are probably more reliable, as the census counted only actually divorced persons. The largest discrepancy is in the percentage of single females; this probably comes from the fact that outside the Seventh Ward the single servant girls form a large part of the Negro population. On the whole it is noticeable that the conjugal condition of the Negroes approaches so nearly that of the whites, when the economic and social history of the two groups has been so strikingly different.

These statistics are the best measurements of the condition and tendencies of the Negro home which we have, and although they are crude and difficult in some cases rightly to interpret, yet they shed much light on the problem. First it must be remembered that the Negro home and the stable marriage state is for the mass of the colored people of the country and for a large per cent of those of Philadelphia, a new social institution. The strictly guarded savage home life of Africa, which with all its shortcomings protected womanhood, was broken up completely by the slave ship, and the promiscuous herding of the West Indian plantation put in its stead. From this evolved the Virginia plantation where the double row of little slave cabins were but parts of a communistic paternalism centring in the Big House which was the real centre of the family life. Even in Pennsylvania where the plantation system never was developed the slave family was dependent in morals as well as work upon the master. With emancipation the Negro family was first made independent and with the migration to cities we see for the first time the thoroughly independent Negro family. On the whole it is a more successful institution than we had a right to expect, even though the Negro has had a couple of centuries of contact with some phases of the monogamic ideal.[4] The great weakness of the Negro family is still lack of respect for the marriage bond, inconsiderate entrance into it, and bad household economy and family government. Sexual looseness then arises as a secondary consequence, bringing adultery and prostitution in its train. And these results come largely from the postponement of marriage among the young. Such are the fruits of sudden social revolution.[5]

NOTES

1. There are many sources of error in these returns: it was found that widows usually at first answered the question "Are you married?" in the negative, and the truth had to be ascertained by a second question; unfortunate women and questionable characters generally reported themselves as married; divorced or separated persons called themselves widowed. Such of these errors as were made through misapprehension, were often corrected by additional questions; in case of designed deception the answer was naturally thrown out if the deception was detected, which of course happened in few cases. The net result of these errors is difficult to ascertain: certainly they increase the apparent number of the truly widowed to some extent at the expense of the single and married.

2. The number of actually divorced persons among the Negroes is naturally insignificant; on the other hand the permanent separations are large in number and an attempt has been made to count them. They do not exactly correspond to the divorce column of ordinary statistics and therefore take something from the married column. The number of widowed is probably exaggerated somewhat, but even allowing for errors, the true figure is high. The markedly higher death rate for males has much to do with this. Cf. Chapter X.

3. Unfortunately Philadelphia has no reliable registration of births, and the illegitimate birth rate of Negroes cannot be ascertained. This is probably high judging from other conditions.

4. And, to tell the truth, contact with some very unsavory phases of it.

5. There can be no doubt but what sexual looseness is to-day the prevailing sin of the mass of the Negro population, and that its prevalence can be traced to bad home life in most cases. Children are allowed on the street night and day unattended; loose talk is often indulged in; the sin is seldom if ever denounced in the churches. The same freedom is allowed the poorly trained colored girl as the white girl who has come through a strict home, and the result is that the colored girl more often falls. Nothing but strict home life can avail in such cases. Of course there is much to be said in palliation: the Negress is not respected by men as white girls are, and consequently has no such general social protection; as a servant, maid, etc., she has peculiar temptations; especially the whole tendency of the situation of the Negro is to kill his self-respect which is the greatest safeguard of female chastity.

CHAPTER VII

◆

Sources of the Negro Population

17. The Seventh Ward—We have seen that there is in Philadelphia a large population of Negroes, largely young unmarried folks with a disproportionate number of women. The question now arises, whence came these people? How far are they native Philadelphians, and how far immigrants, and if the latter, how long have they been here? Much depends on the answer to these questions; no conclusions as to the effects of Northern city conditions on Negroes, as to the effects of long, close contact with modern culture, as to the general question of social and economic survival on the part of this race, can be intelligently answered until we know how long these people have been under the influence of given conditions, and how they were trained before they came.[1]

It is often tacitly assumed that the Negroes of Philadelphia are one homogeneous mass, and that the slums of the Fifth Ward, for instance, are one of the results of long contact with Philadelphia city life on the part of this mass. There is just enough truth and falsehood in such an assumption to make it dangerously misleading. The slums of Seventh and Lombard streets are largely the results of the contact of the Negro with city life, but the Negro in question is a changing variable quantity and has felt city influences for periods varying in different persons from one day to seventy years. A generalization then that includes a North Carolina boy who has migrated to the city for work and has been here for a couple of months, in the same class with a descendant of several generations of Philadelphia Negroes, is apt to make serious mistakes. The first lad may deserve to be pitied if he falls into dissipation and crime, the second ought perhaps to be condemned severely. In other words our judgment of the thousands of Negroes of this city must be in all cases considerably modified by a knowledge of their previous history and antecedents.

Of the 9675 Negroes in the Seventh Ward, 9138 gave returns as to their birthplace. Of these, there were born:

In Philadelphia	2,939 or 32.1 per cent.
In Pennsylvania, outside of Philadelphia	526 or 6.0 "
In the New England and Middle States	485 or 5.3 "
In the South	4,980 or 54.3 "
In the West and in foreign lands	208 or 2.3 "

That is to say, less than one-third of the Negroes living in this ward were born here, and over one-half were born in the South. Separating them by sex and giving their birthplaces more in detail, we have:

BIRTHPLACE OF NEGROES, SEVENTH WARD

BORN IN	MALES	FEMALES	TOTAL
Philadelphia	1,307	1,632	2,939
Pennsylvania, outside of Philadelphia	231	295	526
Virginia.......................................	939	1,012	1,951
Maryland	550	794	1,344
Delaware	168	296	464
New Jersey....................................	141	190	331
District of Columbia	146	165	311
Other parts, and undesignated parts, of the South ..	528	382	910
Other New England and Middle States	62	92	154
Western States	28	27	55
Foreign countries	110	43	153
Unknown	291	246	537
Total	4,501	5,174	9,675

This means that a study of the Philadelphia Negroes would properly begin in Virginia or Maryland and that only a portion have had the opportunity of being reared amid the advantages of a great city. To study this even more minutely let us divide the population according to age periods:

BIRTHPLACE BY AGE PERIODS

BIRTHPLACE	0–9	10–20	21–30	31–40	OVER 40	UNKNOWN	TOTAL
Philadelphia	1,004	737	502	289	396	11	2,939
Pennsylvania	8	52	185	110	168	3	526
Virginia, Maryland, New Jersey, Delaware, District of Columbia ...	137	432	1,564	1,150	1,090	28	4,401
South in general	20	79	375	259	175	2	910
North	11	12	45	36	48	2	154
West	10	9	12	18	6	0	55
Foreign lands	2	2	63	43	42	1	153
Unknown	19	19	142	105	63	189	537
Total	1,211	1,342	2,888	2,010	1,988	236	9,675

That the Negro immigration to the city is not an influx of whole families is shown by the fact that 83 per cent of the children under ten were born in Philadelphia. Of the youth from ten to twenty about one-half were born in the city. The great influx comes in the years from twenty-one to thirty, for of these but 17 per cent were born in the city; of the men and women born between 1856 and 1865, that is, in war time, about one-seventh were born in the city; of the freedmen, that is those born before 1856, a larger portion, one-fifth, were born in Philadelphia. The wave of immigration may therefore be thus plotted:

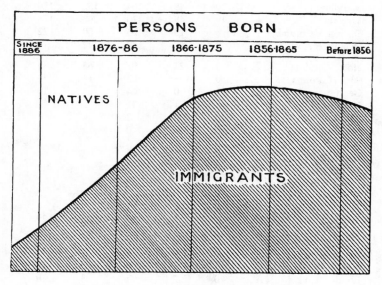

PERSONS	BORN			
SINCE 1886	1876-86	1866-1875	1856-1865	Before 1856

NATIVES

IMMIGRANTS

THE WAVE OF NEGRO IMMIGRATION.

The square represents the Negro population of the Seventh Ward, divided into segments according to age by the upright lines; the shaded portions show the proportion of immigrants.

Further detailed information as to birthplace is given in the next table. (See pages 54 and 55.)

Much of the immigration to Philadelphia is indirect; Negroes come from country districts to small towns; then go to larger towns; eventually they drift to Norfolk, Va., or to Richmond. Next they come to Washington, and finally settle in Baltimore or Philadelphia.[2] The training they receive from such wanderings is not apt to improve young persons greatly, and the custom has undoubtedly helped to swell the numbers of a large migratory criminal class who are often looked upon as the product of particular cities, when, as a matter of fact, they are the offscourings of country districts, sharpened and prepared for crime by the slums of many cities through which they have passed. Besides these, there is the large and well-intentioned class who are seeking to better their lot and are attracted by the larger life of the city.

PHILADELPHIA—NEGROES OF SEVENTH WARD, 1896

BIRTHPLACE—MALES BY FIVE AGE PERIODS

SECTION	PLACE	0–9	10–20	21–30	31–40	OVER 40	UNKNOWN
City	Philadelphia	486	337	208	123	151	2
State	Pennsylvania	5	20	92	49	64	1
Neighboring States	New Jersey	10	14	31	42	44	0
	Maryland	20	48	164	137	176	5
	Virginia	19	48	420	268	178	6
	District of Columbia ...	6	13	55	50	22	0
	Delaware	2	12	40	42	71	1
South	North Carolina	5	21	97	63	35	0
	South Carolina	0	5	22	16	11	1
	Georgia	0	0	14	5	10	0
	Florida	1	1	11	5	1	0
	Alabama	0	0	2	0	4	0
	Mississippi	0	0	0	2	0	0
	Louisiana	0	0	4	1	1	0
	West Virginia	0	1	13	3	4	0
	Kentucky	0	1	2	4	3	0
	Tennessee	0	0	9	3	2	0
	Missouri	0	0	0	0	2	0
	Texas	0	0	1	2	0	0
	"South"	1	5	55	50	29	0
New England and Middle States	Massachusetts	1	2	7	1	4	0
	Connecticut	2	0	1	1	2	0
	New York	1	4	8	5	15	0
	Rhode Island	0	2	1	3	0	0
	Maine	0	0	1	1	0	0
West	Minnesota	1	0	0	0	0	0
	Nebraska	0	1	0	0	0	0
	Ohio	0	4	4	5	3	0
	Michigan	0	1	0	0	0	0
	Illinois	0	0	2	2	0	0
	California	0	0	0	1	0	0
	"West"	0	0	0	2	2	0
Foreign Countries	West Indies	0	0	37	30	24	0
	Canada	2	0	1	1	3	0
	Africa	0	0	3	1	0	0
	Portugal	0	0	2	0	0	0
	Mexico	0	0	1	0	0	0
	East Indies	0	0	0	1	0	0
	Nova Scotia	0	0	0	1	0	0
	South America	0	0	0	2	1	0
?	Unknown	8	7	87	56	25	108

PHILADELPHIA—NEGROES OF SEVENTH WARD, 1896

BIRTHPLACE—FEMALES BY FIVE AGE PERIODS

SECTION	PLACE	0–9	10–20	21–30	31–40	OVER 40	UNKNOWN
City	Philadelphia	518	400	294	166	245	9
State	Pennsylvania	3	32	93	61	104	2
Neighboring States	New Jersey	15	19	44	52	58	2
	Maryland	16	92	254	217	211	4
	Virginia	35	129	431	242	169	6
	District of Columbia ..	13	31	69	29	22	1
	Delaware	1	26	56	71	139	3
South	North Carolina	8	31	66	32	32	0
	South Carolina	1	4	8	12	11	0
	Georgia	2	3	12	4	3	0
	Florida	0	1	5	1	0	1
	Alabama	0	0	6	0	0	0
	Mississippi	0	3	1	3	1	0
	Louisiana	0	0	1	2	2	0
	West Virginia	0	1	7	9	1	0
	Kentucky	0	0	3	1	1	0
	Tennessee	0	0	1	2	4	0
	Missouri	0	0	1	2	2	0
	Texas	0	0	0	1	0	0
	Arkansas	0	0	1	0	0	0
	"South"	2	3	33	36	16	0
New England and Middle States	Massachusetts	2	0	5	4	3	0
	Connecticut	1	0	4	2	10	1
	New York	4	4	17	15	9	1
	Rhode Island	0	0	1	4	2	0
	Maine	0	0	0	0	3	0
West	Minnesota	2	0	0	0	0	0
	Ohio	0	1	6	7	1	0
	Michigan	3	0	0	1	0	0
	Delaware	4	1	0	0	0	0
	Kansas	0	1	0	0	0	0
Foreign Countries	West Indies	0	0	7	1	6	0
	Canada	0	0	3	3	5	0
	South America	0	0	1	0	0	0
	Cuba	0	0	1	0	0	0
	Europe*	0	2	7	3	3	1
?	Unknown	11	12	55	49	38	81

*Intermarried whites.

Much light, therefore, will be thrown on the question of migration if we take the Negro immigrants as a class and inquire how long they have lived in the city; we can separate the immigrants into four classes, corresponding to the waves of immigration: first, the ante-bellum immigrants, resident thirty-five years or more; second, the refugees of war time and the period following, resident twenty-one to thirty-four years; third, the laborers and sightseers of the time of the Centennial, resident ten to twenty years; fourth, the recent immigration, which may be divided into those resident from five to nine years, from one to four years, and those who have been in the city less than a year. Of 5337 immigrants,[3] the following classes may be made:

ARRIVED SINCE DECEMBER 1	RESIDENT	NUMBER	PER CENT		PER CENT	
	Years.					
1895	Under 1	293	5.5	28.7		53.2
1892	1 to 4	1,242	23.2			
1887	5 to 9	1,308	24.5	45.9		
1875	10 to 20	1,143	21.4			46.8
1862	21 to 34	1,040	19.4	25.4		
Before 1860	35 and over	311	6.0			
Before 1896	. . . .	5,337	100	100		100

Thus we see that the majority of the present immigrants arrived since 1887, and nearly 30 per cent since 1892. Carrying out the division by age periods, we have:

AGE YEARS RESIDENT	0–9	10–20	21–30	31–40	OVER 40	UNKNOWN
Under 1 year	40	56	113	60	22	3
1 to 4 years	77	181	648	239	94	3
5 to 9 years	48	139	603	355	157	6
10 to 20 years	0	103	343	449	238	10
21 to 34 years	0	0	107	334	595	4
35 years and over	0	0	0	17	294	0
Total	165	479	1,814	1,454	1,400	26

This table simply confirms the testimony of others as to the recent immigration of young people. Without doubt these statistics of immigration considerably understate the truth; strong social considerations lead many Negroes to give their birthplace as Philadelphia when, as a matter of fact, it may be elsewhere. We may then safely conclude that less than a third of the Negroes in the city were born here, and of the others less than a quarter have been resident twenty years or more. So that half the Negro population can not in any sense be said to be a product of the city, but rather represents raw material, whose transformation forms a pressing series of social problems. Of course, not all immigrants are undesirable material, nor are the native Negroes all creditable to the city; on the contrary, many of the best specimens of Negroes both past and present were not born in the city,[4] while some of the most baffling problems arise as to the young people of native families. Nevertheless, as a whole, it is true that the average of culture and wealth and social efficiency is far lower among immigrants than natives, and that this gives rise to the gravest of the Negro problems.

18. The City—The available figures for the past are not many nor altogether reliable, yet it seems probable that the per cent of immigrants to-day is as large as at any previous time and perhaps larger. In 1848, 57.3 per cent of 15,532 Negroes were natives of the State, and the remaining 42.7 per cent immigrants. In 1890 we have only figures for the whole State, which show that 45 per cent of the Negroes were immigrants mainly from Virginia, Maryland, Delaware, New Jersey, North Carolina, etc.[5] For Philadelphia the percentage would probably be higher.

The new immigrants usually settle in pretty well-defined localities in or near the slums, and thus get the worst possible introduction to city life. In 1848, five thousand of the 6600 immigrants lived in the narrow and filthy alleys of the city and Moyamensing. To-day they are to be found partly in the slums and partly in those small streets with old houses, where there is a dangerous intermingling of good and bad elements fatal to growing children and unwholesome for adults. Such streets may be found in the Seventh Ward, between Tenth and Juniper streets, in parts of the Third and Fourth wards and in the Fourteenth and Fifteenth wards. This mingling swells the apparent size of many slum districts, and at the same time screens the real criminals. Investigators are often surprised in the worst districts to see red-handed criminals and good-hearted, hard-working, honest people living side by side in apparent harmony. Even when the new immigrants seek better districts, their low standard of living and careless appearance make them unwelcome to the better class of blacks and to the great mass of whites. Thus they find themselves hemmed in between the slums and the decent sections, and they easily drift into the happy-go-lucky life of the lowest classes and rear young criminals for our jails. On the whole, then, the sociological effect of the immigration of Negroes is the same as that of illiterate foreigners to this country, save that in this case the brunt of the burden of illiteracy, laziness and inefficiency has been, by reason of peculiar social conditions, put largely upon the shoulders of a group which is least prepared to bear it.

NOTES

1. The chief source of error in the returns as to birthplace are the answers of those who do not desire to report their birthplace as in the South. Naturally there is considerable social distinction between recently arrived Southerners and old Philadelphians; consequently the tendency is to give a Northern birthplace. For this reason it is probable that even a smaller number than the few reported were really born in the city.
2. Compare "The Negroes of Farmville: A Social Study," in *Bulletin* of U. S. Labor Bureau, January, 1898.
3. In the case of lodgers not at home and sometimes of members of families answers could not be obtained to this question. There were in all 862 persons born outside the city from whom answers were not obtained.
4. Absalom Jones, Dorsey, Minton, Henry Jones and Augustin were none of them natives of Philadelphia.

5. Chinese, Japanese and Indians are included in these tables. The exact figures are:

Negro population of Pennsylvania	107,626
Of these, born in Pennsylvania	58,681
Virginia	19,873
Maryland	12,202
Delaware	4,851
New Jersey	1,786
New York	891
North Carolina	1,362
District Columbia	1,131
Unknown	1,804

CHAPTER VIII

◆

Education and Illiteracy

19. The History of Negro Education—Anthony Benezet and the Friends of Philadelphia have the honor of first recognizing the fact that the welfare of the State demands the education of Negro children. On the twenty-sixth of January, 1770, at the Philadelphia Monthly Meeting of Friends, the general situation of the Negroes, and especially the free Negroes, was discussed. On motion of one, probably Benezet, it was decided that instruction ought to be provided for Negro children.[1] A committee was appointed, and on February 30 this committee proposed "that a committee of seven Friends be nominated by the Monthly Meeting, who shall be authorized to employ a schoolmistress of prudent and exemplary conduct, to teach not more at one time than thirty children in the first rudiments of school learning, and in sewing and knitting. That the admission of scholars into the said school be entrusted to the said committee, giving to the children of free Negroes and Mulattoes the preference, and the opportunity of being taught clear of expense to their parents." A subscription of £100 (about $266.67) was recommended for this purpose. This report was adopted, and the school opened June 28, 1770, with twenty-two colored children in attendance. In September the pupils had increased to thirty-six, and a teacher in sewing and knitting was employed. Afterward those who could were required to pay a sum, varying from seven shillings six-pence to ten shillings per quarter, for tuition. The following year a school-house was built on Walnut street, below Fourth—a one-story brick building, 32 by 18 feet.

From 1770 to 1775 two hundred and fifty children and grown persons were instructed. Interest, however, began to wane, possibly under the war-cloud, and in 1775 but five Negro children were in attendance and some white children were admitted. Soon, however, the parents were aroused, and we find forty Negroes and six whites attending.

After the war Benezet took charge of the school and held it in his house at Third and Chestnut. At his death, in 1784, he left a part of his estate to "hire and employ a religious-minded person or persons to teach a number of Negro, Mulatto or Indian children, to read, write, arithmetic, plain accounts, needle-work, etc." Other bequests were received, including one from a Negro, Thomas Shirley, and from this fund the schools, afterward known as the Raspberry street schools, were conducted for many years, and a small school is still maintained. In the early part of the century sixty to eighty scholars attended the school, and a night school was opened. In 1844 a lot on Raspberry street was purchased, and a school-house erected. Here, from 1844 to 1866, eight thousand pupils in all were instructed.

Public schools for Negroes were not established until about 1822, when the Bird school, now known as the James Forten, was opened on Sixth street, above Lombard; in 1830 an unclassified school in West Philadelphia was begun, and in 1833 the Coates street school, now known as the Vaux school, on Coates street (now called Fairmount Avenue), near Fifth, was established. Other schools were opened at Frankford in 1839, at Paschalville in 1841, on Corn street in 1849, and at Holmesburg in 1854. In 1838 the Negro school statistics were as follows:

NEGRO SCHOOL STATISTICS, 1838

SCHOOLS	PUPILS ENROLLED	AVERAGE ATTENDANCE
9 free schools	1,116	713
3 schools, partly free	226	125
3 pay schools, white teachers	102	89
10 pay schools, colored teachers	288	260
25 schools	1,732	1,187
Total children of school age	3,025	

Ten years later school facilities had greatly increased:

NEGRO SCHOOL STATISTICS, 1847

SCHOOLS	PUPILS ENROLLED
Public Grammar School, Lombard street	463
Abolition Society Infant School, Lombard street	70
Public Primary School, Gaskill street	226
Raspberry Street School	155
Public Primary School, Brown street	113
Adelphi School, Wager street	166
Shiloh Baptist Church Infant School, Clifton and Cedar Sts.	207
Bedford Street School	32
Moral Reform School	81
Public School, Oak street, West Philadelphia	12
At undesignated public schools	67
At twenty private schools	296
Total	1,888
At work and apprenticed	504
At home and unaccounted for	2,074
Total Negro children	4,466

This would seem to indicate a smaller percentage of children in school than in the last decade—a natural outcome of the period of depression through which the Negroes had just passed.

In 1850 the United States census reported 3498 adults who could neither read nor write, among the Negroes of the city. The adult population at that time must have been about 8000. There were 2176 children in school. In 1856 we have another set of detailed statistics:

SCHOOLS	TOTAL ENROLLMENT	AVERAGE ATTENDANCE
Public schools	1,031	821
Charity schools	748	491
Benevolent and reformatory schools	211	. .
Private schools	331	. .
Total	2,321	. .
Children from 8 to 18 not in school	1,620	

The schools by this time had increased in number. There were the following public schools:

SCHOOLS AND SITUATIONS	NUMBER TEACHERS	ENROLLMENT	AVERAGE ATTENDANCE
Bird, Sixth above Lombard street, Boys' Department, Grammar School	4	228	208
Bird, Sixth above Lombard street, Girls' Department, Grammar School	4	252	293
Bird, Sixth above Lombard street, Primary Department	3	183	150
Robert Vaux, Coates street, unclassified	2	136	93
West Philadelphia, Oak street, unclassified	2	97	78
Corn street, unclassified	1	47	32
Frankford, unclassified	1	31	25
Holmesburg, unclassified	1	25	19
Banneker, Paschalville, unclassified	1	32	15
Total	19	1,031	913

The public schools seemed to have been largely manned by colored teachers, and were for a long time less efficient than the charity schools. The grammar schools at one time, about 1844, were about to be given up, but were saved, and in 1856 were doing fairly well. The charity schools were as follows:

SCHOOLS	TEACHERS	ENROLLMENT	AVERAGE ATTENDANCE
Institute for Colored Youth, Lombard St.	2	31	26
Raspberry St. schools, Boys' Department	2	90	64
Raspberry St. schools, Girls' Department	2	79	53
Adelphi, Wager Street, Girls' Department	2	70	42
Adelphi, Wager street, Infants' Department . . .	2	95	61
Sheppard, Randolph street	2	60	40
School at the House of Industry	3	100	75
School for Destitute, Lombard street	1	73	45
Infant School, South and Clifton streets	3	150	85
House of Refuge School	3	119	111
Orphans' Shelter School, Thirteenth street	2	73	73
Home for Colored Children, Girard avenue . .	1	19	19
Total	25	959	694

Of the above schools, the House of Refuge, Orphans' Shelter, House of Industry, and Home for Colored Children were schools connected with benevolent and reformatory institutions. The Raspberry school was that founded by Benezet. The Institute for Colored Youth was founded by Richard Humphreys, a West Indian ex-slaveholder, who lived in Philadelphia. On his death, in 1832, he bequeathed the sum of $10,000 to the Friends, to found an institution, "having for its object the benevolent design of instructing the descendants of the African race in school learning, in the various branches of the mechanic arts and trades, and in agriculture, in order to prepare, fit and qualify them to act as teachers." The Institute was accordingly founded in 1837, chartered in 1842, and upon receiving further gifts was temporarily located on Lombard street. In 1866 additional sums were raised, and the Institute located on Bainbridge street, above Ninth, where it is still conducted.

There were in 1856 the following private schools:

Grade	Schools	Enrollment
For high school work	1	30
For grammar school work	2	30
For common branches	10	271
Total	13	331

There were also two night schools, with an attendance of 150 or more.

The percentage of illiteracy in the city was still large. Bacon's investigation showed that of 9021 adults over twenty years of age, 45½ per cent were wholly illiterate, 16½ per cent could read and write and 19 per cent could "read, write and cipher." Detailed statistics for each ward are given in the next table:

ILLITERACY OF PHILADELPHIA NEGROES, 1854–6

Ward	Total Adults over 20 Years of Age	Of these there can Read, Write and Cipher	Read and Write	Read	Totally Illiterate
1	223	25	23	47	128
2	349	36	54	76	183
3	275	60	48	68	99
4	1,427	262	199	273	693
5	1,818	350	285	310	873
6	151	21	25	34	71
7	1,867	431	337	311	788
8	969	204	192	199	374
9	76	20	16	19	21
10	208	40	39	42	87
11	37	2	11	5	19
12	234	53	35	42	104
13	69	15	12	15	27
14	233	34	46	66	87
15	157	20	26	29	82
16	82	17	12	13	40
17	70	13	8	11	38
18	4	1	1	0	2

(Continued)

ILLITERACY OF PHILADELPHIA NEGROES, 1854–6—*Continued*

WARD	TOTAL ADULTS OVER 20 YEARS OF AGE	OF THESE THERE CAN READ, WRITE AND CIPHER	READ AND WRITE	READ	TOTALLY ILLITERATE
19	114	6	20	18	70
20	99	22	12	15	50
21	2	0	0	1	1
22	36	7	4	7	18
23	249	30	43	48	128
24	252	41	34	37	140
Total	9,001	1,710	1,482	1,686	4,123

Separate schools for black and white were maintained from the beginning, barring the slight mixing in the early Quaker schools. Not only were the common schools separate, but there were no public high schools for Negroes, professional schools were closed to them, and within the memory of living men the University of Pennsylvania not only refused to admit Negroes as students, but even as listeners in the lecture halls.[2] Not until 1881 was a law passed declaring it "unlawful for any school director, superintendent or teacher to make any distinction whatever on account of, or by reason of, the race or color of any pupil or scholar who may be in attendance upon, or seeking admission to, any public or common school maintained wholly or in part under the school laws of this commonwealth." This enactment was for some time evaded, and even now some discrimination is practiced quietly in the matter of admission and transfers. There are also schools still attended solely by Negro pupils and taught by Negro teachers, although, of course, the children are at liberty to go elsewhere if they choose. They are kept largely through a feeling of loyalty to Negro teachers. In spite of the fact that several Negroes have been graduated with high marks at the Normal School, and in at least one case "passed one of the best examinations for a supervising principal's certificate that has been accomplished in Philadelphia by any teacher,"[3] yet no Negro has been appointed to a permanent position outside the few colored schools.

20. The Present Condition—There were, in 1896, 5930 Negro children in the public schools of the city, against 6150 in 1895 and 6262 in 1897. Confining ourselves simply to the Seventh Ward, we find the total population of legal school age—six to thirteen in Pennsylvania—was 862 in 1896, of whom 740, or 85.8 per cent, were reported as attending school at some time during the year. Of the persons five to twenty years of age about 48 per cent were in school. Statistics by age and sex are in the next table.[4] (See page 64.)

Some difference is to be noted between the sexes: Of the children six to thirteen years of age, 85 per cent of the boys and nearly 86 per cent of the girls are in school; of the youth fourteen to twenty, 20 per cent of the boys and 21 per cent of the girls are in school. The boys stop school pretty suddenly at sixteen, the girls at seventeen. Nearly 11 per cent of the children in school were in attendance less than the full term;[5] of these attending the whole term there is much irregularity through absences and tardiness. On the whole, therefore, the effective school attendance is less than appears at first sight.

SCHOOL POPULATION AND ATTENDANCE (1896–97) BY AGE
NEGROES OF THE SEVENTH WARD

		MALES		FEMALES	
AGE		SCHOOL POPULATION	SCHOOL ATTENDANCE	SCHOOL POPULATION	SCHOOL ATTENDANCE
Kindergarten	4 years . . .	67	5	66	6
age	5 years . . .	46	11	51	19
Total of Kindergarten age		113	16	117	25
	6 years . . .	50	28	56	35
	7 years . . .	48	40	59	45
Pennsylvania	8 years . . .	53	48	67	59
legal school	9 years . . .	54	50	51	50
age	10 years . . .	49	44	57	52
	11 years . . .	39	38	58	55
	12 years . . .	45	39	62	56
	13 years . . .	53	46	61	55
Total of legal school age		391	333	471	407
	14 years . . .	45	35	52	36
Youth above	15 years . . .	39	22	52	24
legal school	16 years . . .	53	24	71	31
age, and under	17 years . . .	50	6	87	19
voting age	18 years . . .	55	4	80	4
	19 years . . .	56	2	91	1
	20 years . . .	67	0	122	2
Total youth . . .	14–20	365	93	555	117
Total children (Usual school age)	5–20	802	437	1,077	543

The question of illiteracy is a difficult one to have answered without actual tests, especially when the people questioned have some motives for appearing less ignorant than they actually are. The figures for the Seventh Ward, therefore, undoubtedly understate the illiteracy somewhat; nevertheless the error is not probably large enough to deprive the figures of considerable value, and compared with statistics taken in a similar manner they are probably of average reliability.[6] Of 8464 Negroes in the Seventh Ward the returns show that 12.17 per cent are totally illiterate. Comparing this with previous years we have:

1850 . . . . . 44 per cent	1890	18 per cent	
1856 . . . . . 45½ "	1896 (7th Ward) . .	12.17 " [7]	
1870 . . . . . 22 "			

The large number of young people in the Seventh Ward probably brings the average of illiteracy below the level of the whole city. Why this is so may be seen if we take the illiteracy of four age-classes:

AGE	READ AND WRITE	READ	ILLITERATE
Youth, 10 to 20 years of age	94%	2%	4%
Men and women, 21 to 30 years of age . .	90	6	4
Men and women, 31 to 40 years of age . .	77	6	17
Men and women, over 40 years of age . .	61	10	29

The same difference is plain if we take the returns of the census of 1890 for the colored population of the whole city:

AGE	ILLITERATE MALES	ILLITERATE FEMALES	TOTAL ILLITERATES
10 to 19	138	216	354
20 to 34	836	1,096	1,932
35 to 44	1,098	1,571	2,669
45 and over	334	775	1,109
Total (including those of unknown age)	2,450	3,719	6,169
	MALES	FEMALES	COLORED PERSONS
Population over 10	15,981	18,266	34,247
Per cent of total illiteracy	15%	21%	18%

Separating those in the Seventh Ward by sex, we have this table, showing a total illiteracy of 10 per cent among the males and 17 per cent among the females:

ILLITERACY BY SEX AND BY AGE PERIODS—SEVENTH WARD

SEX—AGES	MALES					FEMALES				
	TOTAL	READ AND WRITE	READ	WHOLLY ILLITERATE	UNKNOWN	TOTAL	READ AND WRITE	READ	WHOLLY ILLITERATE	UNKNOWN
Youth, 10 to 20 years	550	514	10	13	13	792	730	16	38	8
Post-bellum men, (born since 1865), 21 to 30 years	1,396	1,229	45	61	61	1,492	1,283	55	116	38
Men of war time (born between 1855 and 1866), 31 to 40 years	978	784	40	111	43	1,032	697	84	211	40
Freedmen (born before 1856), over 40 years	887	625	63	181	18	1,101	558	136	381	26
Of unknown age	120	12	1	3	104	116	24	2	4	86
Total	3,931	3,164	159	369	230	4,533	3,292	293	750	198

Granting that those reporting themselves as able to read should in most cases be included under the illiterate, and that therefore the rate of illiteracy in the Seventh Ward is about 18 per cent, and perhaps 20 per cent for the city, nevertheless the rate is, all things considered, low and places the Philadelphia Negroes in a position not much worse than that of the total population of Belgium (15.9 per cent), so far as actual illiterates are concerned.[8]

The degree of education of those who can read and write can only be indicated in general terms. The majority have only a partial common school education from the country schools of the South or the primary grades of the city; a considerable number have taken grammar school work; a very few have entered the high schools and there have been from fifty to one hundred graduates from colleges and professional schools since the war. Exact figures as to the proportion of students taking higher courses are not easily obtained.

In the Catto School, 1867–96, 11 per cent of those entering the primary grade were promoted to the grammar school; less than 1 per cent of those entering the primary grade of the Vaux School were promoted to the High School. Of those graduating from the course at the Institute for Colored Youth, 8 per cent have taken a college or professional course.[9] Thus it appears that of 1000 colored children entering the primary grade 110 go to the grammar school, ten to the high school and one to college or to a professional school. The basis of induction here is, however, too small for many conclusions.[10]

At present there are in the Seventh Ward thirteen schools for children of all races and sixty-four teachers, with school property valued at $214,382. The schools are: one combined grammar and secondary, three secondary, one combined secondary and primary, four primary and four kindergartens.

In the city the following are the public schools chiefly attended by Negroes:

Coulter street, Twenty-second Section	45 boys,	39 girls,	all colored
J. E. Hill, Germantown	84 "	89 "	"
Robert Vaux, Wood street	67 "	74 "	"
O. V. Catto, Lombard street	140 "	150 "	"
Wilmot, Meadow and Cherry streets	48 "	47 "	"
James Miller, Forty-second and Ludlow sts.,	24 "	13 "	"
J. S. Ramsey, Quince and Pine streets	243 "	253 "	nearly all colored

All the teachers are colored except those in the Ramsey and Miller schools, who are all white. There are a few colored kindergarten teachers in various sections, and large numbers of colored children go to other schools beside those designated. Many of the colored schools have a high reputation for efficient work.[11] There is, theoretically, no discrimination in night schools and some Negroes go to white schools; for the most part, however, the Negroes are in the following night schools:

PHILADELPHIA COLORED NIGHT SCHOOLS, 1895

Name of School	No. Registered at Beginning of Term	No. Registered at End of Term	Average Attendance	Average Per Cent Present During Term	Pupils Under 15 Years	Pupils 15–20 Years	Pupils 21–29 Years	Pupils 30–40 Years	Pupils 40–50 Years	Pupils Over 50 Years	Average Age
O. V. Catto	60	175	69	64	17	47	49	32	25	5	27
Vaux	18	71	25	59	1	12	23	16	9	0	28
Park Avenue	35	95	51	62	14	34	40	3	4	0	21
J. E. Hill	30	112	40	64	4	47	40	11	6	4	24
West Philadelphia .	50	94	38	49	3	14	39	32	6	0	27
Coulter street	48	88	47	68	5	48	24	11	0	0	20
Total night schools of city—white and colored	8,957	2,208	8,352		67	6,172	11,963	2,844	625	183	44	18

The Institute for Colored Youth is still a popular and useful institution. It gives grammar and high school courses. In 1890, by the efforts of both white and colored friends,[12] an industrial department, with eleven teachers, was added. Among the men trained here are Octavius V. Catto, Jacob C. White, Jr., who was for thirty-five years principal of the Vaux School, two ex-ministers from the United States to Haiti, and the young colored physician who recently broke twenty-five years record in the excellence of his examination before the State Board. Under Mr. White, mentioned above, Mr. Henry Tanner, the artist recently honored by the French government, was graduated from the Vaux School.

Considering this testimony as a whole, it seems certain that the Negro problem in Philadelphia is no longer, in the main, a problem of sheer ignorance; to be sure, there is still a very large totally illiterate class of perhaps 6000 persons over ten years of age; then, too, the other 24,000 are not in any sense of the word educated as a mass; most of them can read and write fairly well, but few have a training beyond this. The leading classes among them are mostly grammar school graduates, and a college bred person is very exceptional. Thus the problem of education is still large and pressing; and yet considering their ignorance in the light of history and present experience, it must be acknowledged that there are other social problems connected with this people more pressing than that of education; that a fair degree of persistence in present methods will settle in time the question of ignorance, but other social questions are by no means so near solution.

The only difficulties in the matter of education are carelessness in school attendance, and poverty which keeps children out of school. The former is a matter for the colored people to settle themselves, and is one to which their attention needs to be called. While much has been done, yet it cannot be said that Negroes have fully grasped their great school advantages in the city by keeping their younger children regularly in school, and from this remissness much harm has sprung.

NOTES

1. This account is mainly from the pamphlet: "A Brief Sketch of the Schools for Black People," etc. Philadelphia, 1867.
2. Within a few years a Negro had to fight his way through a prominent dental college in the city.
3. Philadelphia *Ledger*, August 13, 1897.
4. The chief error in the school returns arises from irregularity in attendance. Those reported in school were there sometime during the year, and possibly off and on during the whole year, but many were not steady attendants.
5. Of 647 school children 62 were in school less than nine months—some less than three. Probably many more than this did not attend the full term.
6. As has before been noted, the Negroes are less apt to deceive deliberately than some other peoples. The ability to read, however, is a point of pride with them, and especial pains was taken in the canvass to avoid error; often two or more questions on the point were asked. Nevertheless all depended in the main on voluntary answers.
7. This looks small and yet it probably approximates the truth. My general impression from talking with several thousand Negroes in the Seventh Ward is that the percentage of total illiteracy is small among them.
8. The Seventh Special Report of the United States Commissioner of Labor enables us to make some comparison of the illiteracy of the foreign and Negro populations of the City:

NATIONALITIES	PERSONS ABLE TO READ AND WRITE		ILLITERATES		COMPARISON OF ILLITERACY
Italians, 1894	1,396	36.37 p.c.	2,442	63.63 p.c.	
Russians, 1894	1,128	58.08 "	814	41.92 "	
Poles, 1894	838	59.73 "	565	40.27 "	
Hungarians, 1894	314	69.16 "	140	30.84 "	
Irish, 1894	541	74.21 "	188	25.79 "	
Negroes, 7th W., 1896 . .	6,893	81.44 "	1,571	18.56 "	
Germans, 1894	451	85.26 "	78	14.74 "	

The foreigners here reported include all those living in certain parts of the Third and Fourth Wards of Philadelphia. They are largely recent immigrants. The Russians and Poles are mostly Jews.—ISABEL EATON.

9. Data furnished by two principals of colored schools. At present (1897) there are 58 Negro students in the following schools: Central High, Girls' Normal, Girls' High, Central Manual Training and North East Manual Training; or about one per cent of the total school enrollment.
10. Probably the percentage of children promoted from primary to grammar grades in this case is unusually small.
11. The following report from a member of the Committee on Schools of the City Councils is taken from the Philadelphia *Ledger*, December 2, 1896: On the matter of the needs of the colored population in connection with the schools, Mr. Meehan had to say: "Young women of the colored race are qualifying themselves for public school teachers by taking the regular course through our Normal School. No matter how well qualified they may be to teach, directors do not elect them to positions in the schools. It is taken for granted that only white teachers shall be placed in charge of white children. The colored Normal School graduates might be given a chance by appointments in the centre of some colored population, so that colored people might support their own teachers if so disposed, as they support their own ministers in their separate colored churches. The good result of this arrangement is shown by the experience in the Twenty-second Section, where there are two schools with seven colored teachers, ranking among the most popular in the section."
12. Negroes in the city raised $2000 toward this.

CHAPTER IX

◆

The Occupations of Negroes

21. The Question of Earning a Living—For a group of freedmen the question of economic survival is the most pressing of all questions; the problem as to how, under the circumstances of modern life, any group of people can earn a decent living, so as to maintain their standard of life, is not always easy to answer. But when the question is complicated by the fact that the group has a low degree of efficiency on account of previous training; is in competition with well-trained, eager and often ruthless competitors; is more or less handicapped by a somewhat indefinite but existent and wide-reaching discrimination; and, finally, is seeking not merely to maintain a standard of living but steadily to raise it to a higher plane—such a situation presents baffling problems to the sociologist and philanthropist.

And yet this is the situation of the Negro in Philadelphia; he is trying to better his condition; is seeking to rise; for this end his first need is work of a character to engage his best talents, and remunerative enough for him to support a home and train up his children well. The competition in a large city is fierce, and it is difficult for any poor people to succeed. The Negro, however, has two especial difficulties: his training as a slave and freedman has not been such as make the average of the race as efficient and reliable workmen as the average native American or as many foreign immigrants. The Negro is, as a rule, willing, honest and good-natured; but he is also, as a rule, careless, unreliable and unsteady. This is without doubt to be expected in a people who for generations have been trained to shirk work; but an historical excuse counts for little in the whirl and battle of bread-winning. Of course, there are large exceptions to this average rule; there are many Negroes who are as bright, talented and reliable as any class of workmen, and who in untrammeled competition would soon rise high in the economic scale, and thus by the law of the survival of the fittest we should soon have left at the bottom those inefficient and lazy drones who did not deserve a better fate. However, in the realm of social phenomena the law of survival is greatly modified by human choice, wish, whim and prejudice. And consequently one never knows when one sees a social outcast how far this failure to survive is due to the deficiencies of the individual, and how far to the accidents or injustice of his environment. This is especially the case with the

Negro. Every one knows that in a city like Philadelphia a Negro does not have the same chance to exercise his ability or secure work according to his talents as a white man. Just how far this is so we shall discuss later; now it is sufficient to say in general that the sorts of work open to Negroes are not only restricted by their own lack of training but also by discrimination against them on account of their race; that their economic rise is not only hindered by their present poverty, but also by a widespread inclination to shut against them many doors of advancement open to the talented and efficient of other races.

What has thus far been the result of this complicated situation? What do the mass of the Negroes of the city at present do for a living, and how successful are they in those lines? And in so far as they are successful, what have they accomplished, and where they are inefficient in their present sphere of work, what is the cause and remedy? These are the questions before us, and we proceed to answer the first in this chapter, taking the occupations of the Negroes of the Seventh Ward first, then of the city in a general way, and finally saying a word as to the past.

22. Occupations in the Seventh Ward—Of the 257 boys between the ages of ten and twenty, who were regularly at work in 1896, 39 per cent were porters and errand boys; 25.5 per cent were servants; 16 per cent were common laborers, and 19 per cent had miscellaneous employment. The occupations in detail are as follows:[1]

Total population, males 10 to 20		651	
Engaged in gainful occupations		257	
Porters and errand boys		100	39.0 per cent
Servants		66	25.5 "
Common laborers		40	16.0 "
Teamsters	7		
Apprentices	6		
Bootblacks	6		
Drivers	5		
Newsboys	5		
Peddlers	4		
Typesetters	3		
Actors	2		
Bricklayers	2		
Hostlers	2		
Typewriters	2		
Barber, bartender, bookbinder, factory hand, rubber-worker, sailor, shoemaker—one each . . .	7		
		51	19.5 "
		257	100 per cent

Of the men twenty-one years of age and over, there were in gainful occupations, the following:

In the learned professions	61	2.0 per cent
Conducting business on their own account	207	6.5 "
In the skilled trades	236	7.0 "

Clerks, etc.		159	5.0 per cent
Laborers, better class	602		
Laborers, common class	852		
		1454	45.0 "
Servants		1079	34.0 "
Miscellaneous		11	.5 "
		3207	100 per cent
Total male population, 21 and over			3850[2]

This shows that three-fourths of the male Negroes ten years of age and over in gainful occupations are laborers and servants, while the remaining fourth is equally divided into three parts: one to the trades, one to small business enterprises, and one to professional men, clerks and miscellaneous employments.

Turning now to the females, ten to twenty years of age, we have:

Housewives	38	4.5 per cent
At work[3]	289	36.5 "
At school	333	42.0 "
At home, unoccupied, etc.	133	17.0 "
Total female population 10–20	793	100 per cent

Of the 289 at work there were:

In domestic service	211	73.0 per cent
Doing day's work	32	11.0 "
Dressmakers and seamstresses	16	5.5 "
Servants in public places	12	4.3 "
Apprentices	6	
Musicians	4	
Teachers	3	
Clerks	2	
Actresses	2	
Hairdressers	1	
	18	6.2 "
	289	100 per cent

Taking the occupations of women twenty-one years of age and over, we have:

Domestic servants	1262	37.0 per cent
Housewives and day laborers	937	27.0 "
Housewives	568	17.0 "
Day laborers, maids, etc.	297	9.0 "
In skilled trades	221	6.0 "
Conducting businesses	63	2.0 "
Clerks, etc.	40	1.0 "
Learned professions	37	1.0 "
	3,425	100 per cent
Total female population 21 and over	3,740[4]	

Leaving out housewives who do no outside work and scheduling all women over twenty-one who have gainful occupations, we have:

Professions	37
Working on own account	63
In trades	221
Clerks and agents, etc.	40
Day workers, janitresses, seamstresses, cooks, etc.	1,234
Servants	1,262
	2,857

The following tables gather up all these statistics and give full returns with distinctions of age and sex:

OCCUPATIONS—FEMALES, TEN YEARS OF AGE AND OVER. SEVENTH WARD, 1896

Occupations	10 Years	11 Years	12 Years	13 Years	14 Years	15 Years	16 Years	17 Years	18 Years	19 Years	20 Years	21–30 Years	31–40 Years	Over 40 Years	Unknown Age	Total 10–20 Years	Total 21 and over and unk.
At school	52	55	56	55	36	24	31	19	4	1	2	5	1	0	1	335	7
At home	5	3	5	3	9	16	16	23	22	13	8	..	..	..	..	..	..
Housewives	0	0	0	0	0	0	1	3	4	11	19	246	128	187	7	38	568
Housewives and day workers	0	0	0	0	0	1	0	1	1	4	5	255	329	344	9	12	937
Day workers	0	0	1	0	0	0	1	3	6	5	4	54	24	46	4	20	128
Domestic service	0	0	0	3	7	11	22	28	33	43	64	661	347	240	14	211	1,262
Apprentice to trade	0	0	0	0	0	0	0	4	1	0	1	0	1	0	0	6	1
Janitresses	0	0	0	0	0	0	0	0	0	1	0	7	7	8	0	1	22
Public waitresses	0	0	0	0	0	0	0	1	1	2	1	12	1	0	1	5	14
Office and public maids	0	0	0	0	0	0	0	0	1	0	1	3	5	4	0	2	12
Public cooks	0	0	0	0	0	0	0	0	2	1	1	17	28	27	0	4	72
Musicians	0	0	0	0	0	0	0	2	0	2	0	5	6	1	0	4	12
Hairdressers	0	0	0	0	0	0	0	0	0	0	1	0	1	5	0	1	6
Seamstresses	0	0	0	0	0	0	0	0	0	1	5	23	12	13	0	6	48
Dressmakers	0	0	0	0	0	0	0	0	4	3	3	78	68	57	1	10	204
Actress	0	0	0	0	0	0	0	1	0	0	1	1	0	0	0	2	1
Teachers	0	0	0	0	0	0	0	0	0	1	2	12	6	4	0	3	22
Clerks	0	0	0	0	0	0	0	0	0	1	1	6	4	0	0	2	10
Restaurant keepers	0	0	0	0	0	0	0	0	0	0	0	5	8	4	0	0	17
Milliners	0	0	0	0	0	0	0	0	0	0	0	1	1	1	0	0	3
Nursery keepers	0	0	0	0	0	0	0	0	0	0	0	0	1	2	0	0	3
Trained nurses	0	0	0	0	0	0	0	0	0	0	0	3	0	4	1	0	8
Agents (beneficial soc.)	0	0	0	0	0	0	0	0	0	0	0	3	0	0	0	0	3
Cateresses	0	0	0	0	0	0	0	0	0	0	0	2	8	8	0	0	18
Shrouders of dead	0	0	0	0	0	0	0	0	0	0	0	0	0	4	0	0	4
Stenographers	0	0	0	0	0	0	0	0	0	0	0	1	2	0	0	0	3
Factory employee	0	0	0	0	0	0	0	0	0	0	0	1	0	0	0	0	1
Matron (of Home)	0	0	0	0	0	0	0	0	0	0	0	0	1	1	0	0	2
Manicure	0	0	0	0	0	0	0	0	0	0	0	1	0	0	0	0	1

(Continued)

OCCUPATIONS—FEMALES, TEN YEARS OF AGE AND OVER.
SEVENTH WARD, 1896—*Continued*

Occupations	10 Years	11 Years	12 Years	13 Years	14 Years	15 Years	16 Years	17 Years	18 Years	19 Years	20 Years	21–30 Years	31–40 Years	Over 40 Years	Unknown Age	Total 10–20 Years	Total 21 and over and unk.
Merchants—																	
Cigar store	0	0	0	0	0	0	0	0	0	0	0	1	1	0	0	0	2
Groceries	0	0	0	0	0	0	0	0	0	0	0	0	2	2	0	0	4
Notions, etc.	0	0	0	0	0	0	0	0	0	0	0	0	3	4	0	0	7
Fuel	0	0	0	0	0	0	0	0	0	0	0	0	1	2	0	0	3
Hardware	0	0	0	0	0	0	0	0	0	0	0	0	0	1	0	0	1
Barber	0	0	0	0	0	0	0	0	0	0	0	0	1	0	0	0	1
Undertakers	0	0	0	0	0	0	0	0	0	0	0	0	1	2	0	0	3
Stewardesses	0	0	0	0	0	0	0	0	0	0	0	0	2	2	0	0	4
Missionary	0	0	0	0	0	0	0	0	0	0	0	0	1	0	0	0	1
Prop. Employment Ag.	0	0	0	0	0	0	0	0	0	0	0	0	3	2	0	0	5
Typesetters	0	0	0	0	0	0	0	0	0	0	0	0	1	0	1	0	2
Housekeepers	0	0	0	0	0	0	0	0	0	0	0	0	2	1	0	0	3
Prostitutes	0	0	0	0	0	0	0	2	1	2	3	51	26	11	12	8	100

OCCUPATIONS—MALES, TEN TO TWENTY-ONE YEARS OF AGE. SEVENTH WARD, 1896

Occupations	10 Years	11 Years	12 Years	13 Years	14 Years	15 Years	16 Years	17 Years	18 Years	19 Years	20 Years	Total
Total boys at given age	49	39	45	53	45	39	53	50	55	56	67	463
Total in school	44	38	39	46	35	22	24	6	4	2	0	178
Total at home	5	1	1	2	5	4	11	3	0	2	0	28
Actors	0	0	0	0	0	0	0	0	1	0	1	2
Apprentices to trades	0	0	0	0	0	0	0	1	3	1	1	6
Barber	0	0	0	0	0	0	0	0	0	1	0	1
Bartender	0	0	0	0	0	0	0	0	0	1	0	1
Bookbinder	0	0	0	0	0	0	0	1	0	0	0	1
Bootblacks	0	0	0	0	0	1	1	2	1	1	0	6
Bricklayer	0	0	0	0	0	0	0	0	0	2	0	2
Drivers for Doctors	0	0	0	0	0	0	0	1	0	3	1	5
Errand-boys	0	0	2	2	4	5	6	6	5	1	2	33
Factory laborer	0	0	0	0	0	0	0	0	0	1	0	1
Hostlers	0	0	0	0	0	0	0	1	0	1	0	2
Laborers	0	0	0	1	0	0	1	3	12	12	11	40
Newsboys	0	0	1	0	0	1	2	0	0	1	0	5
Peddlers	0	0	0	0	0	0	1	0	1	1	1	4
Printers	0	0	0	0	0	0	0	0	1	1	1	3
Porters	0	0	1	0	1	4	5	10	15	11	20	67
Rubber worker	0	0	0	0	0	0	0	0	0	1	0	1
Sailor	0	0	0	0	0	0	0	1	0	0	0	1
Service (domestic)	0	0	1	2	0	0	1	11	7	7	18	47
Service (public)	0	0	0	0	0	1	1	1	3	5	8	19
Shoemakers	0	0	0	0	0	0	0	0	0	0	1	1
Teamsters	0	0	0	0	0	1	0	2	2	0	2	7
Typewriters	0	0	0	0	0	0	0	1	0	1	0	2

OCCUPATIONS—MALES, TWENTY-ONE YEARS AND OVER. SEVENTH WARD, 1896

Occupations	21–30 Years	31–40 Years	41 and over	Unk. Age	Total
Actors	4	2	. .	. .	6
Agents (ins. societies and drummers)	6	3	6	. .	15
Apprentice to trade	1	. .	. .	. .	1
Barbers	28	21	15	. .	64
Bartenders	2	3	. .	. .	5
Bellmen	32	10	1	. .	43
Bookbinders	1	1	. .	. .	2
Bootblacks	15	6	1	. .	22
Bricklayers	. .	7	4	. .	11
Brickmakers	2	. .	1	. .	3
Builder and contractor	1	. .	. .	. .	1
Bakers	. .	1	3	. .	4
Boiler-maker	. .	1	. .	. .	1
Blacksmith and wheelwright	. .	. .	1	. .	1
Chiropodists	. .	1	1	. .	2
China repairer	. .	. .	1	. .	1
Compounder of liquors	. .	1	. .	. .	1
Cooper	. .	1	. .	. .	1
Carpenter (ship)	. .	1	. .	. .	1
Carpenters	1	2	2	. .	5
Cashier	. .	1	. .	. .	1
Cabinet-maker	1	. .	. .	. .	1
Candy-makers	1	1	. .	. .	2
Caterers	11	18	36	. .	65
Chemist	1	. .	. .	. .	1
Cigar-makers	17	17	4	1	39
Clerks	7	4	7	. .	18
Clerks (in public service)	3	1	4	. .	8
Clerks (shipping)	1	2	. .	. .	3
Conductor (railroad)*	. .	1	. .	. .	1
Dairymen	. .	2	. .	. .	2
Dancing-masters	1	2	. .	. .	3
Drivers (for doctor)	10	1	1	. .	12
Dyer	. .	. .	1	. .	1
Errand boys	2	. .	. .	. .	2
Engineers (stationary)	7	4	2	. .	13
Elevator men	16	5	1	. .	22
Editor	1	. .	. .	. .	1
Florist	. .	1	. .	. .	1
Frame-makers	2	. .	1	. .	3
Furniture polisher	1	. .	. .	. .	1
Gold beater	. .	. .	1	. .	1
Gamblers	4	3	1	8	16
Hucksters	12	15	10	. .	37
Hostlers	21	12	11	. .	44
Hod carriers	27	23	29	. .	79
Inspector of furniture	. .	1	. .	. .	1
Ice carvers	1	1	. .	. .	2
Janitors	29	20	45	. .	94
Kalsominer	. .	. .	1	. .	1

(Continued)

OCCUPATIONS—MALES, TWENTY-ONE YEARS AND OVER.
SEVENTH WARD, 1896—*Continued*

OCCUPATIONS	21–30 YEARS	31–40 YEARS	41 AND OVER	UNK. AGE	TOTAL
Lodging-house keepers	..	..	3	..	3
Landlord	..	..	1	..	1
Locksmith	..	1	..	..	1
Laborers (casual)	1	4	7	..	12
(soap factory)	2	..	..	..	2
(furnace-setters)	2	..	..	..	2
(on buildings)	3	4	..	..	7
(brickyard)	19	7	7	..	32
(on streets)	33	10	4	..	37
(general)	149	120	120	21	410
(farm)	2	1	..	..	3
(water works and gas, etc.)	9	9	28	1	47
Laundrymen	0	1	1	..	2
Managers and foremen	3	2	1	..	6
Messengers	9	10	12	2	33
Musicians	10	7	3	..	20
Manufacturers	..	..	1	..	1
Nurses	1	1	..	..	2
Oyster openers	2	2	..	..	4
Packers (china)	5	4	5	..	14
Painters	3	4	3	..	10
Paper-hanger	3	..	..	..	23
Porters	135	77	60	2	74
Politicians	1	1	..	..	2
Photographers	1	1	..	..	2
Plasterers	..	3	..	..	3
Printers	6	1	2	..	9
Proprietors—Hotels and restaurants	6	6	10	..	22
Express business	3	4	7	..	14
Printing office	3	1	..	..	4
Cigar store	1	6	..	..	7
Milk-dealing	1	..	..	..	1
Store, notions and fuel	3	9	10	..	22
Grocery	1	1	2	..	4
Employment agency	1	1	1	..	3
Barber shop	..	5	10	..	15
Newspaper	..	1	..	..	1
Pool-room	..	2	1	..	3
Professions—Teachers	1	3	3	..	7
Lawyers	2	2	1	..	5
Clergymen	4	8	10	..	22
Physicians	2	1	3	..	6
Dentists	..	1	2	..	3
Policemen	..	5	..	..	5
Pilot	..	..	1	..	1
Prize fighter	..	1	..	..	1
Rubber workers	2	..	1	..	3
Roofer	1	..	..	..	1
Rag pickers	2	..	4	..	6

(*Continued*)

OCCUPATIONS—MALES, TWENTY-ONE YEARS AND OVER.
SEVENTH WARD, 1896—*Continued*

OCCUPATIONS	21–30 YEARS	31–40 YEARS	41 AND OVER	UNK. AGE	TOTAL
Real estate agents	. .	1	2	. .	3
Root doctors	1	. .	1	. .	2
Service—Domestic	288	161	123	10	582
Hotel and restaurants, etc.	205	126	72	11	414
Public waiters (with caterers)	9	15	13	1	38
Stewards	8	14	9	. .	31
Students	13	4	. .	. .	17
Sailors	14	3	3	1	21
Sextons	1	1	2	. .	4
Shoemakers	4	1	13	. .	18
Stevedores	64	60	40	. .	164
Stone-cutters	1	1	1	. .	3
Tinsmith	. .	1	. .	. .	1
Trainer (horses)	. .	1	. .	. .	1
Tailors	1	3	. .	. .	4
Teamsters	63	38	32	1	134
Upholsterers	2	1	4	. .	7
Undertakers	4	1	1	. .	6
Watchmen	1	4	9	. .	14
Wicker-worker	. .	1	. .	. .	1

*Intermarried white man.

Let us now glance at the occupations as a whole: of the 9675 Negroes in the Seventh Ward, 1212 are children nine years of age or less. Of the remaining 8463 there are:

At work	6,610
In school	609
Housewives	568
Known criminals	116
Unoccupied, at home, defective, unknown, etc.	560
	8,463

The 6610 at work are distributed as follows:

Professions	101
Working on own account	268
In trades	492
Clerks, semi-professional and responsible workers	216
Laborers (select)	778
Laborers (ordinary)	2,111
Servants	2,644
	6,610

We can grasp the true meaning of these figures only by comparing the distribution of occupations among the Negroes with that of the total population of the city; for this purpose we must redistribute the occupations according to the simpler, but in many respects unsatisfactory, divisions of the United States census. We then have:

	Whole Population of Philadelphia, 1890		Negroes of Seventh Ward, 1896	
	Number	Per Cent	Number	Per Cent
Total population over 10	847,283	. .	8,463	. .
Number in gainful occupations	66,791	. .	6,611	. .
Per cent in gainful occupations	55.1	. .	78	. .
Engaged in agriculture	6,497	1.5	11	.2
Engaged in professional service	19,438	4.2	130*	2.0
Engaged in domestic and personal service	106,129	22.7	4,889	74.3
Engaged in trade and transportation	115,462	24.7	1,006	15.3
Engaged in manufacturing and mechanical industries .	219,265	46.9	541	8.2

*Omitting 24 students 21 years of age and over.

Illustrated graphically, this is:

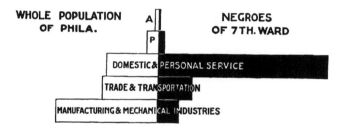

Comparing the whole populations with the Negroes of the Seventh Ward by sex, we have:

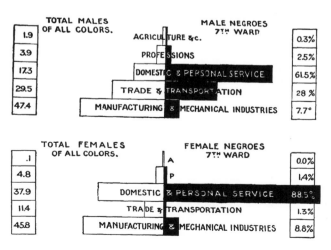

In these statistics and tables we have first to notice the large proportion of these people who work for a living; taking the population ten years of age and over, and we have 78 per cent for the Negroes of the Seventh Ward, and 55.1 per cent for the whole city, white and colored. This is an indication of an absence of accumulated wealth, arising from poverty and low wages; the general causes of poverty are largely historical and well known; to appreciate the cause of low wages, we have only to see the few occupations to which the Negroes are practically limited, and imagine the competition that must ensue. This is true among the men, and especially true among the women, where the limitation is greatest. All the forces that are impelling white women to become bread-winners, are emphasized in the case of Negro women: their chances of marriage are decreased by the low wages of the men and the large excess of their own sex in the great cities; they must work, and if there are few chances open they must suffer from competition in wages. Among the men low wages means either enforced celibacy or irregular and often dissipated lives, or homes where the wife and mother must also be a bread-winner. Statistics curiously illustrate this; 16.3 per cent of the native white women of native parents and of all ages, in Philadelphia are bread-winners;[5] their occupations are restricted, and there is great competition; yet among Negro women, where the restriction in occupation reaches its greatest limit, nevertheless 43 per cent are bread-winners, and their wages are at the lowest point in all cases save in some lines of domestic service where custom holds them at certain figures; even here, however, the tendency is downward.

THE WORKING POPULATION OF PHILADELPHIA, 1890

COLOR, ETC.	NUMBER, TEN YEARS OF AGE AND OVER, IN GAINFUL OCCUPATIONS			PER CENT OF TOTAL POPULATION IN GAINFUL OCCUPATIONS		
	MALE	FEMALE	TOTAL	MALE	FEMALE	TOTAL
Whites,						
(Native, with native parents)	122,332	34,731	157,063	65	16	38
(Native, with foreign parents)	91,280	39,618	130,898	58	24	40
Colored (Negro and Chinese, etc.)	13,650	9,258	22,908	72	43	57
Total Population	344,143	122,648	466,791	..	..	..

The causes of this peculiar restriction in employment of Negroes are twofold: first, the lack of training and experience among Negroes; second, the prejudice of the whites. The first is to be expected in some degree, although undoubtedly carelessness and culpable inefficiency have played their part. The second cause will be discussed at length, later. One point, however, needs mention: the peculiar distribution of employments among whites and Negroes makes the great middle class of white people seldom, if ever, brought into contact with Negroes—may not this be a cause as well as an effect of prejudice?

Another noticeable fact is the absence of child-labor; this is not voluntary on the part of the Negroes, but due to restricted opportunity; there is really very little that Negro children may do. Their chief employment, therefore, is found in helping about the house while the mother is at work. Thus those children scheduled as at home represent child-labor in many cases.

23. Occupations in the City—Turning from the more detailed study of the Seventh Ward, let us glance in a general way over the occupations of Negroes in the city at large.

The Professions—The learned professions are represented among Negroes by clergymen, teachers, physicians, lawyers and dentists, in the order named. Practically all Negroes go to their own churches, where they have, save in a very few cases, clergymen of their own race. There are not less than sixty Negro ministers in the city (possibly a hundred) mostly Methodists and Baptists, with three or four Presbyterians and two Episcopalians. The Presbyterian and Episcopalian clergymen are well trained and educated men in nearly every case. The ministers of the African Methodists vary; those in charge of the larger churches are all men of striking personality, with genius for leadership and organization in some lines, and in some cases, though not in all, they are well-educated men. Practically none of them are illiterate. The Baptist ministers are not on the whole so well trained as the Methodists, although some are well-educated.

Taken on the average the Negro ministers of the city are good representatives of the masses of the Negroes. They are largely chosen by the masses, must cater to their tastes, and must in every way be men whom the rank and file of the race like and understand. Sometimes a strong personality, like the late Theodore Miller, will take a church and lift it to a high level; usually the minister rather follows than leads, and indicates public opinion among his people rather than forms it. The Baptist minister is the elected chairman of a pure democracy, who, if he can command a large enough following, becomes a virtual dictator; he thus has the chance to be a wise leader or a demagogue, or, as in many cases, a little of both. The Methodist minister is the appointed steward of a large corporation, of which his particular church is a small part. His success depends upon the way in which he conducts this church: his financial success, his efforts to increase church membership and his personal popularity. The result is that the colored Methodist minister is generally a wide-awake business man, with something of the politician in his make-up, who is sometimes an inspiring and valuable leader of men; in other cases he may develop into a loud but wily talker, who induces the mass of Negroes to put into fine church edifices money which ought to go to charity or business enterprise.

Ministers receive from $250 a year, in small missions, to $1500 in three or four of the largest churches. The average would be between $600 and $1000.

Next to the clergymen come the teachers, of whom there are about forty in the city:

SCHOOL	PRINCIPALS	ASSISTANT TEACHERS	KINDER- GARTNERS	INDUS'L TEACHERS
Institute for Colored Youth	2	7	0	2
O. V. Catto	1	6	2	0
Vaux	1	3	0	0
J. E. Hill	1	3	1	0
Coulter street	1	1	0	0
Wilmot	1	1	0	0
House of Industry	0	4	0	0
James Forten	0	0	2	0
Berean Church	0	0	1	0
Total	7	25	6	2

These teachers are in nearly every case well equipped and have made good records. Save in the kindergartens, or in one or more temporary cases, they teach Negro children exclusively. The public school teachers receive the same pay as the white teachers.[6]

The Negro physician is to-day just beginning to reap the reward of a long series of attempts and failures. At first thought it would seem natural for Negroes to patronize Negro merchants, lawyers and physicians, from a sense of pride and as a protest against race feeling among whites. When, however, we come to think further, we can see many hindrances. If a child is sick, the father wants a good physician; he knows plenty of good white physicians; he knows nothing of the skill of the black doctor, for the black doctor has had no opportunity to exercise his skill. Consequently for many years the colored physician had to sit idly by and see the 40,000 Negroes healed principally by white practitioners. To-day this has largely changed, and principally through the efforts of the younger class of doctors, who have spared no pains to equip themselves at the best schools of the country. The result is that fully half the Negroes employ Negro physicians, and to a small extent these physicians practice among the whites. There are still many of the old class of root doctors and patent medicine quacks with a lucrative trade among Negroes.[7] Of reputable Negro physicians there are in the city about fifteen, graduated as follows:

University of Pennsylvania	5
Hahnemann (Homeopathic)	2
Women's Medical	2
Medico-Chirurgical	1
Harvard	1
University of Michigan	1
Howard	2
	14

Seven of these have good-sized practice, running from $1500 a year to $3000 or more. Five others have practically just commenced to get practice and are doing fairly well. The other two have outside work and have a limited practice. There are many medical students in the city, and this field is the most attractive open to the Negro among the learned professions.

In contrast to the fair success of the Negro in medicine is his partial failure in law. There are at present about ten practicing Negro lawyers in the city, graduated as follows:

Howard	3
University of Pennsylvania	4
Unknown	3

Two of these are fairly successful practitioners—well versed in law, with some experience, and a small but steady practice. Three others are with difficulty earning a living at criminal practice in police cases; and the rest are having little or no practice. This failure of most Negro lawyers is not in all cases due to lack of ability and push on their part. Its principal cause is that the Negroes furnish little lucrative law business, and a Negro lawyer will seldom be employed by whites. Moreover, while the work of a physician is largely private, depending on individual skill, a lawyer must have co-operation from fellow lawyers and respect and influence in court; thus prejudice or discrimination of any kind is especially felt in this profession. For these reasons Negro lawyers are for the most part confined to petty criminal practice and seldom get a chance to show their ability.

There are three Negro dentists, two being graduated from first-class institutions and enjoying good practice.

On the whole, the professional class of Negroes is creditable to the race. The teachers and physicians would bear comparison with any race; the ranks of the clergy are overcrowded and they present all degrees, from excellent and well-trained spiritual guides to blatant demagogues; the lawyers have little chance to show themselves.

The Entrepreneur—The number of individual undertakers of business enterprise among Negroes is small but growing. Let us first take the Seventh Ward alone and glance over the field. There are in this ward twenty-three establishments for meals and other entertainment, varying from a small one-room restaurant to a twenty-room hotel; some of these on Lombard and South streets have capacious dining-rooms with twenty or more tables; some are little dark places with two or three dubious looking stands. In length of establishment they vary: eight had in 1896 been running a year or less; four, two years; two, three years; four, from four to eight years. They represent investments varying from $40 to $1500, and employ beside the proprietors between fifty and one hundred persons according to the season.

There are in the Seventh Ward twenty-three barbershops varying from two months to forty years in length of establishment; eight are from three to five years old, five over ten years old. They employ beside the proprietors from twenty to forty journeymen more or less regularly. A shop represents an investment varying from $50 to $250 or more. The Negro as a barber is rapidly losing ground in the city. It is difficult to say why this has occurred, but there are several contributory reasons: first the calling was for so long an almost exclusively Negro calling that it came in for a degree of the contempt and ridicule poured on Negroes in general; it therefore grew very unpopular among Negroes, and apprentices became very scarce. To-day one would have to look a long time among young and aspiring Negroes to find one who would willingly become a barber—it smacks perhaps a little too much of domestic service, and is a thing to fall back upon but not to aspire to. In the second place the business became unpopular with Negroes because it compels them to draw a color line. No first-class Negro barber would dare shave his own brother in his shop in Philadelphia on account of the color prejudice. This is peculiarly galling and has led to much criticism and unpopularity for certain leading barbers among their own people. These two reasons led to a lack of interest and enterprise in the business for a long time and it needed but one movement to hasten the collapse, that is, competition. The competition of German and Italian barbers furnished the last and most potent reason for the withdrawal of the Negro; they were skilled workmen, while skilled Negro barbers were becoming scarce; they cut down the customary prices and some of them found business co-operation and encouragement which Negroes could not hope for. For these reasons the business is slipping from the Negro. This is undoubtedly a calamity and unless the Negro in spite of sentiment awakens in time he will find a lucrative employment gone and nothing in its place. Already a white labor union movement is beginning to crowd the Negro, to ask for legislation which will strike him most forcibly and in other ways to bring organized endeavor to bear upon disorganized apathy.

The Seventh Ward has thirteen small Negro grocery stores. They are mostly new ventures, eight being less than a year old; four, one to five years old, and one fifteen years old. Two are co-operative enterprises but have had no great success. All of these stores with two or three exceptions are really experiments and most of them will soon go to the wall and their places be taken by others. The six smaller shops represent investments of $25 to $50; two have $50 and $100 invested; three between $100 and $200, and one from $500 to $1000. The ambition of the middle class of Negroes lies in this direction and their endeavors are laudable. In another age of industrial development they would have already constituted themselves a growing class of small tradesmen; but to-day the department store and stock-company make the competition too great for people with so little commercial training and instinct. Nevertheless the number of Negro groceries will undoubtedly grow considerably in the next decade.

Next come fourteen cigar stores representing a total investment of $1000 to $1500 mostly in sums of $25, $50 and $100. These stores have been established as follows: one year or less, six; two years, four; three to sixteen years, four. They sell cigars and tobacco, and daily papers; some also rent bicycles, or have a boot-blacking stand or pool room attached. One of the proprietors conducts, beside his cigar store, three barber shops and a restaurant, and employs twenty people. Some of these stores are finely equipped. This business is new for Negroes and growing; a few women have ventured into it, and thus in some cases it furnishes a side occupation for wives.

There are four candy and notion shops established respectively five months, six months, one year and three years, and each representing an investment of $10 to $100. They are in most cases in the hands of women and do a small business. There are also numberless places for selling fuel of all kinds, of which about thirteen rise to the dignity of shops. They represent small investments.

Three retail liquor shops and one bottling establishment are conducted by colored people, representing considerable investments. Two of the saloons are old and well conducted, and financially successful. The other saloon and the bottling establishment are not very successful.

Four large employment agencies and some smaller ones are situated in the ward. They conduct lodging houses and in some cases boarding houses in connection. One is sixteen years old; all hire clerks. Their business is to act as agents for persons desiring servants, and to guide unemployed persons to situations; for this they charge a percentage or fixed sum out of the wages. They also often serve as homes for unemployed servants, giving them board and lodging, sometimes on credit. Their work is thus useful and lucrative when properly conducted as in two or three establishments. In one or two others, however, there is some suspicion of unfair dealing; servants are attracted from the South by catchy advertisements and personal letters, only to find themselves eventually penniless and out of work in a large city.[8] Questionable acquaintanceships are also made at the agencies at times, which lead to ruin. These agencies need strict regulation.

There are four undertaking establishments, two of which are conducted by women. They represent investments of $1000–$10,000 and two of them do a business which probably aggregates $8000 or more annually in each case. They are all old establishments—six to thirty-three years—and in no branch of business, save one, has the Negro evinced so much push, taste and enterprise. Two of the establishments will, in equipment, compare favorably with the white businesses in the city; indeed, in fair competition they have gained the great bulk of Negro and some white patronage from white competitors.

Three bakeries, established two and three years respectively are having moderate success. Six printing offices established, one, six months, the others four to seven years, do job work on small presses; two publish weekly papers. These shops are fairly successful and get considerable work from the colored people. One dressmaker has a shop with $150 invested; another runs a dressmaking school.

Four upholsterers have shops, old and well established, and all do a good business; in two cases the business amounts to two to five thousand a year. One sells antique furniture also.

There are a large number of caterers in the ward—eightythree[9] in all. Most of these, however, do a small business, and in some cases have other work also for at least a part of the year. Of the principal caterers there are about ten, of whom the *doyen* was the late Andrew F. Stevens.[10] These ten caterers do a large business, amounting in some cases probably to $3000 to $5000 a year. They have a small co-operative store on Thirteenth street, with a considerable stock of dishes, and such things as olives, pickles, etc. This is conducted by a manager and has one hundred or more members. There is also a caterers' association, which is really a trades union. Its club room serves as a clearing house for business and the employment of waiters. This has been running ten years. The catering business presents many interesting phases to the economist and sociologist. Undoubtedly the pre-eminence of Negroes in this business has declined since the Augustins, Jones and Dorsey passed. Negro caterers are still prominent, but they do not by any means dominate the field, as then. The chief reason for this is the change that has come over American fashionable society in the last twenty-five years, and the application of large capital to the catering business. Philadelphia society is no longer a local affair, but receives its cue as to propriety and fashion from New York, London and Paris; consequently the local caterers can no longer dictate fashion for any single American city; more than this, demands have so risen with increasing wealth that catering establishments like Delmonico's, which would keep in the front rank, represent a large investment of capital—investments far beyond the power of the local Negro caterers of Philadelphia. Thus we find a large business built up by talent and tact, meeting with changed social conditions; the business must therefore change too. It is the old development from the small to the large industry, from the house-industry to the concentrated industry, from the house-industry to the concentrated industry, from the private dining room to the palatial hotel. If the Negro caterers of Philadelphia had been white, some of them would have been put in charge of a large hotel, or would have become co-partners in some large restaurant business, for which capitalists furnished funds. For such business co-operation, however, the time was not ripe, and perhaps only a few of the best Negro caterers would have been capable of entering into it with success. As it was, the change in fashion and mode of business changed the methods of the Negro caterers and their clientele. They began to serve the middle class instead of the rich and exclusive, their prices had to become more reasonable, and their efforts to excel had consequently fewer incentives. Moreover, they now came into sharp competition with a class of small white caterers, who, if they were worse cooks, were better trained in the tricks of the trade. Then, too, with this new and large clientele that personal relationship between the caterer and those served was broken up, and a larger place for color prejudice was made.

It is thus plain that a curious economic revolution in one industry has gone on during twenty-nine years, not unaccompanied by grave social problems. In this case the Negro has emerged in better condition and has shown more capacity for hand-to-hand economic encounter than, for instance, in the barbering business. Yet he has not emerged unscathed; in every such battle, when a Negro is fighting for an economic advantage, there is ever a widespread feeling among all his neighbors that it is inexpedient to allow this class to became wealthy or even well-to-do. Consequently the battle always becomes an *Athanasius contra mundum*, where almost unconsciously the whole countenance and aid of the community is thrown against the Negro.

The three Negro cemetery companies of the city have their headquarters in the Seventh Ward. They arose from the curious prejudice of the whites against allowing Negroes to be buried near their dead. The companies hold valuable property and are fairly well conducted.[11] There are several expressmen in the ward owning their own outfits; one has been established twenty-five years; he has three or four wagons and hires four or five men regularly. There was in 1896 a hardware and furniture business forty-seven years old, on South street, but the proprietor, Robert Adger, has since died.[12] There are several bicycle shops, a flourishing milk, butter and egg store, a china repairing shop, of long standing; a hair goods store, a rubber goods repairing shop, seventeen years old; a second-hand stove store and two patent medicine shops.

To test the accuracy of these statistics and to note changes, a second visit was made in this ward in 1897, with this result:

NEGRO BUSINESS ESTABLISHMENTS, SEVENTH WARD, 1896–97

BUSINESS	1896 (DEC.)	1897 (OCT.)
Restaurants	23	39
Barber shops	23	24
Grocery stores	13	11
Cigar stores	14	11
Candy and notions	4	2
Shoemaker shops	8	13
Upholsterers	4	4
Liquor saloons	3	2
Undertakers	4	4
Newspapers	2	1
Drug store	0	1
Patent medicine stores	2	2
Printing offices	4	4

Such small businesses represent the efforts of a class of poor people to save capital.[13] They are all alike hindered by three great drawbacks: First, the Negro never was trained for business and can get no training now; it is very seldom that a Negro boy or girl can on any terms get a position in a store or other business establishment where he can learn the technique of the work or general business methods. Second, Negro merchants are so rare that it is natural for customers, both white and colored, to take it for granted that their business is poorly conducted without giving it a trial.[14] Third, the Negroes are unused to co-operation with their own people and the process of learning it is long and tedious. Hitherto, their economic activities have been directed almost entirely to the satisfaction of wants of the upper classes of white people, and, too, of personal and household wants; they are just beginning to realize that within their own group there is a vast field for development in economic activity. The 40,000 Negroes of Philadelphia need food, clothes, shoes, hats and furniture; these by proper thrift they see ought to be in part supplied by themselves, and the little business ventures we have noticed are attempts in this direction. These attempts would, however, be vastly more successful in another economic age. To-day, as before noted, the application of large capital to the retail business, the gathering of workmen into factories, the wonderful success of trained talent in catering to the whims and taste of customers almost precludes the effective competition of the small store. Thus the economic condition of the day militates largely against the Negro; it requires more skill and experience to run a small store than formerly and the large store and factory are virtually closed to him on any terms.

Turning now to the other wards of the city let us notice some of the chief business ventures of the Negroes. This list is by no means exhaustive, but it is representative:

WARD	CHARACTER OF BUSINESS	NO. ESTABLISHMENTS
Second	Harness shop	1
Third	Grocery stores	3
	Barber shop	1
Fourth	Barber shops	5
	Second-hand clothing	1
	Second-hand furniture	1
	Coal and wood shops	4
	Newspaper	1
	Restaurants	10
	Hair goods and dressmaking	1
	Expressmen	5
	Decorating and paper-hanging	1
	Job printer	1
	Shoe repair shops	3
	Candy store (manufacture)	1
	Cigar stores	2
	Crockery store	1
	Second-hand stoves	1
Fifth	Barber shops	7
	Pool-room	1
	Shoeblacking shop	1
	Restaurants	8
	Undertaker	1
	Fuel and notions	2
	Cigar store	1
	Publishing house (books and papers)	1
	Blacksmith and wheelwright	1
Eighth	Florist	1
	Watch repairer	1
	Newspaper and job printing	1
	Undertaker	1
	Hotel and liquor saloon	1
	Barber shops	9
	Upholsterers	2
	Rag warehouse	1
	Restaurants	5
	Fuel and newspaper shop	1
	Grocery store	1
	Cigar stores	2
	Employment bureau	1
	Hair dresser for ladies	1
Fourteenth	Barber	1
	Grocery store	1
	Upholsterer	1
	Dealer in mineral water	1
	Second-hand furniture store	1

(Continued)

Ward	Character of Business	No. Establishments
	Fuel and candy store	1
	Restaurants	2
Twentieth	Tailor shop	1
	Shoe-repairing shop	1
	Barber shops	2
Twenty-seventh	Real estate agent	1
	Meat dealer (wholesale)	1
Fifteenth and Twenty-ninth	Carpet cleaning works	1
	Meat and provisions	1
	Barber shops and various small establishments . . .	20
Twenty-sixth and Thirtieth	Second-hand stores	1
	Cigar store	1
	Barber shops	2
	Expressman	1
	Second-hand furniture	1
	Upholsterer	1
	Grocery store	1
	Milk and ice shop	1
	Job printing	1
	Restaurant	1
Twenty-second	Restaurant and lodging house	1
	Grocery stores	2
	Barbers	2
	Upholsterer	1
	Expressman	1
	Steam laundry	1

The most important omissions here are barber shops, on account of the large number, caterers, because their headquarters are mainly in private houses, and many small stores which are easily overlooked and which quickly come and disappear. Some of the businesses are large and important: Three or four caterers do a business of several thousand dollars per year; the well-known Chestnut street florist does a flourishing and well conducted business;[15] the undertaker in the Eighth Ward and the real estate dealer in the Twenty-seventh are unusually successful in their lines. The crockery store in the Fourth Ward is neat and tasty. The three largest enterprises are the provision and wholesale meat businesses in the Fifteenth Ward, and the carpet cleaning works. It is reported that the business of each of these approaches $10,000 a year.

There are five weekly newspapers and a quarterly magazine published in the city by Negroes. Two of the papers are denominational organs for churches; another paper is the official organ of the Odd Fellows; the fourth and fifth are local news sheets. The quarterly is published by the A. M. E. Church. These papers are fairly successful, and are considerably read and reflect the general public opinion pretty well. Most of them have been very weak editorially, though there are some signs of improvement, especially in the case of the quarterly. The publishing house does a business of $15,000 a year.

The Trades—The practical exclusion of the Negro from the trades and industries of a great city like Philadelphia is a situation by no means easy to explain. It is often said simply: the foreigners and trades unions have crowded Negroes out on account of race prejudice and left employers and philanthropists helpless in the matter. This is not strictly true. What the trades unions and white workmen have done is to seize an economic advantage plainly offered them. This opportunity arose from three causes: Here was a mass of black workmen of whom very few were by previous training fitted to become the mechanics and artisans of a new industrial development; here, too, were an increasing mass of foreigners and native Americans who were unusually well fitted to take part in the new industries; finally, most people were willing and many eager that Negroes should be kept as menial servants rather than develop into industrial factors. This was the situation, and here was the opportunity for the white workmen; they were by previous training better workmen on the average than Negroes; they were stronger numerically and the result was that every new industrial enterprise started in the city took white workmen. Soon the white workmen were strong enough to go a step further than this and practically prohibit Negroes from entering trades under any circumstances; this affected not only new enterprises, but also old trades like carpentering, masonry, plastering and the like. The supply of Negroes for such trades could not keep pace with the extraordinary growth of the city and a large number of white workmen entered the field. They immediately combined against Negroes primarily to raise wages; the standard of living of the Negroes lets them accept low wages, and, conversely, long necessity of accepting the meagre wages offered have made a low standard of living. Thus partially by taking advantage of race prejudice, partially by greater economic efficiency and partially by the endeavor to maintain and raise wages, white workmen have not only monopolized the new industrial opportunities of an age which has transformed Philadelphia from a colonial town to a world-city, but have also been enabled to take from the Negro workman the opportunities he already enjoyed in certain lines of work.

If now a benevolent despot had seen the development, he would immediately have sought to remedy the real weakness of the Negro's position, *i.e.*, his lack of training; and he would have swept away any discrimination that compelled men to support as criminals those who might support themselves as workmen.

He would have made special effort to train Negro boys for industrial life and given them a chance to compete on equal terms with the best white workmen; arguing that in the long run this would be best for all concerned, since by raising the skill and standard of living of the Negroes he would make them effective workmen and competitors who would maintain a decent level of wages. He would have sternly suppressed organized or covert opposition to Negro workmen.

There was, however, no benevolent despot, no philanthropist, no far-seeing captain of industry to prevent the Negro from losing even the skill he had learned or to inspire him by opportunities to learn more. As the older Negroes with trades dropped off, there was little to induce younger men to succeed them. On the contrary special effort was made not to train Negroes for industry or to allow them to enter on such a career. Consequently they gradually slipped out of industrial life until in 1890 when the Negroes formed 4 per cent of the population, only 1.1 per cent of 134,709 men in the principal trades of the city were Negroes; of 46,200 women in these trades 1.3 per cent were Negroes; or taking men and women together, 2160 or 1.19 per cent of all were Negroes. This does not, however, tell the whole story, for of this 2160, the barbers, brickmakers, and dressmakers formed 1434. In the Seventh Ward the number in the trades is much larger than the proportion in the city, but here again they are confined to a few trades—barbers, dressmakers, cigarmakers and shoemakers.

How now has this exclusion been maintained? In some cases by the actual inclusion of the word "white" among qualifications for entrance into certain trade unions. More often, however, by leaving the matter of color entirely to local bodies, who make no general rule, but invariably fail to admit a colored applicant except under pressing circumstances. This is the most workable system and is adopted by nearly all trade unions. In sections where Negro labor in certain trades is competent and considerable, the trades union welcomes them, as in Western Pennsylvania among miners and iron-workers, and in Philadelphia among cigarmakers; but whenever there is a trade where good Negro workmen are comparatively scarce each union steadfastly refuses to admit Negroes, and relies on color prejudice to keep up the barrier. Thus the carpenters, masons, painters, iron-workers, etc., have succeeded in keeping out nearly all Negro workmen by simply declining to work with non-union men and refusing to let colored men join the union. Sometimes, in time of strikes, the unions are compelled in self-defence not only to allow Negroes to join but to solicit them; this happened, for instance, in the stone-cutters' strike some years ago.

To repeat, then, the real motives back of this exclusion are plain: a large part is simple race prejudice, always strong in working classes and intensified by the peculiar history of the Negro in this country. Another part, however, and possibly a more potent part, is the natural spirit of monopoly and the desire to keep up wages. So long as a cry against "Irish" or "foreigners" was able to marshal race prejudice in the service of those who desired to keep those people out of some employments, that cry was sedulously used. So to-day the workmen plainly see that a large amount of competition can be shut off by taking advantage of public opinion and drawing the color line. Moreover, in this there is one thoroughly justifiable consideration that plays a great part: namely, the Negroes are used to low wages—can live on them, and consequently would fight less fiercely than most whites against reduction.

The employers in this matter are not altogether blameless. Their objects in conducting business are not, of course, wholly philanthropic, and yet, as a class, they represent the best average intelligence and morality of the community. A firm stand by some of them for common human right might save the city something in taxes for the suppression of crime and vice. There came some time since to the Midvale Steel Works a manager whom many dubbed a "crank;" he had a theory that Negroes and whites could work together as mechanics without friction or trouble.[16] In spite of some protest he put his theory into practice, and to-day any one can see Negro mechanics working in the same gangs with white mechanics without disturbance. A few other cases on a smaller scale have occurred throughout the city. In general, however, the black mechanic who seeks work from a mill owner, or a contractor, or a capitalist is told: "I have no feeling in the matter, but my men will not work with you." Without doubt, in many cases, the employer is really powerless; in many other cases he is not powerless, but is willing to appear so.

The Negroes of the city who have trades either give them up and hire out as waiters or laborers, or they become job workmen and floating hands, catching a bit of carpentering here or a little brick-work or plastering there at reduced wages. Undoubtedly much blame can rightly be laid at the door of Negroes for submitting rather tamely to this organized opposition. If they would meet organization with organization and excellence of work by excellence, they could do much to win standing in the industries of the cities. This is to-day hard to begin, but it is worth the trying, and the Industrial Department of the Institute for Colored Youth, which the Negroes themselves helped equip, is a step in this direction.

Clerks, Semi-professional and Responsible Workers—Under this head has been grouped a miscellaneous mass of occupations: clerks in public and private service, stewards, messengers, musicians, agents, managers and foremen, actors, policemen, etc., *i.e.*, that class of persons whose position demands a degree of attainment in education, reliability, talent or skill. Here the number of Negroes is small, but they are nearly as well represented as in trades—an indication of a rather abnormal development. Of 46,393 men in this class of occupations in the city (*i.e.*, policemen, watchmen, agents, commercial travelers, bankers and brokers, bookkeepers, clerks and salesmen, and barkeepers) 327, or seven-tenths of 1 per cent were Negroes; if we add to this stewards, messengers, musicians, and clerks in government service, they form about 1 per cent of those in the city. Nearly all the clerks and salesmen are to be found in Negro stores, although there are a few exceptions.

CLERKS, SEMI-PROFESSIONAL AND RESPONSIBLE WORKERS
IN PHILADELPHIA, 1890

Occupation	Total	Negroes
Watchmen, policemen and detectives	4,113	62
Bartenders	1,683	32
Agents and collectors	5,049	38
Bankers, brokers, etc.	2,072	6
Bookkeepers, clerks, etc.	23,057	130
Salesmen	10,419	38
Total	46,393	326

There are about sixty colored policemen on the force at present, and the general impression seems to be that they make good average officers. They were first appointed to the police force by Mayor King in 1884. At first there was violent opposition, which would have been listened to had it not been for political complications. The Negro policemen are put on duty mostly in or near the chief Negro settlements and no one of them has yet been promoted from the ranks. The number of Negroes in government service is as follows:

Municipal departments	11
Custom House	1
Post-office	17
Navy yard	1

Beside these there are a number of messengers and ordinary laborers. In many cases these clerks have made very excellent records, as in the case of the discount clerk in the tax office, who has held his position for many years, and is perhaps the most efficient clerk in the office; or again the Negro postmaster and employes in the post-office at Wanamaker's store who have been unusually successful in administrating the second largest sub-station in the city. In a few cases certain Negroes have received office through political influence and have been plainly unfitted for their work.

There are a few clerks in responsible positions—one employed by the Pennsylvania railway company, another in a bank. Such cases, however, are rare.

Laborers—The great mass of the men and a large percentage of the women are manual laborers—*i.e.,* teamsters, janitors, stevedores, hod-carriers, hostlers, elevator-men, sailors, china-packers and night-watchmen. Their wages are usually:

Teamsters	$1 to $1.50 a day.
Janitors	$30 to $60 a month.
Stevedores	20c. to 30c. an hour (irregular employment).
Hod-carriers	$1.50 to $2.50 a day (employed according to season).
Hostlers	$16 to $30 a month.
Elevator-men	$16 to $25 a month.

Besides these there are the ordinary porters, errand boys, newsboys and day-laborers, whose earnings vary considerably, but usually are too small to support a family without much help from wife and children. Stevedores, hod-carriers and day-laborers are especially liable to irregular employment, which makes life hard for them sometimes. The mass of the men are, save in the lower grades, given average wages and meet their greatest difficulty in securing work. The competition in ordinary laboring work is severe in so crowded a city. The women day-laborers are, on the whole, poorly paid, and meet fierce competition in laundry work and cleaning.

The most noticeable thing about the Negro laborers as a whole is their uneven quality. There are some first-class, capable and willing workers, who have held their positions for years and give perfect satisfaction. On the other hand, there are numbers of inefficient and unintelligent laborers on whom employers cannot rely and who are below average American labor in ability. This unevenness arises from two causes: the different training of the various groups of Negroes composing the city population; some are the descendants of generations of free Negroes; some of trained house-servants, long in close contact with their masters' families;

others are the sons of field-hands, untouched and untrained by contact with civilized institutions: all this vast difference in preparation shows vast differences in results. The second reason lies in the increased competition within the group, and the growing lack of incentive to good work, owing to the difficulty of escaping from manual toil into higher and better paid callings; the higher classes of white labor are continually being incorporated into the skilled trades, or clerical workers, or other higher grades of labor. Sometimes this happens with Negroes but not often. The first-class ditcher can seldom become foreman of a gang; the hod-carrier can seldom become a mason; the porter cannot have much hope of being a clerk, or the elevator-boy of becoming a salesman. Consequently we find the ranks of the laborers among Negroes filled to an unusual extent with disappointed men, with men who have lost the incentive to excel, and have become chronic grumblers and complainers, spreading this spirit further than it would naturally go. At the same time this shutting of the natural outlet for ability means an increase of competition for ordinary work.

Without doubt there is not in Philadelphia enough work of the kind that the mass of Negroes can and may do, to employ at fair wages the laborers who at present desire work. The result of this must, of course, be disastrous, and give rise to many loafers, criminals, and casual laborers. The situation is further complicated by the fact that in seasons when work is more plentiful, temporary immigrations from the South swell the number of laborers abnormally; every spring the tide of immigration sets in, consisting of brickmakers, teamsters, asphalt-workers, common laborers, etc., who work during the summer in the city and return to the cheaper living of Virginia and Maryland for the winter. This makes the competition in summer close for Philadelphians, and often brings actual distress in winter. A pressing duty is to see that the opportunities for work in the city are not misrepresented, and to relieve congestion in some avenues by opening others to Negro labor. Nor would this be a boon simply for Negroes: the excessive competition of Negroes in certain lines of work makes more suffering for their white competitors than if that competition were less intense in places and spread over a larger area. White hod-carriers and porters suffer greatly from competition, while other branches of labor are artificially protected—an economic injustice which might be remedied.

Another custom that works much harm to all classes and colors of laborers is the custom of working exclusively white or exclusively colored gangs of workmen. It is unjust to the Negro because it virtually closes the greater part of the field of labor against him, since his numbers are small compared with the population of the city, and it is harder for him to gather gangs than for the whites. It is, however, a fruitful cause of injustice to white laborers; for the contractor who gets a gang of Negroes to work, has a temptation to force down wages which he seldom resists or cares to resist. He knows that the standard of living of the Negroes is low, and their chances for employment limited. He therefore takes on a gang of Negroes, lowers wages, and then if whites wish to regain their places, they must accept the lower wages. The white laborers then blame the Negroes for bringing down wages—a charge with just enough truth in it to intensify existing prejudices. If laborers on ordinary jobs were hired regardless of color and according to efficiency, no doubt both white and black labor would gain, and the employer would not in the long run lose much.

Servants—Probably over one-fourth of the domestic servants of Philadelphia are Negroes, and conversely nearly one-third of the Negroes in the city are servants. This makes the Negro a central problem in any careful study of domestic service, and domestic service a large part of the Negro problems. The matter thus is so important that it has been made the subject of a special study appended to this work. A few general considerations only will be advanced here.

So long as entrance into domestic service involves a loss of all social standing and consideration, so long will domestic service be a social problem. The problem may vary in character with different countries and times, but there will always be some maladjustment in social relations when any considerable part of a population is required to get its support in a manner which the other part despises, or affects to despise. In the United States the problem is complicated by the fact that for years domestic service was performed by slaves, and afterward, up till to-day, largely by black freedmen—thus adding a despised race to a despised calling. Even when white servants increased in number they were composed of white foreigners, with but a small proportion of native Americans. Thus by long experience the United States has come to associate domestic service with some inferiority in race or training.

The effect of this attitude on the character of the service rendered, and the relation of mistress and maid, has been only too evident, and has in late years engaged the attention of some students and many reformers. These have pointed out how necessary and worthy a work the domestic performs, or could perform, if properly trained; that the health, happiness and efficiency of thousands of homes, which are training the future leaders of the republic, depend largely on their domestic service. This is true, and yet the remedy for present ills is not clear until we recognize how far removed the present commercial method of hiring a servant in market is from that which obtained at the time when the daughters of the family, or of the neighbor's family, helped in the housework. In other words, the industrial revolution of the century has affected domestic service along with other sorts of labor, by separating employer and employed into distinct classes. With the Negro the effect of this was not apparent so long as slavery lasted; the house servant remained an integral part of the master's family, with rights and duties. When emancipation broke this relation there went forth to hire a number of trained black servants, who were welcomed South and North; they liked their work, they knew no other kind, they understood it, and they made ideal servants. In Philadelphia twenty or thirty years ago there were plenty of this class of Negro servants and a few are still left.

A generation has, however, greatly altered the face of affairs. There were in the city, in 1890, 42,795 servants, and of these 10,235 were Negroes. Who are these Negroes? No longer members of Virginia households trained for domestic work, but principally young people who were using domestic service as a stepping-stone to something else; who worked as servants simply because they could get nothing else to do; who had received no training in service because they never expected to make it their life-calling. They, in common with their white fellow citizens, despised domestic service as a relic of slavery, and they longed to get other work as their fathers had longed to be free. In getting other work, however, they were not successful, partly on account of lack of ability, partly on account of the strong race prejudice against them. Consequently to-day the ranks of Negro servants, and that means largely the ranks of domestic service in general in Philadelphia, have received all those whom the harsh competition of a great city has pushed down, all whom a relentless color proscription has turned back from other chosen vocations; half-trained teachers and poorly equipped students who have not succeeded; carpenters and masons who may not work at their trades; girls with common school training, eager for the hard work but respectable standing of shop girls and factory hands, and proscribed by their color—in fact, all those young people who, by natural evolution in the case of the whites, would have stepped a grade higher than their fathers and mothers in the social scale, have in the case of the post-bellum generation of Negroes been largely forced back into the great mass of the listless and incompetent to earn bread and butter by menial service.

And they resent it; they are often discontented and bitter, easily offended and without interest in their work. Their attitude and complaint increases the discontent of their fellows who have little ability, and probably could not rise in the world if they might. And, above all, both the disappointed and the incompetents are alike ignorant of domestic service in nearly all its branches, and in this respect are a great contrast to the older set of Negro servants.

Under such circumstances the first far-sighted movement would have been to open such avenues of work and employment to young Negroes that only those best fitted for domestic work would enter service. Of course this is difficult to do even for the whites, and yet it is still the boast of America that, within certain limits, talent can choose the best calling for its exercise. Not so with Negro youth. On the contrary, the field for exercising their talent and ambition is, broadly speaking, confined to the dining room, kitchen and street. If now competition had drained off the talented and aspiring into other avenues, and eased the competition in this one vocation, then there would have been room for a second movement, namely, for training schools, which would fit the mass of Negro and white domestic servants for their complicated and important duties. Such a twin movement—the diversification of Negro industry and the serious training of domestic servants—would do two things: it would take the ban from the calling of domestic service by ceasing to make "Negro" and "servant" synonymous terms. This would make it possible for both whites and blacks to enter more freely into service without a fatal and disheartening loss of self-respect; secondly, it would furnish trained servants—a sad necessity to-day, as any housekeeper can testify.

Such a movement did not, however, take place, but, on the contrary, another movement. English trained servants, the more docile Swedes and better paid white servants were brought into displace Negro servants. One has but to notice the coachmen on the driveways, or the butlers on Rittenhouse Square, or the nursemaids in Fairmount Park, to see how largely white servants have displaced Negroes. How has this displacement been brought about? First, by getting better trained and more willing servants; secondly, by paying servants higher wages.

The Swedish and American servants, in most cases, know more of domestic service than the post-bellum generation of Negroes, and certainly as a class they are far more reconciled to their lot. In the higher branches of domestic service— cooks, butlers and coachmen—the process has been to substitute a man at $50 to $75 a month for one at $30 to $40, and naturally again the result has been gratifying, because a better class of men are attracted by the wages; thus the waiters at the new large hotels are not merely white, but better paid, and undoubtedly ought to render better service. In these ways without doubt domestic service has in some respects improved in the city by a partial substitution of better trained, better paid and more contented white servants for poorly trained, discontented, and in the case of waiters, butlers and coachmen, poorly paid Negroes. Moreover, the substitution has not met with active opposition or economic resistance on the part of the Negroes, because fully one-half of those in domestic service would be only too glad to get other work of any kind.

What now has been the result of these economic changes? The result has undoubtedly been the increase of crime, pauperism and idleness among Negroes: because while they are being to some extent displaced as servants, no corresponding opening for employment in other lines has been made. How long can such a process continue? How long can a community pursue such a contradictory economic policy—first confining a large portion of its population to a pursuit which public opinion persists in looking down upon; then displacing them even there by better trained and better paid competitors. Manifestly such a course is bound to make that portion of the community a burden on the public; to debauch its women, pauperize its men, and ruin its homes; it makes the one central question of the Seventh Ward, not imperative social betterments, raising of the standard of home life, taking advantage of the civilizing institutions of the great city—on the contrary, it makes it a sheer question of bread and butter and the maintenance of a standard of living above that of the Virginia plantation.

Nor has the whole group failed in every case to answer this question: the foregoing statistics show how, slowly and under many discouragements, diversification of employments is taking place among the black population. This, however, is the brighter side and represents the efforts of that determined class among all people that surmount eventually nearly all obstacles. The spirit of the age however looks to-day not to the best and most energetic, but to those on the edge, those who will become effective members of society only when properly encouraged. The great mass of the Negroes naturally belong to this class and when we turn to the darker side of the picture and study the disease, poverty and crime of the Negro population, then we realize that the question of employment for Negroes is the most pressing of the day and that the starting point is domestic service which still remains their peculiar province. First then as before said the object of social reform should be so to diversify Negro employments as to afford proper escape from menial employment for the talented few, and so as to allow the mass some choice in their lifework: this would be not only for the sake of Negro development, but for the sake of a great human industry which must continue to suffer as long as the odium of race is added to a disposition to look down upon the employment under any circumstances; the next movement ought to be to train servants—not toward servility and toadying, but in problems of health and hygiene, in proper cleaning and cooking, and in matters of etiquette and good form.

To this must be added such arousing of the public conscience as shall lead people to recognize more keenly than now the responsibility of the family toward its servants—to remember that they are constituent members of the family group and as such have rights and privileges as well as duties. To-day in Philadelphia the tendency is the other way. Thousands of servants no longer lodge where they work but are free at night to wander at will, to hire lodgings in suspicious houses, to consort with paramours, and thus to bring moral and physical disease to their place of work. A reform is imperatively needed, and here, as in most of the Negro problems, a proper reform will benefit white and black alike—the employer as well as the employed.

24. History of the Occupations of Negroes—There early arose in the colony of Pennsylvania the custom of hiring out slaves, especially mechanics and skilled workmen. This very soon roused the ire of the free white workmen, and in 1708 and 1722 we find them petitioning the legislature against the practice, and receiving some encouragement therefrom. As long, however, as an influential class of slaveholders had a direct financial interest in black mechanics they saw to it that neither law nor prejudice hindered Negroes from working. Thus before and after the Revolution there were mechanics as well as servants among the Negroes. The proportion of servants, however, was naturally very large. We have no figures until 1820, when of, the 7,582 Negroes in the city, 2,585 or 34 per cent were servants; in 1840, 27 per cent were servants. Some of these servants represented families, so that the proportion of those dependent on domestic service was larger even than the percentage indicated. In 1896 in the Seventh Ward the per cent of servants, using the same method of computation, was 27.3 per cent.

Of those not servants, the Negroes themselves declared in 1832, that "notwithstanding the difficulty of getting places for our sons as apprentices to learn mechanical trades, owing to the prejudices with which we have to contend, there are between four and five hundred people of color in the city and suburbs who follow mechanical employments." In 1838 the investigator of the Abolition Society found 997 of the 17,500 Negroes in the county who had learned trades, although only a part of these (perhaps 350) actually worked at their trades at that time. The rest, outside the servants and men with trades, were manual laborers. Many of these mechanics were afterward driven from the city by the mobs.

In 1848 another study of the Negroes found the distribution of the Negroes as follows:

Of 3,358 men, twenty-one years of age and over:

Laborers	1,581
Waiters, cooks, etc.	557
Mechanics	286
Coachmen, carters, etc.	276
Sailors, etc.	240
Shopkeepers, traders, etc.	166
Barbers	156
Various occupations	96
	3,358

Of 4,249 women, twenty-one years and over there were:

Washerwomen	1,970
Seamstresses	486
Day workers	786
In trades	213
Housewives	290
Servants (living at home)	156
Cooks	173
Rag pickers	103
Various occupations	72
	4,249

Of both sexes five to twenty years of age there were:

School children	1,940
Unaccounted for	1,200
At home	484
Helpless	33
Working at home	274
Servants	354
Laborers	253
Sweeps	12
Porters	18
Apprentices	230
	4,798

Besides these there were in white families 3,716 servants.

Just how accurate the statistics of 1847 were it is now difficult to say, probably there was some exaggeration from the well-meant effort of the friends of the Negro to show the best side. Nevertheless it seems as though the diversity of employments at this time was considerable, although of course under such heads as "shopkeepers and traders" street stands more often than stores were meant.

In 1856 the inquiry appears to have been more exhaustive and careful, and the number of Negroes with trades had increased to 1,637—including barbers and dressmakers. Even here, however, some uncertainty enters, for "less than two-thirds of those who have trades follow them. A few of the remainder pursue other avocations from choice, but the greater number are compelled to abandon their trades on account of the unrelenting prejudice against their color." The following table gives these returns:

OCCUPATION OF PHILADELPHIA NEGROES, 1856

MECHANICAL TRADES

Dressmakers	588
Barbers	248
Shoemakers	112
Shirt and dressmakers	70
Brickmakers	53
Carpenters	49

(Continued)

OCCUPATION OF PHILADELPHIA NEGROES, 1856—*Continued*

MECHANICAL TRADES

Milliners and dressmakers	45
Tailors	49
Tanners and curriers	24
Blacksmiths	22
Cabinetmakers	20
Weavers	16
Pastry cooks	10
Plasterers	14
Sailmakers	12
113 other trades with one to nine in each	305

1,637

In the light of such historical testimony it seems certain that the industrial condition of the Negro in the last century has undergone great vicissitudes, although it is difficult sometimes to trace them. A diagram something like this would possibly best represent the historical development for a century:

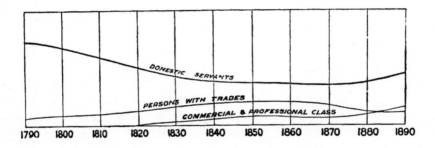

Such a diagram must of course be based largely upon conjecture, but it represents as nearly as the data allow the proportionate—not the absolute—extent to which the Negroes of the city are represented in certain pursuits.

In the half century 1840 to 1890 the proportion of Negroes who are domestic servants has not greatly changed; the mass of the remainder are still laborers; their opportunities for employment have been restricted by three causes: competition, industrial change, color prejudice. The competition has come in later years from the phenomenal growth of cities and the consequent hardening of conditions of life; the Negro has especially felt this change because of all the elements of our urban population he is least prepared by previous training for rough, keen competition; the industrial changes since and just before the emancipation of the slaves have had a great influence on their development, to which little notice has hitherto been given. In the industrial history of nations the change from agriculture to manufacturing and trade has been a long, delicate process: first came house industries—spinning and weaving and the like; then the market with its simple processes of barter and sale; then the permanent stall or shop, and at last the small retail store. In our day this small retail store is in process of evolution to something larger and more comprehensive. When we look at this development and see how suddenly the American city Negro has been snatched from agriculture to the centres of trade and manufactures, it should not surprise us to learn that he has not as yet succeeded in finding a permanent place in that vast system of industrial co-operation. Apart from all questions of race, his problem in this respect is greater than the problem of the white country boy or the European peasant immigrant, because his previous industrial condition was worse than theirs and less calculated to develop the power of self-adjustment, self-reliance and co-operation. All these considerations are further complicated by the fact that the industrial condition of the Negro cannot be considered apart from the great fact of race prejudice—indefinite and shadowy as that phrase may be. It is certain that, while industrial co-operation among the groups of a great city population is very difficult under ordinary circumstances, that here it is rendered more difficult and in some respects almost impossible by the fact that nineteen-twentieths of the population have in many cases refused to co-operate with the other twentieth, even when the co-operation means life to the latter and great advantage to the former. In other words, one of the great postulates of the science of economics—that men will seek their economic advantage—is in this case untrue, because in many cases men will not do this if it involves association, even in a casual and business way, with Negroes. And this fact must be taken account of in all judgments as to the Negro's economic progress.

NOTES

1. The returns as to occupations are on the whole reliable. There was in the first place little room for deception, since the occupations of Negroes are so limited that a false or indefinite answer was easily revealed by a little judicious probing; moreover there was little disposition to deceive, for the Negroes are very anxious to have their limited opportunities for employment known; thus the motives of pride and complaint balanced each other fairly well. Some error of course remains: the number of servants and day workers is slightly understated; the number of caterers and men with trades is somewhat exaggerated by the answers of men with two occupations: *e.g.*, a waiter with a small side business of catering returns himself as caterer; a carpenter who gets little work and makes his living largely as a laborer is sometimes returned as a carpenter, etc. In the main the errors are small and of little consequence.

2. A more detailed list of the occupations of male Negroes, twenty-one years of age and over, living in the Seventh Ward in 1896, is as follows:

ENTREPRENEURS

Caterers	65	Employment Agents	3
Hucksters	37	Lodging House Keepers	3
Proprietors Hotels and Restaurants	22	Proprietors of Pool Rooms	3
Merchants: Fuel and Notions	22	Real Estate Agencies	3
Proprietors of Barber Shops	15	Job Printers	3
Expressmen owning outfit	14	Builder and Contractor	1
Merchants, Cigar Stores	7	Sub-landlord	1
Merchants, Grocery Stores	4	Milk Dealer	1
Proprietors of Undertaking		Publisher	1
Establishments	2		207

IN LEARNED PROFESSIONS

Clergymen	22	Dentists	3
Students	17	Editors	1
Teachers	7		—
Physicians	6		61
Lawyers	5		

IN THE SKILLED TRADES

Barbers	64	Apprentice	1
Cigar Makers	39	Boilermaker	1
Shoemakers	18	Blacksmit	1
Stationary Engineers	13	China Repairer	1
Bricklayers	11	Cooper	1
Printers	10	Cabinetmaker	1
Painters	10	Dyer	1
Upholsterers	7	Furniture Polisher	1
Carpenters	6	Gold Beater	1
Bakers	4	Kalsominer	1
Tailors	4	Locksmith	1
Undertakers	4	Laundryman (steam)	1
Brickmakers	3	Paper Hanger	1
Framemakers	3	Roofer	1
Plasterers	3	Tinsmith	1
Rubber Workers	3	Wicker Worker	1
Stone Cutters	3	Horse Trainer	1
Bookbinders	2	Chemist	1
Candy Makers	2	Florist	1
Chiropodists	2	Pilot	1
Ice Carvers	2		—
Photographers	2		236

CLERKS, SEMI-PROFESSIONAL AND RESPONSIBLE WORKERS

Messengers	33	Policemen	5
Stewards	31	Sextons	4
Musicians	20	Shipping Clerks	3
Clerks	18	Dancing Masters	3
Agents	15	Inspector in Factory	1
Clerks in Public Service	8	Cashier	1
Managers and Foremen	6		—
Actors	6		159
Bartenders	5		

SERVANTS

Domestics	582	Nurses	2
Hotel Help	457		—
Public Waiters	38		1,079

LABORERS (SELECT CLASS)

Stevedores	164	China Packers	14
Teamsters	134	Watchmen	14
Janitors	94	Drivers	12
Hod Carriers	79	Oyster Openers	4
Hostlers	44		——
Elevator Men	22		602
Sailors	21		

LABORERS (ORDINARY)

Common Laborers	493	Casual Laborers	12
Porters	274	Miscellaneous Laborers	4
Laborers for City	47		——
Bootblacks	22		852

MISCELLANEOUS

Rag Pickers	6	Prize Fighter	1
"Politicians"	2		——
Root Doctors	2		11

3. This includes 12 housewives who also work.
4. A more detailed list of the occupations of female Negroes, twenty-one years of age and over, living in the Seventh Ward in 1896, is as follows:

ENTREPRENEURS

Caterers	18	Undertakers	3
Restaurant Keepers	17	Child-Nursery Keepers	3
Merchants	17		——
Employment Agents	5		63

LEARNED PROFESSIONS

Teachers	22	Students	7
Trained Nurses	8		——
			37

SKILLED TRADES

Dressmakers	204	Manicure	1
Hairdressers	6	Barber	1
Milliners	3	Typesetter	1
Shrouders of Dead	4		——
Apprentice	1		221

CLERKS, SEMI-PROFESSIONAL AND RESPONSIBLE WORKERS

Musicians	12	Matrons	2
Clerks	10	Actress	1
Stewardesses	4	Missionary	1
Housekeepers	4		——
Agents	3		40
Stenographers	3		

LABORERS, ETC.

Housewives and Day Workers	937	Janitresses	22
Day Workers	128	Factory Employee	1
Public Cooks	72	Office Maids	12
Seamstresses	48		
Waitresses in Restaurants, etc.	14		1,234

SERVANTS

Domestic Servants 1,262

5. A better comparison here would be made by finding the percentages of the population above 10 years of age; statistics unfortunately are not available for this.
6. This has been the case only in comparatively recent times.
7. Negroes also buy immense quantities of patent medicines, etc.
8. In Norfolk, Va., I once saw the advertisement on a street sign calling for colored "clerks, saleswomen, stenographers," etc., for Northern cities!
9. This total includes a large number of men and women who do some private catering, but for the most part work under other caterers; strictly a large part of them are waiters rather than caterers.
10. Mr. Stevens died in 1898—he was an honest, reliable, business man—of pleasant address, and universally respected. He was easily the successor of Dorsey, Jones and Minton in the catering business.
11. When the caterer Henry Jones died his funeral procession was actually turned back from the cemetery by the refusal of the authorities of Mt. Moriah Cemetery to allow him interment there; he had before his death bought and paid for a lot in the cemetery and the Supreme Court eventually confirmed his title. To-day this absurd prejudice is not so strong and Negroes own lots in the Episcopal Cemetery of St. James the Less and in perhaps one other.
12. The following clipping from the Philadelphia *Ledger*, November 2, 1896, illustrates a typical life:
    "Robert Adger, a colored Abolitionist, died on Saturday, at his home, 835 South street. He was born a slave, in Charleston, S. C., in 1813. His mother, who was born in New York, went to South Carolina about 1810, with some of her relatives, and while there was detained as a slave.
    "When his master died, Mr. Adger, together with his mother and other members of the family, were sold at auction, but, through the assistance of friends, legal proceedings were instituted, and their release finally secured. Mr. Adger then came to this city about 1845, and secured a position as a waiter in the old Merchants' Hotel. Later he was employed as a nurse, and while working in that capacity, saved enough money to start in the furniture business on South street, above Eighth, which he continued to conduct with success until his death. Mr. Adger always took an active interest in the welfare of the people of his race."
13. One enterprising capitalist hires and sub-rents eight different houses with furnished apartments, paying $1,944 annually in rent; he has a bicycle shop which brings in $1,000 a year for an expense of about $330. He also owns a barber shop which brings in about $1,000 a year; one-half the gross receipts of this he pays to a foreman, who pays his journeymen barbers; the owner pays for rent and material. "If I had an education," he said, "I could get on better."
14. Several storekeepers have had white persons enter the store, look at the proprietors and say "Oh! I—er—made a mistake," and go out.
15. Here was a case where some persons sought to drive an enterprising and talented Negro out of business simply because he was colored. A Chestnut street property owner made a special effort to give him a start and now he conducts a business of which no merchant need be ashamed.
16. The large steel manufactory known as the "Midvale Steel Works" is located at Nicetown, near Germantown, in Philadelphia County. This establishment was visited by the writer, and the manager of the establishment interviewed as to the success of the experiment made by him in employing Negroes as workmen along with whites.
    About 1,200 men are employed altogether, and fully 200 of these are Negroes. About 40 per cent of the whole number of employes are American-born, but generally of Irish, English or German

parentage. The remaining 43 per cent are foreign-born, chiefly English, Irish and German, with a few Swedes.

"Our object in putting Negroes on the force," said the manager, "was twofold. First, we believed them to be good workmen; secondly, we thought they could be used to get over one difficulty we had experienced at Midvale, namely, the clannish spirit of the workmen and a tendency to form cliques. In steel manufacture much of the work is done with large tools run by gangs of men; the work was crippled by the different foremen trying always to have the men in their gang all of their own nationality. The English foreman of a hammer gang, for instance, would want only Englishmen, and the Irish Catholics only Irishmen. This was not good for the works, nor did it promote friendliness among the workmen. So we began bringing in Negroes and placing them on different gangs, and at the same time we distributed the other nationalities. Now our gangs have, say, one Negro, one or two Americans, an Englishman, etc. The result has been favorable both for the men and for the works. Things run smoothly, and the output is noticeably greater."

"The manager was especially questioned about the grade of work done by Negroes and their efficiency as skilled workmen. He said: "They do all the grades of work done by the white workmen. Some of this work is of such a nature that it had been supposed that only very intelligent English and American workmen could be trusted with it. We have 100 colored men doing that skilled work now, and they do it as well as any of the others."

As to wages, the manager said no discrimination was made between Negroes and whites. They start as laborers at $1.20 a day and "we try to treat them as individuals, not as a herd; they know that good work gives them a chance for better work and better pay. Thus their ambition is aroused; yesterday, for instance, four Negroes saved a furnace worth $30,000. The furnace was full of molten steel, which had become clogged, so that it could not be gotten out in the usual way. A number of powerful men were required to open the side of the furnace. Four colored men volunteered and saved the steel."

With regard to the relations between white and black workmen the manager said: "We have had no trouble at all. The unions generally hold potential strikes over their employers' heads to keep the Negro out of employment. There has, however, been no strike in this establishment for seventeen years, and Negroes have been employed for the last seven years."

Finally the manager declared that according to his belief the Negro workman does not have half a chance to show his ability. "He does good work and betters his condition when he has any inducement to do so."

ISABEL EATON

CHAPTER X

◆

The Health of Negroes

25. The Interpretation of Statistics—The characteristic signs which usually accompany a low civilization are a high birth rate and a high death rate; or, in other words, early marriages and neglect of the laws of physical health. This fact, which has often been illustrated by statistical research, has not yet been fully apprehended by the general public because they have long been used to hearing more or less true tales of the remarkable health and longevity of barbarous peoples. For this reason the recent statistical research which reveals the large death rate among American Negroes is open to very general misapprehension. It is a remarkable phenomenon which throws much light on the Negro problems and suggests some obvious solutions. On the other hand, it does not prove, as most seem to think, a vast recent change in the condition of the Negro. Reliable data as to the physical health of the Negro in slavery are entirely wanting; and yet, judging from the horrors of the middle passage, the decimation on the West Indian plantations, and the bad sanitary condition of the Negro quarters on most Southern plantations, there must have been an immense death rate among slaves, notwithstanding all reports as to endurance, physical strength and phenomenal longevity. Just how emancipation has affected this death rate is not clear; the rush to cities, where the surroundings are unhealthful, has had a bad effect, although this migration on a large scale is so recent that its full effect is not yet apparent; on the other hand, the better care of children and improvement in home life has also had some favorable effect. On the whole, then, we must remember that reliable statistics as to Negro health are but recent in date and that as yet no important conclusions can be arrived at as to historic changes or tendencies. One thing we must of course expect to find, and that is a much higher death rate at present among Negroes than among whites: this is one measure of the difference in their social advancement. They have in the past lived under vastly different conditions and they still live under different conditions: to assume that, in discussing the inhabitants of Philadelphia, one is discussing people living under the same conditions of life, is to assume what is not true. Broadly speaking, the Negroes as a class dwell in the most unhealthful parts of the city and in the worst houses in those parts; which is of course simply saying that the part of the population having a large degree of poverty, ignorance and general social degradation is usually to be found in the worst portions of our great cities.

Therefore, in considering the health statistics of the Negroes, we seek first to know their absolute condition, rather than their relative status; we want to know what their death rate is, how it has varied and is varying and what its tendencies seem to be; with these facts fixed we must then ask, What is the meaning of a death rate like that of the Negroes of Philadelphia? Is it, compared with other races, large, moderate or small; and in the case of nations or groups with similar death rates, What has been the tendency and outcome? Finally, we must compare the death rate of the Negroes with that of the communities in which they live and thus roughly measure the social difference between these neighboring groups; we must endeavor also to eliminate, so far as possible, from the problem disturbing elements which would make a difference in health among people of the same social advancement. Only in this way can we intelligently interpret statistics of Negro health.

Here, too, we have to remember that the collection of statistics, even in Philadelphia, is by no means perfect. The death returns are to be relied upon, but the returns of births are wide of the true condition; the statistics of causes of death are also faulty.

26. The Statistics of the City—The mortality of Negroes in Philadelphia, according to the best reports, has been as follows:[1]

Date	Average Annual Deaths per 1000 Negroes
1820–1830	47.6
1830–1840	32.5
1884–1890	31.25*
1891–1896	28.02†

*Including still-births; excluding still-births, 29.52.
†Including still-births and assuming the average Negro population, 1891–1896, at the low figure of 41,500.[2] For this period, excluding still-births, 25.41.

The average annual death rate, 1884 to 1890, in the wards having over 1,000 Negro inhabitants, was as follows:

Ward	Negro Population	Death Rate per 1000, excluding Still-births, 1884–90
Fourth	2,573	43.38
Fifth	2,335	48.46
Seventh	8,861	30.54
Eighth	3,011	29.25
Fourteenth	1,379	22.38
Fifteenth	1,751	20.18
Twentieth	1,333	18.64
Twenty-second	1,798	15.91

(Continued)

WARD	NEGRO POPULATION	DEATH RATE PER 1000, EXCLUDING STILL-BIRTHS, 1884–90
Twenty-third	1,026	18.67
Twenty-sixth	1,375	18.15
Twenty-seventh	2,077	39.86
Twenty-ninth	1,476	19.09
Thirtieth	1,789	21.74
Twenty-fourth and Thirty-fourth	2,003	35.11
City	39,371	29.52

Separating the deaths by the sex of the deceased, we have:

Total death rate of Negroes, 1890, (still-births included)	32.42 per 1000
For Negro males	36.02 "
For Negro females	29.23 "

Separating by age, we have:

Total death rate, 1890 (still-births included) all ages	32.42 per 1000
Under fifteen	69.24 "
Fifteen to twenty	13.61 "
Twenty to twenty-five	14.50 "
Twenty-five to thirty-five	15.21 "
Thirty-five to forty-five	17.16 "
Forty-five to fifty-five	29.41 "
Fifty-five to sixty-five	40.09 "
Sixty-five and over	116.49 "

The large infant mortality is shown by the average annual rate of 171.44 (including still-births), for children under five years of age, during the years 1884 to 1890.

These statistics are very instructive. Compared with modern nations the death rate of Philadelphia Negroes is high, but not extraordinarily so: Hungary (33.7), Austria (30.6), and Italy (28.6), had in the years 1871–90 a larger average than the Negroes in 1891–96, and some of these lands surpass the rate of 1884–90. Many things combine to cause the high Negro death rate: poor heredity, neglect of infants, bad dwellings and poor food. On the other hand the age classification of city Negroes with its excess of females and of young people of twenty to thirty-five years of age, must serve to keep the death rate lower than its rate would be under normal circumstances. The influence of bad sanitary surroundings is strikingly illustrated in the enormous death rate of the Fifth Ward—the worst Negro slum in the city, and the worst part of the city in respect to sanitation. On the other hand the low death rate of the Thirtieth Ward illustrates the influences of good houses and clean streets in a district where the better class of Negroes have recently migrated.

The marked excess of the male death rate points to a great difference in the social condition of the sexes in the city, as it far exceeds the ordinary disparity; as, *e. g.*, in Germany where the rates are, males 28.6, females 25.3.[3] The young girls who come to the city have practically no chance for work except domestic service. This branch of work, however, has the great advantage of being healthful; the servant has usually a good dwelling, good food and proper clothing. The boy, on the contrary, usually has to live in a bad part of the city, on poorly prepared or irregular food and is more exposed to the weather. Moreover, his chances of securing any work at all are much smaller than the girls'. Consequently the female death rate is but 81 per cent of the male rate.

When we turn to the statistics of death according to age, we immediately see that, as is usual in such cases, the high death rate is caused by an excessive infant mortality, which ranks very high compared with other groups.

The chief diseases to which Negroes fall victims are:[4]

DISEASE	DEATH RATE PER 100,000, 1890
Consumption	532.52
Diseases of the nervous system	388.86
Pneumonia	356.67
Heart disease and dropsy	257.59
Still-births	203.10
Diarrheal diseases	193.19
Diseases of the urinary organs	133.75
Accidents and injuries	99.07
Typhoid fever	91.64

For the period, 1891–1896, the average annual rate was as follows:

DISEASE	DEATH RATE PER 100,000, 1891–1896
Consumption	426.50
Diseases of the nervous system	307.63
Pneumonia	290.76
Heart disease and dropsy	172.69
Still and premature births	210.12
Typhoid fever	44.98

The strikingly excessive rate here is that of consumption, which is the most fatal disease for Negroes. Bad ventilation, lack of outdoor life for women and children, poor protection against dampness and cold are undoubtedly the chief causes of this excessive death rate. To this must be added some hereditary predisposition, the influence of climate, and the lack of nearly all measures to prevent the spread of the disease.

We find thus a group of people with a high, but not unusual, death rate, which rate has been gradually decreasing, if statistics are reliable, for seventy-five years. This death rate is due principally to infantile mortality and consumption, and these are caused chiefly by conditions of life and poor hereditary physique.

How now does this group compare with the condition of the mass of the community with which it comes in daily contact? Comparing the death rates of whites and Negroes, we have:

DATE	WHITES	NEGROES
1820–1830		47.6
1830–1840	23.7	32.5
1884–1890*	22.69	31.25
1891–1896†	21.20‡	25.41§

* Including still-births.
† Excluding still-births.
‡ Assuming white population, 1891–96, has increased in the same ratio as 1880–90, and that it averaged 1,066,985 in these years.
§ Assuming that the mean Negro population was 41,500.

This shows a considerable difference in death rates, amounting to nearly 10 per cent in 1884–1890, and to 4 per cent by the estimated rates of 1891–1896. If the estimate of population on which the latter rate is based is correct, then the difference in death rate is not larger than would be expected from different conditions of life.[5]

The absolute number of deaths (excluding still-births) has been as follows:

YEAR	WHITES	NEGROES
1891	22,384	983
1892	23,233	1,072
1893	22,621	1,034
1894	21,960	1,030
1895	22,645	1,151
1896	22,903	1,079

Comparing the death rate by wards we have this table:

POPULATION AND DEATH RATE, PHILADELPHIA, 1884–90

WARDS	POPULATION, 1890		DEATH RATE PER 1000, EXCLUDING STILL-BIRTHS	
	WHITE	COLORED	WHITE	COLORED
First	53,057	794	22.08	33.07
Second	31,016	522	23.93	24.21
Third	19,043	861	23.91	21.71

(*Continued*)

POPULATION AND DEATH RATE, PHILADELPHIA, 1884–90—*Continued*

WARDS	POPULATION, 1890		DEATH RATE PER 1000, EXCLUDING STILL-BIRTHS	
	WHITE	COLORED	WHITE	COLORED
Fourth	17,792	2,573	29.98	43.38
Fifth	14,619	2,335	25.67	48.46
Sixth	8,574	125	24.30	49.77
Seventh	21,177	8,861	24.30	30.54
Eighth	13,940	3,011	24.26	29.25
Ninth	9,284	497	25.40	22.32
Tenth	20,495	798	19.88	14.51
Eleventh	12,931	11	28.31	500.00
Twelfth	13,821	338	21.57	44.85
Thirteenth	17,362	539	20.67	28.76
Fourteenth	19,339	1,379	21.47	22.38
Fifteenth	50,954	1,751	20.08	20.18
Sixteenth	16,973	104	28.04	46.38
Seventeenth	19,412	124	28.89	64.95
Eighteenth	29,142	1	24.42	90.91
Nineteenth	55,249	275	23.73	51.33
Twentieth	43,127	1,333	20.77	18.64
Twenty-first	26,800	93	19.45	56.78
Twenty-second	43,512	1,798	17.77	15.91
Twenty-third	34,255	1,026	18.50	18.67
Twenty-fourth	41,600	930	17.95	35.11
Twenty-fifth	35,677	260	24.29	33.33
Twenty-sixth	60,722	1,375	19.48	18.15
Twenty-seventh	30,712	2,077	31.91	39.86
Twenty-eighth	45,727	644	15.56	15.96
Twenty-ninth	53,261	1,476	20.19	19.09
Thirtieth	28,808	1,789	22.12	21.74
Thirty-first	32,944	16	21.46	57.47
Thirty-second	29,662	382	14.61	13.66
Thirty-third	32,975	190	13.07	18.63
Thirty-fourth	22,628	1,073	*	*
Whole city	1,006,590	39,371	21.54	29.52

*Death rate included in that of the Twenty-fourth ward.

From this table we may make some interesting comparisons; take first the worst wards:

WARD	WHITES	NEGROES*
Fourth	29.98	43.38
Fifth	25.67	48.46
Seventh	24.30	30.54
Eighth	24.26	29.25

*Total Negro population, 16,780.

In all these wards there is a large Negro population comprising a considerable per cent of new immigrants; and these wards contain the worst slum districts and most unsanitary dwellings of the city. However, there are in these same wards peculiar circumstances which decrease the death rate of the whites: First, in the Fourth and Fifth wards a large number of foreign immigrants whose death rate, on account of the absence of old people and children, is small; and of Jews whose death rate is, on account of their fine family life, also small; secondly, in the Seventh and Eighth wards there are, as all Philadelphians know, large sections inhabited by the best people of the city, with a death rate below the average.

Taking another set of wards, we have:

WARD	WHITES	NEGROES*
Fourteenth	21.47	22.38
Fifteenth	20.08	20.18
Twenty-sixth	19.48	18.15
Twenty-seventh	31.91	39.86
Thirtieth	22.12	21.74

* Total Negro population, 8,371.

Here we have quite a different tale. These are the wards where the best Negro families have been renting and buying homes in the last ten years, in order to escape from the crowded downtown wards. The Thirtieth and Twenty-sixth wards are the best sections; the statistics of the Fourteenth and Fifteenth wards show the same thing although their validity is somewhat vitiated by the large number of Negro servants there in the prime of life.

A last set of wards is as follows:

WARD	WHITES	NEGROES*
Twentieth	20.77	18.64
Twenty-second	17.77	15.91
Twenty-third	18.50	18.67
Twenty-eighth	15.56	15.96
Twenty-ninth	20.19	19.09

* Total Negro population, 6,277.

In most of these some exceptional circumstances make the Negro death rate abnormally low. Generally this arises from the fact that these are white residential wards and the Negro population is largely composed of servants. These, as has been before noted, have a small death rate because of their ages, and then too, when they are sick they go home to die in the Seventh Ward, or to the hospitals in the Twenty-seventh and other wards.

These tables would seem to adduce considerable proof that the Negro death rate is largely a matter of condition of living.

When we look at the comparative deaths of the races, by sex, we see that the forces operating among Negroes to make a disparity between the death rates of men and women are largely absent among the whites.

Sex	White	Negro	Total
Male	23.85	36.02	24.30
Female	20.79	29.23	21.12

(1890, including still-births.)

The age structure reveals partially the character of the great differences in death rate between the races. (See page 112.)

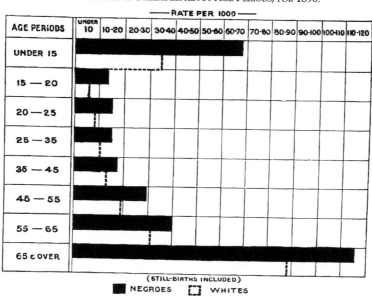

Death Rate of Philadelphia by Age Periods, for 1890.

(STILL-BIRTHS INCLUDED)
■ NEGROES   ☐ WHITES

NUMBER OF DEATHS IN PHILADELPHIA, BY AGES, 1884–1890

WARD	COLOR'D POPULATION	WHITE — DEATHS IN SIX YEARS AT CERTAIN AGES							NEGRO — DEATHS IN SIX YEARS AT CERTAIN AGES						
		ALL AGES	UNDER 5	5–15	15–25	25–65	OVER 65	UNKNOWN	ALL AGES	UNDER 5	5–15	15–25	25–65	OVER 65	UNKN'N
Seventh	8,861	3,225	1,044	139	215	1,148	625	54	1,753	765	95	128	582	165	18
Eighth	3,011	2,191	498	76	168	855	533	61	584	241	33	51	193	59	7
Fourth	2,573	3,346	1,624	164	191	993	338	36	700	336	42	43	216	58	5
Fifth	2,335	2,358	900	81	151	885	320	21	720	265	32	62	285	69	7
Twenty-seventh	2,077	5,425	2,165	148	291	1,785	951	85	477	156	19	60	168	62	12
Twenty-fourth and Thirty-fourth	2,003	6,519	2,549	366	468	1,966	1,094	76	399	147	19	26	77	125	5
Twenty-second	1,798	4,373	1,535	177	338	1,294	94	89	170	84	14	14	41	12	5
Thirtieth	1,789	3,911	1,423	195	313	1,331	591	58	248	118	13	25	74	17	1
Fifteenth	1,751	6,256	2,214	265	458	2,205	1,034	80	214	71	18	39	66	17	3
Twenty-ninth	1,476	6,217	2,200	339	440	2,044	1,120	74	170	86	9	21	44	10	0
Fourteenth	1,379	2,670	931	116	183	875	530	35	203	109	9	16	47	17	5
Twenty-sixth	1,375	6,337	2,957	358	421	1,856	678	67	138	55	9	11	43	19	1
Twentieth	1,333	5,585	1,912	286	416	1,852	1,056	63	159	70	15	13	48	9	4
Twenty-third	1,026	3,603	1,251	208	260	1,128	730	26	110	46	6	9	32	13	4
Third	861	2,836	1,306	138	151	879	329	33	120	53	5	12	42	8	0
Tenth	798	2,614	809	114	163	948	539	41	95	42	2	8	38	4	1
First	794	6,916	3,187	390	463	2,014	789	73	162	75	9	14	49	15	0
Twenty-eighth	644	3,553	1,522	193	221	1,012	557	48	52	27	5	3	11	4	2
Thirteenth	539	2,277	869	90	130	723	446	19	105	56	1	6	33	9	0
Second	522	4,580	1,970	212	357	1,413	572	56	80	37	5	3	21	13	1
Total	39,371	127,556	51,479	6,096	8,787	40,497	19,170	1,527	7,322	3,125	390	624	2,328	768	87

112

DEATH RATE IN PHILADELPHIA, 1890, BY EIGHT AGE PERIODS

COLOR	ALL AGES	UNDER 15	15–20	20–25	25–35	35–45	45–55	55–65	65 AND OVER
Total whites	22.28	34.89	6.17	8.81	10.85	13.60	18.98	31.56	88.88
Total male whites	23.85	37.22	6.49	10.12	11.28	15.30	20.85	36.44	93.51
Total female whites ..	20.79	32.51	5.89	7.64	10.43	11.91	17.20	27.42	85.35
Total Negroes	32.42	69.24	13.61	14.50	15.21	17.16	29.41	40.09	116.49
Total male Negroes ...	36.02	75.81	15.01	19.75	14.12	20.52	33.67	47.70	155.26
Total female Negroes .	29.23	63.12	12.66	10.46	16.24	13.55	25.48	34.57	96.47
Native whites	22.80	36.84	6.20	8.64	10.74	12.55	17.85	29.61	89.23
Native white males ..	24.43	39.37	6.34	9.65	10.95	13.73	19.44	34.04	98.66
Native white females .	21.25	34.25	6.07	7.70	10.55	11.43	16.35	25.82	82.78

For children under five, including still-births, we find these average annual death rates, 1884–1890:

RACE	CITY	SEVENTH WARD
Native white	94.00	111.04
Negro	171.44	188.82
Total population	94.79	132.63

Nothing shows more plainly the poor home life of the Negroes than these figures. A comparison of the differences in death rate from various diseases will complete the picture:

DEATH RATE PER 100,000 FROM SPECIFIED DISEASES, 1890

For Whole City

DISEASE	NEGRO	WHITE
Consumption	532.52	269.42
Pneumonia	356.67	180.31
Diarrheal diseases	193.19	151.40
Diseases of the nervous system	388.86	302.01
Diphtheria and croup	44.58	82.06
Diseases of the urinary system	133.75	60.81
Heart disease and dropsy	257.59	157.16
Cancer and tumor	37.15	56.63
Disease of the liver	12.38	27.82
Malarial fever	7.43	5.66
Typhoid fever	91.64	72.82
Still-births	203.10	135.61
Suicides	3.20	12.99
Other accidents and injuries	99.07	78.78

AVERAGE ANNUAL DEATH RATE OF PHILADELPHIA, 1884–1890,
PER EACH 100,000 OF POPULATION

For Specified Diseases

CAUSES	TOTAL	WHITES TOTAL	NATIVE	FOREIGN	NEGRO
All causes	2,303.43	2,269.19	2,562.31	1,470.26	3,124.81
Scarlet fever	26.18	26.86	35.84	2.39	9.82
Typhoid fever	69.35	69.65	73.10	60.25	62.31
Malarial fever	7.21	7.19	8.22	4.37	7.68
Diphtheria	50.48	51.48	69.30	2.92	26.46
Croup	47.82	49.03	66.41	1.66	18.78
Diarrheal diseases	156.11	155.30	196.16	43.94	195.40
Consumption...................	297.87	287.06	299.29	253.72	557.36
Pneumonia....................	164.17	158.77	174.79	115.13	293.62
Measles	10.67	10.67	14.37	.60	10.67
Whooping-cough	11.39	10.69	14.52	.27	28.17
Cancer and tumor	54.73	55.17	48.15	74.30	44.38
Heart disease and dropsy	146.27	142.10	37.44	154.83	246.25
Childbirth and puerperal diseases .	10.06	9.98	9.61	11.00	11.95
Diseases of liver	27.58	28.32	24.70	38.18	9.82
nervous system	318.83	315.86	373.38	159.07	390.07
urinary organs	74.90	73.44	72.54	75.89	110.11
Old age	46.08	45.99	37.13	70.12	48.23
Still-births....................	117.68	115.38	157.72	.....	172.84
All other causes	656.01	646.23	743.50	381.10	890.67
Unknown	10.02	10.02	10.19	9.54	10.24

The Negroes exceed the white death rate largely in consumption, pneumonia, diseases of the urinary system, heart disease and dropsy, and in still-births; they exceed moderately in diarrheal diseases, diseases of the nervous system, malarial and typhoid fevers. The white death rate exceeds that of Negroes for diphtheria and croup, cancer and tumor, diseases of the liver, and deaths from suicide.

We have side by side and in intimate relationship in a large city two groups of people, who as a mass differ considerably from each other in physical health; the difference is not so great as to preclude hopes of final adjustment; probably certain social classes of the larger group are in no better health than the mass of the smaller group. So too there are without doubt classes in the smaller group whose physical condition is equal to, or superior to the average of the larger group. Particularly with regard to consumption it must be remembered that Negroes are not the first people who have been claimed as its peculiar victims; the Irish were once thought to be doomed by that disease—but that was when Irishmen were unpopular.

Nevertheless, so long as any considerable part of the population of an organized community is, in its mode of life and physical efficiency distinctly and noticeably below the average, the community must suffer. The suffering part furnishes less than its quota of workers, more than its quota of the helpless and dependent and consequently becomes to an extent a burden on the community. This is the situation of the Negroes of Philadelphia to-day: because of their physical health they receive a larger portion of charity, spend a larger proportion of their earnings for physicians and medicine, throw on the community a larger number of helpless widows and orphans than either they or the city can afford. Why is this? Primarily it is because the Negroes are as a mass ignorant of the laws of health. One has but to visit a Seventh Ward church on Sunday night and see an audience of 1500 sit two and three hours in the foul atmosphere of a closely shut auditorium to realize that long formed habits of life explain much of Negro consumption and pneumonia; again the Negroes live in unsanitary dwellings, partly by their own fault, partly on account of the difficulty of securing decent houses by reason of race prejudice. If one goes through the streets of the Seventh Ward and picks out those streets and houses which, on account of their poor condition, lack of repair, absence of conveniences and limited share of air and light, contain the worst dwellings, one finds that the great majority of such streets and houses are occupied by Negroes. In some cases it is the Negroes' fault that the houses are so bad; but in very many cases landlords refuse to repair and refit for Negro tenants because they know that there are few dwellings which Negroes can hire, and they will not therefore be apt to leave a fair house on account of damp walls or poor sewer connections. Of modern conveniences Negro dwellings have few. Of the 2441 families of the Seventh Ward only 14 per cent had water closets and baths, and many of these were in poor condition. In a city of yards, 20 per cent of the families had no private yard and consequently no private outhouses.

Again, in habits of personal cleanliness and taking proper food and exercise, the colored people are woefully deficient. The Southern field-hand was hardly supposed to wash himself regularly, and the house servants were none too clean. Habits thus learned have lingered, and a gospel of soap and water needs now to be preached. Negroes are commonly supposed to eat rather more than necessary. And this perhaps is partially true. The trouble is more in the quality of the food than its quantity, in the wasteful method of its preparation, and in the irregularity in eating.[6] For instance, one family of three living in the depth of dirt and poverty on a crime-stricken street spent for their daily food:

	CENTS
Milk, for child	4
One pound pork chops	10
One loaf bread	5
	19

When we imagine this pork fried in grease and eaten with baker's bread, taken late in the afternoon or at bedtime, what can we expect of such a family? Moreover, the tendency of the classes who are just struggling out of extreme poverty is to stint themselves for food in order to have better looking homes; thus the rent in too many cases eats up physical nourishment.

Finally, the number of Negroes who go with insufficient clothing is large. One of the commonest causes of consumption and respiratory disease is migration from the warmer South to a Northern city without change in manner of dress. The neglect to change clothing after becoming damp with rain is a custom dating back to slavery time.

These are a few obvious matters of habit and manner of life which account for much of the poor health of Negroes. Further than this, when in poor health the neglect to take proper medical advice, or to follow it when given, leads to much harm. Often at the hospital a case is treated and temporary relief given, the patient being directed to return after a stated time. More often with Negroes than with whites, the patient does not return until he is worse off than at first. To this must be added a superstitious fear of hospitals prevalent among the lower classes of all people, but especially among Negroes. This must have some foundation in the roughness or brusqueness of manner prevalent in many hospitals, and the lack of a tender spirit of sympathy with the unfortunate patients. At any rate, many a Negro would almost rather die than trust himself to a hospital.

We must remember that all these bad habits and surroundings are not simply matters of the present generation, but that many generations of unhealthy bodies have bequeathed to the present generation impaired vitality and hereditary tendency to disease. This at first seems to be contradicted by the reputed robustness of older generations of blacks, which was certainly true to a degree. There cannot, however, be much doubt, when former social conditions are studied, but that hereditary disease plays a large part in the low vitality of Negroes to-day, and the health of the past has to some extent been exaggerated. All these considerations should lead to concerted efforts to root out disease. The city itself has much to do in this respect. For so large and progressive a city its general system of drainage is very bad; its water is wretched, and in many other respects the city and the whole State are "woefully and discreditably behind almost all the other States in Christendom."[7] The main movement for reform must come from the Negroes themselves, and should start with a crusade for fresh air, cleanliness, healthfully located homes and proper food. All this might not settle the question of Negro health, but it would be a long step toward it.

The most difficult social problem in the matter of Negro health is the peculiar attitude of the nation toward the well-being of the race. There have, for instance, been few other cases in the history of civilized peoples where human suffering has been viewed with such peculiar indifference. Nearly the whole nation seemed delighted with the discredited census of 1870 because it was thought to show that the Negroes were dying off rapidly, and the country would soon be well rid of them. So, recently, when attention has been called to the high death rate of this race, there is a disposition among many to conclude that the rate is abnormal and unprecedented, and that, since the race is doomed to early extinction, there is little left to do but to moralize on inferior species.

Now the fact is, as every student of statistics knows, that considering the present advancement of the masses of the Negroes, the death rate is not higher than one would expect; moreover there is not a civilized nation to-day which has not in the last two centuries presented a death rate which equaled or surpassed that of this race. That the Negro death rate at present is anything that threatens the extinction of the race is either the bugbear of the untrained, or the wish of the timid.

What the Negro death rate indicates is how far this race is behind the great vigorous, cultivated race about it. It should then act as a spur for increased effort and sound upbuilding, and not as an excuse for passive indifference, or increased discrimination.

NOTES

1. The earlier figures are from Dr. Emerson's reports, in the "Condition," etc., of the Negro, 1838, and from the pamphlet, "Health of Convicts." All the tables, 1884 to 1890, are from Dr. John Billings' report in the Eleventh Census. Later reports are compiled from the City Health Reports, 1890 to 1896.
2. This figure is conjectural, as the real Negro population is unknown. Estimated according to the rate of increase from 1880 to 1890, the average annual population would have been 42,229; I think this is too high, as the rate of increase has been lower in this decade.
3. This and other comparisons are mostly taken from Mayo-Smith, "Statistics and Sociology."
4. For death rate, 1884–1890, Cf. below, p. 159.
5. The official figures of the Board of Health give no estimate of the Negro death-rate alone. They give the following death rate for the city including both whites and blacks, and excluding still-births:

Year	Total Number of Deaths	Death Rate per 1000 of Population
1891	23,367	21.85
1892	24,305	22.25
1893	23,655	21.20
1894	22,680	19.90
1895	23,796	20.44
1896	23,982	20.17

    Average death rate for the six years, 20.97; by my calculation, the rate for the whole population would be 21.63.
6. Cf. Atwater & Woods: "Dietary Studies with reference to the Food of the Negro in Alabama." (Bulletin No. 38, U. S. Dept. of Agriculture), p. 21, and *passim*.
7. Dr. Dudley Pemberton before the State Homeopathic Medical Society.—Philadelphia *Ledger*, October 1, 1896.

CHAPTER XI

◆

The Negro Family

27. The Size of the Family—There were in the Seventh Ward, in 1896, 7,751 members of families (including 171 persons living alone), and 1,924 single lodgers.[1] The average size of the family, without lodgers and boarders, was 3.18.

FAMILIES ACCORDING TO SIZE

NUMBER IN FAMILY	NUMBER OF FAMILIES	PER CENT OF DIFFERENT SIZE FAMILIES	MEMBERS OF FAMILIES
One	171	7.0	171
Two	1,031	42.2	2,062
Three	470 ⎫		1,410
Four	327 ⎪	44.3	1,308
Five	183 ⎬		915
Six	106 ⎭		636
Seven	76	.	532
Eight	28 ⎫	5.8	224
Nine	25 ⎬		225
Ten	13 ⎭		130
Eleven	2 ⎫		22
Twelve	4 ⎪		48
Thirteen	3 ⎬	0.7	39
Fourteen	1 ⎪		14
Fifteen	1 ⎭		15
Total	2,441	100	7,751
Lodgers	. . .	. . .	1,924
Total population	. . .	. . .	9,675
Average size real family	. . .	. . .	3.18
Average size of family, including single lodgers	. . .	. . .	3.96
Average size of census family	. . .	. . .	5.08

With the whole population of the ward included, the average size was about four, and counting married and single lodgers as part of the renting family, the average size is about five.[2] In any case the smallness of the families is remarkable,

118

and is probably due to local causes in the ward, to the general situation in the city and to development in the race at large. The Seventh Ward is a ward of lodgers and casual sojourners; newly married couples settle down here until they are compelled, by the appearance of children, to move into homes of their own, and these in later years are being chosen in the Twenty-sixth, Thirtieth and Thirty-sixth wards, and uptown. Some couples leave their families in the South with grandmothers and live in lodgings here, returning to Virginia or Maryland only temporarily in summer or winter; a good many men come here from elsewhere, live as lodgers and support families in the country; then, too, childless couples often work out, the woman at service and the man lodging in this ward; the woman joins her husband once or twice a week, but does not lodge regularly there, and so is not a resident of the ward; such are the local conditions that affect greatly the size of families.[3]

The size of families in cities is nearly always smaller than elsewhere, and the Negro family follows this rule; late marriages among them undoubtedly act as a check to population; moreover, the economic stress is so great that only the small family can survive; the large families are either kept from coming to the city or move away, or, as is most common, send the breadwinners to the city while they stay in the country. It is of course but conjecture to say how far these causes are working among the general Negro population of the country; but considering that the whole race has to-day begun its great battle for economic survival, and that few of the better class, male or female, can expect to get married early in life, it is fair to expect that for several decades to come the average size of the Negro family will decrease until economic well-being can keep pace with the demands of a rising standard of living; and that then we shall have another era of good-sized though not very large Negro families.[4]

As has before been intimated, the difficulty of earning income enough to afford to marry, has had its ill effects on the sexual morality of city Negroes, especially, too, since their hereditary training in this respect has been lax. It is, therefore, fair to conclude that a number of the families of two are simply more or less permanent cohabitations; and that a large number of families are centres of irregular sexual intercourse. Observation in the ward bears out this conclusion, and shows that fifty-eight of the families of two were certainly unmarried persons.

The result of all these causes is shown in the following table, although the comparison is not strictly allowable; the real family of the Negroes is compared with the census family of other groups, and this exaggerates the proportion of the smaller families among the Negroes:

NUMBER IN FAMILY	NEGROES SEVENTH WARD %	WHOLE POPULATION OF CITY %	BROOKL'N, N. Y. %	UNITED STATES %
One	7.0	1.91	2.71	3.63
Two	42.2	. . .	. . .	. . .
Two to six	86.5	74.67	78.37	73.33
Seven to ten	5.8	21.09	17.53	20.97
Eleven and over	0.7	2.33	1.39	2.07

Further comparison with France may be made:[5]

NUMBER IN FAMILY	NEGROES SEVENTH WARD	FRANCE
One	7.0	14.0
Two to three	61.5	41.3
Four to five	20.9	29.8
Six or more	10.6	14.5

Making allowance for the errors of this comparison, it nevertheless seems true that the conditions of family life in the ward are abnormal and characterized by an unusually large number of families of two persons.

There are no statistics for the Negro families of the whole city such as would serve to eliminate the local peculiarities of the Seventh Ward. General observation would indicate in the Fifth and Eighth wards similar conditions to the Seventh. In most of the other wards conditions are different, and in all probability vary widely from these crowded central wards. Nevertheless, throughout all of them large families are not the rule, the number of bachelors and lodgers is considerable, and there is some cohabitation, although this is, in the city at large, much less prevalent than in the Seventh Ward. It would seem, therefore, that the indications of our study of conjugal condition were here emphasized, and that the Negro urban home has commenced a revolution which will either purify and raise it or more thoroughly debauch it than now; and that the determining factor is economic opportunity. The full picture of this change demands statistics of births and marriages from year to year. These unfortunately are not so registered as to be even partially reliable. Both the birth and marriage rate, however, are in all probability steadily decreasing.[6] The death rate also comes in here as a factor, not only by reason of the great infant mortality but also on account of the excessive death rate of the men. In all this one catches a faint glimpse of the intricacy and far-reaching influence of the Negro problems.

28. Incomes—The economic problem of the Negroes of the city has been repeatedly referred to. We now come directly to the question, What do Negroes earn? In a year about what is the income of an average family? Such a question is difficult to answer with anything like accuracy. Only returns based on actual written accounts would furnish thoroughly reliable statistics; such accounts cannot be had in this case. The few that keep accounts would in many cases naturally be unwilling to produce them. On the other hand, the great mass of people in the lower walks of life scarcely know how much they earn in a year. The tables here presented, therefore, must be regarded simply as careful estimates. These estimates are based on three or more of the following items: (1) The statement of the family as to their earnings. Some of the better class gave a general estimate of their average yearly income; most gave the wages earned per week or month at their usual occupation. (2) The occupations followed by the several members of the family; (3) the time lost from work in the last year or the time usually lost; (4) the apparent circumstances of the family judging from the appearance of the home and inmates, the rent paid, the presence of lodgers, etc.

In most cases the first item was given the greatest weight in settling the matter, but was modified by the others; in other cases, however, either this statement could not be obtained or was vague, and in a few instances evidently false. In such circumstances the second item was decisive: the occupations followed by the mass of Negroes are paid according to a pretty well-known scale of prices; a hotel waiter's income could be pretty accurately fixed without further data. The third item was important in many occupations; stevedores, for instance, receive generally twenty cents per hour; nevertheless, few if any earn $600 a year, because they lose much time between ships and in winter. Finally, as a general corrective to deception or inadvertence the circumstances of home life as seen by the investigator on his visit, the rent paid—an item which could be pretty accurately ascertained—the number of lodgers, the occupation of the housewife and children—all these items served to confirm or throw doubt on the conclusions indicated by the other data, and were given some weight in the final judgment.

Thus it can easily be seen that these returns may contain, and probably do contain, considerable error. On the one hand they cannot be as accurate as returns based on income tax reports, and on the other hand they are probably more reliable than data founded solely on the bare statements of those asked. The personal judgment of the investigator enters into the determination of the figures to a larger extent than is desirable, and yet it has been limited as carefully as the nature of the inquiry permitted.[7]

The income according to size of family is indicated in the next table. From this, making the standard a family of five, and making some allowance for larger and smaller families, we can conclude that 19 per cent of the Negro families in the Seventh Ward earn five dollars and less per week on the average; 48 per cent

INCOMES, ACCORDING TO SIZE OF FAMILY IN SEVENTH WARD, 1896

AMOUNT OF INCOME PER YEAR	SIZE OF FAMILY											TOTAL NUMBER OF FAMILIES
	1	2	3	4	5	6	7	8	9	10	11 TO 15	
$ 50	7	5	1	..	..	..	1	..	..	..	..	14
100	22	18	2	2	1	..	..	..	..	..	..	45
150	31	69	19	4	6	4	..	..	..	..	..	133
200	23	105	35	12	8	4	..	..	..	..	..	187
250	32	95	46	26	7	1	5	2	..	..	..	214
300	10	108	49	33	9	3	1	..	..	..	..	213
350	9	121	46	30	11	10	2	1	..	..	..	230
400	4	95	39	34	22	9	6	..	..	..	..	209
450	1	79	40	26	14	7	3	1	1	..	..	172
500	7	115	47	37	26	17	1	3	2	..	1	256
550	..	23	12	8	4	4	1	0	3	..	..	55
600	1	17	14	8	7	3	3	..	1	..	..	54
650	1	45	26	27	11	7	4	2	1	..	1	125
700	..	10	16	12	9	5	6	3	2	..	..	63
750	3	23	19	16	13	7	9	3	1	..	..	94
800	..	7	7	7	3	2	2	1	..	1	1	31
850	..	3	2	1	3	1	4	2	2	..	..	18
900	..	5	4	8	3	3	5	9	1	1	1	40

(Continued)

INCOMES, ACCORDING TO SIZE OF FAMILY IN SEVENTH WARD, 1896—*Continued*

AMOUNT OF INCOME PER YEAR	1	2	3	4	5	6	7	8	9	10	11 TO 15	TOTAL NUMBER OF FAMILIES
1,000–1,200	..	1	1	1	4	..	..	..	1	3	1	12
1,200–1,500	1	3	10	3	5	7	6	2	5	3	1	46
1,500 and over	2	6	10	12	6	5	10	3	2	4	5	65
Unknown	15	67	17	6	2	2	1	..	..	..	..	110
Unknown							of unknown size					55

earn between $5 and $10; 26 percent, $10–$15, and 8 per cent over $15 per week. Tabulating this we have:

AVERAGE EARNINGS PER WK	No. OF FAMILIES	%	COMPARISON.	
$5 & LESS	420 { 192	8.9	VERY POOR	
	228	9.6	POOR	
$5–10	1088	47.8	FAIR	
$10–15	581	25.5	COMFORTABLE	
$15–20	91	4.	GOOD CIRCUMSTANCES	
$20 & OVER	96	4.2	WELL-TO-DO	
TOTAL	2276	100.00%		

It is difficult to compare this with other groups because of the varying meaning of the terms poor, well-to-do, and the like. Nevertheless, a comparison with Booth's diagram of London will, if not carried too far, be interesting:[8]

POVERTY IN LONDON AND AMONG THE NEGROES OF THE SEVENTH WARD OF PHILADELPHIA.

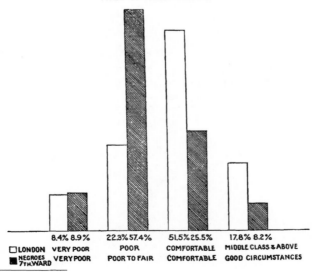

	8.4% 8.9%	22.3% 57.4%	51.5% 25.5%	17.8% 8.2%
☐ LONDON	VERY POOR	POOR	COMFORTABLE	MIDDLE CLASS & ABOVE
■ NEGROES 7TH WARD	VERY POOR	POOR TO FAIR	COMFORTABLE	GOOD CIRCUMSTANCES

The chief difficulty of this comparison lies in the distribution of the population between the "poor" and "comfortable;" probably the former class among the Negroes is here somewhat exaggerated. At any rate, the division between these two grades is in the Seventh Ward much less stable than in London since their economic status is less fixed. In good times perhaps 50 per cent of the Negroes could well be designated comfortable, but in time of financial stress vast numbers of this class fall below the line into the poor and go to swell the number of paupers, and in many cases of criminals. Indeed this whole division into incomes of different classes is, among the Negroes, much less stable than among the whites, just as it used to be less stable among the whites of fifty years ago than it is among those of to-day.

The whole division into "poor," "comfortable" and "well-to-do" depends primarily on the standard of living among a people. Let us, therefore, note something of the income and expenditure of certain families in different grades.[9] The very poor and semi-criminal class are congregated in the slums at Seventh and Lombard Streets, Seventeenth and Lombard, and Eighteenth and Naudain, together with other small back streets scattered over the ward. They live in one- and two-room tenements, scantily furnished and poorly lighted and heated; they get casual labor, and the women do washing. The children go to school irregularly or loaf on the streets. This class does not frequent the large Negro churches, but part of them fill the small noisy missions. The vicious and criminal portion do not usually go to church. Those of this class who are poor but decent are next-door neighbors usually to pronounced criminals and prostitutes. The income and expenditure of some of these families follow.

Family No. 1 lives in one of the worst streets of the ward, surrounded by thieves and prostitutes. There are three persons in the family: a woman of thirty-four, with a son of sixteen and a second husband of twenty-six. Both the husband and son are out of work, the former being a waiter and the latter a bootblack. They live in one filthy room, twelve feet by fourteen, scantily furnished and poorly ventilated. The woman works at service and receives about three dollars a week. They pay twelve dollars a month for three rooms, and sub-rent two of them to other families, which makes their rent about three dollars.

Their food costs them about $1.00 a week and the fuel 56 cents a week during the winter. Their expenditure for other items is varying and indefinite; beer, however, comes in for something. Their whole expenditure is probably $125–$150 a year, of which the woman earns at least $100.

Family No. 2 has a yearly budget as follows for two persons:

Rent, @ $4 a month	$48.00
Food—Bread, pork, tea, etc., @ $1.44 a week	74.88
Fuel, 20–47 cents a week	16.60
	$139.48

Other items would bring this up to about $150 to $175.

Family No. 3, consisting of one person, reports the following budget, not including rent:

Food	$30.00
Fuel	15.00
Clothing	10.00
Amusements	1.50
Sickness, etc	10.00
Other purposes	15.00
Total, per year	$81.50

The rent of such a family would not exceed $40, making the total expenditure about $121.50.

Family No. 4—four persons—man and wife and two babies, living in one room, spend as follows:

Rent, @ $3 a month		$36.00
Food—Weekly: milk	$0.28	
pork	.70	
bread	.35	
	1.33	69.16
Fuel, 20–98 cents a week		18.00
		$123.16

The man has work one and one-half weeks in the month as a wire fence maker, when regularly employed, which is about half the time. The rest of the time he takes care of the babies while his wife works at service. The last two families seem respectable, but unfortunate. The other two are doubtful.

The "poor" are a degree above these cases; they are composed of the inefficient, unfortunate and improvident, and just manage to get enough to eat, a little to wear, and shelter. A specimen family is composed of six persons—man and wife, a widowed daughter, two grandsons of thirteen and eleven, and a nephew of twenty-eight. They live in three rooms, with poor furniture and of fair cleanliness. The father and nephew are laborers, often out of work. The mother does day's work and the daughter is at service. They spend for:

Rent—$8 per month	$96.00
Food—$2.16 a week	112.32
Fuel—50–84 cents a week	31.20
	$239.52

Clothing, etc., will bring this total to $250–$275. This is an honest family, belonging to one of the large Baptist churches.

Family No. 5, a mother and child, expends for

Food	$96.00
Fuel	30.00
Clothing	30.00
Amusements	10.00
Sickness	15.00
Other purposes	25.00
Total	$206.00

To this must be added house-rent, bringing the total to $250 or $275.

We next come to the great hard-working laboring class—the 47 per cent of the population which is, on the whole, most truly representative of the mass. They live in houses with three to six rooms, nearly always well furnished; they spend considerable for food and dress, and for churches and beneficial societies. They are honest and good-natured for the most part, but are not used to large responsibility.

No. 6, a family of three from this class—man, wife and seventeen-year-old son—earn and spend as follows:

INCOME		EXPENSE	
Man—hod-carrier and laborer, $1.25–$2.00 a day—casual— averages $3.00 a week	$150.00	Rent, $22.00 a month, of which $14.00 is repaid by lodgers—net rent, $8.00	$96.00
		Food—$3.50–$4.00 a week	190.00
Wife—washerwoman, Oct. to Mch., earns $5.00 to $6.00 a week, rest of year $1.50–$2.00, average, $3.50,	180.00	Fuel	35.00
			$321.00
Son—porter in office building, $2.50 per week and board 6 days	125.00	Clothing and all other purposes, and savings	134.00
	$455.00		$455.00

This family occupies a seven-room house, but rents out three of the rooms to lodgers. They have a nicely furnished parlor.

Three other families of the same class follow:

No. 7. Expenditure for one year, $338 (not including rent). Number in family, adults 2, children 2.

Food	$110.00
Fuel	40.00
Clothing	50.00
Amusements	35.00
Sickness	40.00
Other purposes	63.00

NO. 8. EXPENDITURE FOR ONE YEAR, $520.00

Number in Family, Adults 3, Children 2

EXPENDITURE FOR	WEEKLY	MONTHLY	YEARLY	EXPENDITURE FOR	WEEKLY	MONTHLY	YEARLY
Rent	...	$16.00	$192.00	Amusements	...	...	$2.00
Food	$4.00	16.00	192.00	Sickness and d'th .	...	...	10.00
Fuel	...	...	34.00	All other purposes .	...	...	30.00
Clothing	...	...	60.00				

NO. 9. EXPENDITURE FOR ONE YEAR, ABOUT $600.00

Number in Family, Adults 2, Children 7

EXPENDITURE FOR	WEEKLY	MONTHLY	YEARLY	EXPENDITURE FOR	WEEKLY	MONTHLY	YEARLY
Rent	...	...	$200.00	Clothing	...	5.00	60.00
Food	$5.00	$20.00	240.00	All other purposes	...	...	$28.00
Fuel	1.50	6.00	72.00				

Three other budgets are appended, representing a still better class:

No. 10.

> Total income, $840.00
>
> | Rent | .... | $192.00 |
> |---|---|---|
> | Food | .... | 260.00 |
> | Fuel | .... | 50.00 |
> | Clothing | .... | 25.00 |
> | Amusements | .... | 15.00 |
> | | | $542.00 |

This is a small family—mother and daughter—who are evidently saving money. The daughter is a teacher.

No. 11. Total expenditure, exclusive of rent, $683.

> | Food | .... | $378.00 |
> |---|---|---|
> | Fuel | .... | 45.00 |
> | Clothing | .... | 100.00 |
> | Amusements | .... | 20.00 |
> | Sickness | .... | 50.00 |
> | Other purposes | .... | 90.00 |

There are four adults and three children in this family.

No. 12. Total expenditure, exclusive of rent, $805.

Food	$420.00
Fuel	60.00
Clothing	150.00
Amusements	20.00
Sickness	5.00
Travel, and other purposes	150.00

This is one of the best families in the city; they keep one servant. There are three adults and two children in the family.

The class to which these last families belong is often lost sight of in discussing the Negro. It is the germ of a great middle class, but in general its members are curiously hampered by the fact that, being shut off from the world about them, they are the aristocracy of their own people, with all the responsibilities of an aristocracy, and yet they, on the one hand, are not prepared for this rôle, and their own masses are not used to looking to them for leadership. As a class they feel strongly the centrifugal forces of class repulsion among their own people, and, indeed, are compelled to feel it in sheer self-defence. They do not relish being mistaken for servants; they shrink from the free and easy worship of most of the Negro churches, and they shrink from all such display and publicity as will expose them to the veiled insult and depreciation which the masses suffer. Consequently this class, which ought to lead, refuses to head any race movement on the plea that thus they draw the very color line against which they protest. On the other hand their ability to stand apart, refusing on the one hand all responsibility for the masses of the Negroes and on the other hand seeking no recognition from the outside world, which is not willingly accorded—their opportunity to take such a stand is hindered by their small economic resources. Even more than the rest of the race they feel the difficulty of getting on in the world by reason of their small opportunities for remunerative and respectable work. On the other hand their position as the richest of their race—though their riches are insignificant compared with their white neighbors—makes unusual social demands upon them. A white Philadelphian with $1500 a year can call himself poor and live simply. A Negro with $1500 a year ranks with the richest of his race and must usually spend more in proportion than his white neighbor in rent, dress and entertainment.

In every class thus reviewed there comes to the front a central problem of expenditure. Probably few poor nations waste more money by thoughtless and unreasonable expenditure than the American Negro, and especially those living in large cities like Philadelphia. First, they waste much money in poor food and in unhealthful methods of cooking. The meat bill of the average Negro family would surprise a French or German peasant or even an Englishman. The crowds that line Lombard street on Sundays are dressed far beyond their means; much money is wasted in extravagantly furnished parlors, dining-rooms, guest chambers and other visible parts of the homes. Thousands of dollars are annually wasted in excessive rents, in doubtful "societies" of all kinds and descriptions, in amusements of various kinds, and in miscellaneous ornaments and gewgaws. All this is a natural heritage of a slave system, but it is not the less a matter of serious import to a people in such economic stress as Negroes now are.

The Negro has much to learn of the Jew and Italian, as to living within his means and saving every penny from excessive and wasteful expenditures.

29. Property—We must next inquire what part of these incomes have been turned into real property. Philadelphia keeps no separate account of her white and Negro real estate owners and it is very difficult to get reliable data on the subject. Even the house-to-house inquiry could but approximate the truth on account of the number of houses owned by Negroes but rented out through white real estate agents. From the returns it appears that 123 of the 2441 families in the Seventh Ward or 5.3 per cent own property in that ward; seventy-four other families own property outside the ward, making in all 197 or 8 per cent of the families who are property holders. It is possible that omissions may raise this total to 10 per cent. The total value of this property is partly conjectural but a careful estimate would place it at about $1,000,000, or 4½ per cent of the valuation of a ward where the Negroes form 42 per cent of the population.

Two estimates for the whole city represent the holdings of the well-to-do Negroes, that is, those having $10,000 and more of property, as follows:[10]

From $10,000 to $15,000	27
" 15,000 to 25,000	10
" 25,000 to 50,000	11
" 50,000 to 100,000	4
" 100,000 to 500,000	1
	53

In all, these persons represent an ownership of at least $1,500,000. The other property holders can only be estimated; the total ownership of property by Philadelphia Negroes must be at least five millions, not including church property. Comparing this with estimates in the past, we have:[11]

1821, real estate, assessed value, $112,464; real value,			$281,162
1832, " "	"	"	357,000
1838, " "	"	"	322,532
1848, " "	"	"	531,809
1855, real and personal estate	"	"	2,685,693
1898, " " " "	"	"	5,000,000

In 1849 the returns of the investigation showed that 7.4 per cent of the Negroes in the county owned property, and 5.5 per cent in the city proper, compared with 5.3 per cent in the Seventh Ward to-day. In this comparison, however, we must consider the enormous increase in the value of Philadelphia real estate.

Taking the heads of the 123 families known to live in the Seventh Ward and to own real estate we find that they were born as follows:

Philadelphia	41	= 41 = 33⅓ per cent
Pennsylvania	7	
Maryland	22	
Virginia	21	
South	13	82 = 66⅔ per cent
Delaware and New Jersey	8	
Other parts of United States and abroad	7	
Unknown	4	
	123	

The eighty-two not born in Philadelphia have lived there as follows:

Over 2 and under 10 years	5
10 to 14 years	7
15 to 19 "	7
20 to 24 "	14
25 to 29 "	8
30 to 34 "	8
35 to 39 "	16
40 to 44 "	4
45 to 49 "	3
50 to 54 "	3
60 years and over	3
Unknown	4
	82

Nineteen have lived less than twenty years in the city and fifty-nine, twenty years or more.

The occupations of the 123 property owners were as follows:

Caterers	22	Hotel keepers and restaurateurs	3
Waiters	12	Cooks	2
Porters and Janitors	10	Undertakers	2
Housewives	9	School-teachers	2
Laundresses	8	Barbers	2
Mechanics	7	Physicians	2
Coachmen	6	Shrouder of dead	1
Clerks in public service	4	Newspaper publisher	1
Drivers and teamsters	4	Real estate dealer	1
Upholsterers	3	Sexton	1
Employment agents	3	No occupation	3
Merchants	3	Unknown	2
Stewards	3		123
Ministers	3		
Hod-carriers and laborers	2		
Policemen and watchmen	2		

This shows that the real estate owners are either Philadelphia born or old residents and that the mass of them are caterers and house servants, with a sprinkling of those representing the newer employments as clerks in public service, merchants, and the like.

Of these one hundred and twenty-three families

62 own the houses they occupy.

20 own the houses they occupy, and also other real estate in the city.

7 own the houses they occupy, own other real estate in the city, and also own real estate elsewhere.

5 own homes outside the city, and other real estate elsewhere.

22 own real estate in the city.

7 own real estate in the city and elsewhere also.

In other words, 89 own homes in the city, and 34 own real estate somewhere.

Returns from forty of these holders indicate a total holding of $250,000, or if we add in one large estate, $650,000. Other less definite but fairly reliable returns raise the total ownership of property in the Seventh Ward to $1,000,000 or more. Sixty-three of the seventy-four owning property outside the city report $49,010 in real estate.[12] In none of these returns has there been any account of the mortgage indebtedness taken, nor is there any means of ascertaining this debt.[13]

On the whole the statistics show comparatively few Negro property holders in Philadelphia. In a city where the percentage of home owners is unusually large, over 94 per cent of the Negroes appear from the imperfect returns available to be renters. There are several reasons for this: first, the Negroes distrust all saving institutions since the fatal collapse of the Freedmen's Bank; secondly, they have difficulty in buying homes in decent neighborhoods; thirdly, the rising price of real estate, and the falling off of wage and industrial opportunity for the Negro must be taken into account. Finally a curious effect of color prejudice, to be discussed later, has had enormous influence in concentrating Negro population in localities where it was hard to buy homes. All these are cogent reasons, and yet they are not enough to excuse the Negroes from not buying much more property than they have. Much of the money that should have gone into homes has gone into costly church edifices, dues to societies, dress and entertainment. If the Negroes had bought little homes as persistently as they have worked to develop a church and secret society system, and had invested more of their earnings in savings-banks and less in clothes they would be in a far better condition to demand industrial opportunity than they are to-day.

This does not mean that the Negro is lazy or a spend-thrift; it simply means misdirected energies which cause the Negro people yearly to waste thousands of dollars in rents and live in poor homes when they might with proper foresight do much better.

There are some signs of awakening to this fact among the Negroes. Lately they are just beginning to understand and profit by the Building and Loan Associations. Forty-one families in the Seventh Ward, or about 2 per cent, belong now to such associations and the number is increasing. Outside the Seventh Ward as large and probably a larger percentage belong to co-operative home-buying societies. The peculiar phenomenon among the colored people, however, is the wide development of beneficial and secret orders. Three hundred and six families, or 17 per cent of the Negroes of the ward, are reported as belonging to beneficial societies and probably 25 per cent or more actually belong. Beside these there are the petty insurance societies, to which 1021 families or 42 per cent belong. In more prosperous times this membership may reach 50 or 60 per cent or a total of at least 4000 men, women and children. The beneficial and secret societies, being organizations of Negroes, will be spoken of later. The petty insurance societies are for the most part conducted by whites. Some of these are reliable enterprises, and by careful management and honest dealing do something to encourage the saving spirit among the Negroes. It is doubtful, however, if they form the best kind of incentive, and probably they stand in the way of the savings-bank and building association.

Only a few deserve this qualified approval. The large majority are little better than licensed gambling operations; it is a disgrace that a great municipality allows them to prey upon the people in the manner they do.[14] They usually rest on no sound business principles; they take any and all risks, generally without medical examination and depend on lapses in payments and bold cheating to make money. Even the best conducted of these societies have to depend on the unreturned contributions of persons who cannot keep up their payments, to make both ends meet.

There were in 1897 thirty-one insurance societies doing business in the Seventh Ward. The following table gives the weekly premiums required for sick and death benefits in one society:

RATES AND DEATH BENEFITS

Weekly Dues for Benefits Payable at Death only

AGE	$100 BENEFIT	$200 BENEFIT
12–15	$0.04	$0.07
15–25	.05	.09
25–30	.06	.11
30–35	.07	.13
35–40	.08	.15
40–45	.10	.18
45–50	.12	.23
50–53	.14	.26
53–55	.15	.28
55–58	.18	.35
58–60	.20	.39

This is at the rate of $46.80 to $52 for a $1000 life policy at the age of 43, which can be had in regular companies for about $35. The excess represents the expense of collection and the gambler's risk.

SICKNESS AND ACCIDENT BENEFITS

Weekly Dues for Specified Sums per Week

AGE NEXT BIRTHDAY	$4.00	$5.00	$6.00	$7.00	$8.00	$10.00
12–20	.10	.13	.16	.19	.22	.25
20–25	.11	.14	.17	.20	.23	.26
25–30	.12	.15	.18	.21	.24	.27
30–35	.14	.17	.20	.23	.26	.29
35–40	.15	.18	.21	.24	.27	.30
40–43	.17	.20	.23	.26	.29	.32
43–45	.18	.21	.24	.27	.30	.33
45–48	.19	.22	.25	.28	.31	.34
48–50	.20	.23	.26	.29	.32	.35
50–53	.22	.25	.28	.31	.34	.37
53–55	.23	.26	.29	.32	.35	.38
55–58	.24	.27	.30	.33	.37	.41
58–60	.28	.31	.34	.37	.41	.44

Children—Age, 2 to 11 years.

Amount payable to children after their certificates have been issued for the following periods: Three months, one-third; six months, one-half; nine months, three-fourths; one year, full amount.

Death benefits, $40.

Weekly dues, 5 cents.

Upon payment of 10 cents weekly dues, children from six to eleven years will be paid weekly sick benefits of $2.50.

Membership fee for children, 50 cents.

Membership fee for adults, $1.

Into these companies a large part of the income of many families goes. For instance, let us examine the expenditures of certain actual families for such insurance, remembering that the total income of these families is in most cases $20 to $40 a month.

		MONTHLY
1.	A family of 2 adults and 2 children (stevedore)	$3.29
2.	A family of 2 adults have for 10 years paid	1.00
3.	A family of 4 adults	2.20
4.	A family of 4 adults	2.40
5.	A family of 1 adult and 1 child	2.00
6.	A family of 4 adults	1.84
7.	A family of 1 adult	$2.57
8.	A family of 2 adults (waiter)	2.20
9.	A family of 2 adults (servant)	1.50
10.	A family of 5 adults and 2 children (laborer)	3.00
11.	A family of 2 adults and 3 children (stevedore)	1.44
12.	A family of 9 adults and 1 child	5.00
13.	A family of 8 adults and 4 children	4.20
14.	A family of 9 adults	4.43
15.	A family of 2 adults	2.50
16.	A family of 2 adults (stevedore)	3.00
17.	A family of 2 adults (stevedore)	3.00
18.	A family of 10 adults	8.50
19.	A family of 2 adults, 1 child (stevedore)	5.00
20.	A family of 5 adults, 1 child	5.00
21.	A family of 3 adults	3.90
22.	A family of 4 adults, 1 child (laborer)	5.00
23.	A family of 2 adults, 3 children (waiter)	4.60

It is impossible to get accurate returns as to the total amount spent by the Negroes of the Seventh Ward for insurance in such societies, but answers to questions on this point indicate a total expenditure of approximately $25,000 annually. For this enormous outlay something comes back in the benefits, but probably much less than half. The method of conducting these societies puts a premium on dishonesty and misrepresentation and a tax on honesty and health. A certain class of the insured get sick regularly and draw benefits and are winked at by the societies as a paying advertisement on the street. Their honest neighbors on the other hand will struggle on and work for years, paying regularly—in some cases five, ten and fifteen or more years in various societies—only to be cheated out of their insurance by rascally agents, or conniving home offices, or their own failure at the last moment to keep up payments. Of course the sum involved is too small, and the cheated persons too unknown and lowly to lead to litigation. Let us take some examples:[15]

1. This family lost $100 paid in for insurance, by final lapse in payments. The woman was sixty years old, and poor.
2. This family belonged to the ——— society ten years and paid $12 a year. Finally fell seven days in arrears with payments, and was dropped. Had received $65 in benefits.
3. This family had paid in $50; was one day behind and was dropped.
4. This family had a woman insured for $2.50 a week, and $50 at death. She received no sick benefits at all, and only $20 at death. They said: "We stint ourselves of our victuals to keep up and then lose it all."
5. A family who put $75 into a society and lost it all.
6. A mother was in the ——— society two years. When she was taken sick, she sent her child to notify them; they took no notice of this on the ground that the notification by a child was not legal, and paid her nothing.
7. This man was a member of the ——— society fifteen years, and his wife seven years; paid in $354 in all and drew out $90 in benefits; the society then "discovered" that the man belonged to the G. A. R., and dropped him and kept the money.
8. This man belonged to a society seven years, at $1.30 per month; received $20 in benefits and lost the rest through a lapse in payments.
9. This family belonged to different societies eight years and lost all the money invested.
10. This person was a member of a society some time, when the collector absconded with the money, and the society refused to bear the responsibility.
11. The mother had paid $54.60 to a society for a death benefit, but at her death the society paid nothing.
12. The society collapsed and this person lost $75.
13. This family invested $1.23 a month with a society for thirteen years in order to receive $200 endowment. This was at the rate of $73.80 annually for a $1,000 policy!
14. This man has paid in $88 so far, and has never received sick or other benefits.
15. This woman had belonged to a society for years and was once taken sick just before the agent called. When he came he was asked to return, as the sick woman was asleep. He did not return, and when a claim for sick benefits was made, it was denied on the ground that the woman had not paid her dues when the agent called.

In many other cases the matter of age is made a loophole for cheating; numbers of the Negroes do not know their exact ages; in such cases the insurance agent will suggest an age, usually below the evident truth, and insert it in the policy; if the insured dies the physician guesses at another age nearer the truth, and inserts it in the death certificate. Thereupon the insurance company points to the discrepancy, alleges an attempt to deceive on the part of the insured, and either refuses to pay any of the policy or generally offers to compound for a half or a third of the amount promised. This is perhaps the most common form of cheating outside the failure to account for the payments of lapsed members. In some cases the home office pays the death claim, and the local office or agent cheats the insured.

Without doubt such societies meet outrageous attempts at deception on the part of the insured; and yet since their methods of business put a premium on this sort of cheating they can hardly complain. The whole business is nothing more than gambling, where one set of sharpers bet against another set, and the honest hard-working but ignorant toilers pay the bill.[16] With all the harm that open policy-playing and other sorts of gambling do, it is to be doubted if their effects on character are more deleterious than this form of insurance business. The Negroes by the crime of the Freedmen's Bank have been long prejudiced against banks, and this business encourages their aversion to the slow, sure methods of saving. If the colored people are ever to learn "forehandedness," in place of the slip-shod chance methods of living, the savings-bank must soon replace the insurance society; and that they could support savings-banks in abundance is shown by the fact that they annually invest between $75,000 and $100,000 in insurance societies in the city of Philadelphia.

It is not generally known how lucrative a business the exploitation of the Negro in various lines has become. In ornaments, clothes, entertainments, books and investment schemes, the shrewd and unscrupulous have a broad field of work, and it is being industriously cultivated, especially by whites and to some extent by certain classes of Negroes. Instead then of a struggling people being met by aid in the direction of their greatest weakness, they are surrounded by agencies which tend to make them more wasteful and dependent on chance than they are now. One has only to watch the pawn-brokers' shops on Saturday night in winter to see how largely Negroes support them; and it is but a step from the insurance society to the pawnshop and thence to the policy shop.

30. Family Life—Among the masses of the Negro people in America the monogamic home is comparatively a new institution, not more than two or three generations old. The Africans were taken from polygamy and transplanted into a plantation where the home life was protected only by the caprice of the master, and practically unregulated polygamy and polyandry was the result, on the plantations of the West Indies. In States like Pennsylvania the marriage institution among slaves was early established and maintained. Consequently one meets among the Philadelphia Negroes the result of both systems—the looseness of plantation life and the strictness of Quaker teaching. Among the lowest class of recent immigrants and other unfortunates there is much sexual promiscuity and the absence of a real home life. Actual prostitution for gain is not as widespread as would at first thought seem natural. On the other hand, there are two widespread systems among the lowest classes, viz., temporary cohabitation and the support of men. Cohabitation of a more or less permanent character is a direct offshoot of the plantation life and is practiced considerably; in distinctly slum districts, like that at Seventh and Lombard, from 10 to 25 per cent of the unions are of this nature. Some of them are simply common-law marriages and are practically never broken. Others are compacts, which last for two to ten years; others for some months; in most of these cases the women are not prostitutes, but rather ignorant and loose. In such cases there is, of course, little home life, rather a sort of neighborhood life, centering in the alleys and on the sidewalks, where the children are educated. Of the great mass of Negroes this class forms a very small percentage and is absolutely without social standing. They are the dregs which indicate the former history and the dangerous tendencies of the masses. The system of supporting men is one common among the prostitutes of all countries, and widespread among the Negro women of the town. Two little colored girls walking along South street stopped before a gaudy pair of men's shoes displayed in a shop window, and one said: "That's the kind of shoes I'd buy my fellow!" The remark fixed their life history; they were from among the prostitutes of Middle Alley, or Ratcliffe street, or some similar resort, where each woman supports some man from the results of her gains. The majority of the well-dressed loafers whom one sees on Locust street near Ninth, on Lombard near Seventh and Seventeenth, on Twelfth near Kater, and in other such localities, are supported by prostitutes and political largesse, and spend their time in gambling. They are absolutely without home life, and form the most dangerous class in the community, both for crime and political corruption.

Leaving the slums and coming to the great mass of the Negro population we see undoubted effort has been made to establish homes. Two great hindrances, however, cause much mischief: the low wages of men and the high rents. The low wages of men make it necessary for mothers to work and in numbers of cases to work away from home several days in the week. This leaves the children without guidance or restraint for the better part of the day—a thing disastrous to manners and morals. To this must be added the result of high rents, namely, the lodging system. Whoever wishes to live in the centre of Negro population, near the great churches and near work, must pay high rent for a decent house. This rent the average Negro family cannot afford, and to get the house they sub-rent a part to lodgers. As a consequence, 38 per cent of the homes of the Seventh Ward have unknown strangers admitted freely into their doors. The result is, on the whole, pernicious, especially where there are growing children. Moreover, the tiny Philadelphia houses are ill suited to a lodging system. The lodgers are often waiters, who are at home between meals, at the very hours when the housewife is off at work, and growing daughters are thus left unprotected. In some cases, though this is less often, servant girls and other female lodgers are taken. In such ways the privacy and intimacy of home life is destroyed, and elements of danger and demoralization admitted. Many families see this and refuse to take lodgers, and move where they can afford the rent without help. This involves more deprivations to a socially ostracized race like the Negro than to whites, since it often means hostile neighbors or no social intercourse. If a number of Negroes settle together, the real estate agents dump undesirable elements among them, which some enthusiastic association has driven from the slums.

There are a large number of waiters, porters and servant girls in the city who naturally have no home life and are exposed to peculiar temptations. The church is the rallying place of the best class of these young people, and it attempts to furnish their amusements. Loafing and promenading the streets is the only other entertainment most of these young folks have. They form a serious problem, to which the lodging system is the only attempted answer, and that a dangerous one. Homes and clubs properly conducted ought to be opened for them. A Young Men's Christian Association which would not degenerate into an endless prayer meeting might meet the wants of the young men.

The home life of the middle laboring class lacks many of the pleasant features of good homes. Traces of plantation customs still persist, and there is a widespread custom of seeking amusement outside the home; thus the home becomes a place for a hurried meal now and then, and lodging. Only on Sundays does the general gathering in the front room, the visits and leisurely dinner, smack of proper home life. Nevertheless, the spirit of home life is steadily growing. Nearly all the housewives deplore the lodging system and the work that keeps them away from home; and there is a widespread desire to remedy these evils and the other evil which is akin to them, the allowing of children and young women to be out unattended at night.

In the better class families there is a pleasant family life of distinctly Quaker characteristics. One can go into such homes in the Seventh Ward and find all the quiet comfort and simple good-hearted fare that one would expect among well-bred people. In some cases the homes are lavishly furnished, in others they are homely and old-fashioned. Even in the best homes, however, there is easily detected a tendency to let the communal church and society life trespass upon the home. There are fewer strictly family gatherings than would be desirable, fewer simple neighborhood gatherings and visits; in their place are the church teas, the hall concerts, or the elaborate parties given by the richer and more ostentatious. These things are of no particular moment to the circle of families involved, but they set an example to the masses which may be misleading. The mass of the Negro people must be taught sacredly to guard the home, to make it the centre of social life and moral guardianship. This it is largely among the best class of Negroes, but it might be made even more conspicuously so than it is. Such emphasis undoubtedly means the decreased influence of the Negro church, and that is a desirable thing.

On the whole, the Negro has few family festivals; birthdays are not often noticed, Christmas is a time of church and general entertainments, Thanksgiving is coming to be widely celebrated, but here again in churches as much as in homes. The home was destroyed by slavery, struggled up after emancipation, and is again not exactly threatened, but neglected in the life of city Negroes. Herein lies food for thought.

NOTES

1. Families who were lodging—and there were many—were counted as families, not as lodgers. They were mostly young couples with one or no children. The lodgers were not counted with the families because of their large numbers, and the shifting of many of them from month to month.
2. This figure is obtained by dividing the total population of the ward by the number of homes directly rented, viz., 1675. There is an error here arising from the fact that some sub-renting families are really lodgers and should be counted with the census family, while others are partially separate families and some wholly separate. This error cannot be eliminated.
3. The excessive infant mortality also has its influence on the average size of families. Cf. Chapter X. Whether infanticide or fœticide is prevalent to any extent there are no means of knowing. Once in a while such a case finds its way to the courts.
4. During the last ten years I have been bidden to a dozen or more weddings among the better class of Negroes. In no case was the bridegroom under 30, or the bride under 20. In most cases the man was about 35, and the woman 25 or more.
5. The figures relative to other groups of city Negroes as collected by the conference at Atlanta University are as follows:

Families of	Atlanta, Ga	Nashville, Tenn	Cambridge, Mass	Other Cities	All Groups
1	6.79	2.04	5.10	4.69	4.75
2	20.06	17.89	25.51	17.91	19.17
2–6	79.63	82.10	83.68	78.04	79.85
7–10	13.58	15.45	11.22	17.06	15.22
11 and Over	0	.41	0	.21	.18

These figures apply to only 1,137 families in the above named and other cities. Cf. "U. S. Bulletin of Labor," May, 1897.

6. The birth rate for the city is given in official returns as follows:
   1894. Total for city: males, 16,185; females, 14,552. Negroes: males, 536; females, 476.
   1895. Total for city: males, 15,618; females, 14,220. Negroes: males, 568; females, 524.
   1896. Total for city: males, 15,534; females, 14,219. Negroes: males, 572; females 514.
   Average per year for whites, 29,013.
   Average per year for Negroes, 1,063.
   White birth rate, 27.2 per thousand.
   Negro birth rate, 25.1 per thousand.
   Assuming white population as 1,066,985.
   Assuming Negro population as 41,500.
   The Department of Health declares these returns considerably below the truth, and the omissions among Negroes are of course large. Nevertheless, the Negro birth rate in Philadelphia is probably not high.
7. There were many families who were undoubtedly tempted to exaggerate their income so as to appear better off than they were; others, on the contrary, understated their resources. In most cases, however, the testimony so far as it went appeared to be candid and honest.
8. Cf. Booth's "Life and Labor of the People," II, 21. In this case I have combined Booth's two lower classes, "lowest" and "very poor." I shall discuss the criminal and lowest class in Chapters XIII and XIV. The separation of the "poor" and "very poor" in the Seventh Ward is somewhat arbitrary. I have called all those receiving $150 and less a year "very poor."
9. Only a few reliable budgets are subjoined, and they are typical. A large number might have been gathered, but they would hardly have added much to these.
10. These estimates are by lifelong residents of Philadelphia, who have had unusual opportunity of knowing the men of whom they speak. One says, "I have . . . prepared an estimate which I herein enclose. I have endeavored to be as conservative as possible. There are, doubtless, several omitted because they are not known, or if known are not now thought of; but I believe the estimate is approximately correct."

11. The figures for 1821 are from assessors' reports, quoted in the investigation of 1838. The figures for 1832 are from a memorial to the Legislature, in which the Negroes say that by reference to the receipts of taxpayers which were "actually produced," they paid at least $2,500 in taxes, and had also $100,000 in church property. From this the inquiry of 1,838 estimates that they owned $357,000 outside church property. The same study estimates the property of Negroes in 1838 as follows:

	REAL ESTATE (TRUE VALUE)	PERSONAL PROPERTY
City	$241,962	$505,322
Northern Liberties	26,700	35,539
Kensington	2,255	3,825
Spring Garden	5,935	21,570
Southwark	15,355	26,848
Moyamensing	30,325	74,755
	$322,532	$667,859
Encumbrances	12,906	
	$309,626	

The report says: "This amount must, of course, be received as only an approximation of the truth." Fifteen church edifices, a cemetery and hall are not included in the above. "Condition," etc., 1838. pp. 7, 8.

The investigation in 1847–48, gave the following results:

	VALUE REAL ESTATE	ENCUMBRANCES
City	$368,842	$78,421
Spring Garden	27,150	11,050
Northern Liberties	40,675	13,440
Southwark	31,544	5,915
Moyamensing	51,973	20,216
West Philadelphia	11,625	1,400
	$531,809	$130,442

This property was distributed as follows:

	WHOLE NUMBER HEADS OF FAMILIES	OWNERS OF REAL ESTATE	PER CENT
City	2562	141	5.5
Spring Garden	272	44	16.1
Northern Liberties	202	23	11.3
Southwark	287	30	10.4
Moyamensing	866	52	6.0
West Philadelphia	73	25	34.4
	4262	315	7.4

The occupations of the 315 freeholders was as follows:

    78 laborers
    49 traders
    41 mechanics
    35 coachmen and hackmen
    28 waiters
    20 barbers
    11 professional men
    53 females
    315

The personal property was as follows.

AMOUNT	CITY	SPRING GARDEN	NORTHERN LIBERTIES	SOUTHWARK	MOYAMENSING	WEST PHILADELPHIA	TOTAL
Under $25	570	66	62		259	5	
$25–$50	772	79	102		160	16	
$50–$100	404	38	63		134	9	
$100–$500	650	19	83	102	291	42	
$500–$20,000	156		5	2	5	1	
No Estate	6				15		
Total personal property	$455,620	$9,562	$34,044	$30,402	$90,553	$12,065	$632,246
Average		$178.63	$47.33	$108.07	$105.30	$106.63	$151.57	$147.52

"Statistical Inquiry," etc. p. 15.

A comparison between 1838 and 1848 was made by Needles' "Progress," etc., pp. 8, 9.

	1837	1847	INCREASE
Real estate, less incumbrances	$309,626	$401,362	$91,736
House and water rents	161,482	200,697	39,225
Taxes	3,253	6,308	3,056

The Inquiry of 1856, pp. 15, 16, declares that the previous year the Negroes owned:

Real and personal property (true value)	$2,685,693.00
Taxes paid	9,766.42
House, water and ground rent	396,782.27

A detailed estimate for 1897 gives the following:

VALUE OF ESTATE	NUMBER OF ESTATES	TOTAL
$250,000–$500,000	1 ..... =	.. $350,000
100,000	1 ..... =	.. 100,000
80,000	1 ..... =	.. 80,000
75,000	1 ..... =	.. 75,000
60,000	1 ..... =	.. 60,000
40,000	4 ..... =	.. 160,000
35,000	3 ..... =	.. 105,000
30,000	4 ..... =	.. 120,000
20,000	10 ..... =	.. 200,000
15,000	11 ..... =	.. 165,000
10,000	16 ..... =	.. 160,000
	52	$1,575,000

The total of $1,575,000 is the estimated wealth of the well-to-do.

This estimate is as reliable as can be obtained, and is probably nor far from the real facts.

12. There is more property than this owned, but only the answers that seemed reliable and definite were recorded. Most of this property is in the country districts of the South.

13. Many efforts were made to get official data on the matter of property, but the authorities had no way of even approximately distinguishing the races.

14. For an account of a partial investigation of this subject and some attempts at reform, see "Report of Citizens' Permanent Relief Committee, etc., 1893–4," pp. 31, ff. Cf. Also the work of the Star Kitchen at Seventh and Lombard streets, Philadelphia.

15. Once in a while the affairs of one of these companies are revealed to the public, as for instance, the following noted in the Public *Ledger*, October 20, 1896. The company became bankrupt, and its affairs were found hopelessly involved.

"This was the scheme, according to the former agent and some of the certificate holders. Upon the payment of ten cents a week for seven years, the subscriber was promised $100, to be paid at the end of the seventh year. In a year ten cents a week would amount to $5.20; in seven years to $36.40. The Keystone Investment Company promised to give $100 for $36.40.

"Later the assessment was raised to fifteen cents a week. This would amount in seven years to $54.60, for which sum $100 was promised in return. Some few of the certificate holders paid twenty cents a week, it is said. This, in seven years, would amount to $72.80, for which sum, according to the agreement, the certificate holder was to be paid $100.

"Just how many subscribers the company had it is impossible to learn from the officers. A gentleman, who has a store next door to the company's office, said yesterday that a great many people went there each week to pay their assessments. They appeared to be poor people, he said. There were a great many Negroes among them, and some of them, he said, came from New Jersey.

"The concern started in business in 1891, and has always occupied its present quarters, which are very unpretentious, by the way, for a financial company of any standing. A lady residing on Girard avenue, east of Hanover street, yesterday related her experience with the company as follows:

" 'I invested in certificates for my mother and my little daughter, paying fifteen cents a week on each. The agreement was that each was to receive $100 at the end of seven years. I have been paying for my little girl nearly three years, and for my mother nearly two years. It will be two years next Christmas. The payments were made regularly. On both certificates I have paid in about $35.' "

16. As before noted, I am aware that a few of these societies do not wholly deserve this sweeping condemnation, and that all of them are defended by certain short-sighted persons as encouraging savings. My observation convinces me, however, of the substantial truth of my conclusions. Of course, all this has nothing to do with the legitimate life insurance business.

CHAPTER XII

◆

The Organized Life of Negroes

31. History of the Negro Church in Philadelphia—We have already followed the history of the rise of the Free African Society, which was the beginning of the Negro Church in the North.[1] We often forget that the rise of a church organization among Negroes was a curious phenomenon. The church really represented all that was left of African tribal life, and was the sole expression of the organized efforts of the slaves. It was natural that any movement among freedmen should centre about their religious life, the sole remaining element of their former tribal system. Consequently when, led by two strong men, they left the white Methodist Church, they were naturally unable to form any democratic moral reform association; they must be led and guided, and this guidance must have the religious sanction that tribal government always has. Consequently Jones and Allen, the leaders of the Free African Society, as early as 1791 began regular religious exercises, and at the close of the eighteenth century there were three Negro churches in the city, two of which were independent.[2]

St. Thomas' Church has had a most interesting history. It early declared its purpose "of advancing our friends in a true knowledge of God, of true religion, and of the ways and means to restore our long lost race to the dignity of men and of Christians."[3] The church offered itself to the Protestant Episcopal Church and was accepted on condition that they take no part in the government of the general church. Their leader, Absalom Jones, was ordained deacon and priest, and took charge of the church. In 1804 the church established a day school which lasted until 1816.[4] In 1849 St. Thomas' began a series of attempts to gain full recognition in the Church by a demand for delegates to the Church gatherings. The Assembly first declared that it was not expedient to allow Negroes to take part. To this the vestry returned a dignified answer, asserting that "expediency is no plea against the violation of the great principles of charity, mercy, justice and truth." Not until 1864 was the Negro body received into full fellowship with the Church. In the century and more of its existence St. Thomas' has always represented a high grade of intelligence, and to-day it still represents the most cultured and wealthiest of the Negro population and the Philadelphia born residents. Its membership has consequently always been small, being 246 in 1794, 427 in 1795, 105 in 1860, and 391 in 1897.[5]

The growth of Bethel Church, founded by Richard Allen, on South Sixth Street, has been so phenomenal that it belongs to the history of the nation rather than to any one city. From a weekly gathering which met in Allen's blacksmith shop on Sixth near Lombard, grew a large church edifice; other churches were formed under the same general plan, and Allen, as overseer of them, finally took the title of bishop and ordained other bishops. The Church, under the name of African Methodist Episcopal, grew and spread until in 1890 the organization had 452,725 members, 2,481 churches and $6,468,280 worth of property.[6]

By 1813[7] there were in Philadelphia six Negro churches with the following membership:[8]

St. Thomas', P. E	560
Bethel, A. M. E	1,272
Zoar, M. E.	80
Union, A. M. E.	74
Baptist, Race and Vine Streets	80
Presbyterian	300
	2,366

The Presbyterian Church had been founded by two Negro missionaries, father and son, named Gloucester, in 1807.[9] The Baptist Church was founded in 1809. The inquiry of 1838 gives these statistics of churches:

DENOMINATION	No CHURCHES	MEMBERS	ANNUAL EXPENSES	VALUE OF PROPERTY	INCUMBRANCE
Episcopalian	1	100	$1,000	$36,000	. . .
Lutheran	1	10	120	3,000	$1,000
Methodist	8	2,860	2,100	50,800	5,100
Presbyterian	2	325	1,500	20,000	1,000
Baptist	4	700	1,300	4,200	. . .
Total	16	3,995	$6,020	$114,000	$7,100

Three more churches were added in the next ten years, and then a reaction followed.[10] By 1867 there were in all probability nearly twenty churches, of which we have statistics of seventeen:[11]

STATISTICS OF NEGRO CHURCHES, 1867

NAME	FOUNDED	NUMBER OF MEMBERS	VALUE OF PROPERTY	PASTORS' SALARY
P. E.—				
St. Thomas'	1792	. . .	. . .	. . .
Methodist—				
Bethel	1794	1,100	$50,000	$600
Union	1827	467	40,000	850
Wesley	1817	464	21,000	700
Zoar	1794	400	12,000	. . .

(Continued)

STATISTICS OF NEGRO CHURCHES, 1867—*Continued*

NAME	FOUNDED	NUMBER OF MEMBERS	VALUE OF PROPERTY	PASTORS' SALARY
John Wesley	1844	42	3,000	No regular salary
Little Wesley	1821	310	11,000	500
Pisgah	1831	116	4,600	430
Zion City Mission	1858	90	4,500	. . .
Little Union	1837	200	. . .	. . .
Baptist—				
First Baptist	1809	360	5,000	. . .
Union Baptist	. .	400	7,000	600
Shiloh	1842	405	16,000	600
Oak Street	1827	137	. . .	. . .
Presbyterian—				
First Presbyterian	1807	200	8,000	. . .
Second Presbyterian . . .	1824	. . .	. . .	. . .
Central Presbyterian . . .	1844	240	16,000	. . .

Since the war the growth of Negro churches has been by bounds, there being twenty-five churches and missions in 1880, and fifty-five in 1897.

So phenomenal a growth as this here outlined means more than the establishment of many places of worship. The Negro is, to be sure, a religious creature—most primitive folk are—but his rapid and even extraordinary founding of churches is not due to this fact alone, but is rather a measure of his development, an indication of the increasing intricacy of his social life and the consequent multiplication of the organ which is the function of his group life—the church. To understand this let us inquire into the function of the Negro church.

32. The Function of the Negro Church—The Negro church is the peculiar and characteristic product of the transplanted African, and deserves especial study. As a social group the Negro church may be said to have antedated the Negro family on American soil; as such it has preserved, on the one hand, many functions of tribal organization, and on the other hand, many of the family functions. Its tribal functions are shown in its religious activity, its social authority and general guiding and co-ordinating work; its family functions are shown by the fact that the church is a centre of social life and intercourse; acts as newspaper and intelligence bureau, is the centre of amusements—indeed, is the world in which the Negro moves and acts. So far-reaching are these functions of the church that its organization is almost political. In Bethel Church, for instance, the mother African Methodist Episcopal Church of America, we have the following officials and organizations:

The Bishop of the District . . . .
The Presiding Elder . . . . } Executive.
The Pastor . . . .
The Board of Trustees . . . . Executive Council.
General Church Meeting . . . . Legislative.

The Board of Stewards	} Financial Board.
The Board of Stewardesses	
The Junior Stewardesses	
The Sunday School Organization	Educational System.
Ladies' Auxiliary, Volunteer Guild, etc.	Tax Collectors.
Ushers' Association	Police.
Class Leaders	} Sheriffs and Magistrates.
Local Preachers	
Choir	Music and Amusement.
Allen Guards	Militia.
Missionary Societies	Social Reformers.
Beneficial and Semi-Secret Societies, etc.	Corporations.

Or to put it differently, here we have a mayor, appointed from without, with great administrative and legislative powers, although well limited by long and zealously cherished custom; he acts conjointly with a select council, the trustees, a board of finance, composed of stewards and stewardesses, a common council of committees and, occasionally, of all church members. The various functions of the church are carried out by societies and organizations. The form of government varies, but is generally some form of democracy closely guarded by custom and tempered by possible and not infrequent secession.

The functions of such churches in order of present emphasis are:

1. The raising of the annual budget.
2. The maintenance of membership.
3. Social intercourse and amusements.
4. The setting of moral standards.
5. Promotion of general intelligence.
6. Efforts for social betterment.

1. The annual budget is of first importance, because the life of the organization depends upon it. The amount of expenditure is not very accurately determined beforehand, although its main items do not vary much. There is the pastor's salary, the maintenance of the building, light and heat, the wages of a janitor, contributions to various church objects, and the like, to which must be usually added the interest on some debt. The sum thus required varies in Philadelphia from $200 to $5,000. A small part of this is raised by a direct tax on each member. Besides this, voluntary contributions by members, roughly gauged according to ability, are expected, and a strong public opinion usually compels payment. Another large source of revenue is the collection after the sermons on Sunday, when, amid the reading of notices and a subdued hum of social intercourse, a stream of givers walk to the pulpit and place in the hands of the trustee or steward in charge a contribution, varying from a cent to a dollar or more. To this must be added the steady revenue from entertainments, suppers, socials, fairs, and the like. In this way the Negro churches of Philadelphia raise nearly $100,000 a year. They hold in real estate $900,000 worth of property, and are thus no insignificant element in the economics of the city.

2. Extraordinary methods are used and efforts made to maintain and increase the membership of the various churches. To be a popular church with large membership means ample revenues, large social influence and a leadership among the colored people unequaled in power and effectiveness. Consequently people are attracted to the church by sermons, by music and by entertainments; finally, every year a revival is held, at which considerable numbers of young people are converted. All this is done in perfect sincerity and without much thought of merely increasing membership, and yet every small church strives to be large by these means and every large church to maintain itself or grow larger. The churches thus vary from a dozen to a thousand members.

3. Without wholly conscious effort the Negro church has become a centre of social intercourse to a degree unknown in white churches even in the country. The various churches, too, represent social classes. At St. Thomas' one looks for the well-to-do Philadelphians, largely descendants of favorite mulatto house servants, and consequently well-bred and educated, but rather cold and reserved to strangers or newcomers; at Central Presbyterian one sees the older, simpler set of respectable Philadelphians with distinctly Quaker characteristics—pleasant but conservative; at Bethel may be seen the best of the great laboring class— steady, honest people, well dressed and well fed, with church and family traditions; at Wesley will be found the new arrivals, the sight-seers and the strangers to the city—hearty and easy-going people, who welcome all comers and ask few questions; at Union Baptist one may look for the Virginia servant girls and their young men; and so on throughout the city. Each church forms its own social circle, and not many stray beyond its bounds. Introductions into that circle come through the church, and thus the stranger becomes known. All sorts of entertainments and amusements are furnished by the churches: concerts, suppers, socials, fairs, literary exercises and debates, cantatas, plays, excursions, picnics, surprise parties, celebrations. Every holiday is the occasion of some special entertainment by some club, society or committee of the church; Thursday afternoons and evenings, when the servant girls are free, are always sure to have some sort of entertainment. Sometimes these exercises are free, sometimes an admission fee is charged, sometimes refreshments or articles are on sale. The favorite entertainment is a concert with solo singing, instrumental music, reciting, and the like. Many performers make a living by appearing at these entertainments in various cities, and often they are persons of training and ability, although not always. So frequent are these and other church exercises that there are few Negro churches which are not open four to seven nights in a week and sometimes one or two afternoons in addition.

Perhaps the pleasantest and most interesting social intercourse takes place on Sunday; the weary week's work is done, the people have slept late and had a good breakfast, and sally forth to church well dressed and complacent. The usual hour of the morning service is eleven, but people stream in until after twelve. The sermon is usually short and stirring, but in the larger churches elicits little esponse other than an "Amen" or two. After the sermon the social features begin; notices on the various meetings of the week are read, people talk with each other in subdued tones, take their contributions to the altar, and linger in the aisles and corridors long after dismission to laugh and chat until one or two o'clock. Then they go home to good dinners. Sometimes there is some special three o'clock service, but usually nothing save Sunday school, until night. Then comes the chief meeting of the day; probably ten thousand Negroes gather every Sunday night in their churches. There is much music, much preaching, some short addresses; many strangers are there to be looked at; many beaus bring out their belles, and those who do not gather in crowds at the church door and escort the young women home. The crowds are usually well behaved and respectable, though rather more jolly than comports with a puritan idea of church services.

In this way the social life of the Negro centres in his church—baptism, wedding and burial, gossip and courtship, friendship and intrigue—all lie in these walls. What wonder that this central club house tends to become more and more luxuriously furnished, costly in appointment and easy of access!

4. It must not be inferred from all this that the Negro is hypocritical or irreligious. His church is, to be sure, a social institution first, and religious afterwards, but nevertheless, its religious activity is wide and sincere. In direct moral teaching and in setting moral standards for the people, however, the church is timid, and naturally so, for its constitution is democracy tempered by custom. Negro preachers are often condemned for poor leadership and empty sermons, and it is said that men with so much power and influence could make striking moral reforms. This is but partially true. The congregation does not follow the moral precepts of the preacher, but rather the preacher follows the standard of his flock, and only exceptional men dare seek to change this. And here it must be remembered that the Negro preacher is primarily an executive officer, rather than a spiritual guide. If one goes into any great Negro church and hears the sermon and views the audience, one would say: either the sermon is far below the calibre of the audience, or the people are less sensible than they look; the former explanation is usually true. The preacher is sure to be a man of executive ability, a leader of men, a shrewd and affable president of a large and intricate corporation. In addition to this he may be, and usually is, a striking elocutionist; he may also be a man of integrity, learning, and deep spiritual earnestness; but these last three are sometimes all lacking, and the last two in many cases. Some signs of advance are here manifest: no minister of notoriously immoral life, or even of bad reputation, could hold a large church in Philadelphia without eventual revolt. Most of the present pastors are decent, respectable men; there are perhaps one or two exceptions to this, but the exceptions are doubtful, rather than notorious. On the whole then, the average Negro preacher in this city is a shrewd manager, a respectable man, a good talker, a pleasant companion, but neither learned nor spiritual, nor a reformer.

The moral standards are therefore set by the congregations, and vary from church to church in some degree. There has been a slow working toward a literal obeying of the puritan and ascetic standard of morals which Methodism imposed on the freedmen; but condition and temperament have modified these. The grosser forms of immorality, together with theatre-going and dancing, are specifically denounced; nevertheless, the precepts against specific amusements are often violated by church members. The cleft between denominations is still wide, especially between Methodists and Baptists. The sermons are usually kept within the safe ground of a mild Calvinism, with much insistence on Salvation, Grace, Fallen Humanity and the like.

The chief function of these churches in morals is to conserve old standards and create about them a public opinion which shall deter the offender. And in this the Negro churches are peculiarly successful, although naturally the standards conserved are not as high as they should be.

5. The Negro churches were the birthplaces of Negro schools and of all agencies which seek to promote the intelligence of the masses; and even to-day no agency serves to disseminate news or information so quickly and effectively among Negroes as the church. The lyceum and lecture here still maintain a feeble but persistent existence, and church newspapers and books are circulated widely. Night schools and kindergartens are still held in connection with churches, and all Negro celebrities, from a bishop to a poet like Dunbar, are introduced to Negro audiences from the pulpits.

6. Consequently all movements for social betterment are apt to centre in the churches. Beneficial societies in endless number are formed here; secret societies keep in touch; co-operative and building associations have lately sprung up; the minister often acts as an employment agent; considerable charitable and relief work is done and special meetings held to aid special projects.[12] The race problem in all its phases is continually being discussed, and, indeed, from this forum many a youth goes forth inspired to work.

Such are some of the functions of the Negro church, and a study of them indicates how largely this organization has come to be an expression of the organized life of Negroes in a great city.

33. The Present Condition of the Churches—The 2,441 families of the Seventh Ward were distributed among the various denominations, in 1896, as follows:

	FAMILIES
Methodists	842
Baptists	577
Episcopalians	156
Presbyterians	74
Catholic	69
Shakers	2
Unconnected and unknown	721
	2,441

Probably half of the "unconnected and unknown" habitually attend church.

In the city at large the Methodists have a decided majority, followed by the Baptists, and further behind, the Episcopalians. Starting with the Methodists, we find three bodies: the African Methodist Episcopal, founded by Allen, the A. M. E. Zion, which sprung from a secession of Negroes from white churches in New York in the eighteenth century; and the M. E. Church, consisting of colored churches belonging to the white Methodist Church, like Zoar.

The A. M. E. Church is the largest body and had, in 1897, fourteen churches and missions in the city, with a total membership of 3,210, and thirteen church edifices, seating 6,117 persons. These churches collected during the year, $27,074.13. Their property is valued at $202,229 on which there is a mortgage indebtedness of $30,000 to $50,000. Detailed statistics are given in the table on the next page.

These churches are pretty well organized, and are conducted with vim and enthusiasm. This arises largely from their system. Their bishops have been in some instances men of piety and ability like the late Daniel A. Payne. In other cases they have fallen far below this standard; but they have always been men of great influence, and had a genius for leadership—else they would not have been bishops. They have large powers of appointment and removal in the case of pastors, and thus each pastor, working under the eye of an inspiring chief, strains every nerve to make his church a successful organization. The bishop is aided by several presiding elders, who are traveling inspectors and preachers, and give advice as to appointments. This system results in great unity and power; the purely spiritual aims of the church, to be sure, suffer somewhat, but after all this peculiar organism is more than a church, it is a government of men.

The headquarters of the A. M. E. Church are in Philadelphia. Their publishing house, at Seventh and Pine, publishes a weekly paper and a quarterly review, besides some books, such as hymnals, church disciplines, short treatises, leaflets and the like. The receipts of this establishment in 1897 were $16,058.26, and its expenditures $14,119.15. Its total outfit and property is valued at $45,513.64, with an indebtedness of $14,513.64.

An episcopal residence for the bishop of the district has recently been purchased on Belmont avenue. The Philadelphia Conference disbursed from the general church funds in 1897, $985 to superannuated ministers, and $375 to widows of ministers. Two or three women missionaries visited the sick during the year and some committees of the Ladies' Mission Society worked to secure orphans' homes.[13] Thus throughout the work of this church there is much evidence of enthusiasm and persistent progress.[14]

There are three churches in the city representing the A. M. E. Zion connection. They are:

Wesley	Fifteenth and Lombard Sts.
Mount Zion	Fifty-fifth above Market St.
Union	Ninth St. and Girard Ave.

No detailed statistics of these churches are available; the last two are small, the first is one of the largest and most popular in the city; the pastor receives $1500 a year and the total income of the church is between $4,000 and $5,000. It does considerable charitable work among its aged members, and supports a large sick and death benefit society. Its property is worth at least $25,000.

Two other Methodist churches of different denominations are: Grace U. A. M. E., Lombard street, above Fifteenth; St. Matthew Methodist Protestant, Fifty-eighth and Vine streets. Both these churches are small, although the first has a valuable piece of property.

A. M. E. CHURCHES IN PHILADELPHIA, 1897

Name of Church	Number of Members	No. of Societies — Missionary	No. of Societies — Church Auxiliary	Parsonage	Seating Capacity	General Church Support	Local Church Expenses	Pastor's Salary	Missionary and Educational	Charity	Total Income	Value of Church Property	Indebtedness
Bethel	1,104	1	21	1	1,500	$924.00	$1,560(?)	$1,500.00	$137.45	$435.87	$4,557.32	$94,000.00	(?)
Murray Chapel	170	2	3	..	350	233.00	697.94	700.00	23.97	50.00	1,704.91	5,000.00	$137.00
Zion Mission	128	1	1	..	350	139.00	481.97	653.49	35.54	50.00	1,360.92	7,000.00	1,093.25
Germantown	119	2	2	1	450	156.87	1,685.26	1,000.00	39.83	41.18	2,913.14	14,500.00	7,400.00
Frankford	127	2	3	1	400	142.50	500(?)	600.00	39.50	15.00	1,297.00	15,000.00	1,869.46
Darby	44	1	1	..	300	86.65	300.07	270.00	18.12	2.26	677.00	3,329.00	203.95
Allen Chapel	378	1	4	..	550	312.82	750(?)	964.75	53.25	132.60	2,213.42	15,000.00	3,651.00
Disney	22	1	4	..	200	35.75	129.36	122.05	8.75	3.00	300.91	2,400.00	904.00
York	48	1	2	..	317	106.50	524.20	600.00	55.40	12.00	1,790.60	6,000.00	2,700.00
Tioga	..	..	..	..	..	10.33	182.42	286.05	..	..	478.80	..	..
Payne	25	..	1	..	200	20.13	583.68	47.62	1.25	8.38	661.46	3,000.00	2,454.00
Union	674	..	5	1	1,000	502.88	2,471.81	1,400.00	93.20	135.00	4,602.89	25,000.00	8,038.62
Mt. Pisgah	315	1	5	1	500	391.85	793.38	1,000.00	79.00	465.67	3,749.90	25,000.00	..
Morris Brown	46	2	2	..	..	74.75	287.58	265.62	8.93	8.88	645.86	12,000.00	7,162.00
Total	3,210	15	54	5	6,117	$3,137.03	$14,665.47	$9,398.58	$594.19	$1,358.84	$27,074.13	$202,229.00	$35,613.28

The Methodist Episcopal Church has six organizations in the city among the Negroes; they own church property valued at $53,700, have a total membership of 1,202, and an income of $16,394 in 1897. Of this total income, $1,235, or 7½ per cent, was given for benevolent enterprises. These churches are quiet and well conducted, and although not among the most popular churches, have nevertheless a membership of old and respected citizens.

COLORED M. E. CHURCHES IN PHILADELPHIA, 1897

Church	Members	Salary, etc., of Pastor	Contributions to Presiding Elders and Bishops	Value of Church	Value of Parsonage	Building and Improvements During Year	Paid on Indebtedness	Present Indebtedness	Current Expenses	Benevolent Collections
Bainbridge Street	354	$1,312	$151	$20,000	...	$190	$601	$4,433	$1,274	$326
Frankford	72	720	35	1,500	...	15	146	130	155	87
Germantown ...	165	828	72	4,000	...	...	400	1,000	270	177
Haven	72	440	39	3,400	...	24	...	3,836	277	25
Waterloo Street .	31	221	27	800	...	450	50	90	22	37
Zoar	508	1,270	220	20,000	$4,000	3,522	2,171	5,800	257	583
Total	1,202	$4,791	544	$49,700	$4,000	$4,201	$3,368	$15,289	$2,255	$1,235

There were in 1896 seventeen Baptist churches in Philadelphia, holding property valued at more than $300,000, having six thousand members, and an annual income of, probably, $30,000 to $35,000. One of the largest churches has in the last five years raised between $17,000 and $18,000.

COLORED BAPTIST CHURCHES OF PHILADELPHIA, 1896

Church	Membership	Value of Property	Expended in Missions Local and Foreign	Annual Income
Monumental	435	$30,000	$7.00	...
Cherry Street	800	50,000	...	...
Union	1,020	50,000	58.10	...
St. Paul	422	25,000	1.00	...
Ebenezer	189	12,000	3.36	...
Macedonia	76	1,000	3.00	...
Bethsaida	78	...	...	...
Haddington	50	...	...	...
Germantown	305	24,800	...	...
Grace	57	2,000	5.50	...
Shiloh	1,000	50,000	...	$3,600
Holy Trinity	287	10,000	3.00	...
Second, Nicetown	164	2,000	9.73	...
Zion	700	40,000	...	...
Providence	...	...	...	...
Cherry Street Mission	...	...	...	...
Tabernacle	...	...	...	...
Total	5,583	$296,800	...	...

The Baptists are strong in Philadelphia, and own many large and attractive churches, such as, for instance, the Union Baptist Church, on Twelfth street; Zion Baptist, in the northern part of the city; Monumental, in West Philadelphia, and the staid and respectable Cherry Street Church. These churches as a rule have large membership. They are, however, quite different in spirit and methods from the Methodists; they lack organization, and are not so well managed as business institutions. Consequently statistics of their work are very hard to obtain, and indeed in many cases do not even exist for individual churches. On the other hand, the Baptists are peculiarly clannish and loyal to their organization, keep their pastors a long time, and thus each church gains an individuality not noticed in Methodist churches. If the pastor is a strong, upright character, his influence for good is marked. At the same time, the Baptists have in their ranks a larger percentage of illiteracy than probably any other church, and it is often possible for an inferior man to hold a large church for years and allow it to stagnate and retrograde. The Baptist policy is extreme democracy applied to church affairs, and no wonder that this often results in a pernicious dictatorship. While many of the Baptist pastors of Philadelphia are men of ability and education, the general average is below that of the other churches—a fact due principally to the ease with which one can enter the Baptist ministry.[15] These churches support a small publishing house in the city, which issues a weekly paper. They do some charitable work, but not much.[16]

There are three Presbyterian churches in the city:

NAME	MEMBERS	VALUE OF PROPERTY	ANNUAL INCOME	
Berean	98	$75,000	$1,135	Parsonage
Central	430	50,000	1,800	Parsonage
First African	105	25,000	1,538	

Central Church is the oldest of these churches and has an interesting history. It represents a withdrawal from the First African Presbyterian Church in 1844. The congregation first worshiped at Eighth and Carpenter streets, and in 1845 purchased a lot at Ninth and Lombard, where they still meet in a quiet and respectable house of worship. Their 430 members include some of the oldest and most respectable Negro families of the city. Probably if the white Presbyterians had given more encouragement to Negroes, this denomination would have absorbed the best elements of the colored population; they seem, however, to have shown some desire to be rid of the blacks, or at least not to increase their Negro membership in Philadelphia to any great extent. Central Church is more nearly a simple religious organization than most churches; it listens to able sermons, but does little outside its own doors.[17]

Berean Church is the work of one man and is an institutional church. It was formerly a mission of Central Church and now owns a fine piece of property bought by donations contributed by whites and Negroes, but chiefly by the former. The conception of the work and its carrying out, however, is due to Negroes. This church conducts a successful Building and Loan Association, a kindergarten, a medical dispensary and a seaside home, beside the numerous church societies. Probably no church in the city, except the Episcopal Church of the Crucifixion, is doing so much for the social betterment of the Negro.[18] The First African is the oldest colored church of this denomination in the city.

The Episcopal Church has, for Negro congregations, two independent churches, two churches dependent on white parishes, and four missions and Sunday schools. Statistics of three of these are given in the table on page 153.

The Episcopal churches receive more outside help than others and also do more general mission and rescue work. They hold $150,000 worth of property, have 900–1,000 members and an annual income of $7,000 to $8,000. They represent all grades of the colored population. The oldest of the churches is St. Thomas'. Next comes the Church of the Crucifixion, over fifty years old and perhaps the most effective church organization in the city for benevolent and rescue work. It has been built up virtually by one Negro, a man of sincerity and culture, and of peculiar energy. This church carries on regular church work at Bainbridge and Eighth and at two branch missions; it helps in the Fresh Air Fund, has an ice mission, a vacation school of thirty-five children, and a parish visitor. It makes an especial feature of good music with its vested choir. One or two courses of University Extension lectures are held here each year, and there is a large beneficial and insurance society in active operation, and a Home for the Homeless on Lombard street. This church especially reaches after a class of neglected poor whom the other colored churches shun or forget and for whom there is little fellowship in white churches. The rector says of this work:

"As I look back over nearly twenty years of labor in one parish, I see a great deal to be devoutly thankful for. Here are people struggling from the beginning of one year to another, without ever having what can be called the necessaries of life. God alone knows what a real struggle life is to them. Many of them must always be 'moving on,' because they cannot pay the rent or meet other obligations.

"I have just visited a family of four, mother and three children. The mother is too sick to work. The eldest girl will work when she can find something to do. But the rent is due, and there is not a cent in the house. This is but a sample. How can such people support a church of their own? To many such, religion often becomes doubly comforting. They seize eagerly on the promises of a life where these earthly distresses will be forever absent.

"If the other half only knew how this half is living—how hard and dreary, and often hopeless, life is—the members of the more favored half would gladly help to do all they could to have the gospel freely preached to those whose lives are so devoid of earthly comforts.

"Twenty or thirty thousand dollars (and that is not much), safely invested, would enable the parish to do a work that ought to be done and yet is not being done at present. The poor could then have the gospel preached to them in a way that it is not now being preached."

The Catholic church has in the last decade made great progress in its work among Negroes and is determined to do much in the future. Its chief hold upon the colored people is its comparative lack of discrimination. There is one Catholic

COLORED PROTESTANT EPISCOPAL CHURCHES IN PHILADELPHIA*, 1897

Church	Members	Rectors and Assistants	Church Societies	Offerings of Church For Parish	Offerings of Church Purposes Outside of Parish	Total Income	Expenditures Salary of Rector	Current Expense	Poor	Total Parochial Expenses	Diocesan	General Missions, etc	Total Expense	Value Real and Personal Estate	Encumbrances	Endowment
Independent { Crucifixion and One Mission	310	2	9	$437.58	$879.40	$2,995.93	$1,200	$2,477.98	$73	$2,632.98	$35.00	$101.37	$2,769.35	$45,000	. . .	$11,000
Independent { St. Thomas'	391	1	9	1,457.90	10.00	2,347.53	. . .	2,008.00	70	2,475.81	. . .	. . .	2,582.98	60,000	$5,388.73	. . .
St. Michael and All Angels	90	1	9	227.08	6.67	1,270.79	760	1,381.89	. . .	1,411.89	6.50	. . .	1,420.56	25,000	1,200.00	. . .

* Besides these, there are the following Churches, from which statistics were not obtained: St. Mark's, Zion Sunday school, St. Faith's Mission, and St. Simon's Chapel. The first is supported mainly by a white parish, and has a new building; the second and third are small Missions; the fourth is a promising outgrowth of the Church of the Crucifixion.

church in the city designed especially for Negro work—St. Peter Clavers at Twelfth and Lombard—formerly a Presbyterian church; recently a parish house has been added. The priest in charge estimates that 400 or 500 Negroes regularly attend Catholic churches in various parts of the city. The Mary Drexel Home for Colored Orphans is a Catholic institution near the city which is doing much work. The Catholic church can do more than any other agency in humanizing the intense prejudice of many of the working class against the Negro, and signs of this influence are manifest in some quarters.

We have thus somewhat in detail reviewed the work of the chief churches. There are beside these continually springing up and dying a host of little noisy missions which represent the older and more demonstrative worship. A description of one applies to nearly all; take for instance one in the slums of the Fifth Ward:

"The tablet in the gable of this little church bears the date 1837. For sixty years it has stood and done its work in the narrow lane. What its history has been all this time it is difficult to find out, for no records are on hand, and no one is here to tell the tale.

"The few last months of the old order was something like this: It was in the hands of a Negro congregation. Several visits were paid to the church, and generally a dozen people were found there. After a discourse by a very illiterate preacher, hymns were sung, having many repetitions of senseless sentiment and exciting cadences. It took about an hour to work up the congregation to a fervor aimed at. When this was reached a remarkable scene presented itself. The whole congregation pressed forward to an open space before the pulpit, and formed a ring. The most excitable of their number entered the ring, and with clapping of hands and contortions led the devotions. Those forming the ring joined in the clapping of hands and wild and loud singing, frequently springing into the air, and shouting loudly. As the devotions proceeded, most of the worshipers took off their coats and vests and hung them on pegs on the wall. This continued for hours, until all were completely exhausted, and some had fainted and been stowed away on benches or the pulpit platform. This was the order of things at the close of sixty years' history. * * * When this congregation vacated the church, they did so stealthily, under cover of darkness, removed furniture not their own, including the pulpit, and left bills unpaid."[19]

There are dozens of such little missions in various parts of Philadelphia, led by wandering preachers. They are survivals of the methods of worship in Africa and the West Indies. In some of the larger churches noise and excitement attend the services, especially at the time of revival or in prayer meetings. For the most part, however, these customs are dying away.

To recapitulate, we have in Philadelphia fifty-five Negro churches with 12,845 members owning $907,729 worth of property with an annual income of at least $94,968. And these represent the organized efforts of the race better than any other organizations. Second to them however come the secret and benevolent societies, which we now consider.

34. Secret and Beneficial Societies, and Co-operative Business—The art of organization is the one hardest for the freedman to learn, and the Negro shows his greatest deficiency here; whatever success he has had has been shown most conspicuously in his church organizations, where the religious bond greatly facilitated union. In other organizations where the bond was weaker his success has been less. From early times the precarious economic condition of the free Negroes led to many mutual aid organizations. They were very simple in form: an initiation fee of small amount was required, and small regular payments; in case of sickness, a weekly stipend was paid, and in case of death the members were assessed to pay for the funeral and help the widow. Confined to a few members, all personally known to each other, such societies were successful from the beginning. We hear of them in the eighteenth century, and by 1838 there were 100 such small groups, with 7,448 members, in the city. They paid in $18,851, gave $14,172 in benefits, and had $10,023 on hand. Ten years later about eight thousand members belonged to 106 such societies. Seventy-six of these had a total membership of 5,187. They contributed usually 25 cents to 37½ cents a month; the sick received $1.50 to $3.00 a week, and death benefits of $10.00 to $20.00 were allowed. The income of these seventy-six societies was $16,814.23; 681 families were assisted.[20]

These societies have since been superceded to some extent by other organizations; they are still so numerous, however, that it is impractical to catalogue all of them; there are probably several hundred of various kinds in the city.

To these were early added the secret societies, which naturally had great attraction for Negroes. A Boston lodge of black Masons received a charter direct from England, and independent orders of Odd Fellows, Knights of Pythias, etc., grew up. During the time that Negroes were shut out of the public libraries there were many literary associations with libraries. These have now disappeared. Outside the churches the most important organizations among Negroes to-day are: Secret societies, beneficial societies, insurance societies, cemeteries, building and loan associations, labor unions, homes of various sorts and political clubs. The most powerful and flourishing secret order is that of the Odd Fellows, which has two hundred thousand members among American Negroes. In Philadelphia there are 19 lodges with a total membership of 1,188, and $46,000 worth of property. Detailed statistics are in the table on page 156.[21]

This order owns two halls in the city worth perhaps $40,000. One is occupied by the officers of the Grand Lodge, which employs several salaried officials and clerks. The order conducts a newspaper called the *Odd Fellows' Journal*.

There are 19 lodges of Masons in the city, 6 chapters, 5 commanderies, 3 of the Scottish Rite, and 1 drill corp. The Masons are not so well organized and conducted as the Odd Fellows, and detailed statistics of their lodges are not available. They own two halls worth at least $50,000, and probably distribute not less than $3,000 to $4,000 annually in benefits.

Beside these chief secret orders there are numerous others, such as the American Protestant Association, which has many members, the Knights of Pythias, the Galilean Fishermen, the various female orders attached to these, and a number of others. It is almost impossible to get accurate statistics of all these orders, and any estimate of their economic activity is liable to considerable error. However, from general observation and the available figures, it

COLORED ODD FELLOWS' LODGES IN PHILADELPHIA, 1896

NAME	ORGANIZED	MEMBERS	SICK BENEFIT TO MEMBERS	DEATH BENEFIT	WIDOWS RELIEVED	WIDOWS BURIED	ORPHANS BURIED	AMOUNT PAID FOR SICK	AMOUNT PAID FOR FUNERALS	AMOUNT PAID WIDOWS	AMOUNT PAID IN CHARITY	WHOLE AMOUNT PAID OUT	AMOUNT INVESTED	VALUE OF PROPERTY	BALANCE IN FUND	TOTAL PROPERTY, FUNDS, ETC
Unity	1844	121	.	.	2			$291.85	$25.00	$6.80	.	$627.07	$763.75	$660.00	$42.97	$2,547.61
Good Samaritan	1864	80	3	.				104.00	85.00		$10.00	307.96	712.99	113.85	18.66	845.50
Fraternal	1864	88	7	1				84.00			28.36	249.42	452.50	250.00	820.84	1,522.34
Phoenix	1846	98	3	.				98.50	121.00	7.50	5.00	419.65	1,420.30	100.00	163.11	1,620.30
Covenant	1847	77	5	.				214.00	160.00		6.00	547.50	450.00	550.00	86.00	1,036.50
Friendship	1847	24	.	1	1			43.50				98.93		200.00	5.00	205.00
Carthagenian	1848	113	15	1	1			272.00	70.00	5.00	16.00	798.19	2,362.50	583.65	2,281.25	5,227.40
Mt. Olive	1848	70	7	.				109.00			12.00	383.51	62.50	600.00	587.39	1,633.40
Good Hope	1855	46	4	1	1	1	2	36.00	10.00	15.00		348.44	248.00	1,500.00	60.72	1,809.82
Mt. Lebanon	1857	36	3	1	1	3	1	22.20	149.50	10.00		245.32	50.00	50.00	50.00	150.00
Equity	1867	173	6	1				134.55	175.00	25.00		415.99	200.00	20,000.00	100.00	28,300.00
St. Albans	1875	31	1	.				6.20	30.00			78.95		2,500.00	25.00	275.00
Keystone	1873	15	2	.					20.00						4.00	4.00
Gideon	1875	17	2	1	1			56.00	40.00	4.00	10.00	144.00		50.00	10.00	60.00
Beth Eden	1876	31	5	1	1			54.00	13.00	8.00	3.50	133.05		75.00	20.00	95.00
Philadelphia	1886	36	2	1	1			32.00	40.00	10.00		181.06		350.00	5.24	355.24
Pennsylvania	1889	.	.	.												
John Rhodes	1891	15	.									15.00	10.00		40.00	40.00
Quaker City	1892	96	10					220.18	20.00	5.00	10.00	417.00		33.00	67.00	100.00
Total	. . .	1,167	75	7	8	3	3	$1,777.98	$958.50	$96.30	$100.86	$5,381.04	$6,732.54	$27,615.50	$4,387.18	$45,827.11

seems fairly certain that at least four thousand Negroes belong to secret orders, and that these orders annually collect at least $25,000, part of which is paid out in sick and death benefits, and part invested. The real estate, personal property and funds of these orders amount to no less than $125,000.

The function of the secret society is partly social intercourse and partly insurance. They furnish pastime from the monotony of work, a field for ambition and intrigue, a chance for parade, and insurance against misfortune. Next to the church they are the most popular organizations among Negroes.

Of the beneficial societies we have already spoken in general. A detailed account of a few of the larger and more typical organizations will now suffice. The Quaker City Association is a sick and death benefit society, seven years old, which confines its membership to native Philadelphians. It has 280 members and distributes $1,400 to $1,500 annually. The Sons and Daughters of Delaware is over fifty years old. It has 106 members, and owns $3,000 worth of real estate. The Fraternal Association was founded in 1861; it has 86 members, and distributes about $300 a year. It "was formed for the purpose of relieving the wants and distresses of each other in the time of affliction and death, and for the furtherance of such benevolent views and objects as would tend to establish and maintain a permanent and friendly intercourse among them in their social relations in life." The Sons of St. Thomas was founded in 1823 and was originally confined to members of St. Thomas' Church. It was formerly a large organization, but now has 80 members, and paid out in 1896, $416 in relief. It has $1,500 invested in government bonds. In addition to these there is the Old Men's Association, the Female Cox Association, the Sons and Daughters of Moses, and a large number of other small societies.

There is arising also a considerable number of insurance societies, differing from the beneficial in being conducted by directors. The best of these are the Crucifixion connected with the Church of the Crucifixion, and the Avery, connected with Wesley A. M. E. Z. Church; both have a large membership and are well conducted. Nearly every church is beginning to organize one or more such societies, some of which in times past have met disaster by bad management. The True Reformers of Virginia, the most remarkable Negro beneficial organization yet started, has several branches here. Beside these there are numberless minor societies, as the Alpha Relief, Knights and Ladies of St. Paul, the National Co-operative Society, Colored Women's Protective Association, Loyal Beneficial, etc. Some of these are honest efforts and some are swindling imitations of the pernicious white petty insurance societies.

There are three building and loan associations conducted by Negroes. Some of the directors in one are white, all the others are colored. The oldest association is the Century, established October 26, 1886. Its board of directors is composed of teachers, upholsterers, clerks, restaurant keepers and undertakers, and it has had marked success. Its income for 1897 was about $7,000. It has $25,000 in loans outstanding.

The Berean Building and Loan Association was established in 1888 in connection with Berean Presbyterian Church; 13 of the 19 officers and directors are colored. Its income for 1896 was nearly $30,000, and it had $60,000 in loans; 43 homes have been bought through this association.[22]

The Pioneer Association is composed entirely of Negroes, the directors being caterers, merchants and upholsterers. It was founded in 1888 and has an office on Pine street. Its receipts in 1897 were $9,000, and it had about $20,000 in loans. Nine homes are at present being bought in this association.

There are arising some loan associations to replace the pawn-shops and usurers to some extent. The Small Loan Association, for instance, was founded in 1891, and has the following report for 1898:

Shares sold	$1,144.00
Assessments on shares	114.40
Repaid loans	4,537.50
Interest	417.06
Cash in treasury	275.54
Dividends paid	222.67
Loans made	4,626.75
Expenses	82.02

The Conservative is a similar organization, consisting of ten members.

This account has attempted to touch only the chief and characteristic organizations, and makes no pretensions to completeness. It shows, however, how intimately bound together the Negroes of Philadelphia are. These associations are largely experiments, and as such, are continually reaching out to new fields. The latest ventures are toward labor unions, co-operative stores and newspapers. There are the following labor unions, among others: The Caterers' Club, the Private Waiters' Association, the Coachmen's Association, the Hotel Brotherhood (of waiters), the Cigar-makers' Union (white and colored), the Hod-Carriers' Union, the Barbers' Union, etc.

Of the Caterers' Club we have already heard.[23] The Private Waiters' Association is an old beneficial order with well-to-do members. The private waiter is really a skilled workman of high order, and used to be well paid. Next to the guild of caterers he ranked as high as any class of Negro workmen before the war—indeed the caterer was but a private waiter further developed. Consequently this labor union is still jealous and exclusive and contains some members long retired from active work. The Coachmen's Association is a similar society; both these organizations have a considerable membership, and make sick and death benefits and social gatherings a feature. The Hotel Brotherhood is a new society of hotel waiters and is conducted by young men on the lines of the regular trades unions, with which it is more or less affiliated in many cities. It has some relief features and considerable social life. It strives to open and keep open work for colored waiters and often arranges to divide territory with whites, or to prevent one set from supplanting the other. The Cigar-makers' Union is a regular trades union with both white and Negro members. It is the only union in Philadelphia where Negroes are largely represented. No friction is apparent. The Hod-Carriers' Union is large and of considerable age but does not seem to be very active. A League of Colored Mechanics was formed in 1897 but did not accomplish anything. There was before the war a league of this sort which flourished, and there undoubtedly will be attempts of this sort in the future until a union is effected.[24]

The two co-operative grocery stores, and the caterers' supply store have been mentioned.[25] There was a dubious attempt in 1896 to organize a co-operative tin-ware store which has not yet been successful.[26]

With all this effort and movement it is natural that the Negroes should want some means of communication. This they have in the following periodicals conducted wholly by Negroes:

A. M. E. Church *Review*, quarterly, 8vo, about ninety-five pages.

Christian Recorder, eight-page weekly newspaper. (Both these are organs of the A. M. E. Church.)

Baptist *Christian Banner*, four-page weekly newspaper. (Organ of the Baptists.)

Odd Fellows' *Journal*, eight-page weekly newspaper. (Organ of Odd Fellows.)

Weekly *Tribune*, eight-page weekly newspaper, seventeen years established.

The *Astonisher*, eight-page weekly newspaper (Germantown).

The *Standard-Echo*, four-page weekly newspaper (since suspended).

The *Tribune* is the chief news sheet and is filled generally with social notes of all kinds, and news of movements among Negroes over the country. Its editorials are usually of little value chiefly because it does not employ a responsible editor. It is in many ways however an interesting paper and represents pluck and perseverance on the part of its publisher. The *Astonisher* and *Standard Echo* are news sheets. The first is bright but crude. The *Recorder, Banner* and *Journal* are chiefly filled with columns of heavy church and lodge news. The *Review* has had an interesting history and is probably the best Negro periodical of the sort published; it is often weighted down by the requirements of church politics, and compelled to publish some trash written by aspiring candidates for office; but with all this it has much solid matter and indicates the trend of thought among Negroes to some extent. It has greatly improved in the last few years. Many Negro newspapers from other cities circulate here and widen the feeling of community among the colored people of the city.

One other kind of organization has not yet been mentioned, the political clubs, of which there are probably fifty in the city. They will be considered in another chapter.

35. Institutions—The chief Negro institutions of the city are: The Home for Aged and Infirmed Colored Persons, the Douglass Hospital and Training School, the Woman's Exchange and Girls' Home, three cemetery companies, the Home for the Homeless, the special schools, as the Institute for Colored Youth, the House of Industry, Raspberry street schools and Jones's school for girls, the Y.M.C.A., and University Extension Centre.

The Home for the Aged, situated at the corner of Girard and Belmont avenues, was founded by a Negro lumber merchant, Steven Smith, and is conducted by whites and Negroes. It is one of the best institutions of the kind; its property is valued at $400,000, and it has an annual income of $20,000. It has sheltered 558 old people since its foundation in 1864.

The Douglass Memorial Hospital and Training School is a curious example of the difficult position of Negroes: for years nearly every hospital in Philadelphia has sought to exclude Negro women from the course in nurse-training, and no Negro physician could have the advantage of hospital practice. This led to a movement for a Negro hospital; such a movement however was condemned by the whites as an unnecessary addition to a bewildering number of charitable institutions; by many of the best Negroes as a concession to prejudice and a drawing of the color line. Nevertheless the promoters insisted that colored nurses were efficient and needed training, that colored physicians needed a hospital, and that colored patients wished one. Consequently the Douglass Hospital has been established and its success seems to warrant the effort.[27]

The total income for the year 1895–96 was $4,656.31; sixty-one patients were treated during the year, and thirty-two operations performed; 987 out-patients were treated. The first class of nurses was graduated in 1897.

The Woman's Exchange and Girls' Home is conducted by the principal of the Institute for Colored Youth at 756 South Twelfth street. The exchange is open at stated times during the week, and various articles are on sale. Cheap lodging and board is furnished for a few school girls and working girls. So far the work of the exchange has been limited but it is slowly growing, and is certainly a most deserving venture.[28]

The exclusion of Negroes from cemeteries has, as before mentioned, led to the organization of three cemetery companies, two of which are nearly fifty years old. The Olive holds eight acres of property in the Twenty-fourth Ward, claimed to be worth $100,000. It has 900 lot owners; the Lebanon holds land in the Thirty-sixth Ward, worth at least $75,000. The Merion is a new company which owns twenty-one acres in Montgomery County, worth perhaps $30,000. These companies are in the main well-conducted, although the affairs of one are just now somewhat entangled.

The Home for the Homeless is a refuge and home for the aged connected with the Church of the Crucifixion. It is supported largely by whites but not entirely. It has an income of about $500. During 1896, 1,108 lodgings were furnished to ninety women, 8,384 meals given to inmates, 2,705 to temporary lodgers, 2,078 to transients, and 812 to invalids.

The schools have all been mentioned before. The Young Men's Christian Association has had a checkered history, chiefly as it would seem from the wrong policy pursued; there is in the city a grave and dangerous lack of proper places of amusement and recreation for young men. To fill this need a properly conducted Young Men's Christian Association, with books and newspapers, baths, bowling alleys and billiard tables, conversation rooms and short, interesting religious services is demanded; it would cost far less than it now costs the courts to punish the petty misdemeanors of young men who do not know how to amuse themselves. Instead of such an institution however the Colored Y. M. C. A. has been virtually an attempt to add another church to the numberless colored churches of the city, with endless prayer-meetings and loud gospel hymns, in dingy and uninviting quarters. Consequently the institution is now temporarily suspended. It had accomplished some good work by its night schools, and social meetings.

Since the organization of the Bainbridge Street University Extension Centre, May 10, 1895, lectures have been delivered at the Church of the Crucifixion, Eighth and Bainbridge streets, by Rev. W. Hudson Shaw, on English History; by Thomas

Whitney Surette, on the Development of Music; by Henry W. Elson, on American History, and by Hilaire Belloc, on Napoleon. Each of these lecturers, except Mr. Belloc, has given a course of six lectures on the subject stated, and classes have been held in connection with each course. The attendance has been above the average as compared with other Centres in the city.

Beside these efforts there are various embryonic institutions: A day nursery in the Seventh Ward by the Woman's Missionary Society, a large organization which does much charitable work; an industrial school near the city, etc. There are, too, many institutions conducted by whites for the benefit of Negroes, which will be mentioned in another place.

Much of the need for separate Negro institutions has in the last decade disappeared, by reason of the opening of the doors of the public institutions to colored people. There are many Negroes who on this account strongly oppose efforts which they fear will tend to delay further progress in these lines. On the other hand, thoughtful men see that invaluable training and discipline is coming to the race through these institutions and organizations, and they encourage the formation of them.

36. The Experiment of Organization—Looking back over the field which we have thus reviewed—the churches, societies, unions, attempts at business cooperation, institutions and newspapers—it is apparent that the largest hope for the ultimate rise of the Negro lies in this mastery of the art of social organized life. To be sure, compared with his neighbors, he has as yet advanced but a short distance; we are apt to condemn this lack of unity, the absence of carefully planned and laboriously executed effort among these people, as a voluntary omission—a bit of carelessness. It is far more than this, it is lack of social education, of group training, and the lack can only be supplied by a long, slow process of growth. And the chief value of the organizations studied is that they are evidences of growth. Of actual accomplishment they have, to be sure, something to show, but nothing to boast of inordinately. The churches are far from ideal associations for fostering the higher life—rather they combine too often intrigue, extravagance and show, with all their work, saving and charity; their secret societies are often diverted from their better ends by scheming and dishonest officers, and by the temptation of tinsel and braggadocio; their beneficial associations, along with all their good work, have an unenviable record of business inefficiency and internal dissension. And yet all these and the other agencies have accomplished much, and their greatest accomplishment is stimulation of effort to further and more effective organization among a disorganized and headless host. All this world of co-operation and subordination into which the white child is in most cases born is, we must not forget, new to the slave's sons. They have been compelled to organize before they knew the meaning of organization; to co-operate with those of their fellows to whom co-operation was an unknown term; to fix and fasten ideas of leadership and authority among those who had always looked to others for guidance and command. For these reasons the present efforts of Negroes in working together along various lines are peculiarly promising for the future of both races.

NOTES

1. Cf. Chapter III.
2. St. Thomas', Bethel and Zoar. The history of Zoar is of interest. It "extends over a period of one hundred years, being as it is an offspring of St. George's Church, Fourth and Vine streets, the first Methodist Episcopal church to be established in this country, and in whose edifice the first American Conference of that denomination was held. Zoar Church had its origin in 1794, when members of St. George's Church established a mission in what was then known as Campingtown, now known as Fourth and Brown streets, at which place its first chapel was built. There it remained until 1883, when economic and sociological causes made necessary the selection of a new site. The city had grown, and industries of a character in which the Negroes were not interested had developed in the neighborhood, and, as the colored people were rapidly moving to a different section of the city, it was decided that the church should follow, and the old building was sold. Through the liberality of Colonel Joseph M. Bennett a brick building was erected on Melon street, above Twelfth.

   "Since then the congregation has steadily increased in numbers, until in August of this year it was found necessary to enlarge the edifice. The corner-stone of the new front was laid two months ago. The present membership of the church is about 550."—*Public Ledger*, November 15, 1897.
3. See Douglass' "Annals of St. Thomas'."
4. It was then turned into a private school and supported largely by an English educational fund.
5. St. Thomas' has suffered often among Negroes from the opprobrium of being "aristocratic," and is to-day by no means a popular church among the masses. Perhaps there is some justice in this charge, but the church has nevertheless always been foremost in good work and has many public spirited Negroes on its rolls.
6. Cf. U. S. Census, Statistics of Churches, 1890.
7. In 1809 the leading Negro churches formed a "Society for Suppressing Vice and Immorality," which received the endorsement of Chief Justice Tilghman, Benjamin Franklin, Jacob Rush, and others.
8. "Condition of Negroes, 1838," pp. 39–40.
9. Cf. Robert Jones' "Fifty years in Central Church." John Gloucester began preaching in 1807 at Seventh and Bainbridge.
10. In 1847 there were 19 churches; 12 of these had 3974 members; 11 of the edifices cost $67,000. "Statistical Inquiry," 1848, pp. 29, 30.

    In 1854 there were 19 churches reported and 1677 Sunday-school scholars. Bacon, 1856.
11. See Inquiry of 1867.
12. Cf. Publications of Atlanta University No. 3, "Efforts of American Negroes for Social Betterment."
13. An account of the present state of the A. M. E. Church from its own lips is interesting, in spite of its somewhat turgid rhetoric. The following is taken from the minutes of Philadelphia Conference, 1897:

REPORT ON STATE OF THE CHURCH

"To the Bishop and Conference: We your Committee on State of the Church beg leave to submit the following:

"Every truly devoted African Methodist is intensely interested in the condition of the church that was handed down to us as a precious heirloom from the hands of a God-fearing, self-sacrificing ancestry; the church that Allen planted in Philadelphia, a little over a century ago has enjoyed a marvelous development. Its grand march through the procession of a hundred years has been characterized by a series of brilliant successes, completely refuting the foul calumnies cast against it and overcoming every obstacle that endeavored to impede its onward march, giving the strongest evidence that God was in the midst of her; she should not be moved.

"From the humble beginnings in the little blacksmith shop, at Sixth and Lombard streets, Philadelphia, the Connection has grown until we have now fifty-five annual conferences, beside mission fields, with over four thousand churches, the same number of itinerant preachers, near six hundred thousand communicants, one and a half million adherents, with six regularly organized and well-manned departments, each doing a magnificent work along special lines, the whole under the immediate supervision of eleven bishops, each with a marked individuality and all laboring together for the further development and perpetuity of the church. In this the Mother Conference of the Connection, we have every reason to be grateful to Almighty God for the signal blessings. He has so graciously poured out upon us. The spiritual benedictions have been many. In response to earnest effort and faithful prayers by both pastors and congregations, nearly two thousand persons have professed faith in Christ, during this conference year. Five thousand dollars have been given by the membership and friends of the Connectional interests to carry on the machinery of the church, besides liberal contributions for the cause of missions, education, the Sunday-school Union and Church Extension Departments, and beside all this, the presiding elder and pastors have been made to feel that the people are perfectly willing to do what they can to maintain the preaching of the word, that tends to elevate mankind and glorify God.

"The local interests have not been neglected; new churches have been built, parsonages erected, church mortgages have been reduced, auxiliary societies to give everybody in the church a chance to work for God and humanity, have been more extensively organized than ever before.

"The danger signal that we see here and there cropping out, which is calculated to bring discredit upon the Church of Christ, is the unholy ambition for place and power. The means ofttimes used to bring about the desired results, cause the blush of shame to tinge the brow of Christian manhood. God always has and always will select those He designs to use as the leaders of his Church.

"Political methods that are in too many instances resorted to, are contrary to the teaching and spirit of the Gospel of Christ. Fitness and sobriety will always be found in the lead.

"Through mistaken sympathy we find that several incompetent men have found their way into the ministerial ranks; men who can neither manage the financial nor spiritual interests of any church or bring success along any line, who are continuously on the wing from one conference to the other. The time has come when the strictest scrutiny must be exercised as to purpose and fitness of candidates, and if admitted and found to be continuous failures, Christian charity demands that they be given an opportunity to seek a calling where they can make more success than in the ministry. These danger signals that flash up now and then must be observed and everything contrary to the teachings of God's word and the spirit of the discipline weeded out. The church owes a debt of gratitude to the fathers who have always remained loyal and true; who labored persistently and well for the upbuilding of the connection, that they can never repay.

"Particular care should be taken that no honorable aged minister of our great Church should be allowed to suffer for the necessaries of life. We especially commend to the consideration of every minister the Ministers' Aid Association, which is now almost ready to be organized, the object of which is to help assuage the grief and dry the tears of those who have been left widowed and fatherless.

"Our Publication Department is making heroic efforts for the larger circulation of our denominational papers and literature generally. These efforts ought to be, and must needs be heartily seconded by the Church. Lord Bacon says: 'Talking makes a ready man, writing an exact man, but reading makes a full man.' We want our people at large to be brimful of information relative to the growth of the church, the progress of the race, the upbuilding of humanity and the glory of God.

"Our missionary work must not be allowed to retrograde. The banner that Allen raised must not be allowed to trail, but must go forward until the swarthy sons of Ham everywhere shall gaze with a longing and loving look upon the escutcheon that has emblazoned on it, as its motto: 'The Fatherhood of God and the Brotherhood of man,' and the glorious truth flashing over the whole world that Jesus Christ died to redeem the universal family of mankind. Disasters and misfortunes may come to us, but strong men never quail before adversities. The clouds of to-day may be succeeded by the sunshine of to-morrow."

14. Cf., *e.g.*, the account of the founding of new missions in the minutes of the Philadelphia Conference, 1896.

15. Baptists themselves recognize this. One of the speakers in a recent association meeting, as reported by the press, "deprecated the spirit shown by some churches in spreading their differences to their detriment as church members, and in the eyes of their white brethren; and he

recommended that unworthy brethren from other States, who sought an asylum of rest here, be not admitted to local pulpits except in cases where the ministers so applying are personally known or vouched for by a resident pastor. The custom of recognizing as preachers men incapable of doing good work in the pulpit, who were ordained in the South after they had failed in the North, was also condemned, and the President declared that the times demand a ministry that is able to preach. The practice of licensing incapable brethren for the ministry, simply to please them, was also looked upon with disfavor, and it was recommended that applicants for ordination be required to show at least ability to read intelligently the Word of God or a hymn."

16. One movement deserves notice—the Woman's Auxiliary Society. It consists of five circles, representing a like number of colored Baptist churches in this city, viz., the Cherry Street, Holy Trinity, Union, Nicetown and Germantown, and does general missionary work.

17. See, Jones' "Fifty Years in Central Street Church," etc. The system and order in this church is remarkable. Each year a careful printed report of receipts and expenditures is made. The following is an abstract of the report for 1891:

Receipts

Finance Committee	$977.39	
Pew Rents	709.75	
Legacy	760.77	
Other Receipts	329.54	
	———	$2,777.45

Expenditures

Pastor's Salary	$1,000.00	
Other Salaries	476.00	
Repayment of Loan	409.00	
Interest on Mortgage	60.96	
Donations to General Church	31.57	
General Expenses, etc.	759.23	
	———	$2,736.76
Balance		$40.69

18. For history and detailed account of this work see Anderson's "Presbyterianism and the Negro."

19. Rev. Charles Daniel, in the *Nazarene*. The writer hardly does justice to the weird witchery of those hymns sung thus rudely.

20. Cf. report of inquiries in above years.

21. From Report of Fourth Annual Meeting of the District Grand Lodge of Pennsylvania, G. U. of O. F., 1896.

22. This association has issued a valuable little pamphlet called "Helpful Hints on Home," which it distributes. This explains the object and methods of building and loan associations.

23. See *supra*, p. 119 ff.

24. The College Settlement was interested in this organization, but the movement was evidently premature.

25. See *supra*, p. 117 and p. 119.

26. An interesting advertisement of this venture is appended; it is a curious mixture of business, exhortation and simplicity. The present state of the enterprise is not known:

"NOTICE TO ALL.

"WE CALL YOUR ATTENTION

"TO THIS WORK.

"THE UNION TIN-WARE MANUFACTURING CO.

"Is now at work, chartered under the laws of the States of New Jersey and Pennsylvania.

"The purpose of said Company is to manufacture everything in the TIN-WARE LINE that the law allows, and to sell stock all over the United States of America; and put in members enough in every city to open a Union Tin-Ware Store, and if the promoter finds that he has not enough members in a city to open a Tin-Ware Store, then he shall open it with money from the factory. SHARES are $10.00, they can be paid on installment plan; and you do not have any monthly dues to pay, but on the 20th of every December or whenever the Stockholders appoint the time, the dividend will be declared.

"We will make this one of the grandest organizations ever witnessed by the Race, if you lend us your aid. This Store will contain Groceries, Dry Goods and Tin-Ware, and you can do your dealing at your own store. This factory will give you work, and learn you a trade."

27. Since the opening of the hospital colored nurses have had less trouble in white institutions, and one colored physician has been appointed intern in a large hospital. Dr. N. F. Mossell was chiefly instrumental in founding the Douglass Hospital.

28. In connection with this work, Bethel Church often holds small receptions for servant girls on their days off, when refreshments are served and a pleasant time is spent. The following is a note of a similar enterprise at another church: "The members of the Berean Union have opened a 'Y' parlor, where young colored girls employed as domestics can spend their Thursday afternoon both pleasantly and profitably. The parlor is open from 4 until 10 p. m., every Thursday, and members of the Union are present to welcome them. A light supper is served for ten cents. The evening is spent in literary exercises and social talk. The parlor is in the Berean Church, South College avenue, near Twentieth street."

CHAPTER XIII

◆

The Negro Criminal

37. History of Negro Crime in the City[1]—From his earliest advent the Negro, as was natural, has figured largely in the criminal annals of Philadelphia. Only such superficial study of the American Negro as dates his beginning with 1863 can neglect this past record of crime in studying the present. Crime is a phenomenon of organized social life, and is the open rebellion of an individual against his social environment. Naturally then, if men are suddenly transported from one environment to another, the result is lack of harmony with the new conditions; lack of harmony with the new physical surroundings leading to disease and death or modification of physique; lack of harmony with social surroundings leading to crime. Thus very early in the history of the colony characteristic complaints of the disorder of the Negro slaves is heard. In 1693, July 11, the Governor and Council approved an ordinance, "Upon the Request of some of the members of Council, that an order be made by the Court of Quarter Sessions for the Countie of philadelphia, the 4th July instant (proceeding upon a presentment of the Grand Jurie for the bodie of the sd countie), agt the tumultuous gatherings of the Negroes of the towne of philadelphia, on the first dayes of the weeke, ordering the Constables of philadelphia, or anie other person whatsoever, to have power to take up Negroes, male or female, whom they should find gadding abroad on the said first dayes of the weeke, without a ticket from their Mr. or Mris., or not in their Compa, or to carry them to gaole, there to remain that night, and that without meat or drink, and to Cause them to be publically whipt next morning with 39 Lashes, well Laid on, on their bare backs, for which their sd. Mr. or Mris. should pay 15d. to the whipper," etc.[2]

Penn himself introduced a law for the special trial and punishment of Negroes very early in the history of the colony, as has been noted before.[3] The slave code finally adopted was mild compared with the legislation of the period, but it was severe enough to show the unruly character of many of the imported slaves.[4]

Especially in Philadelphia did the Negroes continue to give general trouble, not so much by serious crime as by disorder. In 1732, under Mayor Hasel, the City Council "taking under Consideration the frequent and tumultuous meetings of the Negro Slaves, especially on Sunday, Gaming, Cursing, Swearing, and committing many other Disorders, to the great Terror and Disquiet of the Inhabitants of this city," ordered an ordinance to be drawn up against such disturbances.[5] Again, six years later, we hear of the draft of another city ordinance for "the more Effectual suppressing Tumultuous meetings and other disorderly doings of the Negroes, Mulattos and Indian servts. and slaves." [6] And in 1741, August 17, "frequent complaints having been made to the Board that many disorderly persons meet every ev'g about the Court house of this city, and great numbers of Negroes and others sit there with milk pails and other things late at night, and many disorders are there committed against the peace and good government of this city," Council ordered the place to be cleared "in half an hour after sunset." [7]

Of the graver crimes by Negroes we have only reports here and there which do not make it clear how frequently such crimes occurred. In 1706 a slave is arrested for setting fire to a dwelling; in 1738 three Negroes are hanged in neighboring parts of New Jersey for poisoning people, while at Rocky Hill a slave is burned alive for killing a child and burning a barn. Whipping of Negroes at the public whipping post was frequent, and so severe was the punishment that in 1743 a slave brought up to be whipped committed suicide. In 1762 two Philadelphia slaves were sentenced to death for felony and burglary; petitions were circulated in their behalf but Council was obdurate.[8]

Little special mention of Negro crime is again met with until the freedmen under the act of 1780 began to congregate in the city and other free immigrants joined them. In 1809 the leading colored churches united in a society to suppress crime and were cordially endorsed by the public for this action. After the war immigration to the city increased and the stress of hard times bore heavily on the lower classes. Complaints of petty thefts and murderous assaults on peaceable citizens now began to increase, and in numbers of cases they were traced to Negroes. The better class of colored citizens felt the accusation and held a meeting to denounce crime and take a firm stand against their own criminal class. A little later the Negro riots commenced, and they received their chief moral support from the increasing crime of Negroes; a Cuban slave brained his master with a hatchet, two other murders by Negroes followed, and gambling, drunkenness and debauchery were widespread wherever Negroes settled. The terribly vindictive insurrection of Nat Turner in a neighboring State frightened the citizens so thoroughly that when some black fugitives actually arrived at Chester from Southampton County, Virginia, the Legislature was hastily appealed to, and the whole matter came to a climax in the disfranchisement of the Negro in 1837, and the riots in the years 1830 to 1840.[9]

Some actual figures will give us an idea of this, the worst period of Negro crime ever experienced in the city. The Eastern Penitentiary was opened in 1829 near the close of the year. The total number of persons received here for the most serious crimes is given in the next table. This includes prisoners from the Eastern counties of the State, but a large proportion were from Philadelphia:[10]

YEARS	TOTAL COMMITMENTS	NEGROES	PER CENT OF NEGROES	PER CENT OF NEGROES OF TOTAL POPULATION
1829–34	339	99	29.0	8.27 (1830)
1835–39	878	356	40.5	7.39 (1840)

(Continued)

Years	Total Commitments	Negroes	Per Cent of Negroes	Per Cent of Negroes of Total Population
1840–44	701	209	29.8	7.39 (1840)
1845–49	633	151	23.8	4.83 (1850)
1850–54	664	106	16.0	4.83 (1850)

Or to put it differently the problem of Negro crime in Philadelphia from 1830 to 1850 arose from the fact that less than one-fourteenth of the population was responsible for nearly a third of the serious crimes committed.

These figures however are apt to relate more especially to a criminal class. A better measure of the normal criminal tendencies of the group would perhaps be found in the statistics of Moyamensing, where ordinary cases of crime and misdemeanor are confined and which contains only county prisoners. The figures for Moyamensing prison are:

Years	Total White Prisoners Received	Total Negro Prisoners Received	Per Cent of Negroes of Total Prisoners	Per Cent of Negroes of Total Population
1836–45	1,164	1,087	48.29	7.39 (1840)
1846–55	1,478	696	32.01	4.83 (1850)
Total	2,642	1,783	. . .	. . . . . .

Here we have even a worse showing than before; in 1896 the Negroes forming 4 per cent of the population furnish 9 per cent of the arrests, but in 1850 being 5 per cent of the population they furnished 32 per cent of the prisoners received at the county prison. Of course there are some considerations which must not be overlooked in interpreting these figures for 1836–55. It must be remembered that the discrimination against the Negro was much greater then than now: he was arrested for less cause and given longer sentences than whites.[11] Great numbers of those arrested and committed for trial were never brought to trial so that their guilt could not be proven or disproven; of 737 Negroes committed for trial in six months of the year 1837, it is stated that only 123 were actually brought to trial; of the prisoners in the Eastern Penitentiary, 1829 to 1846, 14 per cent of the whites were pardoned and 2 per cent of the Negroes. All these considerations increase the statistics to the disfavor of the Negro.[12] Nevertheless making all reasonable allowances it is undoubtedly true that the crime of Negroes in this period reached its high tide for this city.

The character of the crimes committed by Negroes compared with whites is shown by the following table, which covers the offences of 1359 whites and 718 Negroes committed to the Eastern Penitentiary, 1829–1846. If we take simply petty larceny we find that 48.8 per cent of the whites and 55 per cent of the Negroes were committed for this offence.[13]

KINDS OF CRIME	WHITES		NEGROES	
	NUMBER	PER CENT	NUMBER	PER CENT
Offences *vs.* the person	166	11.4	89	12.4
Offences *vs.* property with violence	191	13.1	165	22.9
Offences *vs.* property without violence ...	873	59.8	432	60.2
Malicious offences *vs.* property	22	1.5	14	2.0
Offences *vs.* Currency and forgery	167	11.5	7	1.0
Miscellaneous	40	27.0	11	1.5
All offences	1,359	100	718	100

38. Negro Crime Since the War—Throughout the land there has been since the war a large increase in crime, especially in cities. This phenomenon would seem to have sufficient cause in the increased complexity of life, in industrial competition, and the rush of great numbers to the large cities. It would therefore be natural to suppose that the Negro would also show this increase in criminality and, as in the case of all lower classes, that he would show it in greater degree. His evolution has, however, been marked by some peculiarities. For nearly two decades after emancipation he took little part in many of the great social movements about him for obvious reasons. His migration to city life, therefore, and his sharing in the competition of modern industrial life, came later than was the case with the mass of his fellow citizens. The Negro began to rush to the cities in large numbers after 1880, and consequently the phenomena attendant on that momentous change of life are tardier in his case. His rate of criminality has in the last two decades risen rapidly, and this is a parallel phenomenon to the rapid rise of the white criminal record two or three decades ago. Moreover, in the case of the Negro there were special causes for the prevalence of crime: he had lately been freed from serfdom, he was the object of stinging oppression and ridicule, and paths of advancement open to many were closed to him. Consequently the class of the shiftless, aimless, idle, discouraged and disappointed was proportionately larger.

In the city of Philadelphia the increasing number of bold and daring crimes committed by Negroes in the last ten years has focused the attention of the city on this subject. There is a widespread feeling that something is wrong with a race that is responsible for so much crime, and that strong remedies are called for. One has but to visit the corridors of the public buildings, when the courts are in session, to realize the part played in law-breaking by the Negro population. The various slum centres of the colored criminal population have lately been the objects of much philanthropic effort, and the work there has aroused discussion. Judges on the bench have discussed the matter. Indeed, to the minds of many, this is the real Negro problem.[14]

That it is a vast problem a glance at statistics will show;[15] and since 1880 it has been steadily growing. At the same time crime is a difficult subject to study, more difficult to analyze into its sociological elements, and most difficult to cure or suppress. It is a phenomenon that stands not alone, but rather as a symptom of countless wrong social conditions.

The simplest, but crudest, measure of crime is found in the total arrests for a period of years. The value of such figures is lessened by the varying efficiency and diligence of the police, by discrimination in the administration of law, and by unwarranted arrests. And yet the figures roughly measure crime. The total arrests and the number of Negroes is given in the next table for thirty-two years, with a few omissions:

ARRESTS IN PHILADELPHIA, 1864–96

Date	Total Number Arrested	Total Negroes Arrested	Percentage of Negroes
1864	34,221	3,144	9.1
1865	43,226	2,722	6.3
1869	38,749	2,907	7.5
1870	31,717	2,070	6.5
1873	30,400	1,380	4.5
1874	32,114	1,257	3.9
1875	34,553	1,539	4.5
1876	. . .	. . .	. . .
1877	44,220	2,524	5.7
1879	40,714	2,360	5.8
1880	44,097	2,204	4.98
1881	45,129	2,327	5.11
1882	46,130	2,183	4.73
1883	45,295	2,022	4.46
1884	49,468	2,134	4.31
1885	51,418	2,662	5.11
1886	. . .	. . .	. . .
1887	57,951	3,256	5.61
1888	46,899	2,910	6.20
1889	42,673	2,614	6.10
1890	49,148	3,167	6.44
1891	53,184	3,544	6.66
1892	52,944	3,431	6.48
1893	57,297	4,078	7.11
1894	61,478	4,805	7.81
1895	60,347	5,137	8.5
1896	58,072	5,302	9.1

We find that the total arrests in the city per annum have risen from 34,221 in 1864 to 61,478 in 1894, an increase of 80 per cent in crime, parallel to an increase of 85 per cent in population. The Negroes arrested have increased from 3,114 in 1864 to 4,805 in 1894, an increase of 54 per cent in crime, parallel to an increase of 77 per cent in the Negro population of the city. So, too, the percentage of Negroes in the total arrests is less in 1894 than in 1864. If, however, we follow the years between these two dates we see an important development: 1864 was the date bounding the ante-bellum period of crime; thereafter the proportion of Negro arrests fell steadily until, in 1874, the Negroes came as nearly as ever furnishing their normal quota of arrests, 3.9 per cent from 3.28 per cent (1870) of the population. Then slowly there came a change. With the Centennial Exposition in 1876 came a stream of immigrants, and once started the stream increased in speed by its own momentum. With this immigration the proportion of Negro arrests arose rapidly at first as a result of the exposition; falling off a little in the early eighties, but with 1885 rising again steadily and quickly to over 6 per cent in 1888, 6.4 per cent in 1890, 7 per cent in 1893, 8.5 per cent in 1895, 9 per cent in 1896. This is, as has been said before, but a rough indication of the amount of crime for which the Negro is responsible; it must not be relied on too closely, for the number of arrests cannot in any city accurately measure wrongdoing save in a very general way; probably increased efficiency in the police force since 1864 has had large effect; and yet we can draw the legitimate conclusion here that Negro crime in the city is far less, according to population, than before the war; that after the war it decreased until the middle of the seventies and then, coincident with the beginning of the new Negro immigration to cities,[16] it has risen pretty steadily.

These same phenomena can be partially verified by statistics of Moyamensing prison. If we take the tried and untried prisoners committed to this county prison from 1876 to 1895 we find the same gradual increase of crime:

MOYAMENSING PRISON

Both Tried and Untried Prisoners

DATE	TOTAL RECEPTIONS	NEGROES	PER CENT OF NEGROES
1876	21,736	1,530	7.8
1877	22,666	1,460	6.44
1878	22,147	1,356	6.12
1879	20,736	1,136	5.48
1880	22,487	1,030	4.58
1881	22,478	1,168	5.19
1882	24,176	1,274	5.27
1883	23,245	1,175	5.05
1884	25,081	1,218	4.86
1885	24,725	1,427	5.77
1886	27,286	1,708	6.26
1887	28,964	1,724	5.97
1888	21,399	1,399	6.54
1889	18,476	1,338	7.24
1890	20,582	1,611	7.83
1891	22,745	1,723	7.57
1892	22,460	1,900	8.46
1893	25,209	2,234	8.86
1894	25,777	2,452	9.51
1895	22,584	2,317	10.26
Total	464,959	31,180	6.70
1876–1885	229,477	12,774	5.57
1886–1895	235,482	18,406	7.81

If we compare in this table the period 1876–85 with that of 1886–95 we find that the proportion of Negro criminals in the first period was 5.6 per cent, in the second 7.8 per cent.

The statistics of inmates of the House of Correction, where mild cases and juveniles are sent, for the last few years go to tell the same tale:

Year	Total Receptions	Negroes	Percentage of Negroes
1891	5,907	274	4.6
1892	5,297	254	4.8
1893	. . .	. . .	. . .
1894	6,579	1,055	16.0
1895	7,548	672	8.9

Gathering up the statistics presented let us make a rough diagram of some of the results. First let us scan the record of the Negro in serious crime, such as entails incarceration in the Eastern Penitentiary. In these figures the Philadelphia convicts are not separated from those in the eastern counties of the state prior to 1885. A large proportion of the prisoners however are from Philadelphia; perhaps the net result of the error is somewhat to reduce the apparent proportion of Negroes in the earlier years. Taking then the proportion of Negro prisoners received to total receptions since the founding of the Penitentiary we have this diagram:

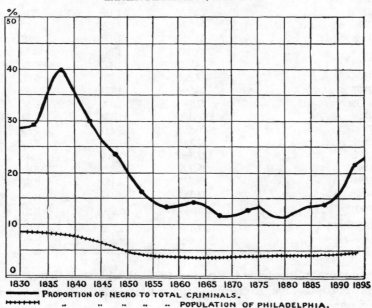

PROPORTION OF NEGROES TO TOTAL CONVICTS RECEIVED AT THE
EASTERN PENITENTIARY, 1829–1895.

The general rate of criminality may be graphically represented from the proportion of Negroes in the county prison, although changes in the policy of the courts make the validity of this somewhat uncertain:

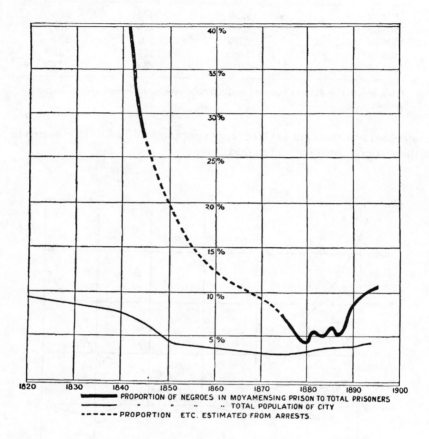

PROPORTION OF NEGROES IN MOYAMENSING PRISON TO TOTAL PRISONERS
"   "   "   "   " TOTAL POPULATION OF CITY
PROPORTION ETC. ESTIMATED FROM ARRESTS.

It thus seems certain[17] that general criminality as represented by commitments to the county prison has decreased markedly since 1840, and that its rapid increase since 1880 leaves it still far behind the decade 1830 to 1840. Serious crime as represented by commitments to the penitentiary shows a similar decrease but one not so marked indicating the presence of a pretty distinct criminal class.

CONVICTS COMMITTED TO THE EASTERN PENITENTIARY

Years	Total Commitments	Negroes	Percentage of Negroes
1835–39	878	356	40.5
1855–59	941	126	13.4
1860–64	909	129	14.2
1865–69	1,474	179	12.1

(*Continued*)

CONVICTS COMMITTED TO THE EASTERN PENITENTIARY—*Continued*

Years	Total Commitments	Negroes	Percentage of Negroes
1870–74	1,291	174	13.4
1875–79	2,347	275	11.7
1880–84	2,282	308	13.5
1885–89*	1,583	223	14.09
1890–95*	1,418	318	22.43

*Only convicts from Philadelphia; the statistics for the year 1891 are not available and are omitted.

The record of arrests per 1,000 of Negro population 1864 to 1896 seems to confirm these conclusions for that period:

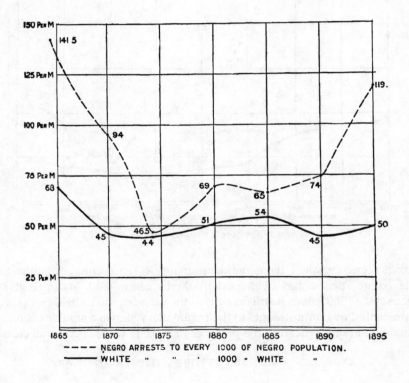

The increase in crime between 1890 and 1895 is not without pretty adequate explanation in the large Negro immigration cityward and especially in "the terrible business depression of 1893" to which the police bureau attributes the increase of arrests. The effect of this would naturally be greater among the economic substrata.

This brings us to the question, Who are the Negro criminals and what crimes do they commit? To obtain an answer to this query let us make a special study of a typical group of criminals.

39. A Special Study in Crime[18]—During ten years previous to and including 1895, there were committed to the Eastern Penitentiary, the following prisoners from the city of Philadelphia:

PHILADELPHIA WHITES AND NEGROES COMMITTED TO THE
EASTERN PENITENTIARY

DATE	TOTAL CONVICTIONS	NEGROES	PER CENT OF NEGROES	
1885	313	40	12.78	
1886	347	45	12.97	
1887	363	53	14.60	14.9
1888	269	39	14.49	
1889	291	46	15.81	
1890	271	63	23.25	
1891*	. .	. .	. .	
1892	213	42	19.71	
1893	320	74	23.13	22.43
1894	329	69	20.97	
1895	285	70	24.56	
Total	3,001	541	18.2 average	

*Statistics for this year were not available. Throughout this section, therefore, this year is omitted.

Let us now take the 541 Negroes who have been the perpetrators of the serious crimes charged to their race during the last ten years and see what we may learn. These are all criminals convicted after trial for periods varying from six months to forty years. It seems plain in the first place that the 4 per cent of the population of Philadelphia having Negro blood furnished from 1885 to 1889, 14 per cent of the serious crimes, and from 1890 to 1895, 22½ per cent. This of course assumes that the convicts in the penitentiary represent with a fair degree of accuracy the crime committed. The assumption is not wholly true; in convictions by human courts the rich always are favored somewhat at the expense of the poor, the upper classes at the expense of the unfortunate classes, and whites at the expense of Negroes. We know for instance that certain crimes are not punished in Philadelphia because the public opinion is lenient, as for instance embezzlement, forgery, and certain sorts of stealing; on the other hand a commercial community is apt to punish with severity petty thieving, breaches of the peace, and personal assault or burglary. It happens, too, that the prevailing weakness of ex-slaves brought up in the communal life of the slave plantation, without acquaintanceship with the institution of private property, is to commit the very crimes which a great centre of commerce like Philadelphia especially abhors. We must add to this the influences of social position and connections in procuring whites pardons or lighter sentences. It has been charged by some Negroes that color prejudice plays some part, but there is no tangible proof of this, save perhaps that there is apt to be a certain presumption of guilt when a Negro is accused, on the part of police, public and judge.[19] All these considerations modify somewhat our judgment of the moral status of the mass of Negroes. And yet, with all allowances, there remains a vast problem of crime.

The chief crimes for which these prisoners were convicted were:

Theft	243
Serious assaults on persons	139
Robbery and burglary	85
Rape	24
Other sexual crimes	23
Homicide	16
All other crimes	11
Total	541

Following these crimes from year to year we have:

CRIME	1885	1886	1887	1888	1889	1890	1892	1893	1894	1895	TOTAL
Theft, etc.	20	21	23	13	24	39	20	32	23	28	243
Robbery and burglary	2	8	8	5	5	9	7	14	19	8	85
Serious assaults ...	10	9	11	15	9	12	9	19	18	27	139
Homicide	..	..	3	2	5	..	2	1	1	2	16
Sexual crimes	6	7	7	4	4	4	4	5	3	3	47
All others	2	..	1	1	..	..	..	2	3	2	11
Total	40	45	53	40	47	64	42	73	67	70	541

The course of the total serious crime for this period may be illustrated by this diagram:

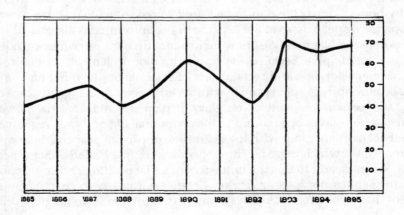

Drawing a similar diagram for the different sorts of crime we have:

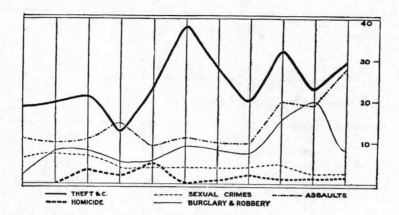

In ten years convictions to the penitentiary for theft have somewhat increased, robbery, burglary and assault have considerably increased, homicide has remained about the same, and sexual crimes have decreased. Detailed statistics are given in the following table:

CRIMES OF 541 CONVICTS IN EASTERN PENITENTIARY, 1885–1895

Crimes	1885	1886	1887	1888	1889	1890	1892	1893	1894	1895
Assault and battery	3	.	1	2	.	1	.	.	.	.
Aggravated assault and battery	3	3	3	7	3	6	3	6	6	9
Assault to kill	4	6	7	6	6	5	4	13	11	17
Manslaughter	.	.	.	1	3	.	1	1	.	1
Murder	.	.	3	1	2	.	1	.	1	1
Assault to murder	.	.	1	.	.	.	.	.	.	.
Assault to steal	.	.	.	.	.	.	2	.	1	1
Larceny	20	21	23	13	24	39	17	27	22	28
Robbery	2	3	3	1	.	4	3	5	9	6
Burglary	.	5	5	4	5	5	4	9	10	2
Embezzlement	.	.	.	.	.	.	.	1	.	.
Sodomy	2	1	1	3	2	3	2	.	.	1
Abortion	1	.	.	.	.	.	1	.	.	.
Rape	1	.	.	.	1	.	.	2	1	.
Attempt to rape	1	6	1	1	1	1	1	3	2	1
Incest	1	.	.	.	.	.	.	.	.	.
Keeping bawdy house	.	.	4	.	.	.	.	.	.	1
Enticing female child	.	.	1	.	1	.	.	.	.	.
Carrying concealed weapons	1	.	.	.	.	.	.	1	.	.
Forgery	1	.	.	.	.	.	.	.	1	1
False pretense	.	.	.	1	.	.	1	.	1	.
Receiving stolen goods	.	.	.	.	.	.	2	4	1	.

(Continued)

CRIMES OF 541 CONVICTS IN EASTERN PENITENTIARY, 1885–1895—*Continued*

CRIMES	1885	1886	1887	1888	1889	1890	1892	1893	1894	1895
Mayhem	.	.	.	.	.	.	.	1	.	.
Indecent exposure	.	.	.	.	.	.	.	.	.	1
Conspiracy	.	.	.	.	.	.	.	.	1	.
Total	40	45	53	40	47	64	42	73	67	70

The total crime can be classified also in this way:

Crimes against property	328	60.63	per cent
" persons	157	29.02	"
" persons and property	8	1.48	"
Sexual crimes	48	8.87	"
	541	100	per cent

Let us now turn from the crime to the criminals. 497 of them (91.87 per cent) were males and 44 (8.13 per cent) were females. 296 (54.71 per cent) were single, 208 (34.45 per cent) were married, and 37 (6.84 per cent) were widowed. In age they were divided as follows:

AGE	NUMBER	PER CENT	
15–19	58	10.73	
20–24	170	56.19	66.92
25–29	132		
30–39	132	24.03	
40–49	34	6.29	34.08
50–59	10	1.85	
60 and over	5	.91	
Total	541	100	

The mass of criminals are, it is easy to see, young single men under thirty. Detailed statistics of sex and age and conjugal condition are given in the next tables.

AGE AND SEX OF CONVICTS IN EASTERN PENITENTIARY
NEGROES, 1885–1895

AGES	MALES	FEMALES	TOTAL
15–19	53	5	58
20–24	153	17	170
25–29	119	13	132
30–34	80	5	85
35–39	45	2	47
40–44	21	1	22
45–49	11	1	12
50–59	3	.	3
60 and over	15	.	15
Total	497	44	541

CONJUGAL CONDITION OF CONVICTS IN EASTERN PENITENTIARY

	MALES			FEMALES		
AGE	SINGLE	MARRIED	WIDOWED	SINGLE	MARRIED	WIDOWED
15–19	48	5	0	4	1	0
20–24	117	35	0	7	9	1
25–29	59	54	8	3	10	0
30–34	30	38	6	0	4	1
35–39	11	30	4	0	0	2
40–49	8	16	8	0	2	0
50–59	3	3	4	0	0	0
60 and over	0	2	3	0	0	0

The convicts were born in the following States:

Philadelphia	114
Other parts of Pennsylvania	48
New Jersey	21
Maryland	99
Virginia	77
Delaware	37
District of Columbia	35
North Carolina	19
New York	11
South Carolina	9
Georgia	8
Other parts of the North	13
" " " " South	22
The West	13
Foreign Countries	15
	541

Altogether 21 per cent were natives of Philadelphia; 217 were born in the North, and 309, or 57 per cent, were born in the South. Two-thirds of the Negroes of the city, judging from the Seventh Ward, were born outside the city, and this part furnishes 79 per cent of the serious crime. 54 per cent were born in the South, and this part furnishes 57 per cent of the crime, or more, since many giving their birthplace as in the North were really born in the South.

The total illiteracy of this group reaches 26 per cent or adding in those who can read and write imperfectly, 34 per cent compared with 18 per cent for the Negroes of the city in 1890. In other words the illiterate fifth of the Negro population furnished a third of the worst criminals.

Naturally as the general intelligence of a community increases the general intelligence of its criminals increases, though seldom in the same proportion, showing that some crime may justly be attributed to pure ignorance. The number of criminals able to read and write has increased from 50 per cent in 1885 to 79 per cent in 1895. The number of colored men from fifteen to thirty who can read and write was about 90 per cent in the Seventh Ward in 1896. This shows how little increased

ILLITERACY OF CONVICTS IN THE EASTERN STATE PENITENTIARY

YEAR	READ AND WRITE		READ AND WRITE IMPERFECTLY		TOTALLY ILLITERATE	
	NUMBER	PER CENT	NUMBER	PER CENT	NUMBER	PER CENT
1885	20	50.0	6	15.0	14	35.0
1886	25	55.55	4	8.88	16	35.55
1887	27	50.94	13	24.53	13	24.53
1888	25	64.10	6	15.38	8	20.51
1889	26	56.52	10	21.74	10	21.74
1890	43	68.25	3	4.76	17	26.98
1892	33	78.57	0	0	9	21.43
1893	55	74.32	0	0	19	25.68
1894	49	71.01	0	0	20	28.99
1895	55	78.57	0	0	15	21.43
Total	358	66.17	42	7.76	141	26.06

intelligence alone avails to stop crime in the face of other powerful forces. It would of course be illogical to connect these phenomena directly as cause and effect and make Negro crime the result of Negro education—in that case we should find it difficult to defend the public schools in most modern lands. Crime comes either in spite of intelligence or as a result of misdirected intelligence under severe economic and moral strain. Thus we find here, as is apparently true in France, Italy and Germany, increasing crime and decreasing illiteracy as concurrent phenomena rather than as cause and effect. However the rapid increase of intelligence in Negro convicts does point to some grave social changes: first, a large number of young Negroes are in such environment that they find it easier to be rogues than honest men; secondly, there is evidence of the rise of more intelligent and therefore more dangerous crime from a trained criminal class, quite different from the thoughtless, ignorant crime of the mass of Negroes.

A separation of criminals according to sex and age and the kind of crime is of interest. (See p. 182 for males.)

CRIMINALS IN EASTERN STATE PENITENTIARY—FEMALES, BY AGE AND CRIME

AGES	CRIMES							
	LARCENY	ASSAULT AND BATTERY	AGGRAVATED ASSAULT	ASSAULT TO KILL	MURDER	BAWDY AND DISORDERLY HOUSES	ACCESSORY TO MURDER	ABDUCTION
15–19	5	..	..	..	..	..	..	..
20–24	10	1	3	2	1	..	..	..
25–29	11	..	1	..	..	1	..	..
30–34	3	..	..	..	..	..	1	1
35–39	1	..	..	..	..	1	..	..
40–44	1	..	..	..	..	..	..	..
45–49	1	..	..	..	..	..	..	..

The women are nearly all committed for stealing and fighting. They are generally prostitutes from the worst slums. The boys of fifteen to nineteen are sentenced largely for petty thieving:

Whole number of male convicts, 15–19 years of age		53
Convicted for larceny	27	
" " assault and fighting	8	
" " sexual crimes	5	
" " burglary	5	
" " other crimes	8	
		53

Making a similar table for two other age periods we have:

Men, 20–24 Years		Men, 25–29 Years	
Larceny	62	Larceny	45
Assault	41	Assault	33
Burglary and robbery	30	Burglary and robbery	22
Sexual crimes	6	Sexual crimes	13
Other crimes	14	Homicide	4
		Other crimes	3
	153		119

There is here revealed no especial peculiarity: stealing and fighting are ever the besetting sins of half-developed races.

It would be very instructive to know how many of the 541 criminals had been in the hands of the law before. This is however very difficult to ascertain correctly since in many, if not the majority of cases, the word of the prisoner must be taken. Even these methods however reveal the startling fact that only 315 or 58 per cent of these 541 convicts are reported as being incarcerated for the first time. 226 or 42 per cent can be classed as habitual criminals, who have been convicted as follows:

Twice	105	46.5	per cent
Three times	60	26.5	"
Four "	24	11.0	"
Five "	19	8.0	"
Six "	9	4.0	"
Seven "	4	1.8	"
Nine "	1		
Ten "	1	2.2	"
Eleven "	2		
Twelve "	1		
	226	100	per cent

When we realize that probably a large number of the other convicts are on their second or third term we begin to get an idea of the real Negro criminal class.[20]

CRIMINALS IN EASTERN STATE PENITENTIARY—MALES, BY AGE AND CRIME

AGES	CRIMES																							
	LARCENY	ASSAULT AND BATTERY	RECEIVING STOLEN GOODS	ASSAULT TO STEAL	CONCEALED WEAPONS	AGGRAVATED ASSAULT AND BATTERY	ASSAULT TO KILL	BURGLARY	ROBBERY	SODOMY	ASSAULT TO RAPE	RAPE	MANSLAUGHTER	FORGERY	MURDER	CONSPIRACY	FALSE PRETENSE	EMBEZZLEMENT	MAYHEM	BAWDY HOUSES	ENTICEMENT TO RAPE	INDECENT EXPOSURE	INCEST	ABORTION
15–19	27	1	2	1	1	2	4	5		1	3	1	1	1	3									
20–24	62	4	2	1	1	16	24	14	16	4	1	1	1		1	1	2	1	1					
25–29	45	1	1	2		9	22	12	10	3	3	4	1		3					1	2			
30–34	23	1	1			6	17	12	9	3	2		1	1	2					1		1		
35–39	23		1			6	3	3			4		1	1			1			1			1	
40–44	9					4	2	1	1		2		1											1
45–49	3					2	2	1		1	1		1											
50–59	2				1		1	2	1	3														
60 and over	3						1																	1
Total	197	7	7	4	3	45	76	50	37	15	16	6	7	3	9	1	3	1	1	3	2	1	1	2

A few other facts are of interest: if we tabulate crime according to the illiteracy of its perpetrators, we have:

Larceny	31	per cent of illiteracy
Assault, burglary and homicide	34	"
Sexual crimes	55	"

Or in other words, the more serious and revolting the crime the larger part does ignorance play as a cause. If we separate prisoners convicted for the above crimes according to length of sentence, we have:

Under five years	464	90.5 per cent
Five and under ten years	40	8.0 "
Ten years and over	9	1.5 "
	513	

Of the 49 sentenced for 5 years and over, 18 or 37 per cent were illiterate; of those sentenced for less than 5 years, 160 or 35 per cent were illiterate.

From this study we may conclude that young men are the perpetrators of the serious crime among Negroes; that this crime consists mainly of stealing and assault; that ignorance, and immigration to the temptations of city life, are responsible for much of this crime but not for all; that deep social causes underlie this prevalence of crime and they have so worked as to form among Negroes since 1864 a distinct class of habitual criminals; that to this criminal class and not to the great mass of Negroes the bulk of the serious crime perpetrated by this race should be charged.

40. Some Cases of Crime—It is difficult while studying crime in the abstract to realize just what the actual crimes committed are, and under what circumstances they take place. A few typical cases of the crimes of Negroes may serve to give a more vivid idea than the abstract statistics give. Most of these cases are quoted from the daily newspapers.

First let us take a couple of cases of larceny:

Edward Ashbridge, a colored boy, pleaded guilty to the larceny of a quart of milk, the property of George Abbott. The boy's mother said he was incorrigible, and he was committed to the House of Refuge.

William Drumgoole, colored, aged thirty-one years, of Lawrenceville, Va., was shot in the back and probably fatally wounded late yesterday afternoon by William H. McCalley, a detective, employed in the store of John Wanamaker, Thirteenth and Chestnut streets. Drumgoole, it is alleged, stole a pair of shoes from the store, and was followed by McCalley to the corner of Thirteenth and Chestnut streets, where he placed him under arrest. Drumgoole broke away from the detective's grasp, and running down Thirteenth street turned into Drury street, a small thoroughfare above Sansom street. McCalley started in pursuit, calling upon him to stop, but the fugitive darted into an alleyway, and when his pursuer came up within a few yards of him, he threatened to "do him up" if he followed him any further. McCalley drew his revolver from his pocket, and as Drumgoole again broke into a run he pointed the weapon at his legs and fired. Drumgoole fell to the ground, and when McCalley came up to him he was unable to rise. McCalley saw at a glance that, instead of wounding him in the leg, as he had intended, the bullet had lodged in the man's back. He hurriedly sought assistance, and had the wounded man taken to the Jefferson Hospital. McCalley then surrendered himself to Reserve Policeman Powell, and was taken to the Central Station.

Fighting and quarreling among neighbors and associates is common in the slum districts:

Etta Jones, colored, aged twenty-one years, residing on Hirst street, above Fifth, was stabbed near her home last night, it is alleged, by Lottie Lee, also colored, of Second and Race streets. The other woman was taken to the Pennsylvania Hospital, where her injuries were found to consist of several cuts on the left shoulder and side, none of which are dangerous. Her assailant was arrested later by Policeman Dean and locked up in the Third and Union streets station house. The assault is said by the police to have been the outcome of an old grudge.

Joseph Cole, colored, aged twenty-four years, residing in Gillis' alley, was dangerously stabbed shortly before midnight on Saturday, as is alleged, by Abraham Wheeler, at the latter's house, on Hirst street. Cole was taken to the Pennsylvania Hospital, where it was found the knife had penetrated to within a short distance of the right lung. Wheeler fled from the house after the cutting and eluded arrest until yesterday afternoon, when he was captured by Policeman Mitchell, near Fifth and Lombard streets. When brought to the station house Wheeler denied having cut Cole, but acknowledged having struck him because he was insulting his wife. He was locked up, however, to await the result of Cole's injuries.

Sometimes servants are caught pilfering:

Theodore Grant, colored, residing on Burton street, attempted to pledge a woman's silk dress for $15 at McFillen's, Seventeenth and Market streets, several days ago. The pawnbroker refused, under his rule, to take women's raiment from a man, and told Grant to bring the owner. Grant went away and returned with Ella Jones, a young colored woman, who consented to take $7 for the dress. Since that time C. F. Robertson, residing at Sixtieth and Spruce streets, made complaint to the police of the loss of the dress, and as the result of an investigation made by Special Policemen Gallagher and Ewing, Grant and Ella Jones were arrested yesterday charged with the larceny of the silk dress, which was recovered. Grant admitted to the special policemen that Ella had given him the dress to pawn, but asserted that he had nothing to do with the matter except to offer to pledge the article. At a hearing before Magistrate Jermon, at the City Hall, yesterday, Mr. Robertson stated that the girl had made a statement to him, saying that Grant had induced her to take the dress. He said the girl had been perfectly trustworthy up to the time of her acquaintance with Grant, and had been left in full charge of the house, and that nothing was ever missed. He said he also expected to show that Grant had been concerned in two or three robberies. Ella Jones, a neatly dressed girl, who said she came from Maryland, stated to the magistrate that Grant had been coming to see her for about a year past. She said he had been importuning her to take something and let him pawn it, so that he could raise some money, until she finally consented. After she started to go to her mistress' room to get the dress her heart failed and she turned back, but he persuaded her, telling her that Mrs. Robertson would not miss it, and then she took the dress. Mr. Robertson informed the magistrate, and Ella assented to the statement, that Grant had taken every cent of her earnings from her for weeks past and had also pawned all of her clothing, so that at the present time she was penniless and had not a single garment except what she wore. The magistrate said it was undoubtedly a hard case, but he would have to hold Grant and Ella on the charge of larceny, and Grant under additional bail for a further hearing next Thursday on the charges referred to by Mr. Robertson. The police say that Grant, who is a smooth-faced, cross-eyed mulatto, is a "crap fiend," and that whatever money he has managed to obtain by threats and cajolery from his victim, Ella Jones, has gone into the pockets of the small-fry gamblers.

There is growing evidence of the appearance of a set of thieves of intelligence and cunning: sneak thieves, confidence-men, pickpockets, and "sharpers." Some typical cases follow:

Marion Shields and Alice Hoffman, both colored and residing on Fitzwater street, above Twelfth, had a further hearing yesterday before Magistrate South, at the City Hall, and were held for trial on the charge of pilfering wearing apparel, money, vases, umbrellas, surgical instruments, and other portable property from physicians' offices and houses, where they had made visits, under the pretence of desiring to hold consultations with the doctors. The Magistrate said there were ten cases against Marion Shields individually on which she would be placed under $2,500 bail, and six cases against both women on which the bail would be $1,500. For her frankness, Marion Shields was given the lighter sentence, one year in the Eastern Penitentiary, and Alice Hoffman was sentenced to eighteen months in the same institution.

Two daring thieves yesterday entered the jewelry store of Albert Baudschopfs, 468½ North Eighth street, and secured a number of articles of jewelry from under the very eyes of the proprietor. They had left the store and proceeded leisurely down the street before the jeweller discovered his loss, with the result that before an alarm could be given the thieves had traveled a considerable distance. One of the men was captured after a long chase, but the other's whereabouts is unknown. About half-past one o'clock two colored men entered the store and upon their request were shown trays of various articles. One of the men engaged the proprietor in conversation while the other continued to inspect the jewelry. They said they did not intend buying then and would call again and opening the door walked hurriedly down the street. Mr. Baudschopfs says the men got away with a gold-filled watch case, a silver watch, three gold lockets, each set with a small diamond; two dozen ladies' gold rings, not jewelled; a gold scarf pin and a man's gold watch.

A crime for which Negroes of a certain class have become notorious is that of snatching pocketbooks on the streets:

While passing down Eleventh street, near Mount Vernon, shortly after nine o'clock, Mrs. K. Nichun, of 1947 Warnock street, was approached from behind by a Negro, who snatched a pocketbook containing $2 from her hand and ran down a small thoroughfare towards Tenth street. Very few pedestrians were upon the street at the time, but two men, who were attracted by the woman's scream, started in pursuit of the thief. The latter had too much of a start, however, and escaped.

William Williams, colored, of Dayton, O., was locked up in the Central Station yesterday, by Reserve Policeman A. Jones, on the charge of snatching a pocketbook from the hands of Mrs. Mary Tevis, of 141 Mifflin street. The theft occurred at Eighth and Market streets. After securing the pocketbook Williams ran until he reached the old office of the city solicitor, at Sixth and Locust streets. He was followed by Reserve Jones, who captured him in the cellar of the building. Williams was taken to Eighth and Sansom streets to await the arrival of the patrol wagon, and while getting into the vehicle the pocketbook dropped from out of his trousers.

Detectives Bond and O'Leary and Special Policeman Duffy, of the Eighth and Lombard streets station, arrested last night Sylvester Archer, of Fifth street, below Lombard, William Whittington, alias "Piggy," of Florida street, and William Carter, of South Fifteenth street, all colored and about twenty-one years of age, on the charge of assault upon and robbery of Mrs. Harrington Fitzgerald, wife of the editor of the *Evening Item*. The assault occurred on Monday at noon. As Mrs. Fitzgerald was passing Thirteenth and Spruce streets, a purse which she carried in her hand, and which contained $20, was snatched from her by one of three colored men. They took advantage of the crowd to strike her after the robbery had been perpetrated and escaped before her outcry was heard. When the men were brought to the Central Station last night and questioned by Captain of Detectives Miller, Whittington, it is said, confessed complicity in the crime. He told the captain that they had been following a band up Thirteenth street, and as they reached Spruce street Carter said, "There's a pocketbook; I'm going to get it." "All right; get it," came the response. Carter ran up to Mrs. Fitzgerald and in a moment shouted, "I've got it!" Then he and Archer ran up Thirteenth street. Each man has a criminal record, and the picture of each is in the Rogues' Gallery. Carter has just completed a six months' sentence for purse-snatching, while Williams and Archer have each served time for larceny.

So frequent have these crimes become that sometimes Negroes are wrongfully suspected; whoever snatches a pocketbook on a dark night is supposed to be black.

A favorite method of stealing is to waylay and rob the frequenters of bawdy houses; very little of this sort of crime, naturally, is reported. Here are some cases of such "badger thieves," as they are called:

William Lee, colored, and Kate Hughes, a white woman, were convicted of robbing Vincenzo Monacello of $10. Lee was sentenced to three years and three months in the Eastern Penitentiary and his accomplice to three years in the county prison. Mary Roach, jointly indicted with them, was acquitted. Monacello testified that, while walking along Christian street, between Eighth and Ninth streets, on Thursday night of last week, he was accosted by Mary Roach and accompanied her to her home on Essex street. Here he met Lee and Kate Hughes and they all drank considerable beer. Later in the night he started with Kate Hughes, at her suggestion, to a house further up the street. While on their way the prosecutor said he was struck in the face with a brick by Lee, after which the money was stolen from him. Mary Roach took the stand against the other two defendants and the case against her was abandoned.

Ella Jones, colored, claiming to be from Baltimore, was arrested yesterday by Policeman Dean on the charge of the larceny of a $10 bill from Joseph Gosch, a

Pole, who came from Pittsburg on Sunday, and claims that while he was looking for lodging he was taken to the woman's house and robbed.

From pocketbook snatching to highway robbery is but a step:

Before Judge Yerkes, in Court No. 1, Samuel Buckner, a young colored man, was convicted of robbing George C. Goddard of a gold watch and chain and a pocketbook containing $3. He was sentenced to ten years in the Eastern Penitentiary. Mr. Goddard, with his head swathed in bandages, was called to the stand. He said that a few minutes past midnight of November 28 he was returning to his home, No. 1220 Spruce street, after a visit. He placed his hand in his pocket, drew out his key and was about to mount the steps when a dark form appeared from Dean street, a small, poorly-lighted thoroughfare, next door but one to his home, and at the same instant he was struck a violent blow full in the face with a brick. He sank to the pavement unconscious. When he recovered his senses he was in the Pennsylvania Hospital. There was a long, deep cut on his right cheek, another across the forehead, both eyes were blackened and swollen, and his nose was also bruised. At the same time he discovered the loss of his pocketbook and jewelry. Judge Yerkes reviewed the facts of the case, and in imposing sentence said: "When you committed this offence you were absolutely indifferent as to the consequences of your cowardly attack. You rifled this man's person of all his valuables and left him lying unconscious on the pavement, and for aught you knew he might have been dead. It is necessary not only that society be protected from the depredations of such fiends as you, but also that an example be made of such ruffians. The sentence of the Court is that you undergo an imprisonment of ten years at labor in the Eastern Penitentiary, and stand committed until this sentence shall be complied with." The official record shows that Buckner was arrested on December 11, 1893, by policeman Logan, of the Lombard street station, on the charge of the larceny of a purse from Mrs. Caroline Lodge, of 2416 North Fifteenth street, on the street, and was sentenced December 14, 1893, by Judge Biddle, to one year's imprisonment.

Cases of aggravated assaults, for various reasons, are frequent:

Rube Warren, colored, thirty years, of Foulkrod and Cedar streets, was held in $1000 bonds, by Magistrate Eisenbrown, for an alleged aggravated assault and battery on Policeman Haug, of the Frankford station, during a dog fight about a month ago. The policeman attempted to stop the fight when Warren, it is charged, assisted by several companions, assaulted him, broke his club and took away his revolver. During the free fight that followed, in which other policemen took part, Warren escaped and went to Baltimore. There, it is said, he was sent to prison for thirty days. As soon as he was released he went back to Frankford, where he was arrested on Saturday night.

William Braxton, colored, aged twenty-eight years, of Irving street, above Thirty-seventh, was yesterday held in $800 bail for a further hearing, charged with having committed an aggravated assault on William Keebler, of South Thirtieth street. The assault occurred about three o'clock yesterday morning on Irving street, near Thirty-seventh, where the colored folks of the neighborhood were having a party. Keebler and two friends, none of whom were colored, forced their company on the invited guests, it is said, and a fight ensued. Keebler was found a short time afterward lying in the snow with one eye almost gouged out. He was conveyed to the University Hospital and the police of the Woodland avenue station, under Acting Sergeant Ward, upon being notified of the affair, hurried to the Irving street house and arrested twenty of the guests just in the height of their merrymaking. All of them, however, were discharged at the hearing, upon Braxton's being recognized as the man who struck Keebler. The physician at the hospital says that the injured man will very likely lose the sight of one eye.

Gambling goes on almost openly in the slum sections and occasions, perhaps, more quarreling and crime than any other single cause. Reporters declared in 1897 that—

"Policy playing is rampant in Philadelphia. Under the very noses of the police officials and, it is safe to say, with the knowledge of some of them, policy shops are conducted openly and with amazing audacity. They are doing a 'land office' business. Hundreds of poor people every day place upon the infatuating lottery money that had better be spent for food and clothing. They actually deny themselves the necessaries of life to gamble away their meagre income with small chance of getting any return. Superintendent of Police Linden, discussing the general subject of policy playing with a *Ledger* reporter, said: 'There are not words enough in the dictionary to express my feelings upon this matter. I regard policy as the worst evil in a large city among the poor people. There are several reasons for this. One is that women and children may play. Another is that players may put a few cents on the lottery. Policy may do more harm than all the saloons and "speak easies" in the city. The price of a drink of liquor is five or ten cents and the cost of a "growler" is ten cents, but a man or a woman can buy two cents' worth of policy. The effect of this is obvious. Persons who have not the price of a drink may gamble away the few pennies they do possess in a policy shop. Then the drain is constant. Policy "fiends" play twice a day, risking from two cents to a dollar upon the chance. They become so infatuated with the play that they will spend their last cent upon it in the hope of making a "hit." Many children go hungry and with insufficient clothing as a result of policy playing. I have heard of young children engaging in this sort of gambling. Of course the effect of this is very bad. The policy evil is, to my mind, the very worst that exists in our large cities as affecting the poorer classes of people.' " [21]

Once in a while gambling houses are raided:

Twenty-three colored men, who were arrested in a raid of the police on an alleged gambling house, on Rodman street, above Twelfth, had a hearing yesterday, before Magistrate South, at the City Hall. One man, residing on Griscom street, testified that the house was supposed to be a "club," and that it was customary to pay a dollar before admission could be secured, and that he had been gambling at "crap" and a card game known as "five-up," and had lost $18. He said there was a president, marshal and sergeant-at-arms. He pointed out Bolling, Jordan and Phillips as the principals. Special Policeman Duffy testified that the crowd was playing "crap" with dice on the floor when he headed the raid on Monday night. He said he had notified Bolling, as the head of the house, three months ago, when he had heard that gambling was going on there, to stop it. On cross-examination the witness said he did not know that it was a social club called the "Workingmen's Club." Patrolman William Harvey testified that he went to the house on last Saturday night and got in readily, and was not called on to pay a dollar initiation fee, as had been claimed was the rule. He said he played "sweat" and lost twenty-five cents, but did not win anything. He said Bolling was running the game. He said that when he entered the house somebody called out "Sam's got a new man," and that was all that was said.

More and more frequently in the last few years, have crime, excess, and disappointment led to attempted suicide:

> Policeman Wynne, of the Fifth and Race streets station, last evening found an unknown colored woman lying unconscious in an alleyway at Delaware avenue and Race street. Beside the woman was an empty bottle labeled benzine. Wynne immediately summoned the patrol wagon and had the woman removed to the Pennsylvania Hospital, where her condition was said to be critical. The physicians said there was no doubt the woman had drunk the contents of the bottle, and narcotics were at once administered to counteract the effect of the poison. At midnight the woman showed signs of returning consciousness and it was thought that she would recover. The police have no clue to her identity, as she could not tell her name, and the alleyway where she was found is surrounded by business houses, and no one could be found who knew her.

It is but fair to add that many unsustained charges of crime are made against Negroes, and possibly more in proportion than against other classes. Some typical cases of this sort are of interest:

> W. M. Boley, colored, thirty years old, who said he resided in Mayesville, South Carolina, was a defendant before Magistrate Jermon, at the City Hall, yesterday, on the charge of assault with intent to steal. Detective Gallagher and Special Policeman Thomas testified that their attention was attracted to the prisoner by his actions in a crowd at the New York train gate at Broad street station on Saturday. He had with him several parcels which he laid on the floor near the gate, and they said they saw him make several attempts to pick women's pockets, and arrested him. The man however proved by documentary evidence that he was a clergyman, a graduate of Howard University, and financial agent of a Southern school. He was released.
>
> Under instructions from Judge Finletter, a jury rendered a verdict of not guilty in the case of George Queen, a young colored man, charged with the murder of Joseph A. Sweeney and John G. O'Brien. Dr. Frederick G. Coxson, pastor of the Pitman Methodist Episcopal Church, at Twenty-third and Lombard streets, testified that on the night in question he was about to retire, when he heard a disturbance on the street. Upon going out he saw three young men, two of whom were leading the other and persuading him to come with them. At the same time the prisoner, Queen, came along in the middle of the street, walking leisurely. Immediately upon seeing him the three men attacked him, and were shortly afterward joined by three others, and the entire crowd, among whom were Sweeney and O'Brien, continued beating and striking the colored man. Suddenly the crowd scattered and Queen was placed under arrest; he had fatally stabbed two of his assailants. This testimony showed that the accused was not the aggressor, and without hearing the defence Judge Finletter ordered the jury to render a verdict of

not guilty. The case, he said, was one of justifiable homicide, the defendant having a right to resist the attack by force. The judge further said he thought the case would have a tendency to repel the brutal attacks made on inoffensive persons in the community, and to make the streets safe for every man to walk on at any hour without fear.

Leaving for a moment the question of the deeper social causes of crime among Negroes, let us consider two closely allied subjects, pauperism and the use of alchoholic liquors.

NOTES

1. Throughout this chapter the basis of induction is the number of prisoners received at different institutions and *not* the prison population at particular times. This avoids the mistakes and distortions of the latter method. (Cf. Falkner: "Crime and the Census," Publications of the American Academy of Political and Social Science, No. 190). Many writers on Crime among Negroes, as *e.g.*, F. L. Hoffman, and all who use the Eleventh Census uncritically, have fallen into numerous mistakes and exaggerations by carelessness on this point.
2. "Pennsylvania Colonial Records," I, 380–81.
3. See Chapter III, and Appendix B.
4. Cf. "Pennsylvania Statutes at Large," Ch. 56.
5. Watson's "Annals," I, 62.
6. *Ibid.*
7. *Ibid.*, pp. 62–63.
8. "Pennsylvania Colonial Records," II, 275; IX, 6; "Watson's Annals," I, 309.
9. Cf. Chapter IV.
10. Reports Eastern Penitentiary.
11. Average length of sentences for whites in Eastern Penitentiary during nineteen years, 2 years 8 months 2 days; for Negroes, 3 years 3 months 14 days. Cf. "Health of Convicts" (pam.), pp. 7, 8.
12. *Ibid.*, "Condition of Negroes," 1838, pp. 15–18; "Condition," etc., 1848, pp. 26, 27.
13. "Condition of Negroes," 1849, pp. 28, 29. "Condition," etc., 1838, pp. 15–18.
14. "The large proportion of colored men who, in April, had been before the criminal court, led Judge Gordon to make a suggestion when he yesterday discharged the jurors for the term. 'It would certainly seem,' said the Court, 'that the philanthropic colored people of the community, of whom there are a great many excellent and intelligent citizens sincerely interested in the welfare of their race, ought to see what is radically wrong that produces this state of affairs and correct it, if possible. There is nothing in history that indicates that the colored race has a propensity to acts of violent crime; on the contrary, their tendencies are most gentle, and they submit with grace to subordination.'" Philadelphia *Record*, April 29, 1893; Cf. *Record*, May 10 and 12; *Ledger*, May 10, and *Times*, May 22, 1893.
15. Except as otherwise noted, the statistics of this section are from the official reports of the police department.
16. Cf. Chapters IV and VII.
17. The chief element of uncertainty lies in the varying policy of the courts, as for instance, in the proportion of prisoners sent to different places of detention, the severity of sentence, etc. Only the general conclusions are insisted on here.
18. For the collection of the material here compiled, I am indebted to Mr. David N. Fell, Jr., a student of the Senior Class, Wharton School, University of Pennsylvania, in the year '96–'97. As before noted the figures in this Section refer to the number of prisoners received at the Eastern Penitentiary, and not to the total prison population at any particular time.
19. Witness the case of Marion Stuyvesant accused of the murder of the librarian Wilson, in 1897.
20. The following Negroes were measured by the Bertillon system in Philadelphia during the last three years:

1893 . . . . 64 (Whites 101).
1894 . . . . 66 (Whites 248).
1895 . . . . 56 (Whites 267).
1896 . . . . 75 (Whites 347).

The arrests by detectives for five years are given below.

CRIMES OF NEGROES ARRESTED BY DETECTIVES, 1887–1892

CRIMES	1887	1888	1889	1890	1891	1892
Fugitives from justice	. . .	10	2	4	4	9
Larceny	10	19	17	19	18	29
Pickpocket	7	4	1	. . .	. . .	13
Burglary	1	. . .	2	. . .	2	4
Professional thief	1	4	2	1	2	3
Sodomy	. . .	. . .	. . .	. . .	. . .	1
Misdemeanor	. . .	1	. . .	1	. . .	1
Absconding	. . .	. . .	. . .	. . .	. . .	1
Assault to kill	5	6	1	1	4	4
Stabbing	. . .	. . .	. . .	. . .	. . .	1
False pretense	. . .	2	. . .	1	. . .	1
Forgery	. . .	. . .	. . .	. . .	. . .	1
Receiving stolen goods	1	4	8	. . .	3	. . .
Murder	3	2	1	3	2	. . .
Abortion	. . .	. . .	. . .	1	1	. . .
Breach of peace	. . .	. . .	. . .	2	. . .	. . .
Abandonment	. . .	. . .	1	1	. . .	. . .
Gambling house	. . .	4	. . .	5	. . .	. . .
Fornication and adultery	. . .	. . .	1	. . .	. . .	. . .
Infanticide	. . .	1	. . .	. . .	. . .	. . .
House robbery	. . .	1	. . .	. . .	. . .	. . .
Lottery	1	8	. . .	. . .	. . .	. . .
Embezzlement	. . .	1	. . .	. . .	. . .	. . .
Perjury	. . .	1	. . .	. . .	. . .	. . .
Seduction	1	. . .	. . .	. . .	. . .	. . .
Bawdy house	1	. . .	. . .	. . .	. . .	. . .

21. Although the police lieutenants have reported to the Superintendent that few policy shops exist, the *Ledger* has information which leads it to state that such is not the fact. Many complaints against the evil have been received at this office. A reporter found it easy to locate and gain admittance to a number of houses where policy is written. A policy writer who is thoroughly informed as to the inside working of the system is authority for the statement that at no time in recent years has policy playing been so prevalent or the business carried on as openly as it is now.

While the locations of the policy shops are well known and the writers familiar to many persons, the backers, who, after all, are the substantial part of the system, are hard to reach, for they exercise an unusual cunning in the direction of the business. There are several backers in Philadelphia of greater or less pretensions, but a young man who resides uptown and operates principally in the territory north of Girard avenue, is said to be the heaviest backer of the game in this city. He owns sixty or seventy "books," and his income from their combined receipts is sufficient to support himself and several relatives in magnificent style.

A *Ledger* reporter spent one day last week looking up the policy shops in one of the sections where this backer operates. He found, in addition to several places where policy is written, the rendezvous of the writers and the headquarters of the policy king himself.

The writers who hold "books" from the backer in question meet twice every day, Sundays excepted, in a mean, dirty little house overlooking the Reading tracks, just below Montgomery avenue. They enter by the rear through a narrow alley leading off Delhi street, several yards below Montgomery avenue. At noon and at 6 o'clock in the evening the writers hurry to this rendezvous.

The unusual number of men gathering at this point at regular intervals, and the business-like manner in which they go through the alley and back gate is enough to attract the attention of the Twelfth District policeman on this beat and arouse his suspicions. Whether he notices it or not, these proceedings have been going on for months.

Each writer, when he reaches this central point, turns in his "book" and receipts. There are two drawings daily, hence the two meetings. Two relatives of the backer receive the "books" and the money. A copy of each writer's "book" and all the money are carried by one of these men to the house of an ex-special policeman, a few squares away, and there turned over to the backer, who has received a telegram from Cincinnati stating the numbers that have come out at that drawing.

The "books" are carefully gone over, to see if there are any "hits." If there are they are computed, and the backer sends to each writer the amount necessary to pay his losses. The numbers that appear at each drawing are printed with rubber stamps in red ink, on slips of white paper and given to the writers to distribute among the players.

These drawings are usually carried to the rendezvous by the ex-policeman. The backer pockets the half day's receipts, mounts his bicycle and rides away.

To establish beyond a doubt the character of the building in which the writers meet, the reporter made his way into it on the afternoon in question. It is a well-known policy shop, conducted by a colored man, who has been writing policy for years. He is president of a colored political club, with headquarters near by. On the occasion of the visit the back gate was ajar. Pushing it open, the reporter walked in without challenge—From the *Public Ledger*, December 3, 1897.

CHAPTER XIV

◆

Pauperism and Alcoholism

41. Pauperism—Emancipation and pauperism must ever go hand in hand; when a group of persons have been for generations prohibited from self-support, and self-initiative in any line, there is bound to be a large number of them who, when thrown upon their own resources, will be found incapable of competing in the race of life. Pennsylvania from early times, when emancipation of slaves in considerable numbers first began, has seen and feared this problem of Negro poverty. The Act of 1726 declared: "Whereas free Negroes are an idle and slothful people and often prove burdensome to the neighborhood and afford ill examples to other Negroes, therefore be it enacted * * * * that if any master or mistress shall discharge or set free any Negro, he or she shall enter into recognizance with sufficient securities in the sum of £30 to indemnify the county for any charge or incumbrance they may bring upon the same, in case such Negro through sickness or otherwise be rendered incapable of self-support."

The Acts of 1780 and 1788 took pains to provide for Negro paupers in the county where they had legal residence, and many decisions of the courts bear upon this point. About 1820 when the final results of the Act of 1780 were being felt, an act was passed "To prevent the increase of pauperism in the Commonwealth;" it provided that if a servant was brought into the state over twenty-eight years of age (the age of emancipation) his master was to be liable for his support in case he became a pauper.[1]

Thus we can infer that much pauperism was prevalent among the freedmen during these years although there are no actual figures on the subject. In 1837, 235 of the 1673 inmates of the Philadelphia County Almshouse were Negroes or 14 per cent of paupers from 7.4 per cent of the population. These paupers were classed as follows:[2]

MALES		FEMALES	
Under 21 years	18	Under 18 years	33
21 to 50 "	57	18 to 40 "	59
50 to 75 "	18	40 to 60 "	17
Unknown	13	60 " and over	10
		Unknown	10
	106		129

Lunatics and defective	16 males,	31 females,
Defective from exposure	11 "	11 "
Consumption, rheumatism, etc.	9 "	
Pleurisy, typhus fever, etc.	12 "	
Destitute	13 "	
Paupers	32 "	35 "
Unclassed	13 "	28 "
Women lying-in, children and orphans, ...		24 "
	106 males	129 females

Ten years later there were 196 Negro paupers in the Almshouse, and those receiving outdoor relief were reported as follows:[3]

In the City:
Of 2562 Negro families, 320 received assistance.
In Spring Garden:
Of 202 Negro families, 3 received assistance.
In Northern Liberties:
Of 272 Negro families, 6 received assistance.
In Southwark:
Of 287 Negro families, 7 received assistance.
In West Philadelphia:
Of 73 Negro families, 2 received assistance.
In Moyamensing:
Of 866 Negro families, 104 received assistance.
Total, of 4262 Negro families, 442 received assistance, or 10 per cent.

This practically covers the available statistics of the past; it shows a large amount of pauperism and yet perhaps not more than could reasonably be expected.

To-day it is very difficult to get any definite idea of the extent of Negro poverty; there is a vast amount of alms-giving in Philadelphia, but much of it is unsystematic and there is much duplication of work; and, at the same time, so meagre are the records kept that the real extent of pauperism and its causes are very hard to study.[4]

The first available figures are those relating to lodgers at the station houses— *i. e.,* persons without shelter who have applied for and been given lodging:[5]

1891, total lodgers	13,600, of whom	365, or 2.7 per cent were Negroes
1892, "	.... 11,884, "	345, or 2.9 " " "
1893, "	.... 20,521, "	622, or 3.0 " " "
1894, "	.... 43,726, "	1,247, or 2.9 " " "
1895, "	.... 45,788, "	2,247, or 4.9 " " "
1896, "	.... 46,121, "	2,359, or 5.0 " " "

Somewhat similar statistics are furnished by the report of arrests by the vagrant detective for the last ten years:

1887	total arrests, 581. Negroes	55	9.5 per cent
1888	" 574. "	48	8.4 "
1889	" 588. "	36	6.1 "
1890	" 523. "	48	9.1 "

1891 . . . . total arrests, 554. Negroes . . . . 47 8.5 per cent
1892 . . . .   "   505.   "   . . . . 65 12.9   "
1893 . . . .   "   586.   "   . . . . 67 11.0   "
1894 . . . .   "   688.   "   . . . . 66 9.6   "
1895 . . . .   "   557.   "   . . . . 56 10.3   "
1896 . . . .   "   629.   "   . . . . 59 9.3   "

The Negro vagrants arrested during the last six years were thus disposed of:

DISPOSAL	1891	1892	1893	1894	1895	1896
Given temporary shelter	21	27	29	39	26	32
Transported from city	3	2	5	4	2	3
Arrested for vagrancy, beggary, etc.	5	10	4	4	2	5
Arrested for vicious conduct, etc.	15	10	16	11	14	5
Sent to House of Refuge	3	14	7	2	5	0
Sent to societies and institutions	0	2	6	6	7	13

These records give a vague idea of that class of persons just hovering between pauperism and crime—tramps, loafers, defective persons and unfortunates—a class difficult to deal with because made up of diverse elements.

Turning to the true paupers, we have the record of the paupers admitted to the Blockley Almshouse during six years:

ADULTS–SIXTEEN YEARS OF AGE AND OVER

YEAR	TOTAL RECEPTIONS	NEGROES	PER CENT OF NEGROES
1891	6764	569	8.4
1892	6231	537	8.8
1893	6451	567	8.8
1894	6108	569	9.3
1895	6318	606	9.3
1896	6414	593	9.2

CHILDREN UNDER SIXTEEN YEARS OF AGE

YEAR	TOTAL RECEPTIONS	NEGROES	PER CENT OF NEGROES
1891	380	38	12.3
1892	262	38	14.5
1893	295	38	12.9
1894	304	35	11.1
1895	401	42	10.5
1896	410	51	12.4

In 1891, 4.2 per cent of the whites admitted were insane and 2.3 per cent of the Negroes; in 1895, 8.3 per cent of the whites and 8.6 per cent of the Negroes:

THE INSANE

	WHITES		NEGROES	
YEAR	TOTAL RECEPTIONS	INSANE	TOTAL RECEPTIONS	INSANE
1891	6,195	264	569	13
1892	5,694	450	537	45
1893	5,884	427	567	39
1894	5,539	441	569	38
1895	5,712	463	606	52

We have already seen that in the Seventh Ward about 9 per cent of the Negroes can be classed as the "very poor," needing public assistance in order to live. From this we may conclude that between three and four thousand Negro families in the city may be classed among the semi-pauper class. Thus it is plain that there is a large problem of poverty among the Negro problems; 4 per cent of the population furnish according to the foregoing statistics at least 8 per cent of the poverty. Considering the economic difficulties of the Negro, we ought perhaps to expect rather more than less than this. Beside these permanently pauperized families there is a considerable number of persons who from time to time must receive temporary aid, but can usually get on without it. In time of stress as during the year 1893 this class is very large.

There is especial suffering and neglect among the children of this class of people: in the last ten years the Children's Aid Society has received the following children:[6]

FROM 1887 TO 1897	NEGROES	TOTAL
Received from judges and magistrates (so-called delinquents)	19	181
Deserted babies	7	55
Orphans	4	147
Half-orphans, including those with mothers in delicate health and worthless fathers; also both parents worthless	12	448
From Blockley Almshouse	7	
From Blockley Almshouse (foundlings)	12	362
From Society for Prevention of Cruelty to Children	3	45
From County Poor Boards	26	151
	110	1,389

The total receptions during these ten years have been 1389, of which the Negroes formed 8 per cent. This but emphasizes the fact of poor family life among the lower classes which we have spoken of before.

A little better light can be thrown on the problem of poverty by a study of concrete cases; for this purpose 237 families have been selected. They live in the Seventh Ward and are composed of those families of Negroes whom the Charity Organization Society, Seventh District, has aided for at least two winters.[7] First, we must notice that this number nearly corresponds with the previously estimated per cent of the "very poor."[8] Arranging these families according to size, we have:

NUMBER IN FAMILY	FAMILIES	PERSONS
1	48	48
2	61	122
3	54	162
4	31	124
5	19	95
6	10	60
7	1	7
11	1	11
Unknown	9	?
Total	234	638

The reported causes of poverty, which were in all cases verified by visitors so far as possible, were as follows:

Lack of work .... 115 families.
Sickness, accident, or physical disability 39   "
Death of bread-winner and old age 24   "
Probable gambling, criminal shiftlessness, etc., ... 16   "
Desertion of bread-winner 15   "
Laziness and improvidence 10   "
Intemperate use of alcoholic liquors 8   "
Financial reverses 7   "
234 families

From as careful a consideration of these cases as the necessarily meagre information of records and visitors permit, it seems fair to say that Negro poverty in the Seventh Ward was, in these cases, caused as follows:

By sickness and misfortune .... 40 per cent.
By lack of steady employment 30   "
By laziness, improvidence and intemperate drink 20   "
By crime 10   "

Of course this is but a rough estimate; many of these causes indirectly influence each other: crime causes sickness and misfortune; lack of employment causes crime; laziness causes lack of work, etc.

Several typical families will illustrate the varying conditions encountered:

No. 1.—South Eighteenth street. Four in the family; husband intemperate drinker; wife decent, but out of work.

No. 2.—South Tenth street. Five in the family; widow and children out of work, and had sold the bed to pay for expense of a sick child.

No. 3.—Dean street. A woman paralyzed; partially supported by a colored church.

No. 4.—Carver street. Worthy woman deserted by her husband five years ago; helped with coal, but is paying the Charity Organization Society back again.

No. 5.—Hampton street. Three in family; living in three rooms with three other families. "No push, and improvident."

No. 6.—Stockton street. The woman has just had an operation performed in the hospital, and cannot work yet.

No. 7.—Addison street. Three in family; left their work in Virginia through the misrepresentations of an Arch street employment bureau; out of work.

No. 8.—Richard street. Laborer injured by falling of a derrick; five in the family. His fellow workmen have contributed to his support, but the employers have given nothing.

No. 9.—Lombard street. Five in family; wife white; living in one room; hard cases; rum and lies; pretended one child was dead in order to get aid.

No. 10.—Carver street. Woman and demented son; she was found very drunk on the street; plays policy.

No. 11.—Lombard street. Worthy woman sick with a tumor; given temporary aid.

No. 12.—Ohio street. Woman and two children deserted by her husband; helped to pay her rent.

No. 13.—Rodman street. A widow and child; out of work. "One very little room, clean and orderly."

No. 14.—Fothergill street. Two in the family; the man sick, half-crazy and lazy; "going to convert Africa and didn't want to cook;" given temporary help.

No. 15.—Lombard street. An improvident young couple out of work; living in one untidy room, with nothing to pay rent.

No. 16.—Lombard street. A poor widow of a wealthy caterer; cheated out of her property; has since died.

No. 17.—Ivy street. A family of four; husband was a stevedore, but is sick with asthma, and wife out of work; decent, but improvident.

No. 18.—Naudain street. Family of three; the man, who is decent, has broken his leg; the wife plays policy.

No. 19.—South Juniper street. Woman and two children; deserted by her husband, and in the last stages of consumption.

No. 20.—Radcliffe street. Family of three; borrowed of Charity Organization Society $1.00 to pay rent, and repaid it in three weeks.

No. 21.—Lombard street. "A genteel American white woman married to a colored man; he is at present in the South looking for employment; have one child;" both are respectable.

No. 22.—Fothergill street. Wife deserted him and two children, and ran off with a man; he is out of work; asked aid to send his children to friends.

No. 23.—Carver street. Man of twenty-three came from Virginia for work; was run over by cars at Forty-fifth street and Baltimore avenue, and lost both legs and right arm; is dependent on colored friends and wants something to do.

No. 24.—Helmuth street. Family of three; man out of work all winter, and wife with two and one-half days' work a week; respectable.

No. 25.—Richard street. Widow, niece and baby; the niece betrayed and deserted. They ask for work.

42. The Drink Habit—The intemperate use of intoxicating liquors is not one of the Negro's special offences; nevertheless there is considerable drinking and the use of beer is on the increase. The Philadelphia liquor saloons are conducted under an unusually well-administered system, and are not to so great an extent centres of brawling and loafing as in other cities; no amusements, as pool and billiards, are allowed in rooms where liquor is sold. This is not an unmixed good for the result is that much of the drinking is thus driven into homes, clubs and "speakeasies." The increase of beer-drinking among all classes, black and white, is noticeable; the beer wagons deliver large numbers of bottles at private residences, and much is carried from the saloons in buckets.

An attempt was made in 1897 to count the frequenters of certain saloons in the Seventh Ward during the hours from 8 to 10 on a Saturday night. It was impracticable to make this count simultaneously or to cover the whole ward, but eight or ten were watched each night.[9] The results are a rough measurement of the drinking habits in this ward.

There are in the ward 52 saloons of which 26 were watched in districts mostly inhabited by Negroes. In these two hours the following record was made:
Persons entering the saloons:
Negroes—male, 1,373; female, 213. Whites—male, 1,445; female, 139.
Of those entering, the following are known to have carried liquor away:
Negroes—male, 238; female, 125. Whites—male, 275; female, 81.
3,170 persons entered half the saloons of the Seventh Ward in the hours from 8 to 10 of one Saturday night in December, 1897; of these, 1,586 were Negroes, and 1,584 were whites; 2,818 were males, and 352 were females.[10] Of those entering these saloons at this time a part carried away liquor—mostly beer in tin buckets; of those thus visibly carrying away liquor there were in all 719; of these 363 were Negroes, and 356 were whites; 513 were males, and 206 were females.

The observers stationed near these saloons saw, in the two hours they were there, 79 drunken persons.

The general character of the saloons and their frequenters can best be learned from a few typical reports. The numbers given are the official license numbers:

No. 516. Persons entering saloon:
Men—white, 40; Negro, 68. Women—white, 12; Negro, 12.
Persons carrying liquor away:
Men—white, 8; Negro, 16. Women—white, 1; Negro, 3 Drunken persons seen, 12.

General character of saloon and frequenters:—"A small corner saloon, kept by a white man. The saloon appears to be a respectable one and has three entrances: one on Thirteenth street and the two on a small court. The majority of the colored patrons are poor people and of the working class. The white patrons are, for the greater part, of the better class. Among the latter very few were intoxicated."

No. 488. Persons entering:
Men—white, 24; Negro, 102. Women—white, 2; Negro, 3.
Carrying liquor away, 12; drunken persons seen, 8.

General character:—"The saloon was none too orderly; policemen remained near all the time; the Negro men entering were as a rule well dressed—perhaps one-third were laborers; the white men were well dressed but suspicious looking characters."

No. 515. Persons entering:
Men—white, 81; Negro, 59. Women—white, 4; Negro, 10.
Persons carrying liquor away:
Men—white, 15 (one a boy of 12 or 14 years of age); Negro, 11. Women—white, 4; Negro, 8.
Drunken persons seen, 2 (to one nothing was sold).
General character of saloon and frequenters:—"There were two Negro men and seven white men in saloon when the count was started. The place has three doors but all are easily observed. Trade is largely in distilled liquors, and a great deal is sold in bottles—a 'barrel shop.'"

No. 527. Persons entering saloon:

	8 TO 9 P.M.	9 TO 10 P.M.	TOTAL
Men, White	49	54	104
" Negro	29	37	68
Women, White	3	3	6
" Negro	5	2	7
	88	97	185

Persons carrying liquor away:

Men, White	6	11	17
" Negro	4	9	13
Women, White	0	1	1
" Negro	4	0	4
Boys, "	1	0	1
	15	21	36

Drunken persons seen, none.
General character of saloon and frequenters:—"Quiet, orderly crowd—quick trade—no loafing. Three boys were among those entering."

No. 484. Persons entering saloon:
Men—white, 70; Negro, 32. Women—white, 10; Negro, 1.
Persons carrying liquor away:
Men—white, 10; Negro, 12. Women—white, 4; Negro, 0.
Drunken persons seen, 11, six of whom were white and five black. "I cannot say that the saloon was responsible for all of them, but they were all in or about it."
This saloon is in the worst slum section of the ward and is of bad character. Frequenters were a mixed lot, "fast, tough, criminal and besotted."

No. 487. Persons entering:

Men—white, 79; Negro, 129. Women—white, 13; Negro, 34.

Persons carrying liquor away:

Men—white, 15; Negro, 25. Women—white, 5; Negro, 8.

"No drunken men seen. Frequented by a sharp class of criminals and loafers. Near the notorious 'Middle Alley.'"

No. 525.

Total Negroes entering, 14; total whites entering, 13.

"No loafers about the front of the saloon. Streets well lighted and neighborhood quiet, according to the policeman. There was a barber shop next door and a saloon on the corner ten doors below. Very few drunken people were seen. Trade was most brisk between eight and nine o'clock. In two hours one more Negro than white entered. Two more Negroes, men, than whites carried away liquor. One white man, a German, returned three times for beer in a kettle. Two Negro women carried beer away in kettles; one white woman (Irish) made two trips. All women entered by side door. The saloon is under a residence, three stories, corner of Waverly and Eleventh streets. Waverly street has a Negro population which fairly swarms—good position for Negro trade. Proprietor and assistant were both Irish. The interior of the saloon was finished in white pine stained to imitate cherry. Extremely plain. Barkeeper said, 'A warm night, but we are doing very well.' One beggar came in, a colored 'Auntie;' she wanted bread, not gin. Negroes were well dressed, as a rule, many smoking. The majority of frequenters by their bustling air and directness with which they found the place, showed long acquaintance with the neighborhood; especially this corner."

No. 500. Persons entering saloon:

Men—white, 40; Negro, 73. Women—white, 4; Negro, 6.

Persons carrying liquor away:

Men—white, 6; Negro, 23. Women—white, 5; Negro, 4.

Drunken persons seen, 1.

General character of saloon and frequenters:—"Four story building, plain and neat; three entrances; iron awning; electric and Welsbach lights. Negroes generally tidy and appear to be pretty well-to-do. Whites not so tidy as Negroes and generally mechanics. Almost all smoke cigars. Liquor carried away openly in pitchers and kettles. Three of the white women, carrying away liquor, looked like Irish servant girls. Some of the Negroes carried bundles of laundry and groceries with them."

Few general conclusions can be drawn from this data. The saloon is evidently not so much a moral as an economic problem among Negroes; if the 1,586 Negroes who went into the saloons within two hours Saturday night spent five cents apiece, which is a low estimate, they spent $79.30. If, as is probable, at least $100 was spent that Saturday evening throughout the ward, then in a year we would not be wrong in concluding their Saturday night's expenditure was at least $5,000, and their total expenditure could scarcely be less than $10,000, and it may reach $20,000—a large sum for a poor people to spend in liquor.

43. The Causes of Crime and Poverty—A study of statistics seems to show that the crime and pauperism of the Negroes exceeds that of the whites; that in the main, nevertheless, it follows in its rise and fall the fluctuations shown in the records of the whites, i. e., if crime increases among the whites it increases among Negroes, and *vice versa*, with this peculiarity, that among the Negroes the change is always exaggerated—the increase greater, the decrease more marked in nearly all cases. This is what we would naturally expect: we have here the record of a low social class, and as the condition of a lower class is by its very definition worse than that of a higher, so the situation of the Negroes is worse as respects crime and poverty than that of the mass of whites. Moreover, any change in social conditions is bound to affect the poor and unfortunate more than the rich and prosperous. We have in all probability an example of this in the increase of crime since 1890; we have had a period of financial stress and industrial depression; the ones who have felt this most are the poor, the unskilled laborers, the inefficient and unfortunate, and those with small social and economic advantages: the Negroes are in this class, and the result has been an increase in Negro crime and pauperism; there has also been an increase in the crime of the whites, though less rapid by reason of their richer and more fortunate upper classes.

So far, then, we have no phenomena which are new or exceptional, or which present more than the ordinary social problems of crime and poverty—although these, to be sure, are difficult enough. Beyond these, however, there are problems which can rightly be called Negro problems: they arise from the peculiar history and condition of the American Negro. The first peculiarity is, of course, the slavery and emancipation of the Negroes. That their emancipation has raised them economically and morally is proven by the increase of wealth and co-operation, and the decrease of poverty and crime between the period before the war and the period since; nevertheless, this was manifestly no simple process: the first effect of emancipation was that of any sudden social revolution: a strain upon the strength and resources of the Negro, moral, economic and physical, which drove many to the wall. For this reason the rise of the Negro in this city is a series of rushes and backslidings rather than a continuous growth. The second great peculiarity of the situation of the Negroes is the fact of immigration; the great numbers of raw recruits who have from time to time precipitated themselves upon the Negroes of the city and shared their small industrial opportunities, have made reputations which, whether good or bad, all their race must share; and finally whether they failed or succeeded in the strong competition, they themselves must soon prepare to face a new immigration.

Here then we have two great causes for the present condition of the Negro: Slavery and emancipation with their attendant phenomena of ignorance, lack of discipline, and moral weakness; immigration with its increased competition and moral influence. To this must be added a third as great—possibly greater in influence than the other two, namely the environment in which a Negro finds himself—the world of custom and thought in which he must live and work, the physical surrounding of house and home and ward, the moral encouragements and discouragements which he encounters. We dimly seek to define this social environment partially when we talk of color prejudice—but this is but a vague characterization; what we want to study is not a vague thought or feeling but its concrete manifestations. We know pretty well what the surroundings are of a young white lad, or a foreign immigrant who comes to this great city to join in its organic life. We know what influences and limitations surround him, to what he may attain, what his companionships are, what his encouragements are, what his drawbacks.

This we must know in regard to the Negro if we would study his social condition. His strange social environment must have immense effect on his thought and life, his work and crime, his wealth and pauperism. That this environment differs and differs broadly from the environment of his fellows, we all know, but we do not know just how it differs. The real foundation of the difference is the widespread feeling all over the land, in Philadelphia as well as in Boston and New Orleans, that the Negro is something less than an American and ought not to be much more than what he is. Argue as we may for or against this idea, we must as students recognize its presence and its vast effects.

At the Eastern Penitentiary where they seek so far as possible to attribute to definite causes the criminal record of each prisoner, the vast influence of environment is shown. This estimate is naturally liable to error, but the peculiar system of this institution and the long service and wide experience of the warden and his subordinates gives it a peculiar and unusual value. Of the 541 Negro prisoners previously studied 191 were catalogued as criminals by reason of "natural and inherent depravity." The others were divided as follows:

Crimes due to

(*a*) Defects of the law:

Laxity in administration	33	
Unsuitable laws for minor offences	48	
Inefficient police	22	
License given to the young	16	
Inefficient laws in regard to saloons	11	
Poor institutions and lack of institutions	12	
		142

(*b*) Immediate environment:

Association	53	
Amusements	16	
Home and family influences	25	
		94

(*c*) Lack of training, lack of opportunity, lack of desire to work	56	
(*d*) General environment	6	
(*e*) Disease	16	
(*f*) Moral weakness and unknown	36	
		114

This rough judgment of men who have come into daily contact with five hundred Negro criminals but emphasizes the fact alluded to; the immense influence of his peculiar environment on the black Philadelphian; the influence of homes badly situated and badly managed, with parents untrained for their responsibilities; the influence of social surroundings which by poor laws and inefficient administration leave the bad to be made worse; the influence of economic exclusion which admits Negroes only to those parts of the economic world where it is hardest to retain ambition and self-respect; and finally that indefinable but real and mighty moral influence that causes men to have a real sense of manhood or leads them to lose aspiration and self-respect.

For the last ten or fifteen years young Negroes have been pouring into this city at the rate of a thousand a year; the question is then what homes they find or make, what neighbors they have, how they amuse themselves, and what work they engage in? Again, into what sort of homes are the hundreds of Negro babies of each year born? Under what social influences do they come, what is the tendency of their training, and what places in life can they fill? To answer all these questions is to go far toward finding the real causes of crime and pauperism among this race; the next two chapters, therefore, take up the question of environment.

NOTES

1. See Appendix B for these various laws.
2. "Condition," etc., 1838.
3. "Condition," etc., 1848.
4. Cf. The "Civic Club Digest" for general information.
5. From reports of police department. Many other official reports might be added to these, but they are easily accessible.
6. From the Society records, by courtesy of the officers.
7. From the C. O. S. records, Seventh District, by courtesy of Miss Burke.
8. This coincidence in figures was entirely unnoticed until both had been worked out by independent methods.
9. I am indebted to Dr. S. M. Lindsay and the students of the Wharton School for the carrying out of this plan.
10. No comparison of the number of Negroes and whites for the ward can be made, because many of the saloons omitted are frequented by whites principally.

CHAPTER XV

◆

The Environment of the Negro

44. Houses and Rent—The inquiry of 1848 returned quite full statistics of rents paid by the Negroes.[1] In the whole city at that date 4019 Negro families paid $199,665.46 in rent, or an average of $49.68 per family each year. Ten years earlier the average was $44 per family. Nothing better indicates the growth of the Negro population in numbers and power when we compare with this the figures for 1896 for one ward; in that year the Negroes of the Seventh Ward paid $25,699.50 each month in rent, or $308,034 a year, an average of $126.19 per annum for each family. This ward may have a somewhat higher proportion of renters than most other wards. At the lowest estimate, however, the Negroes of Philadelphia pay at least $1,250,000 in rent each year.[2]

The table of rents for 1848 is as follows (see page 206):

We see that in 1848 the average Negro family rented by the month or quarter, and paid between four and five dollars per month rent. The highest average rent for any section was less than fifteen dollars a month. For such rents the poorest accommodations were afforded, and we know from descriptions that the mass of Negroes had small and unhealthful homes, usually on the back streets and alleys. The rents paid to-day in the Seventh Ward, according to the number of rooms, are tabulated on page 207.

Condensing this table somewhat we find that the Negroes pay rent as follows:

Under $5 per month	490 families, or 21.9 per cent			
$5 and under $10	643 "	" 28.7	"
$10 " " $15	380 "	" 17.0	"
$15 " " $20	252 "	" 11.3	"
$20 " " $30	375 "	" 17.0	"
$30 and over	95 "	" 4.1	"

The lodging system so prevalent in the Seventh Ward makes some rents appear higher than the real facts warrant. This ward is in the centre of the city, near the places of employment for the mass of the people and near the centre of their social life; consequently people crowd here in great numbers. Young couples just married engage lodging in one or two rooms; families join together

RENTS PAID BY NEGROES OF PHILADELPHIA, 1848

	City	Spring Garden	Northern Liberties	Southwark	Moyamensing	West Philadelphia	Total
Total rent paid annually	$124,979.37	$8,697.06	$11,128.00	$11,924.15	$40,809.51	$2,127.37	$199,665.46
Number tenements rented by the year	4	4	5	7	18	12	50
Annual average rent paid for same	$147.81	$125.00	$167.40	$148.43	$163.00	$66.60	. . .
Number tenements rented by the quarter	1,131	35	73	79	210	19	1,547
Annual average rent paid for same	$58.80	$56.97	$58.41	$55.37	$67.23	$37.48	. . .
Number tenements rented by the month	1,078	98	143	139	373	16	1,847
Annual average rent paid for same	$45.20	$46.68	$38.53	$38.78	$43.08	$32.78	. . .
Number tenements rented by the week	248	38	34	34	205	4	563
Annual average rent paid for same	$36.47	$42.84	$30.00	$32.94	$35.47	$22.84	. . .
Number tenements rented by the night	. . .	. . .	. . .	. . .	12	. . .	12
Annual average rent paid for same	. . .	. . .	. . .	. . .	$34.68	. . .	. . .
Number persons whose rent is repaid by sub-tenants	6	1	. . .	. . .	. . .	. . .	7
Number who pay tax for rent	. . .	. . .	3	. . .	. . .	. . .	3
Rent free	2	1	1	. . .	1	. . .	5
Own their houses	88	23	38	28	44	20	241
Not reported	5	3	. . .	. . .	3	. . .	11
Average annual rent per family	. . .	. . .	. . .	. . .	. . .	. . .	$49.68
Sums for 1837	. . .	. . .	. . .	. . .	. . .	. . .	$44.00

NEGRO HOMES, ACCORDING TO RENTS AND ROOMS[3]

Seventh Ward, Philadephia

NUMBER OF ROOMS

Amount of Rent per Month	One and Less	Two	Three	Four	Five	Six	Seven	Eight	Nine	Ten	Eleven and Over	Unknown	Grand Total Rent
Free	.	4	1	1	.	.	.	.	.	.	.	.	. . .
$1.00	.	.	.	.	.	.	.	.	.	.	.	.	. . .
1.50	2	.	.	.	.	.	.	.	.	.	.	.	$3.00
2.00	5	.	.	.	.	.	.	.	.	.	.	1	12.00
2.50	6	.	.	.	.	.	.	.	.	.	.	.	15.00
3.00	36	.	.	.	.	.	.	.	.	.	.	.	108.00
3.50	17	.	.	.	.	.	.	.	.	.	.	.	59.50
4.00	161	4	.	.	.	.	.	.	.	.	.	.	660.00
4.50	237	11	3	1	.	.	.	.	.	.	.	.	1,134.00
5.50	14	2	.	.	.	.	.	.	.	.	.	.	88.00
6.00	175	18	15	.	.	.	.	.	.	.	.	1	1,254.00
6.50	6	4	.	.	.	.	.	.	.	.	.	.	65.00
7.00	39	11	47	.	.	.	.	.	.	.	.	.	679.00
7.50	2	1	5	1	.	.	.	.	.	.	.	.	67.50
8.00	88	28	76	9	4	.	.	.	.	.	.	1	1648.0
8.50	.	2	10	.	.	.	.	.	.	.	.	.	102.00
9.00	3	2	68	9	.	1	.	.	.	.	.	.	747.00
9.50	.	.	1	.	.	.	.	.	.	.	.	.	9.50
10.00	17	8	43	32	7	3	1	.	.	.	.	.	1,110.00
10.50	.	.	2	.	.	.	.	.	.	.	.	.	21.00
11.00	.	1	19	10	3	.	.	.	.	.	.	.	363.00
11.50	.	.	2	.	.	.	.	.	.	.	.	.	23.00
12.00	.	8	48	46	25	11	1	.	.	.	.	.	139.00
13.00	.	.	11	18	10	3	1	.	.	.	.	.	569.00
14.00	.	.	8	17	13	9	3	.	.	.	.	.	700.00
15.00	.	.	10	15	18	31	2	1	1	.	.	.	1,170.00
16.00	.	.	.	5	21	28	5	1	.	.	.	.	960.00
17.00	.	.	.	.	3	8	1	1	.	.	.	.	221.00
18.00	.	1	.	1	8	52	20	6	2	.	.	.	1,620.00
19.00	.	.	.	.	.	6	2	2	1	.	.	.	209.00
20.00	.	.	.	2	4	50	35	16	7	1	.	.	2,300.00
21.00	.	.	.	.	.	3	5	4	2	.	.	.	294.00
22.00	.	.	.	.	.	11	12	5	2	.	.	.	660.00
23.00	.	.	.	.	2	8	8	18	7	1	.	.	1,012.00
24.00	.	.	.	.	.	3	1	1	.	.	.	.	120.00
25.00	.	.	.	1	2	21	27	38	21	12	9	.	3,275.00
26.00–28.00 . .	.	.	.	.	2	1	4	9	15	3	2	.	972.00
30.00	.	.	.	.	1	2	6	8	15	7	10	.	1,470.00
35.00	.	.	.	.	.	1	2	3	4	6	9	.	875.00
40.00	.	.	.	.	.	1	1	1	1	4	6	.	560.00
45.00	.	.	.	.	.	.	.	.	1	1	1	.	135.00
50.00	.	.	.	.	.	.	.	.	.	1	1	.	100.00
65.00	.	.	.	.	.	.	.	.	.	.	1	.	65.00
75.00	.	.	.	.	.	.	.	.	.	1	.	.	75.00
Owned and unknown . .	21	.	3	2	4	12	12	29	16	12	14	51	. . .

Total rent per month	$25,699.50	Aver. rent per year per family	$126.19
Total rent per year	$308,034.00	Aver. rent per year per individual,	$31.83
Aver. rent per month per family,	$10.50+		

and hire one house; and numbers of families take in single lodgers; thus the population of the ward is made up of

Families owning or renting their homes and living
    alone . . . .   738, or 31 per cent
Families owning or renting their homes, who take
    lodgers or sub-renters . . . .   937, " 38 "
Families sub-renting under other families . . . .   766, " 31 "

    Total individuals 7,751   100   "
    Total families   2,441
Individuals lodging with families 1,924

    Total individuals 9,675

The practice of sub-renting is found of course in all degrees: from the business of boarding-house keeper to the case of a family which rents out its spare bed-chamber. In the first case the rent is practically all repaid, and must in some cases be regarded as income; in the other cases a small fraction of the rent is repaid and the real rent and the size of the home reduced. Let us endeavor to determine what proportion of the rents of the Seventh Ward are repaid in sub-rents, omitting some boarding and lodging-houses where the sub-rent is really the income of the housewife. In most cases the room-rent of lodgers covers some return for the care of the room. The next table gives detailed statistics:

PROPORTION OF RENT REPAID IN SUB-RENT

Negroes of Seventh Ward, Philadelphia

| | MONTHLY RENT PAID: DOLLARS | | | | | | | | | | | | |
PROPORTION REPAID IN SUB-RENT	5 AND UNDER	OVER 5 AND UNDER 8	8 AND UNDER 10	10 AND UNDER 12	12 AND UNDER 15	15 AND UNDER 18	18 AND UNDER 20	20 AND UNDER 25	25 AND UNDER 30	30 AND OVER	UNKNOWN	TOTAL FAMILIES	APPROXIMATE TOTAL SUB-RENT: DOLLARS
One-eighth rep'd	.	.	1	1	.	.	.	4	7	6	.	19	61.08
One-sixth "	.	.	.	.	.	.	.	.	1	1	.	2	9.16
One-fourth "	1	.	1	1	8	23	16	31	9	8	1	99	460.51
One-third "	2	3	18	16	45	26	8	17	23	11	.	170	871.33
One-half "	2	17	37	20	17	26	23	55	31	14	1	243	1,748.75
Two-thirds "	.	2	11	6	24	11	10	7	21	6	1	109	1,246.33
Three-fourths "	.	2	4	2	6	11	7	23	19	6	.	80	1,201.08
Four-fifths "	.	.	.	.	.	.	.	1	.	1	.	2	48.00
Whole rent "	.	2	11	3	12	8	13	19	14	10	1	94	3,167.00
More than the whole rent repaid	1	.	4	3	5	2	2	14	13	13	.	57	
Unknown	.	.	.	.	.	.	.	.	.	.	62	62	. . .
Total families	.	.	.	.	.	.	.	.	.	.	.	937	. . .
Approximate total of sub-rent repaid monthly . .	.	.	.	.	.	.	.	.	.	.	.	.	8,813.24

It appears from this table that nearly $9,000 is paid by the sub-renting families and lodgers to the renting families. A part of this ought to be subtracted from the total rent paid if we would get at the net rent; just how much, however, should be called wages for care of room, or other conveniences furnished sub-renters, it is difficult to say. Possibly the net rent of the ward is $20,000, and of the city about $1,000,000.[4]

The accommodations furnished for the rent paid must now be considered. The number of rooms occupied is the simplest measurement, but is not very satisfactory in this case owing to the lodging system which makes it difficult to say how many rooms a family really occupies. A very large number of families of two and three rent a single bedroom and these must be regarded as one-room tenants, and yet this renting of a room often includes a limited use of a common kitchen; on the other hand this sub-renting family cannot in justice be counted as belonging to the renting family. The figures are:

```
829 families live in 1 room, including families lodging, or 35.2 per cent
104    "      "    "  2 rooms . . . . . . . . . . . . . .  or  4.4    "
371    "      "    "  3   "     . . . . . . . . . . . . . . . . or 15.7    "
170    "      "    "  4   "  ⎫
127    "      "    "  5   "  ⎬  . . . . . . . . . . . . . .  or 12.7    "
754    "      "    "  6   "  ⎭  or more . . . . . . . . . .  or 32.0    "
```

The number of families occupying one room is here exaggerated as before shown by the lodging system; on the other hand the number occupying six rooms and more is also somewhat exaggerated by the fact that not all sub-rented rooms have been subtracted, although this has been done as far as possible.

Of the 2,441 families only 334 had access to bathrooms and water-closets, or 13.7 per cent. Even these 334 families have poor accommodations in most instances. Many share the use of one bathroom with one or more other families. The bath-tubs usually are not supplied with hot water and very often have no water-connection at all. This condition is largely owing to the fact that the Seventh Ward belongs to the older part of Philadelphia, built when vaults in the yards were used exclusively and bathrooms could not be given space in the small houses. This was not so unhealthful before the houses were thick and when there were large back yards. To-day, however, the back yards have been filled by tenement houses and the bad sanitary results are shown in the death rate of the ward.

Even the remaining yards are disappearing. Of the 1,751 families making returns, 932 had a private yard 12 × 12 feet, or larger; 312 had a private yard smaller than 12 × 12 feet; 507 had either no yard at all or a yard and outhouse in common with the other denizens of the tenement or alley.

Of the latter only sixteen families had water-closets. So that over 20 per cent and possibly 30 per cent of the Negro families of this ward lack some of the very elementary accommodations necessary to health and decency. And this too in spite of the fact that they are paying comparatively high rents. Here too there comes another consideration, and that is the lack of public urinals and water-closets in this ward and, in fact, throughout Philadelphia. The result is that the closets of tenements are used by the public. A couple of diagrams will illustrate this; the houses of older Philadelphia were built like this:

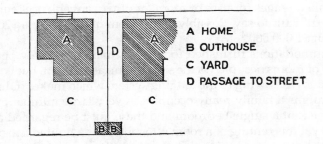

A HOME
B OUTHOUSE
C YARD
D PASSAGE TO STREET

When, however, certain districts like the Seventh Ward became crowded and given over to tenants, the thirst for money-getting led landlords in large numbers of cases to build up their back yards like this:

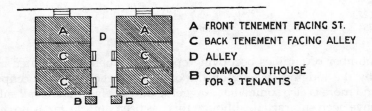

A FRONT TENEMENT FACING ST.
C BACK TENEMENT FACING ALLEY
D ALLEY
B COMMON OUTHOUSÉ FOR 3 TENANTS

This is the origin of numbers of the blind alleys and dark holes which make some parts of the Fifth, Seventh and Eighth Wards notorious. The closets in such cases are sometimes divided into compartments for different tenants, but in many cases not even this is done; and in all cases the alley closet becomes a public resort for pedestrians and loafers. The back tenements thus formed rent usually for from $7 to $9 a month, and sometimes for more. They consist of three rooms one above the other, small, poorly lighted and poorly ventilated. The inhabitants of the alley are at the mercy of its worst tenants; here policy shops abound, prostitutes ply their trade, and criminals hide. Most of these houses have to get their water at a hydrant in the alley, and must store their fuel in the house. These tenement abominations of Philadelphia are perhaps better than the vast tenement houses of New York, but they are bad enough, and cry for reform in housing.

The fairly comfortable working class live in houses of 3–6 rooms, with water in the house, but seldom with a bath. A three room house on a small street rents from $10 up; on Lombard street a 5–8 room house can be rented for from $18 to $30 according to location. The great mass of comfortably situated working people live in houses of 6–10 rooms, and sub-rent a part or take lodgers. A 5–7 room house on South Eighteenth street can be had for $20; on Florida street for $18; such houses have usually a parlor, dining room and kitchen on the first floor and two to four bedrooms, of which one or two are apt to be rented to a waiter or coachman for $4 a month, or to a married couple at $6–10 a month. The more elaborate houses are on Lombard street and its cross streets.

The rents paid by the Negroes are without doubt far above their means and often from one-fourth to three-fourths of the total income of a family goes in rent. This leads to much non-payment of rent both intentional and unintentional, to frequent shifting of homes, and above all to stinting the families in many necessities of life in order to live in respectable dwellings. Many a Negro family eats less than it ought for the sake of living in a decent house.

Some of this waste of money in rent is sheer ignorance and carelessness. The Negroes have an inherited distrust of banks and companies, and have long neglected to take part in Building and Loan Associations. Others are simply careless in the spending of their money and lack the shrewdness and business sense of differently trained peoples. Ignorance and carelessness however will not explain all or even the greater part of the problem of rent among Negroes. There are three causes of even greater importance: these are the limited localities where Negroes may rent, the peculiar connection of dwelling and occupation among Negroes and the social organization of the Negro. The undeniable fact that most Philadelphia white people prefer not to live near Negroes[5] limits the Negro very seriously in his choice of a home and especially in the choice of a cheap home. Moreover, real estate agents knowing the limited supply usually raise the rent a dollar or two for Negro tenants, if they do not refuse them altogether. Again, the occupations which the Negro follows, and which at present he is compelled to follow, are of a sort that makes it necessary for him to live near the best portions of the city; the mass of Negroes are in the economic world purveyors to the rich—working in private houses, in hotels, large stores, etc.[6] In order to keep this work they must live near by; the laundress cannot bring her Spruce street family's clothes from the Thirtieth Ward, nor can the waiter at the Continental Hotel lodge in Germantown. With the mass of white workmen this same necessity of living near work, does not hinder them from getting cheap dwellings; the factory is surrounded by cheap cottages, the foundry by long rows of houses, and even the white clerk and shop girl can, on account of their hours of labor, afford to live further out in the suburbs than the black porter who opens the store. Thus it is clear that the nature of the Negro's work compels him to crowd into the centre of the city much more than is the case with the mass of white working people. At the same time this necessity is apt in some cases to be overestimated, and a few hours of sleep or convenience serve to persuade a good many families to endure poverty in the Seventh Ward when they might be comfortable in the Twenty-fourth Ward. Nevertheless much of the Negro problem in this city finds adequate explanation when we reflect that here is a people receiving a little lower wages than usual for less desirable work, and compelled, in order to do that work, to live in a little less pleasant quarters than most people, and pay for them somewhat higher rents.

The final reason of the concentration of Negroes in certain localities is a social one and one peculiarly strong: the life of the Negroes of the city has for years centred in the Seventh Ward; here are the old churches, St. Thomas', Bethel, Central, Shiloh and Wesley; here are the halls of the secret societies; here are the homesteads of old families. To a race socially ostracised it means far more to move to remote parts of a city, than to those who will in any part of the city easily form congenial acquaintances and new ties. The Negro who ventures away from the mass of his people and their organized life, finds himself alone, shunned and taunted, stared at and made uncomfortable; he can make few new friends, for his neighbors however well-disposed would shrink to add a Negro to their list of acquaintances. Thus he remains far from friends and the concentred social life of the church, and feels in all its bitterness what it means to be a social outcast. Consequently emigration from the ward has gone in groups and centred itself about some church, and individual initiative is thus checked. At the same time color prejudice makes it difficult for groups to find suitable places to move to—one Negro family would be tolerated where six would be objected to; thus we have here a very decisive hindrance to emigration to the suburbs.

It is not surprising that this situation leads to considerable crowding in the homes, *i.e.*, to the endeavor to get as many people into the space hired as possible. It is this crowding that gives the casual observer many false notions as to the size of Negro families, since he often forgets that every other house has its subrenters and lodgers. It is however difficult to measure this crowding on account of this very lodging system which makes it very often uncertain as to just the number of rooms a given group of people occupy. In the following table therefore it is likely that the number of rooms given is somewhat greater than is really the case and that consequently there is more crowding than is indicated. This error however could not be wholly eliminated under the circumstances; a study of the table (page 213) shows that in the Seventh Ward there are 9,302 rooms occupied by 2,401 families, an average of 3.8 rooms to a family, and 1.04 individuals to a room. A division by rooms will better show where the crowding comes in.

Families occupying five rooms and less: 1,648, total rooms per family, 2.17; total individuals per room, 1.53.

Families occupying three rooms and less: 1,350, total rooms per family, 1.63; total individuals per room, 1.85.

The worst cases of crowding are as follows:

Two cases of 10 persons in 1 room.
One case of   9   "   1   "
Five cases of 7   "   1   "
Six cases of   6   "   1   "
Twenty-five cases of 5 persons in 1 room.
One case of   9 persons in 2 rooms.
One case of 16   "   3   "
One case of 13   "   3   "
One case of 11   "   3   "

As said before, this is probably something under the real truth, although perhaps not greatly so. The figures show considerable overcrowding, but not nearly as much as is often the case in other cities. This is largely due to the character of Philadelphia houses, which are small and low, and will not admit many inmates. Five persons in one room of an ordinary tenement would be almost suffocating. The large number of one-room tenements with two persons should

HOMES ACCORDING TO ROOMS AND PERSONS LIVING IN THEM

Persons

Rooms	One	Two	Three	Four	Five	Six	Seven	Eight	Nine	Ten	Eleven	Twelve	Thirteen	Fourteen	Fifteen	Sixteen	Seventeen and Over	Unknown	Homes, Total	Total Rooms
One	47	572	154	58	25	6	5	·	1	2	·	·	·	·	·	·	·	·	870	870
Two	5	38	33	19	6	1	2	·	1	·	·	·	·	·	·	·	·	·	105	210
Three	13	54	69	87	60	36	25	17	8	2	1	1	1	·	·	1	·	·	375	1,125
Four	6	24	35	42	19	19	7	7	5	4	·	3	·	·	·	·	·	·	171	684
Five	1	11	20	21	21	17	14	8	7	5	3	·	·	·	1	1	·	·	127	635
Six	1	5	14	46	38	47	40	24	20	9	10	5	2	1	1	·	·	·	263	1,578
Seven	·	2	10	26	19	23	13	12	14	7	7	5	3	3	2	·	4	·	148	1,036
Eight	4	9	7	17	17	19	12	15	11	8	6	9	2	3	·	·	3	·	143	1,144
Nine	·	1	10	13	8	14	10	8	12	7	5	2	1	2	1	1	·	·	95	855
Ten	·	2	5	6	2	4	5	4	·	5	2	3	3	1	1	1	4	·	48	480
Eleven	·	·	1	1	5	3	4	2	3	2	·	1	1	·	1	4	·	·	28	308
Twelve and over	·	1	2	1	1	1	2	1	4	4	2	1	2	1	2	·	7	·	28	377
Unknown	·	·	·	·	·	·	·	·	·	·	·	·	·	·	·	·	·	32	40	....
Total	76	720	360	341	222	190	139	98	86	55	36	29	15	8	7	9	18	32	2,441	9,302

be noted. These 572 families are for the most part young or childless couples, sub-renting a bedroom and working in the city.[7]

45. Sections and Wards—The spread of Negro population in the city during the nineteenth century is worth studying. In 1793,[8] one-fourth of the black inhabitants—or 538 persons—lived north of Market street and south of Vine, and were either in the homes of white families as servants, or in the alleys, as Shively's, Pewter Platter, Croomb's, Sugar, Cresson's, etc. Between Market and South lived one-half of the blacks, crowded in a region that centred at Sixth and Lombard: in Strawberry alley and lane, Elbow lane, Grey's alley, Shippen's alley, etc., besides in the families of the whites on Walnut, Spruce, Pine, etc. The remaining fourth of the population was in Southwark, south of South street, and in the Northern Liberties, north of Vine. Details are given in the next table:

NUMBER AND DISTRIBUTION OF THE NEGRO INHABITANTS OF PHILADELPHIA IN 1793—OCTOBER TO DECEMBER

(Taken from the Census of the Plague Committee)

BETWEEN MARKET AND VINE STREETS

STREETS, ETC.	NEGROES	STREETS, ETC.	NEGROES
Market	63	Quarry	4
Water	31	Cherry alley	25
Front	40	South alley	1
Second	29	North alley	4
Third	37	Sugar alley	14
Fourth	42	Appletree alley	7
Fifth	24	Cresson's alley	10
Sixth	32	Shively's alley	11
Seventh	8	Pewter Platter alley	3
Eighth	13	Croomb's alley	5
Ninth	3	Baker's alley	7
Arch	56	Brooks' court	1
Race	38	Priest's alley	6
Vine (south side)	9	Says alley	6
New	3		
Church alley	2	Total	538

BETWEEN MARKET AND SOUTH STREETS

STREETS, ETC.	NEGROES	STREETS, ETC.	NEGROES
Water	12	Penn	11
Front	129	Chestnut	50
Second	116	Walnut	83
Third	66	Spruce	66
Fourth	81	Pine	31
Fifth	63	South (north side)	32
Sixth	37	Strawberry lane	4
Seventh	0	Strawberry alley	2
Eighth	16	Elbow lane	10
Ninth	0	Beetles' alley	5

(Continued)

NUMBER AND DISTRIBUTION OF THE NEGRO INHABITANTS OF PHILADELPHIA IN
1793—OCTOBER TO DECEMBER—*Continued*

STREETS, ETC.	NEGROES	STREETS, ETC.	NEGROES
Grey's alley	13	Willing's alley	1
Norris alley	4	Blackberry alley	2
Dock	5	Carpenter	7
Union	32	Gaskill	7
Cypress alley	1	Georges to South	5
Pear	5	Little Water	5
Lombard	57	Stamper's alley	8
Emslie's alley	6	Taylor's alley	1
Laurel court	1	York court	7
Shippen's alley	26		
		Total	1,007

NORTHERN LIBERTIES

STREETS, ETC.	NEGROES	STREETS, ETC.	NEGROES
Water	1	Green	6
Front	59	Coates	32
Second	41	Brown	15
Third	1	Cable lane	1
Fourth	3	St. John	6
Fifth	1	St. Tammany	2
Vine (north side)	18	Willow	1
Callowhill	10	Wood's alley	1
Noble, or Bloody lane	4	Crown	3
Artillery lane (or Duke)	26		
		Total	233

DISTRICT OF SOUTHWARK

STREETS, ETC.	NEGROES	STREETS, ETC.	NEGROES
Swanson	22	Christian	6
South Penn	3	Queen	5
Front	15	Meade's alley	10
Second	22	German	3
Third	34	Plumb	5
Fifth	5	Moll Tuller's alley	4
Cedar court (south side)	19	George	8
Shippen	50	Ball alley	3
Almond	9	Crabtree alley	2
Catharine	33		
		Total	258

SUMMARY

Between Market and Vine streets	538
Between Market and South streets	1,007
North of Vine street	233
South of South street	258
Total	2,036
Total inhabitants of county by census of 1790	2,489

The changes from 1793 to 1838, nearly a half century, may thus be shown:

Place	1793	1838	
City	1,545—75.0%	8,462—60%	
Northern Liberties		878 ⎫	
Kensington	233—11.5%	359 ⎬	1,744—15%
Spring Garden		507 ⎭	
Southwark	258—13.5%	931 ⎫	3,385—25%
Moyamensing		2,454 ⎭	
Total	2036	13,591 + 5,000 servants	

Thus we see in 1838 that the centre of Negro population had gone southward toward Moyamensing. The Cedar, Locust, Newmarket, Pine and South Wards, as they were then called, had the bulk of the population, and they corresponded approximately to the Fourth, Fifth, Seventh and Eighth Wards of to-day.

Ten years later than this, in 1848,[9] we have a more detailed account of the distribution of the Negroes in the various sections of the city. They were mostly crowded into narrow courts and alleys. The colored population north of Vine and east of Sixth streets consisted of 272 families with 1,285 persons. One hundred and one families of these (415 persons) lived on Apple street and its courts, and in Paschall's alley (now Lynd street). Apple street itself, including Hick's court, had 37 families, with 138 persons, living in 16 houses; Shotwell's row, on the same street, had 16 families with 65 persons in 7 houses; the rooms were about 8 feet square. Paschall's alley contained 48 families with 212 persons, in 28 houses; one house had 7 families, 33 persons, living in 13 rooms, 8 feet square. The rent of the whole house was $266 per year; "yet all of them [i.e., these families] have comfortable beds and bedding."

About a third of the total Negro population of Moyamensing (the district "south of Cedar street and west of Passyunk road") was crowded into the space between Fifth and Eighth streets, and South and Fitzwater; for instance:

	FAMILIES		FAMILIES
Shippen street	55	Black Horse alley	5
Bedford street	63	Hutton's court	9
Small street	73	Yeager's court	9
Baker street	21	Dickerson's court	5
Seventh and South streets	14	Britton's court	5
Spafford street	16	Cryder's court	4
Freytag's alley	9	Sherman's court	13
Prosperous alley	11		
		Total	302

"It is in this district and in the adjoining portion of the city, especially Mary street and its vicinity, that the great destitution and wretchedness exist." The personal property of 176 of the above 302 families is returned as $603.50, or

$3.43 per family; 15 families (42 persons) on Small street (Alaska street) above Sixth, have their whole property valued at $7. Most of these Negroes were rag-pickers, and 29 out of 42 families were not natives of the State. Mary street and its courts had 80 families, with 281 persons living in 35 houses. Some were industrious and temperate, but there was "much surrounding misery." In Gile's alley (from Cedar to Lombard street) were 42 families, 147 persons, in 20 houses. Eighty-three of these persons were not natives of the State, and 13 of the families received public charity. A description of this district in 1847 is interesting:

"The vicinity of the place we sought was pointed out by a large number of colored people congregated on the neighboring pavements. We first inspected the rooms, yards and cellars of the four or five houses next above Baker street on Seventh. The cellars were wretchedly dark, damp and dirty, and were generally rented for twelve and a half cents per night. These are occupied by one or more families at the present time, but in the winter season when the frost drives those who in summer sleep abroad in fields, in boardyards and in sheds, to seek more effectual shelter, they often contain from twelve to twenty lodgers per night. Commencing at the back of each house are small wooden buildings roughly put together, about six feet square, without windows or fireplaces, a hole about a foot square being left in front along side of the door to let in fresh air and light, and to let out foul air and smoke. These desolate pens, the roofs of which are generally leaky, and their floors so low that more or less water comes in on them from the yard in rainy weather, would not give comfortable winter accommodations to a cow. Although as dismal as dirt, damp and insufficient ventilation can make them, they are nearly all inhabited. In one of the first we entered, we found the dead body of a large Negro man who had died suddenly there. This pen was about eight feet deep by six wide. There was no bedding in it, but a box or two around the sides furnished places where two colored persons, one said to be the wife of the deceased, were lying either drunk or fast asleep. The body of the dead man was on the wet floor beneath an old torn coverlet."[10]

In 1853 a similar description of the crime, filth and poverty of this district shows us that the present slums do not compare with those in misfortune and depravity.[11] Much of this poverty and degradation could in 1847 be laid at the door of the new immigrants, and although some of the immigrants were in good circumstances, yet in general most of the poverty was found where most of the immigrants were. The immigrants formed the following percentages of the total population in 1847:

City	47.7 per cent
Moyamensing	46.3 "
Southwark	35.9 "
West Philadelphia	34.3 "
Spring Garden	31.4 "
Northern Liberties	14.2 "

The historic centre of Negro settlement in the city can thus be seen to be at Sixth and Lombard. From this point it moved north, as is indicated for instance by the establishment of Zoar Church in 1794. Immigration of foreigners and the rise of industries, however, early began to turn it back and it found outlet in the alleys of Southwark and Moyamensing. For a while about 1840 it was bottled up here, but finally it began to move west. A few early left the mass and settled in West Philadelphia; the rest began a slow steady movement along Lombard street. The influx of 1876 and thereafter sent the wave across Broad street to a new centre at Seventeenth and Lombard. There it divided into two streams; one went north and joined remnants of the old settlers in the Northern Liberties and Spring Garden. The other went south to the Twenty-sixth, Thirtieth and Thirty-sixth Wards. Meantime the new immigrants poured in at Seventh and Lombard, while Sixth and Lombard down to the Delaware was deserted to the Jews, and Moyamensing partially to the Italians. The Irish were pushed on beyond Eighteenth to the Schuylkill, or emigrated to the mills of Kensington and elsewhere. The course may be thus graphically represented (see page 219):

This migration explains much that is paradoxical about Negro slums, especially their present remnant at Seventh and Lombard. Many people wonder that the mission and reformatory agencies at work there for so many years have so little to show by way of results. One answer is that this work has new material continually to work upon, while the best classes move to the west and leave the dregs behind. The parents and grandparents of some of the best families of Philadelphia Negroes were born in the neighborhood of Sixth and Lombard at a time when all Negroes, good, bad and indifferent, were confined to that and a few other localities. With the greater freedom of domicile which has since come, these slum districts have sent a stream of emigrants westward. There has, too, been a general movement from the alleys to the streets and from the back to the front streets. Moreover it is untrue that the slums of Seventh and Lombard have not greatly changed in character; compared with 1840, 1850 or even 1870 these slums are much improved in every way. More and more every year the unfortunate and poor are being sifted out from the vicious and criminal and sent to better quarters.

And yet with all the obvious improvement, there are still slums and dangerous slums left. Of the Fifth Ward and adjoining parts of the Seventh, a city health inspector says:

"Few of the houses are underdrained, and if the closets have sewer connections the people are too careless to keep them in order. The streets and alleys are strewn with garbage, excepting immediately after the visit of the street cleaner. Penetrate into one of these houses and beyond into the back yard, if there is one (frequently there is not), and there will be found a pile of ashes, garbage and filth, the accumulation of the winter, perhaps of the whole year. In such heaps of refuse what disease germ may be breeding?"[12]

To take a typical case:

"Gillis' Alley, famed in the Police Court, is a narrow alley, extending from Lombard street through to South street, above Fifth street, cobbled and without sewer connections. Houses and stables are mixed promiscuously. Buildings are of frame and of brick. No.—looks both outside and in like a Southern Negro's

MIGRATION OF THE NEGRO POPULATION, 1790–1890.

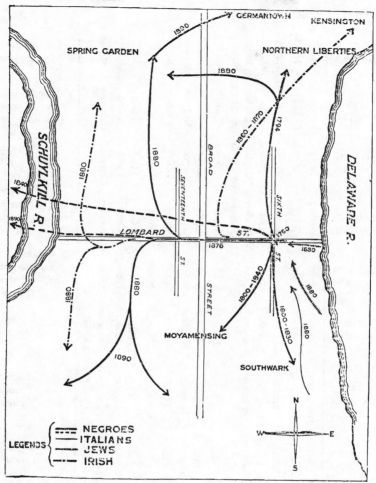

cabin. In this miserable place four colored families have their homes. The aggregate rent demanded is $22 a month, though the owner seldom receives the full rent. For three small dark rooms in the rear of another house in this alley, the tenants pay, and have paid for thirteen years, $11 a month. The entrance is by a court not over two feet wide. Except at midday the sun does not shine in the small open space in the rear that answers for a yard. It is safe to say that not one house in this alley could pass an inspection without being condemned as prejudicial to health. But if they are so condemned and cleaned, with such inhabitants how long will they remain clean?"[13]

Some of the present characteristics of the chief alleys where Negroes live are given in the following table:

SOME ALLEYS WHERE NEGROES LIVE

	GOVETT'S COURT	HINES' COURT	ALLEN'S COURT	HORSTMAN'S COURT	LOMBARD ROW	TURNER'S COURT	ALLEY OFF CARVER STREET	McCANN'S COURT	CROSS ALLEY
General Character	Poor	Poor	Very Poor	Squalid	Fair	Wretched	Fair	Poor	Bad
Width, in feet	3	3–6	6	12	9	3–12	6	12	12
Paved with	Bricks	Bricks	Bricks	Bricks	Bricks	Bricks	Bricks	Bricks	Asphalt
Character of Dwelling	Poor	Back Yard Tenements	Back Yard Tenements	Back Yard Tenements	Fair	Old Wooden Houses	Old Brick Tenements	Old Brick Tenements	Wood and Brick
Number of Stories in Houses	3	3	3	2 and 3	3	1 to 3	3	2 to 3	2 to 3
Inhabitants	All Negroes	All Negroes	All Negroes	All Negroes	Negroes and Jews	All Negroes	Jews and Negroes	All Negroes	Jews and Negroes
Cleanliness, etc.	Fair	Fair	Dirty	Dirty	Fair	Fair	Fair	Fair	Dirty
Width of Sidewalk . . feet.	4	5	6	None	None	None	None	None	None
Lighted by	No Lights	No Lights	No Lights	1 Gas Lamp	1 Gas Lamp	1 Gas Lamp	1 Gas Lamp	1 Gas Lamp	No Lights
Privies in Common or Private	Common	2 for whole Alley	1/2 for each House	5 in open Court	Private	Common	Common	Common	Common
Remarks		Emigrants from 5th Ward slums	Poor and Doubtful Characters	Very Poor People	Respectable Homes mingled with Gamblers and Prostitutes	Many Empty Houses; Poor and Doubtful People	"Blind" Alley; Fairly Respectable	Poor People and some Questionable	Some Bad Characters

The general characteristics and distribution of the Negro population at present in the different wards can only be indicated in general terms. The wards with the best Negro population are parts of the Seventh, Twenty-sixth, Thirtieth and Thirty-sixth, Fourteenth, Fifteenth, Twenty-fourth, Twenty-seventh and Twenty-ninth. The worst Negro population is found in parts of the Seventh, and in the Fourth, Fifth and Eighth. In the other wards either the classes are mixed or there are very few colored people. The tendency of the best migration to-day is toward the Twenty-sixth, Thirtieth and Thirty-sixth Wards, and West Philadelphia.

46. Social Classes and Amusements—Notwithstanding the large influence of the physical environment of home and ward, nevertheless there is a far mightier influence to mold and make the citizen, and that is the social atmosphere which surrounds him: first his daily companionship, the thoughts and whims of his class; then his recreations and amusements; finally the surrounding world of American civilization, which the Negro meets especially in his economic life. Let us take up here the subject of social classes and amusements among Negroes, reserving for the next chapter a study of the contact of the Whites and Blacks.

There is always a strong tendency on the part of the community to consider the Negroes as composing one practically homogeneous mass. This view has of course a certain justification: the people of Negro descent in this land have had a common history, suffer to-day common disabilities, and contribute to one general set of social problems. And yet if the foregoing statistics have emphasized any one fact it is that wide variations in antecedents, wealth, intelligence and general efficiency have already been differentiated within this group. These differences are not, to be sure, so great or so patent as those among the whites of to-day, and yet they undoubtedly equal the difference among the masses of the people in certain sections of the land fifty or one hundred years ago; and there is no surer way of misunderstanding the Negro or being misunderstood by him than by ignoring manifest differences of condition and power in the 40,000 black people of Philadelphia.

And yet well-meaning people continually do this. They regale the thugs and whoremongers and gamblers of Seventh and Lombard streets with congratulations on what the Negroes have done in a quarter century, and pity for their disabilities; and they scold the caterers of Addison street for the pickpockets and paupers of the race. A judge of the city courts, who for years has daily met a throng of lazy and debased Negro criminals, comes from the bench to talk to the Negroes about their criminals: he warns them first of all to leave the slums and either forgets or does not know that the fathers of the audience he is speaking to, left the slums when he was a boy and that the people before him are as distinctly differentiated from the criminals he has met, as honest laborers anywhere differ from thieves.

Nothing more exasperates the better class of Negroes than this tendency to ignore utterly their existence. The law-abiding, hard-working inhabitants of the Thirtieth Ward are aroused to righteous indignation when they see that the word Negro carries most Philadelphians' minds to the alleys of the Fifth Ward or the police courts. Since so much misunderstanding or rather forgetfulness and carelessness on this point is common, let us endeavor to try and fix with some definiteness the different social classes which are clearly enough defined among Negroes to deserve attention. When the statistics of the families of the Seventh Ward were gathered, each family was put in one of four grades as follows:

Grade 1. Families of undoubted respectability earning sufficient income to live well; not engaged in menial service of any kind; the wife engaged in no occupation save that of house-wife, except in a few cases where she had special employment at home. The children not compelled to be bread-winners, but found in school; the family living in a well-kept home.

Grade 2. The respectable working-class; in comfortable circumstances, with a good home, and having steady remunerative work. The younger children in school.

Grade 3. The poor; persons not earning enough to keep them at all times above want; honest, although not always energetic or thrifty, and with no touch of gross immorality or crime. Including the very poor, and the poor.

Grade 4. The lowest class of criminals, prostitutes and loafers; the "submerged tenth."

Thus we have in these four grades the criminals, the poor, the laborers, and the well-to-do.[14] The last class represents the ordinary middle-class folk of most modern countries, and contains the germs of other social classes which the Negro has not yet clearly differentiated. Let us begin first with the fourth class.

The criminals and gamblers are to be found at such centres as Seventh and Lombard streets, Seventeenth and Lombard, Twelfth and Kater, Eighteenth and Naudain, etc. Many people have failed to notice the significant change which has come over these slums in recent years; the squalor and misery and dumb suffering of 1840 has passed, and in its place have come more baffling and sinister phenomena: shrewd laziness, shameless lewdness, cunning crime. The loafers who line the curbs in these places are no fools, but sharp, wily men who often outwit both the Police Department and the Department of Charities. Their nucleus consists of a class of professional criminals, who do not work, figure in the rogues' galleries of a half-dozen cities, and migrate here and there. About these are a set of gamblers and sharpers who seldom are caught in serious crime, but who nevertheless live from its proceeds and aid and abet it. The headquarters of all these are usually the political clubs and pool-rooms; they stand ready to entrap the unwary and tempt the weak. Their organization, tacit or recognized, is very effective, and no one can long watch their actions without seeing that they keep in close touch with the authorities in some way. Affairs will be gliding on lazily some summer afternoon at the corner of Seventh and Lombard streets; a few loafers on the corners, a prostitute here and there, and the Jew and Italian plying their trades. Suddenly there is an oath, a sharp altercation, a blow; then a hurried rush of feet, the silent door of a neighboring club closes, and when the policeman arrives only the victim lies bleeding on the sidewalk; or at midnight the drowsy quiet will be suddenly broken by the cries and quarreling of a half-drunken gambling table; then comes the sharp, quick crack of pistol shots—a scurrying in the darkness, and only the wounded man lies awaiting the patrol-wagon. If the matter turns out seriously, the police know where in Minster street and Middle alley to look for the aggressor; often they find him, but sometimes not.[15]

The size of the more desperate class of criminals and their shrewd abettors is of course comparatively small, but it is large enough to characterize the slum districts. Around this central body lies a large crowd of satellites and feeders: young idlers attracted by excitement, shiftless and lazy ne'er-do-wells, who have sunk from better things, and a rough crowd of pleasure seekers and libertines. These are the fellows who figure in the police courts for larceny and fighting, and drift thus into graver crime or shrewder dissoluteness. They are usually far more ignorant than their leaders, and rapidly die out from disease and excess. Proper measures for rescue and reform might save many of this class. Usually they are not natives of the city, but immigrants who have wandered from the small towns of the South to Richmond and Washington and thence to Philadelphia. Their environment in this city makes it easier for them to live by crime or the results of crime than by work, and being without ambition—or perhaps having lost ambition and grown bitter with the world—they drift with the stream.

One large element of these slums, a class we have barely mentioned, are the prostitutes. It is difficult to get at any satisfactory data concerning such a class, but an attempt has been made. There were in 1896 fifty-three Negro women in the Seventh Ward known on pretty satisfactory evidence to be supported wholly or largely by the proceeds of prostitution; and it is probable that this is not half the real number;[16] these fifty-three were of the following ages:

14 to 19	2
20 to 24	11
25 to 29	9
30 to 39	17
40 to 49	3
50 and over	2
Unknown	9
Total	53

Seven of these women had small children with them and had probably been betrayed, and had then turned to this sort of life. There were fourteen recognized bawdy houses in the ward; ten of them were private dwellings where prostitutes lived and were not especially fitted up, although male visitors frequented them. Four of the houses were regularly fitted up, with elaborate furniture, and in one or two cases had young and beautiful girls on exhibition. All of these latter were seven- or eight-room houses for which $26 to $30 a month was paid. They are pretty well-known resorts, but are not disturbed. In the slums the lowest class of street walkers abound and ply their trade among Negroes, Italians and Americans. One can see men following them into alleys in broad daylight. They usually have male associates whom they support and who join them in "badger" thieving. Most of them are grown women though a few cases of girls under sixteen have been seen on the street.

This fairly characterizes the lowest class of Negroes. According to the inquiry in the Seventh Ward at least 138 families were estimated as belonging to this class out of 2,395 reported, or 5.8 per cent. This would include between five and six hundred individuals. Perhaps this number reaches 1000 if the facts were known, but the evidence at hand furnishes only the number stated. In the whole city the number may reach 3,000, although there is little data for an estimate.[17]

The next class are the poor and unfortunate and the casual laborers; most of these are of the class of Negroes who in the contact with the life of a great city have failed to find an assured place. They include immigrants who cannot get steady work; good-natured, but unreliable and shiftless persons who cannot keep work or spend their earnings thoughtfully; those who have suffered accident and misfortune; the maimed and defective classes, and the sick; many widows and orphans and deserted wives; all these form a large class and are here considered. It is of course very difficult to separate the lowest of this class from the one below, and probably many are included here who, if the truth were known, ought to be classed lower. In most cases, however, they have been given the benefit of the doubt. The lowest ones of this class usually live in the slums and back streets, and next door or in the same house often, with criminals and lewd women. Ignorant and easily influenced, they readily go with the tide and now rise to industry and decency, now fall to crime. Others of this class get on fairly well in good times, but never get far ahead. They are the ones who earliest feel the weight of hard times and their latest blight. Some correspond to the "worthy poor" of most charitable organizations, and some fall a little below that class. The children of this class are the feeders of the criminal classes. Often in the same family one can find respectable and striving parents weighed down by idle, impudent sons and way-ward daughters. This is partly because of poverty, more because of the poor home life. In the Seventh Ward 30½ per cent of the families or 728 may be put into this class, including the very poor, the poor and those who manage just to make ends meet in good times. In the whole city perhaps ten to twelve thousand Negroes fall in this third social grade.

Above these come the representative Negroes; the mass of the servant class, the porters and waiters, and the best of the laborers. They are hard-working people, proverbially good-natured; lacking a little in foresight and forehanded-ness, and in "push." They are honest and faithful, of fair and improving morals, and beginning to accumulate property. The great drawback to this class is lack of congenial occupation especially among the young men and women, and the consequent wide-spread dissatisfaction and complaint. As a class these persons are ambitious; the majority can read and write, many have a common school training, and all are anxious to rise in the world. Their wages are low compared with corresponding classes of white workmen, their rents are high, and the field of advancement opened to them is very limited. The best expression of the life of this group is the Negro church, where their social life centres, and where they discuss their situation and prospects.

A note of disappointment and discouragement is often heard at these discussions and their work suffers from a growing lack of interest in it. Most of them are probably best fitted for the work they are doing, but a large percentage deserve better ways to display their talent, and better remuneration. The whole class deserves credit for its bold advance in the midst of discouragements, and for the distinct moral improvement in their family life during the last quarter century. These persons form 56 per cent or 1,252 of the families of the Seventh Ward, and include perhaps 25,000 of the Negroes of the city. They live in 5–10-room houses, and usually have lodgers. The houses are always well furnished with neat parlors and some musical instrument. Sunday dinners and small parties, together with church activities, make up their social intercourse. Their chief trouble is in finding suitable careers for their growing children.

Finally we come to the 277 families, 11.5 per cent of those of the Seventh Ward, and including perhaps 3,000 Negroes in the city, who form the aristocracy of the Negro population in education, wealth and general social efficiency. In many respects it is right and proper to judge a people by its best classes rather than by its worst classes or middle ranks. The highest class of any group represents its possibilities rather than its exceptions, as is so often assumed in regard to the Negro. The colored people are seldom judged by their best classes, and often the very existence of classes among them is ignored. This is partly due in the North to the anomalous position of those who compose this class; they are not the leaders or the ideal-makers of their own group in thought, work, or morals. They teach the masses to a very small extent, mingle with them but little, do not largely hire their labor. Instead then of social classes held together by strong ties of mutual interest we have in the case of the Negroes, classes who have much to keep them apart, and only community of blood and color prejudice to bind them together. If the Negroes were by themselves either a strong aristocratic system or a dictatorship would for the present prevail. With, however, democracy thus prematurely thrust upon them, the first impulse of the best, the wisest and richest is to segregate themselves from the mass. This action, however, causes more of dislike and jealousy on the part of the masses than usual, because those masses look to the whites for ideals and largely for leadership. It is natural therefore that even to-day the mass of Negroes should look upon the worshipers at St. Thomas' and Central as feeling themselves above them, and should dislike them for it. On the other hand it is just as natural for the well-educated and well-to-do Negroes to feel themselves far above the criminals and prostitutes of Seventh and Lombard streets, and even above the servant girls and porters of the middle class of workers. So far they are justified; but they make their mistake in failing to recognize that, however laudable an ambition to rise may be, the first duty of an upper class is to serve the lowest classes. The aristocracies of all peoples have been slow in learning this and perhaps the Negro is no slower than the rest, but his peculiar situation demands that in his case this lesson be learned sooner. Naturally the uncertain economic status even of this picked class makes it difficult for them to spare much time and energy in social reform; compared with their fellows they are rich, but compared with white Americans they are poor, and they can hardly fulfill their duty as the leaders of the Negroes until they are captains of industry over their people as well as richer and wiser. To-day the professional class among them is, compared with other callings, rather over-represented, and all have a struggle to maintain the position they have won.

This class is itself an answer to the question of the ability of the Negro to assimilate American culture. It is a class small in numbers and not sharply differentiated from other classes, although sufficiently so to be easily recognized.

Its members are not to be met with in the ordinary assemblages of the Negroes, nor in their usual promenading places. They are largely Philadelphia born, and being descended from the house-servant class, contain many mulattoes. In their assemblies there are evidences of good breeding and taste, so that a foreigner would hardly think of ex-slaves. They are not to be sure people of wide culture and their mental horizon is as limited as that of the first families in a country town. Here and there may be noted, too, some faint trace of careless moral training. On the whole they strike one as sensible, good folks. Their conversation turns on the gossip of similar circles among the Negroes of Washington, Boston and New York; on questions of the day, and, less willingly, on the situation of the Negro. Strangers secure entrance to this circle with difficulty and only by introduction. For an ordinary white person it would be almost impossible to secure introduction even by a friend. Once in a while some well-known citizen meets a company of this class, but it is hard for the average white American to lay aside his patronizing way toward a Negro, and to talk of aught to him but the Negro question; the lack, therefore, of common ground even for conversation makes such meetings rather stiff and not often repeated. Fifty-two of these families keep servants regularly; they live in well-appointed homes, which give evidence of taste and even luxury.[18]

Something must be said, before leaving this subject, of the amusements of the Negroes. Among the fourth grade and the third, gambling, excursions, balls and cake-walks are the chief amusements. The gambling instinct is widespread, as in all low classes, and, together with sexual looseness, is their greatest vice; it is carried on in clubs, in private houses, in pool-rooms and on the street. Public gambling can be found at a dozen different places every night at full tilt in the Seventh Ward, and almost any stranger can gain easy access. Games of pure chance are preferred to those of skill, and in the larger clubs a sort of three-card monte is the favorite game, played with a dealer who gambles against all comers. In private houses in the slums, cards, beer and prostitutes can always be found. In the public pool-rooms there is some quiet gambling and playing for prizes. For the new comer to the city the only open places of amusement are these pool-rooms and gambling clubs; here are crowds of young fellows, and once started in this company no one can say where they may not end.

The most innocent amusements of this class are the balls and cake-walks, although they are accompanied by much drinking, and are attended by white and black prostitutes. The cake-walk is a rhythmic promenade or slow dance, and when well done is pretty and quite innocent. Excursions are frequent in summer, and are accompanied often by much fighting and drinking.

The mass of the laboring Negroes get their amusement in connection with the churches. There are suppers, fairs, concerts, socials and the like. Dancing is forbidden by most of the churches, and many of the stricter sort would not think of going to balls or theatres. The younger set, however, dance, although the parents seldom accompany them, and the hours kept are late, making it often a dissipation. Secret societies and social clubs add to these amusements by balls and suppers, and there are numbers of parties at private houses. This class also patronizes frequent excursions given by churches and Sunday schools and secret societies;

they are usually well conducted, but cost a great deal more than is necessary. The money wasted in excursions above what would be necessary for a day's outing and plenty of recreation, would foot up many thousand dollars in a season.

In the upper class alone has the home begun to be the centre of recreation and amusement. There are always to be found parties and small receptions, and gatherings at the invitations of musical or social clubs. One large ball each year is usually given, which is strictly private. Guests from out of town are given much social attention.

Among nearly all classes of Negroes there is a large unsatisfied demand for amusement. Large numbers of servant girls and young men have flocked to the city, have no homes, and want places to frequent. The churches supply this need partially, but the institution which will supply this want better and add instruction and diversion, will save many girls from ruin and boys from crime. There is to-day little done in places of public amusement to protect colored girls from designing men. Many of the idlers and rascals of the slums play on the affections of silly servant girls, and either ruin them or lead them into crime, or more often live on a part of their wages. There are many cases of this latter system to be met in the Seventh Ward.

It is difficult to measure amusements in any enlightening way. A count of the amusements reported by the *Tribune*, the chief colored paper, which reports for a select part of the laboring class, and the upper class, resulted as follows for nine weeks:[19]

Parties at homes in honor of visitors	16
" " homes	11
" " " with dancing	10
Balls in halls	10
Concerts in churches	7
Church suppers, etc.	7
Weddings	7
Birthday parties	7
Lectures and literary entertainments at churches	6
Card parties	4
Fairs at churches	3
Lawn parties and picnics	3
	91

These, of course, are the larger parties in the whole city, and do not include the numerous small church socials and gatherings. The proportions here are largely accidental, but the list is instructive.

NOTES

1. "Condition," etc., 1848, p. 16.
2. Not taking into account sub-rent repaid by sub-tenants; subtracting this and the sum would be, perhaps, $1,000,000—see *infra*, p. 291. That paid by single lodgers ought not, of course, to be subtracted as it has not been added in.
3. The returns as to rents paid are among the most reliable of the statistics gathered. The amount of rent is always well known, and there are few motives for deception. Moreover in Philadelphia there is a tendency to build rows and streets of houses with the same general design. These rent for the

same sum, and thus particular instances of false report are easily detected. One feature of the returns must be noted, *i.e.*, the large number of cases where high rents are paid for one- and two-room tenements. In nearly all of these cases this rent is paid for large front bedrooms in good localities, and often includes furniture. Sometimes a limited use of the family kitchen is also included. In such cases it is misleading to call these one-room tenements. No other arrangement, however, seemed practical in these tables.

4. Here, again, the proportion paid by single lodgers must not be subtracted as it has not been added in before.

5. The sentiment has greatly lessened in intensity during the last two decades, but it is still strong; cf. section 47.

6. At the same time, from long custom and from competition, their wages for this work are not high.

7. One room under such circumstances may not by any means denote excessive poverty or indecency; the room is usually rented in a good locality and is well furnished. Cf. note 3.

8. During the plague of that year a census of the inhabitants remaining in the city was taken. Five-sixths of the Negroes remained, so the census gives a good idea of the distribution of the Negro population. The results are published in the report printed afterward by order of Councils.

9. The figures for 1838 and 1848 are from the inquiries of those dates; cf. census of 1840.

10. "Condition of Negroes," 1848, pp. 34–41.

11. "Mysteries and Miseries of Philadelphia." (Pamphlet.)

12. Dr. Frances Van Gasken in a tract published by the Civic Club.

13. *Ibid.*

14. It will be noted that this classification differs materially from the economic division in Chapter XI. In that case grade four and a part of three appear as the "poor;" grade two and the rest of grade three, as the "fair to comfortable;" and a few of grade two and grade one as the well-to-do. The basis of division there was almost entirely according to income; this division brings in moral considerations and questions of expenditure, and consequently reflects more largely the personal judgment of the investigator.

15. The investigator resided at the College Settlement, Seventh and Lombard streets, some months, and thus had an opportunity to observe this slum carefully.

16. These figures were taken during the inquiry by the visitor to the houses.

17. This includes not simply the actual criminal class, but its aiders and abettors, and the class intimately associated with it. It would, for instance, include much more than Charles Booth's class A in London.

18. A comparison of the size of families in the highest and lowest class may be of interest:

Number in Family	First Grade	Fourth Grade
One	22 — 8%	17 — 12%
Two	66 — 24%	58 — 42%
Three	54 — 19%	27 — 20%
Four	48	21
Five	25 — 33%	6 — 24%
Six	18	6
Seven	20	2
Eight	7 — 12%	0 — 2%
Nine	5	1
Ten	7	0
Eleven	0 4%	0 — 0%
Twelve or more	5	0
Total	277	138

Average size of family, first grade, 4.07%; fourth grade, 2.08%.

This certainly looks like the survival of the fittest, and is hardly an argument for the extinction of the civilized Negro.

19. These weeks were not consecutive but taken at random.

CHAPTER XVI

◆

The Contact of the Races

47. Color Prejudice—Incidentally throughout this study the prejudice against the Negro has been again and again mentioned. It is time now to reduce this somewhat indefinite term to something tangible. Everybody speaks of the matter, everybody knows that it exists, but in just what form it shows itself or how influential it is few agree. In the Negro's mind, color prejudice in Philadelphia is that widespread feeling of dislike for his blood, which keeps him and his children out of decent employment, from certain public conveniences and amusements, from hiring houses in many sections, and in general, from being recognized as a man. Negroes regard this prejudice as the chief cause of their present unfortunate condition. On the other hand most white people are quite unconscious of any such powerful and vindictive feeling; they regard color prejudice as the easily explicable feeling that intimate social intercourse with a lower race is not only undesirable but impracticable if our present standards of culture are to be maintained; and although they are aware that some people feel the aversion more intensely than others, they cannot see how such a feeling has much influence on the real situation or alters the social condition of the mass of Negroes.

As a matter of fact, color prejudice in this city is something between these two extreme views: it is not to-day responsible for all, or perhaps the greater part of the Negro problems, or of the disabilities under which the race labors; on the other hand it is a far more powerful social force than most Philadelphians realize. The practical results of the attitude of most of the inhabitants of Philadelphia toward persons of Negro descent are as follows:

1. As to getting work:

No matter how well trained a Negro may be, or how fitted for work of any kind, he cannot in the ordinary course of competition hope to be much more than a menial servant.

He cannot get clerical or supervisory work to do save in exceptional cases.

He cannot teach save in a few of the remaining Negro schools.

He cannot become a mechanic except for small transient jobs, and cannot join a trades union.

A Negro woman has but three careers open to her in this city: domestic service, sewing, or married life.

2. As to keeping work:

The Negro suffers in competition more severely than white men.

Change in fashion is causing him to be replaced by whites in the better paid positions of domestic service.

Whim and accident will cause him to lose a hard-earned place more quickly than the same things would affect a white man.

Being few in number compared with the whites the crime or carelessness of a few of his race is easily imputed to all, and the reputation of the good, industrious and reliable suffer thereby.

Because Negro workmen may not often work side by side with white workmen, the individual black workman is rated not by his own efficiency, but by the efficiency of a whole group of black fellow workmen which may often be low.

Because of these difficulties which virtually increase competition in his case, he is forced to take lower wages for the same work than white workmen.

3. As to entering new lines of work:

Men are used to seeing Negroes in inferior positions; when, therefore, by any chance a Negro gets in a better position, most men immediately conclude that he is not fitted for it, even before he has a chance to show his fitness.

If, therefore, he set up a store, men will not patronize him.

If he is put into public position men will complain.

If he gain a position in the commercial world, men will quietly secure his dismissal or see that a white man succeeds him.

4. As to his expenditure:

The comparative smallness of the patronage of the Negro, and the dislike of other customers makes it usual to increase the charges or difficulties in certain directions in which a Negro must spend money.

He must pay more house-rent for worse houses than most white people pay.

He is sometimes liable to insult or reluctant service in some restaurants, hotels and stores, at public resorts, theatres and places of recreation; and at nearly all barber shops.

5. As to his children:

The Negro finds it extremely difficult to rear children in such an atmosphere and not have them either cringing or impudent: if he impresses upon them patience with their lot, they may grow up satisfied with their condition; if he inspires them with ambition to rise, they may grow to despise their own people, hate the whites and become embittered with the world.

His children are discriminated against, often in public schools.

They are advised when seeking employment to become waiters and maids.

They are liable to species of insult and temptation peculiarly trying to children.

6. As to social intercourse:

In all walks of life the Negro is liable to meet some objection to his presence or some discourteous treatment; and the ties of friendship or memory seldom are strong enough to hold across the color line.

If an invitation is issued to the public for any occasion, the Negro can never know whether he would be welcomed or not; if he goes he is liable to have his feelings hurt and get into unpleasant altercation; if he stays away, he is blamed for indifference.

If he meet a lifelong white friend on the street, he is in a dilemma; if he does not greet the friend he is put down as boorish and impolite; if he does greet the friend he is liable to be flatly snubbed.

If by chance he is introduced to a white woman or man, he expects to be ignored on the next meeting, and usually is.

White friends may call on him, but he is scarcely expected to call on them, save for strictly business matters.

If he gain the affections of a white woman and marry her he may invariably expect that slurs will be thrown on her reputation and on his, and that both his and her race will shun their company.[1]

When he dies he cannot be buried beside white corpses.

7. The result:

Any one of these things happening now and then would not be remarkable or call for especial comment; but when one group of people suffer all these little differences of treatment and discriminations and insults continually, the result is either discouragement, or bitterness, or over-sensitiveness, or recklessness. And a people feeling thus cannot do their best.

Presumably the first impulse of the average Philadelphian would be emphatically to deny any such marked and blighting discrimination as the above against a group of citizens in this metropolis. Every one knows that in the past color prejudice in the city was deep and passionate; living men can remember when a Negro could not sit in a street car or walk many streets in peace. These times have passed, however, and many imagine that active discrimination against the Negro has passed with them. Careful inquiry will convince any such one of his error. To be sure a colored man to-day can walk the streets of Philadelphia without personal insult; he can go to theatres, parks and some places of amusement without meeting more than stares and discourtesy; he can be accommodated at most hotels and restaurants, although his treatment in some would not be pleasant. All this is a vast advance and augurs much for the future. And yet all that has been said of the remaining discrimination is but too true.

During the investigation of 1896 there was collected a number of actual cases, which may illustrate the discriminations spoken of. So far as possible these have been sifted and only those which seem undoubtedly true have been selected.[2]

1. As to getting work.

It is hardly necessary to dwell upon the situation of the Negro in regard to work in the higher walks of life: the white boy may start in the lawyer's office and work himself into a lucrative practice; he may serve a physician as office boy or enter a hospital in a minor position, and have his talent alone between him and affluence and fame; if he is bright in school, he may make his mark in a university, become a tutor with some time and much inspiration for study, and eventually fill a professor's chair. All these careers are at the very outset closed to the Negro on account of his color; what lawyer would give even a minor case to a Negro assistant? or what university would appoint a promising young Negro as tutor? Thus the young white man starts in life knowing that within some limits and barring accidents, talent and application will tell. The young Negro starts knowing that on all sides his advance is made doubly difficult if not wholly shut off by his color. Let us come, however, to ordinary occupations which concern more nearly the mass of Negroes. Philadelphia is a great industrial and business centre, with thousands of foremen, managers and clerks—the lieutenants of industry who direct its progress. They are paid for thinking and for skill to direct, and naturally such positions are coveted because they are well paid, well thought-of and carry some authority. To such positions Negro boys and girls may not aspire no matter what their qualifications. Even as teachers and ordinary clerks and stenographers they find almost no openings. Let us note some actual instances:

A young woman who graduated with credit from the Girls' Normal School in 1892, has taught in the kindergarten, acted as substitute, and waited in vain for a permanent position. Once she was allowed to substitute in a school with white teachers; the principal commended her work, but when the permanent appointment was made a white woman got it.

A girl who graduated from a Pennsylvania high school and from a business college sought work in the city as a stenographer and typewriter. A prominent lawyer undertook to find her a position; he went to friends and said, "Here is a girl that does excellent work and is of good character; can you not give her work?" Several immediately answered yes. "But," said the lawyer, "I will be perfectly frank with you and tell you she is colored;" and not in the whole city could he find a man willing to employ her. It happened, however, that the girl was so light in complexion that few not knowing would have suspected her descent. The lawyer therefore gave her temporary work in his own office until she found a position outside the city. "But," said he, "to this day I have not dared to tell my clerks that they worked beside a Negress." Another woman graduated from the high school and the Palmer College of Shorthand, but all over the city has met with nothing but refusal of work.

Several graduates in pharmacy have sought to get their three years required apprenticeship in the city and in only one case did one succeed, although they offered to work for nothing. One young pharmacist came from Massachusetts and for weeks sought in vain for work here at any price; "I wouldn't have a darky to clean out my store, much less to stand behind the counter," answered one druggist. A colored man answered an advertisement for a clerk in the suburbs. "What do you suppose we'd want of a nigger?" was the plain answer. A graduate of the University of Pennsylvania in mechanical engineering, well recommended, obtained work in the city, through an advertisement, on account of his excellent record. He worked a few hours and then was discharged because he was found to be colored. He is now a waiter at the University Club, where his white fellow graduates dine.[3] Another young man attended Spring Garden Institute and studied drawing for lithography. He had good references from the institute and elsewhere, but application at the five largest establishments in the city could secure him no work. A telegraph operator has hunted in vain for an opening, and two graduates of the Central High School have sunk to menial labor. "What's the use of an education?" asked one. Mr. A——has elsewhere been employed as a traveling salesman. He applied for a position here by letter and was told he could have one. When they saw him they had no work for him.

Such cases could be multiplied indefinitely. But that is not necessary; one has but to note that, notwithstanding the acknowledged ability of many colored men, the Negro is conspicuously absent from all places of honor, trust or emolument, as well as from those of respectable grade in commerce and industry.

Even in the world of skilled labor the Negro is largely excluded. Many would explain the absence of Negroes from higher vocations by saying that while a few may now and then be found competent, the great mass are not fitted for that sort of work and are destined for some time to form a laboring class. In the matter of the trades, however, there can be raised no serious question of ability; for years the Negroes filled satisfactorily the trades of the city, and to-day in many parts of the South they are still prominent. And yet in Philadelphia a determined prejudice, aided by public opinion, has succeeded nearly in driving them from the field:

A——, who works at a bookbinding establishment on Front street, has learned to bind books and often does so for his friends. He is not allowed to work at the trade in the shop, however, but must remain a porter at a porter's wages.

B——is a brushmaker; he has applied at several establishments, but they would not even examine his testimonials. They simply said: "We do not employ colored people."

C——is a shoemaker; he tried to get work in some of the large department stores. They "had no place" for him.

D——was a bricklayer, but experienced so much trouble in getting work that he is now a messenger.

E——is a painter, but has found it impossible to get work because he is colored.

F——is a telegraph line man, who formerly worked in Richmond, Va. When he applied here he was told that Negroes were not employed.

G——is an iron puddler, who belonged to a Pittsburg union. Here he was not recognized as a union man and could not get work except as a stevedore.

H——was a cooper, but could get no work after repeated trials, and is now a common laborer.

I——is a candy-maker, but has never been able to find employment in the city; he is always told that the white help will not work with him.

J——is a carpenter; he can only secure odd jobs or work where only Negroes are employed.

K——was an upholsterer, but could get no work save in the few colored shops, which had workmen; he is now a waiter on a dining car.

L——was a first-class baker; he applied for work some time ago near Green street and was told shortly, "We don't work no niggers here."

M——is a good typesetter; he has not been allowed to join the union and has been refused work at eight different places in the city.

N——is a printer by trade, but can only find work as a porter.

O——is a sign-painter, but can get but little work.

P——is a painter and gets considerable work, but never with white workmen.

Q——is a good stationary engineer, but can find no employment; is at present a waiter in a private family.

R——was born in Jamaica; he went to England and worked fifteen years in the Sir Edward Green Economizing Works in Wakefield, Yorkshire. During dull times he emigrated to America, bringing excellent references. He applied for a place as mechanic in nearly all the large iron working establishments in the city. A locomotive works assured him that his letters were all right, but that their men would not work with Negroes. At a manufactory of railway switches they told him they had no vacancy and he could call again; he called and finally was frankly told that they could not employ Negroes. He applied twice to a foundry company: they told him: "We have use for only one Negro—a porter," and refusing either further conversation or even to look at his letters showed him out. He then applied for work on a new building; the man told him he could leave an application, then added: "To tell the truth, its no use, for we don't employ Negroes." Thus the man has searched for work two years and has not yet found a permanent position. He can only support his family by odd jobs as a common laborer.

S——is a stone-cutter; he was refused work repeatedly on account of color. At last he got a job during a strike and was found to be so good a workman that his employer refused to dismiss him.

T——was a boy, who, together with a white boy came to the city to hunt work. The colored boy was very light in complexion, and consequently both were taken in as apprentices at a large locomotive works; they worked there some months, but it was finally disclosed that the boy was colored; he was dismissed and the white boy retained.

These all seem typical and reliable cases. There are, of course, some exceptions to the general rule, but even these seem to confirm the fact that exclusion is a matter of prejudice and thoughtlessness which sometimes yields to determination and good sense. The most notable case in point is that of the Midvale Steel Works, where a large number of Negro workmen are regularly employed as mechanics and work alongside whites.[4] If another foreman should take charge there, or if friction should arise, it would be easy for all this to receive a serious set-back, for ultimate success in such matters demands many experiments and a widespread public sympathy.

There are several cases where strong personal influence has secured colored boys positions; in one cabinet-making factory, a porter who had served the firm thirty years, asked to have his son learn the trade and work in the shop. The workmen objected strenuously at first, but the employer was firm and the young man has been at work there now seven years. The S. S. White Dental Company has a colored chemist who has worked up to his place and gives satisfaction. A jeweler allowed his colored fellow-soldier in the late war to learn the gold beaters' trade and work in his shop. A few other cases follow:

A——was intimately acquainted with a merchant and secured his son a position as a typewriter in the merchant's office.

B——, a stationary engineer, came with his employer from Washington and still works with him.

C——, a plasterer, learned his trade with a firm in Virginia who especially recommended him to the firm where he now works.

D—— is a boy whose mother's friend got him work as cutter in a bag and rope factory; the hands objected but the friend's influence was strong enough to keep him there.

All these exceptions prove the rule, viz., that without strong effort and special influence it is next to impossible for a Negro in Philadelphia to get regular employment in most of the trades, except he work as an independent workman and take small transient jobs.

The chief agency that brings about this state of affairs is public opinion; if they were not intrenched, and strongly intrenched, back of an active prejudice or at least passive acquiescence in this effort to deprive Negroes of a decent livelihood, both trades unions and arbitrary bosses would be powerless to do the harm they now do; where, however, a large section of the public more or less openly applaud the stamina of a man who refuses to work with a "Nigger," the results are inevitable. The object of the trades union is purely business-like; it aims to restrict the labor market, just as the manufacturer aims to raise the price of his goods. Here is a chance to keep out of the market a vast number of workmen, and the unions seize the chance save in cases where they dare not as in the case of the cigar-makers and coal-miners. If they could keep out the foreign workmen in the same way they would; but here public opinion within and without their ranks forbids hostile action. Of course, most unions do not flatly declare their discriminations; a few plainly put the word "white" into their constitutions; most of them do not and will say that they consider each case on its merits. Then they quietly black-ball the Negro applicant. Others delay and temporize and put off action until the Negro withdraws; still others discriminate against the Negro in initiation fees and dues, making a Negro pay $100, where the whites pay $25. On the other hand in times of strikes or other disturbances cordial invitations to join are often sent to Negro workmen.[5]

At a time when women are engaged in bread-winning to a larger degree than ever before, the field open to Negro women is unusually narrow. This is, of course, due largely to the more intense prejudices of females on all subjects, and especially to the fact that women who work dislike to be in any way mistaken for menials, and they regard Negro women as menials *par excellence*.

A——, a dressmaker and seamstress of proven ability, sought work in the large department stores. They all commended her work, but could not employ her on account of her color.

B——is a typewriter, but has applied at stores and offices in vain for work; "very sorry" they all say, but they can give her no work. She has answered many advertisements without result.

C—— has attended the Girls, High School for two years, and has been unable to find any work; she is washing and sewing for a living now.

D——is a dressmaker and milliner, and does bead work. "Your work is very good," they say to her, "but if we hired you all of our ladies would leave."

E——, a seamstress, was given work from a store once, to do at home. It was commended as satisfactory, but they gave her no more.

F—— had two daughters who tried to get work as stenographers, but got only one small job.

G—— is a graduate of the Girls, High School, with excellent record; both teachers and influential friends have been seeking work for her but have not been able to find any.

H——a girl, applied at seven stores for some work not menial; they had none.

I—— started at the Schuylkill, on Market street, and applied at almost every store nearly to the Delaware for work; she was only offered scrubbing.[6]

2. So much for the difficulty of getting work. In addition to this the Negro is meeting difficulties in keeping the work he has, or at least the better part of it. Outside of all dissatisfaction with Negro work there are whims and fashions that affect his economic position; to-day general European travel has made the trained English servant popular and consequently well-shaven white men-servants, whether English or not, find it easy to replace Negro butlers and coachmen at higher wages. Again, though a man ordinarily does not dismiss all his white mill-hands because some turn out badly, yet it repeatedly happens that men dismiss all their colored servants and condemn their race because one or two in their employ have proven untrustworthy. Finally, the antipathies of lower classes are so great that it is often impracticable to mix races among the servants. A young colored girl went to work temporarily in Germantown; "I should like so much to keep you permanently," said the mistress, "but all my other servants are white." She was discharged. Usually now advertisements for help state whether white or Negro servants are wanted, and the Negro who applies at the wrong place must not be surprised to have the door slammed in his face.

The difficulties encountered by the Negro on account of sweeping conclusions made about him are manifold; a large building, for instance, has several poorly paid Negro janitors, without facilities for their work or guidance in its prosecution. Finally the building is thoroughly overhauled or rebuilt, elevators and electricity installed and a well paid set of white uniformed janitors put to work under a responsible salaried chief. Immediately the public concludes that the improvement in the service is due to the change of color. In some cases, of course, the change is due to a widening of the field of choice in selecting servants; for assuredly one cannot expect that one twenty-fifth of the population can furnish as many good workmen or as uniformly good ones as the other twenty-four twenty-fifths. One actual case illustrates this tendency to exclude the Negro without proper consideration from even menial employment:

A great church which has a number of members among the most respectable Negro families in the city has recently erected a large new building for its offices, etc., in the city. As the building was nearing completion a colored clergy-man of that sect was surprised to hear that no Negroes were to be employed in the building; he thought that a peculiar stand for a Christian church to take and so he went to the manager of the building; the manager blandly assured him that the rumor was true; and that there was not the shadow of a chance for a Negro to get employment under him, except one woman to clean the water-closet. The reason for this, he said, was that the janitors and help were all to be uniformed and the whites would not wear uniforms with Negroes. The clergyman thereupon went to a prominent member of the church who was serving on the building committee; he denied that the committee had made any such decision, but sent him to another member of the committee; this member said the same thing and referred to the third, a blunt business man. The business man said: "That building is called the —— Church House, but it is more than that, it is a business enterprise, to be run on business principles. We hired a man to run it so as to get the most out of it. We found such a man in the present manager, and put all power in his hands." He acknowledged then, that while the committee had made no decision, the question of hiring Negroes had come up and it was left solely to the manager's decision. The manager thought most Negroes were dishonest and untrustworthy, etc. And thus the Christian church joins hands with trades unions and a large public opinion to force Negroes into idleness and crime.

Sometimes Negroes, by special influence, as has been pointed out before, secure good positions; then there are other cases where colored men have by sheer merit and pluck secured positions. In all these cases, however, they are liable to lose their places through no fault of their own and primarily on account of their Negro blood. It may be that at first their Negro descent is not known, or other causes may operate; in all cases the Negro's tenure of office is insecure:

A—— worked in a large tailor's establishment on Third street for three weeks. His work was acceptable. Then it became known he was colored and he was discharged as the other tailors refused to work with him.

B——, a pressman, was employed on Twelfth street, but a week later was discharged when they knew he was colored; he then worked as a door-boy for five years, and finally got another job in a Jewish shop as pressman.

C—— was nine years a painter in Stewart's Furniture Factory, until Stewart failed four years ago. Has applied repeatedly, but could get no work on account of color. He now works as a night watchman on the streets for the city.

D—— was a stationary engineer; his employer died, and he has never been able to find another.

E—— was light in complexion and got a job as driver; he "kept his cap on," but when they found he was colored they discharged him.

F—— was one of many colored laborers at an ink factory. The heads of the firm died, and now whenever a Negro leaves a white man is put in his place.

G—— worked for a long time as a typesetter on Taggart's *Times*; when the paper changed hands he was discharged and has never been able to get another job; he is now a janitor.

H—— was a brickmason, but his employers finally refused to let him lay brick longer as his fellow workmen were all white; he is now a waiter.

L—— learned the trade of range-setting from his employer; the employer then refused him work and he went into business for himself; he has taught four apprentices.

M—— is a woman whose husband was janitor for a firm twenty years; when they moved to the new Betz Building they discharged him as all the janitors there were white; after his death they could find no work for his boy.

N—— was a porter in a book store and rose to be head postmaster of a substation in Philadelphia which handles $250,000, it is said, a year; he was also at the head of a very efficient Bureau of Information in a large department store.

Recently attempts have been made to displace him, for no specified fault but because "we want his place for another [white] man."

O— is a well-known instance; an observer in 1898 wrote: "If any Philadelphian who is anxious to study the matter with his own eyes, will walk along South Eleventh street, from Chestnut down, and will note the most tasteful and enter-prising stationery and periodical store along the way, it will pay him to enter it. On entering he will, according to his way of thinking, be pleased or grieved to see that it is conducted by Negroes. If the proprietor happens to be in he may know that this keen-looking pleasant young man was once assistant business manager of a large white religious newspaper in the city. A change of management led to his dismissal. No fault was found, his work was commended, but a white man was put into his place, and profuse apologies made.

"The clerk behind the counter is his sister; a neat lady-like woman, educated, and trained in stenography and typewriting. She could not find in the city of Philadelphia, any one who had the slightest use for such a colored woman.

"The result of this situation is this little store, which is remarkably successful. The proprietor owns the stock, the store and the building. This is one tale of its sort with a pleasant ending. Other tales are far less pleasing."

Much discouragement results from the persistent refusal to promote colored employees. The humblest white employee knows that the better he does his work the more chance there is for him to rise in the business. The black employee knows that the better he does his work the longer he may do it; he cannot often hope for promotion. This makes much of the criticism aimed against Negroes, because some of them want to refuse menial labor, lose something of its point. If the better class of Negro boys could look on such labor as a stepping-stone to something higher it would be different; if they must view it as a lifework we cannot wonder at their hesitation:

A—— has been a porter at a great locomotive works for ten years. He is a car-penter by trade and has picked up considerable knowledge of machinery; he was formerly allowed to work a little as a machinist; now that is stopped and he has never been promoted and probably never will be.

B—— has worked in a shop eight years and never been promoted from his porter's position, although he is a capable man.

C—— is a porter; he has been in a hardware store six years; he is bright and has repeatedly been promised advancement but has never got it.

D—— was for seven years in a gang of porters in a department store, and part of the time acted as foreman. He had a white boy under him who disliked him; eventually the boy was promoted but he remained a porter. Finally the boy became his boss and discharged him.

E——, a woman, worked long in a family of lawyers; a white lad went into their office as office-boy and came to be a member of the firm; she had a smart, ambitious son and asked for any sort of office work for him—anything in which he could hope for promotion. "Why don't you make him a waiter?" they asked.

F—— has for twenty-one years driven for a lumber firm; speaks German and is very useful to them, but they have never promoted him.

G—— was a porter; he begged for a chance to work up; offering to do clerical work for nothing, but was refused. White companions were repeatedly promoted over his head. He has been a porter seventeen years.

H—— was a servant in the family of one of the members of a large dry goods firm; he was so capable that the employer sent him down to the store for a place which the manager very reluctantly gave him. He rose to be registering clerk in the delivering department where he worked fourteen years and his work was commended. Recently without notice or complaint he was changed to run an elevator at the same wages. He thinks that pressure from other members of the firm made him lose his work.

Once in a while there are exceptions to this rule. The Pennsylvania Railroad has promoted one bright and persistent porter to a clerkship, which he has held for years. He had, however, spent his life hunting chances for promotion and had been told "You have ability enough, George, if you were not colored ——."

There is much discrimination against Negroes in wages.[7] The Negroes have fewer chances for work, have been used to low wages, and consequently the first thought that occurs to the average employer is to give a Negro less than he would offer a white man for the same work. This is not universal, but it is widespread. In domestic service of the ordinary sort there is no difference, because the wages are a matter of custom. When it comes to waiters, butlers and coachmen, however, there is considerable difference made; while white coachmen receive from $50–$75, the Negroes do not get usually more than $30–$60. Negro hotel waiters get from $18–$20, while whites receive $20–$30. Naturally when a hotel manager replaces $20 men with $30 men he may expect, outside any question of color, better service.

In ordinary work the competition forces down the wages outside mere race reasons, though the Negro is the greatest sufferer; this is especially the case in laundry work. "I've counted as high as seven dozen pieces in that washing," said a weary black woman, "and she pays me only $1.25 a week for it." Persons who throw away $5 a week on a gew-gaws will often haggle over twenty-five cents with a washerwoman. There are, however, notable exceptions to these cases, where good wages are paid to persons who have long worked for the same family.

Very often if a Negro is given a chance to work at a trade his wages are cut down for the privilege. This gives the workingman's prejudice additional intensity:

A—— got a job formerly held by a white porter; the wages were reduced from $12 to $8.

B—— worked for a firm as china packer, and they said he was the best packer they had. He, however, received but $6 a week while the white packers received $12.

C—— has been porter and assistant shipping clerk in an Arch street store for five years. He receives $6 a week and whites get $8 for the same work.

D—— is a stationary engineer; he learned his trade with this firm and has been with them ten years. Formerly he received $9 a week, now $10.50; whites get $12 for the same work.

E—— is a stationary engineer and has been in his place three years. He receives but $9 a week.

F—— works with several other Negroes with a firm of electrical engineers. The white laborers receive $2 a day: "We've got to be glad to get $1.75."

G—— was a carpenter, but could get neither sufficient work nor satisfactory wages. For a job on which he received $15 a week, his white successor got $18.

H——, a cementer, receives $1.75 a day; white workmen get $2–$3. He has been promised more next fall.

I——, a plasterer, has worked for one boss twenty-seven years. Regular plasterers get $4 or more a day; he does the same work, but cannot join the union and is paid as a laborer—$2.50 a day.

J—— works as a porter in a department store; is married, and receives $8 a week. "They pay the same to white unmarried shop girls, who stand a chance to be promoted."

3. If a Negro enters some line of employment in which people are not used to seeing him, he suffers from an assumption that he is unfit for the work. It is reported that a Chestnut street firm once took a Negro shop girl, but the protests of their customers were such that they had to dismiss her. A great many merchants hesitate to advance Negroes lest they should lose custom. Negro merchants who have attempted to start business in the city at first encounter much difficulty from this prejudice:

A—— has a bakery; white people sometimes enter and finding Negroes in charge abruptly leave.

B—— is a baker and had a shop some years on Vine street, but prejudice against him barred him from gaining much custom.

C—— is a successful expressman with a large business; he is sometimes told by persons that they prefer to patronize white expressmen.

D—— is a woman and keeps a hair store on South street. Customers sometimes enter, look at her, and leave.

E—— is a music teacher on Lombard street. Several white people have entered and seeing him, said: "Oh! I thought you were white—excuse me!" or "I'll call again!"

Even among the colored people themselves some prejudice of this sort is met. Once a Negro physician could not get the patronage of Negroes because they were not used to the innovation. Now they have a large part of the Negro patronage. The Negro merchant, however, still lacks the full confidence of his own people though this is slowly growing. It is one of the paradoxes of this question to see a people so discriminated against sometimes add to their misfortunes by discriminating against themselves. They themselves, however, are beginning to recognize this.

4. This chief discrimination against Negroes in expenditure is in the matter of rents. There can be no reasonable doubt but that Negroes pay excessive rents:

A—— paid $13 a month where the preceding white family had paid $10.

B—— paid $16; "heard that former white family paid $12."

C—— paid $25; "heard that former white family paid $20."

D—— paid $12; neighbors say that former white family paid $9.

E—— paid $25, instead of $18.

F—— paid $12, instead of $10.

G——, the Negro inhabitants of the whole street pay $12 to $14 and the whites $9 and $10. The houses are all alike.

H——, whites on this street pay $15–$18; Negroes pay $18–$21.

Not only is there this pretty general discrimination in rent, but agents and owners will not usually repair the houses of the blacks willingly or improve them. In addition to this agents and owners in many sections utterly refuse to rent to Negroes on any terms. Both these sorts of discrimination are easily defended from a merely business point of view; public opinion in the city is such that the presence of even a respectable colored family in a block will affect its value for renting or sale; increased rent to Negroes is therefore a sort of insurance, and refusal to rent a device for money-getting. The indefensible cruelty lies with those classes who refuse to recognize the right of respectable Negro citizens to respectable houses. Real estate agents also increase prejudice by refusing to discriminate between different classes of Negroes. A quiet Negro family moves into a street. The agent finds no great objection, and allows the next empty house to go to any Negro who applies. This family may disgrace and scandalize the neighborhood and make it harder for decent families to find homes.[8]

In the last fifteen years, however, public opinion has so greatly changed in this matter that we may expect much in the future. To-day the Negro population is more widely scattered over the city than ever before. At the same time it remains true that as a rule they must occupy the worst houses of the districts where they live. The advance made has been a battle for the better class of Negroes. An ex-Minister to Hayti moved to the northwestern part of the city and his white neighbors insulted him, barricaded their steps against him, and tried in every way to make him move; to-day he is honored and respected in the whole neighborhood. Many such cases have occurred; in others the result was different. An estimable young Negro, just married, moved with his bride into a little street. The neighborhood rose in arms and besieged the tenant and the landlord so relentlessly that the landlord leased the house and compelled the young couple to move within a month. One of the bishops of the A. M. E. Church recently moved into the newly purchased Episcopal residence on Belmont avenue, and his neighbors have barricaded their porches against his view.

5. The chief discrimination against Negro children is in the matter of educational facilities. Prejudice here works to compel colored children to attend certain schools where most Negro children go, or to keep them out of private and higher schools.

A— tried to get her little girl into the kindergarten nearest to her, at Fifteenth and Locust. The teachers wanted her to send it down across Broad to the kindergarten chiefly attended by colored children and much further away from its home. This journey was dangerous for the child, but the teachers refused to receive it for six months, until the authorities were appealed to.

In transfers from schools Negroes have difficulty in getting convenient accommodations; only within comparatively few years have Negroes been allowed to complete the course at the High and Normal Schools without difficulty. Earlier than that the University of Pennsylvania refused to let Negroes sit in the Auditorium and listen to lectures, much less to be students. Within two or three years a Negro student had to fight his way through a city dental school with his fists, and was treated with every indignity. Several times Negroes have been asked to leave schools of stenography, etc., on account of their fellow students. In 1893 a colored woman applied at Temple College, a church institution, for admission and was refused and advised to go elsewhere. The college then offered scholarships to churches, but would not admit applicants from colored churches. Two years later the same woman applied again. The faculty declared that they did not object, but that the students would; she persisted and was finally admitted with evident reluctance.

It goes without saying that most private schools, music schools, etc., will not admit Negroes and in some cases have insulted applicants.

Such is the tangible form of Negro prejudice in Philadelphia. Possibly some of the particular cases cited can be proven to have had extenuating circumstances unknown to the investigator; at the same time many not cited would be just as much in point. At any rate no one who has with any diligence studied the situation of the Negro in the city can long doubt but that his opportunities are limited and his ambition circumscribed about as has been shown. There are of course numerous exceptions, but the mass of the Negroes have been so often refused openings and discouraged in efforts to better their condition that many of them say, as one said, "I never apply—I know it is useless." Beside these tangible and measurable forms there are deeper and less easily described results of the attitude of the white population toward the Negroes: a certain manifestation of a real or assumed aversion, a spirit of ridicule or patronage, a vindictive hatred in some, absolute indifference in others; all this of course does not make much difference to the mass of the race, but it deeply wounds the better classes, the very classes who are attaining to that to which we wish the mass to attain. Notwithstanding all this, most Negroes would patiently await the effect of time and commonsense on such prejudice did it not to-day touch them in matters of life and death; threaten their homes, their food, their children, their hopes. And the result of this is bound to be increased crime, inefficiency and bitterness.

It would, of course, be idle to assert that most of the Negro crime was caused by prejudice; the violent economic and social changes which the last fifty years have brought to the American Negro, the sad social history that preceded these changes, have all contributed to unsettle morals and pervert talents. Nevertheless it is certain that Negro prejudice in cities like Philadelphia has been a vast factor in aiding and abetting all other causes which impel a half-developed race to recklessness and excess. Certainly a great amount of crime can be without doubt traced to the discrimination against Negro boys and girls in the matter of employment. Or to put it differently, Negro prejudice costs the city something.

The connection of crime and prejudice is, on the other hand, neither simple nor direct. The boy who is refused promotion in his job as porter does not go out and snatch somebody's pocketbook. Conversely the loafers at Twelfth and Kater streets, and the thugs in the county prison are not usually graduates of high schools who have been refused work. The connections are much more subtle and dangerous; it is the atmosphere of rebellion and discontent that unrewarded merit and reasonable but unsatisfied ambition make. The social environment of excuse, listless despair, careless indulgence and lack of inspiration to work is the growing force that turns black boys and girls into gamblers, prostitutes and rascals. And this social environment has been built up slowly out of the disappointments of deserving men and the sloth of the unawakened. How long can a city say to a part of its citizens, "It is useless to work; it is fruitless to deserve well of men; education will gain you nothing but disappointment and humiliation?" How long can a city teach its black children that the road to success is to have a white face? How long can a city do this and escape the inevitable penalty?

For thirty years and more Philadelphia has said to its black children: "Honesty, efficiency and talent have little to do with your success; if you work hard, spend little and are good you may earn your bread and butter at those sorts of work which we frankly confess we despise; if you are dishonest and lazy, the State will furnish your bread free." Thus the class of Negroes which the prejudices of the city have distinctly encouraged is that of the criminal, the lazy and the shiftless; for them the city teems with institutions and charities; for them there is succor and sympathy; for them Philadelphians are thinking and planning; but for the educated and industrious young colored man who wants work and not platitudes, wages and not alms, just rewards and not sermons—for such colored men Philadelphia apparently has no use.

What then do such men do? What becomes of the graduates of the many schools of the city? The answer is simple: most of those who amount to anything leave the city, the others take what they can get for a livelihood. Let us for a moment glance at the statistics of three colored schools:[9]

1. The O. V. Catto Primary School.
2. The Robert Vaux Grammar School.
3. The Institute for Colored Youth.

There attended the Catto school, 1867–97, 5,915 pupils. Of these there were promoted from the full course, 653. 129 of the latter are known to be in positions of higher grade; or taking out 93 who are still in school, there remain 36 as follows: 18 teachers, 10 clerks, 2 physicians, 2 engravers, 2 printers, 1 lawyer and 1 mechanic.

The other 524 are for the most part in service, laborers and housewives. Of the 36 more successful ones fully half are at work outside of the city.

Of the Vaux school there were, 1877–89, 76 graduates. Of these there are 16 unaccounted for; the rest are:

Teachers	27	Barbers	4
Musicians	5	Clerks	3
Merchants	3	Physician	1
Mechanic	1	Deceased	8
Clergymen	3	Housewives	5
	47		

From one-half to two-thirds of these have been compelled to leave the city in order to find work; one, the artist, Tanner, whom France recently honored, could not in his native land much less in his native city find room for his talents. He taught school in Georgia in order to earn money enough to go abroad.

The Institute of Colored Youth has had 340 graduates, 1856–97; 57 of these are dead. Of the 283 remaining 91 are unaccounted for. The rest are:

Teachers	117	Electrical Engineer	1
Lawyers	4	Professor	1
Physicians	4	Government clerks	5
Musicians	4	Merchants	7
Dentists	2	Mechanics	5
Clergymen	2	Clerks	23
Nurses	2	Teacher of cooking	1
Editor	1	Dressmakers	4
Civil Engineer	1	Students	7
			192

Here, again, nearly three-fourths of the graduates who have amounted to anything have had to leave the city for work. The civil engineer, for instance, tried in vain to get work here and finally had to go to New Jersey to teach.

There have been 9, possibly 11, colored graduates of the Central High School. These are engaged as follows:

Grocer	1	Porter	1
Clerks in service of city	2	Butler	1
Caterer	1	Unknown	3 or 5

It is high time that the best conscience of Philadelphia awakened to her duty; her Negro citizens are here to remain; they can be made good citizens or burdens to the community; if we want them to be sources of wealth and power and not of poverty and weakness then they must be given employment according to their ability and encouraged to train that ability and increase their talents by the hope of reasonable reward. To educate boys and girls and then refuse them work is to train loafers and rogues.[10]

From another point of view it could be argued with much cogency that the cause of economic stress, and consequently of crime, was the recent inconsiderate rush of Negroes into cities; and that the unpleasant results of this migration, while deplorable, will nevertheless serve to check the movement of Negroes to cities and keep them in the country where their chance for economic development is widest. This argument loses much of its point from the fact that it is the better class of educated Philadelphia-born Negroes who have the most difficulty in obtaining employment. The new immigrant fresh from the South is much more apt to obtain work suitable for him than the black boy born here and trained in efficiency. Nevertheless it is undoubtedly true that the recent migration has both directly and indirectly increased crime and competition. How is this movement to be checked? Much can be done by correcting misrepresentations as to the opportunities of city life made by designing employment bureaus and thoughtless persons; a more strict surveillance of criminals might prevent the influx of undesirable elements. Such efforts, however, would not touch the main stream of immigration. Back of that stream is the world-wide desire to rise in the world, to escape the choking narrowness of the plantation, and the lawless repression of the village, in the South. It is a search for better opportunities of living, and as such it must be discouraged and repressed with great care and delicacy, if at all. The real movement of reform is the raising of economic standards and increase of economic opportunity in the South. Mere land and climate without law and order, capital and skill, will not develop a country. When Negroes in the South have a larger opportunity to work, accumulate property, be protected in life and limb, and encourage pride and self-respect in their children, there will be a diminution in the stream of immigrants to Northern cities. At the same time if those cities practice industrial exclusion against these immigrants to such an extent that they are forced to become paupers, loafers and criminals, they can scarcely complain of conditions in the South. Northern cities should not, of course, seek to encourage and invite a poor quality of labor, with low standards of life and morals. The standards of wages and respectability should be kept up; but when a man reaches those standards in skill, efficiency and decency no question of color should, in a civilized community, debar him from an equal chance with his peers in earning a living.

48. **Benevolence**[11]—In the attitude of Philadelphia toward the Negro may be traced the same contradictions so often apparent in social phenomena; prejudice and apparent dislike conjoined with widespread and deep sympathy; there can, for instance, be no doubt of the sincerity of the efforts put forth by Philadelphians to help the Negroes. Much of it is unsystematic and ill-directed and yet it has behind it a broad charity and a desire to relieve suffering and distress. The same Philadelphian who would not let a Negro work in his store or mill will contribute handsomely to relieve Negroes in poverty and distress. There are in the city the following charities exclusively designed for Negroes:

Home for Aged and Infirm Colored Persons, Belmont and Girard avenues.[12]

Home for Destitute Colored Children, Berks street and Old Lancaster road.

St. Mary Day Nursery, 1627 Lombard street.

The Association for the Care of Colored Orphans, Forty-fourth and Wallace streets.

Frederick Douglass Memorial Hospital and Training School, 1512 Lombard street.[13]

Magdalen Convent House of the Good Shepherd (Roman Catholic), Penn and Chew streets, Germantown.

St. Mary's Mission for Colored People, 1623–29 Lombard street.

Raspberry Street School, 229 Raspberry street.

The Star Kitchen, and allied enterprises, Seventh and Lombard streets.

Colored Industrial School, Twentieth street, below Walnut.

Sisters of the Blessed Sacrament, for Indians and Colored People, Cornwell's Station, Pa.

Men's Guild House, 1628 Lombard street.

House of St. Michael and All Angels, 613 North Forty-third street.

The Industrial Exchange Training School and Dormitory, 756 South Twelfth street.[13]

Fifty-nine of the charities mentioned in the Civic Club Digest discriminate against colored persons. Fifty-one societies profess to make no discrimination; in the case of the larger and better known societies this is true, as, for instance, the Home Missionary Society, the Union Benevolent Association, the Protestant Episcopal City Mission, the Charity Organization Society, the Children's Aid Society, the Society to Prevent Cruelty to Children, etc. Others, however, exercise a silent policy against Negroes. The Country Week Association, for instance, would rather Negroes should not apply, although it sends a few away each summer. Colored applicants at the building of the Young Woman's Christian Association are not very welcome. So with many other societies and institutions. This veiled discrimination is very unjust, for it makes it seem as though the Negro had more help than he does. On the other hand between donors, prejudiced persons, friends of the Negro, and the beneficiaries, the managers of many of these enterprises find it by far the easiest method silently to draw the color line.

Fifty-seven other charities make no explicit statement as to whether they discriminate or not. To sum up then:

Charitable agencies exclusively for Negroes				14
"	"	"	" Whites	59
"	"	which profess not to discriminate, but in some cases do	.	51
"	"	which make no statements, but usually discriminate	....	57
				181

On the whole it is fair to say that about one half of the charities of Philadelphia, so far as mere numbers are concerned, are open to Negroes. In the different kinds of charity, however, some disproportion is noticeable. Of direct almsgiving, the most questionable and least organized sort of charity, the Negroes receive probably far more than their just proportion, as a study of the work of the great distributing societies clearly shows. On the other hand, protective, rescue and reformatory work is not applied to any great extent among them. Consequently, while actual poverty and distress among Negroes is quickly relieved, there are only a few agencies to prevent the better classes from sinking or to reclaim the fallen or to protect the helpless and the children. Even the agencies of this sort open to the Negroes are not always taken advantage of, partly through ignorance and carelessness, partly because they fear discrimination or because they are apt to be treated the same whether they be from Addison street or Middle alley.

Much of the benevolence of the whites has been checked because the classes on whom it has been showered have not appreciated it, and because there has been no careful attempt to discriminate between different sorts of Negroes. After all, the need of the Negro, as of so many unfortunate classes, is "not alms but a friend."

There are a few homes, asylums, nurseries, hospitals and the like for work among Negroes, which are doing excellent work and deserve commendation. It is to be hoped that this sort of work will receive needed encouragement.

49. The Intermarriage of the Races—For years much has been said on the destiny of the Negro with regard to intermarriage with the whites. To many this seems the difficulty that differentiates the Negro question from all other social questions which we face, and makes it seemingly insoluble; the questions of ignorance, crime and immorality, these argue, may safely be left to the influence of time and education; but will time and training ever change the obvious fact that the white people of the country do not wish to mingle socially with the Negroes or to join blood in legal wedlock with them? This problem is, it must be acknowledged, difficult. Its difficulty arises, however, rather from an ignorance of surrounding facts than from the theoretic argument. Theory in such case is of little value; the white people as members of the races now dominant in the world naturally boast of their blood and accomplishments, and recoil from an alliance with a people which is to-day represented by a host of untrained and uncouth ex-slaves. On the other hand, whatever his practice be, the Negro as a free American citizen must just as strenuously maintain that marriage is a private contract, and that given two persons of proper age and economic ability who agree to enter into that relation, it does not concern any one but themselves as to whether one of them be white, black or red. It is thus that theoretical argument comes to an unpleasant standstill, and its further pursuit really settles nothing, nay, rather unsettles much, by bringing men's thoughts to a question that is, at present at least, of little practical importance. For in practice the matter works itself out: the average white person does not marry a Negro; and the average Negro, despite his theory, himself marries one of his race, and frowns darkly on his fellows unless they do likewise. In those very circles of Negroes who have a large infusion of white blood, where the freedom of marriage is most strenuously advocated, white wives have always been treated with a disdain bordering on insult, and white husbands never received on any terms of social recognition.

Notwithstanding theory and the practice of whites and Negroes in general, it is nevertheless manifest that the white and black races have mingled their blood in this country to a vast extent. Such facts puzzle the foreigner and are destined to puzzle the future historian. A serious student of the subject gravely declares in one chapter that the races are separate and distinct and becoming more so, and in another that by reason of the intermingling of white blood the "original type of the African has almost completely disappeared;"[14] here we have reflected the prevailing confusion in the popular mind. Race amalgamation is a fact, not a theory; it took place, however, largely under the institution of slavery and for the most part, though not wholly, outside the bonds of legal marriage. With the abolition of slavery now, and the establishment of a self-protecting Negro home the question is, what have been the tendencies and the actual facts with regard to the intermarriage of races? This is the only question with which students have to do, and this singularly enough has been the one which they, with curious unanimity, have neglected. We do not know the facts with regard to the mingling of white and black blood in the past save in a most general and unsatisfactory way; we do not know the facts for to-day at all. And yet, of course, without this knowledge all philosophy of the situation is vain; only long observation of the course of intermarriage can furnish us that broad knowledge of facts which can serve as a basis for race theories and final conclusions.[15]

The first legal obstacle to the intermarriage of whites and blacks in Pennsylvania was the Act of 1726, which forbade such unions in terms that would seem to indicate that a few such marriages had taken place. Mulattoes early appeared in the State, and especially in Philadelphia, some being from the South and some from up the State. Sailors from this port in some cases brought back English, Scotch and Irish wives, and mixed families immigrated here at the time of the Haytian revolt. Between 1820 and 1860 many natural children were sent from the South and in a few cases their parents followed and were legally married here. Descendants of such children in many cases forsook the mother's race; one became principal of a city school, one a prominent sister in a Catholic church, one a bishop, and one or two officers in the Confederate army.[16] Some marriages with Quakers took place, one especially in 1825, when a Quakeress married a Negro, created much comment. Descendants of this couple still survive. Since the War the number of local marriages has considerably increased.

In this work there was originally no intention of treating the subject of intermarriage, for it was thought that the data would be too insignificant to be enlightening. When, however, in one ward of the city thirty-three cases of mixed marriages were found, and it was known that there were others in that ward, and probably a similar proportion in many other wards, it was thought that a study of these thirty-three families might be of interest and be a small contribution of fact to a subject where facts are not easily accessible.

The size of these families varies, of course, with the question as to what one considers a family; if we take the "census family," or all those living together under circumstances of family life in one home, the average size of the thirty-three families of the Seventh Ward in which there were intermarried whites was 3.5. If we take simply the father, mother and children, the average size was 2.9. There were ninety-seven parents and children in these families, and twenty other relatives living with them, making 117 individuals in the families. Tabulated they are as follows:

NUMBER OF PERSONS IN THE REAL FAMILY	NUMBER OF PERSONS IN THE CENSUS FAMILY						TOTAL REAL FAMILIES	TOTAL INDIVIDUALS IN REAL FAMILY
	2	3	4	5	6	13		
Two	11	4	1	1	. .	. .	17	34
Three	. .	5	. .	. .	. .	1	6	18
Four	. .	. .	6	. .	. .	. .	6	24
Five	. .	. .	. .	2	1	. .	3	15
Six	. .	. .	. .	. .	1	. .	1	6
Total Census Families	11	9	7	3	2	1	33	97
Total Individuals in Census Family	22	27	28	15	12	13		117 Individuals in Census Family

Of the intermarried whites there are four husbands and twenty-nine wives. Let us first consider the families having the four white husbands:

FOUR WHITE HUSBANDS

	No. 1	No. 2	No. 3	No. 4
Age	48	52	31	32
Birthplace	Philadelphia	Georgia	Cuba?	?
No. of years resident in Philadelphia	48	7	?	12
Reads and Writes?	Reads	Yes	Yes	Yes
Occupation	Street car driver, laborer	Motorman on electric cars	Tobacconist	Painter
No. of Children by this Marriage ..	4	0	0	0
Social grade	Third	Second	Fourth	?

THEIR FOUR NEGRO WIVES

	No. 1	No. 2	No. 3	No. 4
Age	38	29	30	28
Birthplace	Maryland	Georgia	?	Virginia
Years resident in Philadelphia	25	7	?	11
Reads and Writes	No	Reads	Yes	Yes
Occupation	Housewife and day's work	Housewife	Housewife	Cook
Children by this Marriage ...	4	0	0	0
Social grade	Third	Second	Fourth	?

The third family may be simply a case of cohabitation, and not enough is known of the fourth to make any judgment. The second family lives in a comfortable home and appears contented. The first family is poor and the man lazy and good-natured.

The twenty-nine white wives were of the following ages:

15 to 19	1	40 to 49	3
20 to 24	7	50 and over	1
25 to 29	8	Unknown	1
30 to 39	8		
		Total	29

They were born as follows:

Philadelphia	6	Hungary	1
Ireland	6	Virginia	1
England	3	Maryland	1
Scotland	2	Delaware	1
New York	2	Unknown	3
Germany	2		
Canada	1	Total	29

By rearranging this table we have for the known cases:

Born in Philadelphia	6
" " the United States	11
" " " North	8
" " " South	3
" " foreign lands	15

Those not born in Philadelphia have resided there as follows:

Less than 1 year	1
One to three years	1
Five to ten years	3
Over ten years	8
Unknown	10
	23
Born in Philadelphia	6
	29

These wives are occupied as follows:

Housewives	18
" and day's work	3
Waitresses	2
No occupation or unknown	3
Cook	1
Merchant	1
Service	1
	29

Only one of these women was reported as illiterate, and in the case of three no return was made as to illiteracy.

Fourteen of these wives had no children by this marriage; 6 had 1 child, 6 had 2 children, 3 had 3 children; making 27 children in all. Of the 14 having no children 5 were women under twenty-five recently married; 2 were women over forty and probably past child-bearing. Several of the remaining 7 were, in all probability, lewd.

Of the colored husbands of these white wives we have the following statistics:

Age—20 to 24	2	50 and over	1
25 to 29	5	Unknown	2
30 to 39	12		
40 to 49	7	Total	29

Birthplace—Philadelphia	5	North Carolina	1
Maryland	5	Massachusetts	1
Virginia	5	Alabama	1
District of Columbia	3	New York	1
Delaware	2	Unknown	2
Kentucky	1		
New Jersey	1	Total	29
Texas	1		

Born in Philadelphia 5
   " " North 8
   " " South 19

Illiteracy—Can read and write 23
   Illiterate 4
   Unknown 2
   Total 29

Occupations—

Waiter	9	Baker and Merchant	1
Porter	3	Stationary Engineer	1
Barber	2	Laborer	1
Steward	2	Stevedore	1
Cook	2	Caterer	1
Restaurant Keeper	2	Messenger	1
Helper and Engineer	1	Bootblack	1
		Unknown	1
		Total	29

The social grade of thirty-two of these families is thought to be as follows:

First grade, four families. These all live well and are comfortable; the wife stays at home and the children at school. Everything indicates comfort and contentment.

Second grade, fifteen families. These are ordinary working-class families; the wife in some cases helps as a bread-winner; none of them are in poverty, many are young couples just starting in married life. All are decent and respectable.

Third grade, six families. These are poor families of low grade, but not immoral; some are lazy, some unfortunate.

Fourth grade, seven families. Many of these are cases of permanent cohabitation and the women for the most part are or were prostitutes. They live in the slums mostly, and in some cases have lived together many years. None of them have children, or at least have none living with them at present.

Let us now glance a moment at the 31 children of these mixed marriages: 27 born of white mothers by Negro husbands, and 4 of Negro mothers by white husbands:

AGE	MALE	FEMALE	TOTAL
Under 1 year	0	3	3
1–2	2	3	5
3–5	4	3	7
6–10	3	5	8
11–15	3	1	4
16–19	2	—	2
20–29	2	—	2
Total	16	15	31

Of school age, 5–20 14
Number in school 12
Number over 10 who are illiterate 0
At work, 1, as porter.

The homes occupied by these families and the rents paid monthly are:

NUMBER OF ROOMS	$5 AND UNDER	$6–10	$11–15	$16–20	OVER $20	TOTAL FAMILIES
1 (tenant)	2	2	—	—	—	4
1 (lodging)	3	—	—	—	—	3
2.................	—	—	—	—	—	—
3.................	—	5	4	—	—	9
4.................	—	—	4	—	—	4
5.................	—	—	2	—	—	2
6.................	—	—	3	1	2	6
7.................	—	—	—	—	2	2
8 or more	—	—	—	—	3	3
Total	5	7	13	1	7	33

One family owns real estate (building lots).

One family belongs to a building and loan association.

The data here presented constitute too narrow a basis for many general conclusions even for a single city. Of the 2,441 families in the ward these families represent 1.35 per cent. There are two or more other cases in the Seventh Ward not catalogued. If this percentage holds good in the remaining parts of the city there would be about one hundred and fifty such marriages in the city; there are no data on this point.

It is often said that only the worst Negroes and lowest whites intermarry. This is certainly untrue in Philadelphia; to be sure among the lowest classes there is a large number of temporary unions and much cohabitation. In the case of the Seventh Ward several of such cases were not noticed at all in the above record as they savor more of prostitution than of marriage. On the other hand it is an error certainly in this ward to regard marriages of this sort as confined principally to the lower classes; on the contrary they take place most frequently in the laboring classes, and especially among servants, where there is the most contact between the races. Among the best class of Negroes and whites such marriages seldom occur although one notable case occurred in 1897 in Philadelphia, where there could be no question of the good social standing of the parties.

As to the tendencies of the present, and the general result of such marriages there are no reliable data. That more separations occur in such marriages than in others is very probable. It is certainly a strain on affections to have to endure not simply the social ostracism of the whites but of the blacks also. Undoubtedly this latter acts as a more practical deterrent than the first. For, while a Negro expects to be ostracized by the whites, and his white wife agrees to it by her marriage vow, neither of them are quite prepared for the cold reception they invariably meet with among the Negroes. This is the consideration that makes the sacrifice in such marriages great, and makes it perfectly proper to give the aphoristic marriage advice of Punch to those contemplating such alliances. Nevertheless one must candidly acknowledge that there are respectable people who are thus married and are apparently contented and as happy as the average of mankind. It is difficult to see whose concern their choice is but their own, or why the world should see fit to insult or slander them.

NOTES

1. Cf. Section 49.
2. One of the questions on the schedule was: "Have you had any difficulty in getting work?" another: "Have you had any difficulty in renting houses?" Most of the answers were vague or general. Those that were definite and apparently reliable were, so far as possible, inquired into further, compared with other testimony and then used as material for working out a list of discriminations; single and isolated cases without corroboration were never taken. I believe those here presented are reliable, although naturally I may have been deceived in some stories. Of the general truth of the statement I am thoroughly convinced.
3. And is, of course, pointed out by some as typifying the educated Negro's success in life.
4. Cf. Section 23.
5. Two newspaper clippings will illustrate the attitude of the workmen; the first relates to the Chinese apprentices taken into the Baldwin Locomotive Works:

    The announcement that the Baldwins had taken five Chinese apprentices made quite a stir among labor leaders. Some of them worked themselves into quite a fever of indignation. Charles P. Patrick, grand organizer of the Boilermakers' Union, was quite outspoken on the subject.

    He said: "All this plan of putting Chinamen in to learn trades sounds nice and charitable to the Christian League, but how does it sound to the ears of American mechanics who are walking the streets in search of employment? I have traveled all over this country and Mexico, and I have never before seen Chinamen given places over the heads of Americans. In the West and in Mexico, Chinese labor is plentiful, but the Chinamen are given only menial positions. They are servants, helpers in the mines and laborers. I never before heard of a Chinaman being given a place as an apprentice in a shop.

    "Our government excludes Chinese labor from this country, yet here is the Christian League seeking to put forbidden immigrants in a position where they, with their peculiarly cheap, even beggarly style of living, can compete with American labor. I have only been in this city for a few days, but I venture to say I have seen more beggars and men out of work around Eighth and Market streets than I have seen in the whole City of Mexico."

    Missionary Frederic Poole disposed of this argument in a few words. He said: "It is not my idea, nor the idea of Mr. Converse, that these men should at any time compete with American workingmen. It is not the wish of the men themselves. Mr. Converse would not have given them employment had any such thing been intended.

    "To-day China is building a vast railroad to Pekin that will open up all the wealthy and fertile region of Central China. The enterprise is under the direction of the government. It will be in operation in about four years. Men of intelligence will be needed for engineers, and there my five protégés will find their life work. It is not unlikely that the Chinese Government will send for them before their apprenticeship is over."

    John H. Converse was rather interested when he learned of objections to his Chinese apprentices. "We might have expected such objections from professional agitators," he said, "but I do not think you will learn of any among our employees."

    Continuing, he said: "The Baldwin Locomotive Works is now constructing eight locomotives for the Chinese Government, which will be the first to run over the great new railroad being built from Pekin to Tien-Tsin. American workingmen would be very narrow indeed if they cannot see that it is to their own immediate advantage that Chinese mechanics fit to look after American locomotives shall be trained at once, for the time is coming when thousands of American workingmen may be kept busy from the extension of railroad building in China.

    "These five boys are Philadelphians. They were not brought here, and every broad-minded mechanic will believe that their apprenticeship in our shops, should they, as they probably will, return to China, must mean something for the American locomotive. They are the first to be admitted to a locomotive works in this country, and the news will in all likelihood create a more friendly feeling in the railroad department of the Chinese Government for American products."

Mr. Converse said that his firm had no thought of extending the privilege beyond the present number of Chinese apprentices.—Philadelphia *Public Ledger*, January 5, 1897.

No Negro apprentices have ever been admitted.

The other clipping is a report of the discussion in the annual meeting of the Federation of Labor:

The Negro question occupied the major portion of the session, and a heated discussion was brought on by a resolution by Henry Lloyd, reaffirming the declarations of the Federation that all labor, without regard to color, is welcome to its ranks—denouncing as untrue in fact the reported statements of Booker T. Washington that the trades unions were placing obstacles in the way of the material advancement of the Negro, and appealing to the records of the Federation Conventions as complete answers to such false assertions.

This resolution caused much spirited discussion. Delegate Jones, of Augusta, Ga., spoke, claiming that the white laborer could not compete with the Negro laborer, though organization would improve conditions materially. President Gompers took part in the discussion, explaining that the movement was not against the Negro laborer, but against the cheap laborer, and that the textile workers of the East had been compelled to contribute most of their means to teach laborers in the South the benefits of organization.

He also made the point that the capitalist would profit by the failure of the Negro laborers to organize, thus making the Negro an impediment to labor movements.

C. P. Frahey, a Nashville delegate, insisted that the Negro was not the equal of the white man socially or industrially. He grew warm in speaking of President Gompers' remarks regarding the Negro in the labor movement, and stated that the President had not revoked the commission of a National Organizer who had patronized a non-union white barber shop in preference to a union Negro barber shop.

The organizer had simply been allowed to resign and no publicity had been given the matter. In answer to a question desiring the name of the party, Frahey stated it was Jesse Johnson, president of the pressmen.

James O'Connell and P. J. McGuire spoke for the resolution. The latter insisted that Booker T. Washington was attempting to put the Negro before the public as the victim of gross injustice, and himself as the Moses of the race. M. D. Rathford insisted that drawing the color line would be a blow to the miners' organization.

W. D. Mahon charged that Jones was not a representative of Southern trades unionism, having just joined the ranks. Jones then, in his own defence, declared he did not oppose the Negro, but did contend that the Negro laborer was lower than the white, citing an Atlanta case, where whites and blacks had been jointly employed and the whites struck.

He wanted to know if there had been any efforts made in the East to organize Chinese who came in conflict with the union labor. President Gompers then ruled that the discussion must cease.

The resolution which had caused the heated debate was adopted, and the delegates went into executive session.—*Public Ledger*, December 17, 1897.

6. From the facts tabulated, it appears that one-twentieth of the colored domestic servants of Philadelphia have trades, while in addition to this one-tenth have had some higher school training and are presumably fitted to be something more than ordinary domestics. Why then do they not enter these fields instead of drifting into or deliberately choosing domestic service as a means of livelihood? The answer is simple. In a majority of cases the reason why they do not enter other fields is because they are colored not because they are incompetent. Many instances might be cited in proof of this, were proof needed. The following cases are only some of those that were personally encountered by the investigator in one ward of one city.

One very fair young girl, apparently a white girl, was employed as a clerk in one of the large department stores for over two years, so that there was no question of her competency as a clerk. At the end of this time it was discovered that she had colored blood and she was promptly discharged. One young woman who had been a teacher and is now a school janitress, teaching occasionally when extra help is needed, states that she had received an appointment as typewriter in a certain Philadelphia office, on the strength of her letter of application and when she appeared and was seen to be a colored girl, the position was refused her. She said that her brother—whom people usually take to be a white man—after serving in the barbershop of a certain hotel for more than ten years, was summarily discharged when it was learned that he was of Negro birth. One woman, who was a seamstress and dressmaker, stated that she had on several occasions gotten work from a certain church home when she wore a heavy veil, on making her application at the office, but that on the first occasion when she wore no veil her application was refused and had been every time since. Of course many of the men in domestic service have had similar experiences. Ten men out of one hundred and fifty-six had trades, but none of them were members of the trades unions.

Mr. McGuire, vice-president of the Federation of Labor, stated to the present investigator that the Federation claims that colored men may be members of any trade union represented in the Federation. But what this profession amounts to may be judged from Mr. McGuire's further statement, quoted verbatim: "A majority are willing to have them admitted, but a strong minority will oppose it. Not a word will be said against it in discussion, but quietly at the ballot they will rule them out."

How this profession of admission, which amounts to practical exclusion, looks from the workingman's point of view is shown in the experience of a first-rate colored carpenter and builder in the Seventh Ward who was induced to apply for admission to the Carpenters' Union. He asked an officer of the Amalgamated Association of Carpenters and Joiners, one of the allied societies of the American Federation of Labor, if it would be of any use for him to apply to the Union for membership. "If you know your trade and are a carpenter in good and regular standing, I see no reason why you should not become a member," said the officer. "So he sent me to the present secretary of the association, and when I put the question to him, he said, 'Well, he didn't know whether I could join or not, because they had never *had* a colored man in the Union, but he would report it to the association here [Philadelphia] and would write to headquarters in New York to see if it would be admissible to enter a colored man.' He put it on the ground of my color, you see." This application was made in December, 1896. The applicant was told that the matter would be acted on in the Union on a certain night in January, 1897, and every attempt was made to send a man to report that particular meeting, but without success. What occurred is not hard to guess, however, since the colored carpenter whose case was then considered has received no word from the Union from that day to this. He has called at the secretary's office three or four times and left word that he would like to hear what action was taken regarding his application for admission to the Union, but December 1, 1897, he had received no answer to his application made in December, 1896.

The effect of this is well illustrated by the case of a young colored "waiter man" on Pine street, whose case may be taken as typical. He had studied three years at Hampton, where he had learned in that time the stone-cutter's trade. He could practice this in Georgia, he said, but in the South stone-cutters get only $2.00 a day as compared with $3.50, sometimes $4.00 a day, in the North. So he came North with the promise of a job of stone-cutting for a new block of buildings to be erected by a Philadelphian he had met in Georgia. He received $3.50 a day, but when the block was done he could get no other job at stone-cutting and so went into domestic service, where he is receiving $6.25 a week instead of the $21.00 a week he should be receiving as a stone-cutter.

The effect on domestic service is to swell its already over-full ranks with discontented young men and women whom one would naturally expect to find rendering half-hearted service because they consider their domestic work only a temporary makeshift employment. One sometimes hears it said that "our waiter has graduated from such and such a school, but we notice that he is not even a very good waiter." Such comments give rise to the speculation as to the success in ditch digging which would be likely to attend upon the labors of college professors, or indeed, how many of the young white men who have graduated from college and from law schools would show themselves excellent waiters, particularly if they took up the work simply as a temporary expedient. A "match" between Yale and Hampton, where mental activities must be confined to the walls of the butler's pantry, and where there were to be no "fumbles' with soup plates, might bring out interesting and suggestive points.

ISABEL EATON.

7. "In the case of the Colored people, the number of mother wage-earners more than doubles the number of widows. This is due to the small average wage of the Colored husband—the smallest among the twenty-seven nationalities. The laundress is the economic supplement of the porter. . . . It is not because the Colored husband of this district neglects his responsibility as a wage-winner that so many Colored women are forced into supplemental toil, for 98.7 per cent of the Colored husbands are wage-earners, and only 92.2 per cent of the American, 90.3 per cent of the Irish, 96 per cent of the German, 93.7 per cent of the Italian, 93.1 per cent of the French. The Danes, 80 per cent; Canadians, 81.8 per cent; Russians, 85.7 per cent, and Hungarians, 88.8 per cent, have the smallest percentages. Of the more largely represented nationalities, the French most nearly approach the Colored people in the percentage of their wives who are wage-earners; but while the French percentage is 21.6 per cent, the Colored people's percentage is 53.6 per cent." Dr. W. Laidlaw in the "Report of a Sociological Canvass of the Nineteenth Assembly District," a slum section of New York City, in 1897.

8. Undoubtedly certain classes of Negroes bring much deserved criticism on themselves by irregular payment or default of rent, and by the poor care they take of property. They must not, however, be confounded with the better classes who make good customers; this is again a place for careful discrimination.

9. Kindly furnished by the principals of these schools.

10. Cf. on this point the interesting article of John Stevens Durham in the *Atlantic Monthly*, 1898.

11. No attempt has been made here to make any intensive study of the efforts to help Negroes, which are widespread and commendable; they need, however, a study which would extend the scope of this inquiry too far.

12. Founded, and supported in part, by Negroes. Cf. Chap. XII.

13. Founded, and supported in part, by Negroes. Cf. Chap. XII.

14. Hoffman's "Race Traits and Tendencies," etc., pp. 1 and 177.

15. Hoffman has the results of some intermarriages recorded, but they are chiefly reports of criminals in the newspapers, and thus manifestly unfair for generalization.

16. From a personal letter of a life long Philadelphian, whose name I am not at liberty to quote.

CHAPTER XVII

Negro Suffrage

50. The Significance of the Experiment—The indiscriminate granting of universal suffrage to freedmen and foreigners was one of the most daring experiments of a too venturesome nation. In the case of the Negro its only justification was that the ballot might serve as a weapon of defence for helpless ex-slaves, and would at one stroke enfranchise those Negroes whose education and standing entitled them to a voice in the government. There can be no doubt but that the wisest provision would have been an educational and property qualification impartially enforced against ex-slaves and immigrants. In the absence of such a provision it was certainly more just to admit the untrained and ignorant than to bar out all Negroes in spite of their qualifications; more just, but also more dangerous.

Those who from time to time have discussed the results of this experiment have usually looked for their facts in the wrong place, *i.e.*, in the South. Under the peculiar conditions still prevailing in the South no fair trial of the Negro voter could have been made. The "carpet-bag" governments of reconstruction time were in no true sense the creatures of Negro voters, nor is there to-day a Southern State where free untrammeled Negro suffrage prevails. It is then to Northern communities that one must turn to study the Negro as a voter, and the result of the experiment in Pennsylvania while not decisive is certainly instructive.

51. The History of Negro Suffrage in Pennsylvania—The laws for Pennsylvania agreed upon in England in 1682 declared as qualified electors "every inhabitant in the said province, that is or shall be a purchaser of one hundred acres of land or upwards, . . . and every person that hath been a servant or bondsman, and is free by his service, that shall have taken up his fifty acres of land, and cultivated twenty thereof;" and also some other taxpayers.[1]

These provisions were in keeping with the design of partially freeing Negroes after fourteen years service and contemplated without doubt black electors, at least in theory. It is doubtful if many Negroes voted under this provision although that is possible. In the call for the Convention of 1776 no restriction as to color was mentioned,[2] and the constitution of that year gave the right of suffrage to "every freeman of the full age of twenty-one years, having resided in this State for the space of one whole year."[3] Probably some Negro electors in Pennsylvania helped choose the framers of the Constitution.

In the Convention of 1790 no restriction as to color was adopted and the suffrage article as finally decided upon read as follows:

"Article III, Section I. In elections by the citizens, every freeman of the age of twenty-one years, having resided in the State two years next before the election, and within that time paid a State or county tax, which shall have been assessed at least six months before the election, shall enjoy the rights of an elector."[4]

Nothing in the printed minutes of the convention indicates any attempt in the convention to prohibit Negro suffrage, but Mr. Albert Gallatin declared in 1837: "I have a lively recollection that in some stages of the discussion the proposition pending before the convention limited the right of suffrage to 'free white citizens,' etc., and that the word white was struck out on my motion."[5]

It was alleged afterward that in 1795 the question came before the High Court of Errors and Appeals and that its decision denied the right to Negroes. No written decision of this sort was ever found, however, and it is certain that for nearly a half century free Negroes voted in parts of Pennsylvania.[6]

As the Negro population increased, however, and ignorant and dangerous elements entered, and as the slavery controversy grew warmer, the feeling against Negroes increased and with it opposition to their right to vote. In July, 1837, the Supreme Court sitting at Sunbury took up the celebrated case of Hobbs *et al.* against Fogg. Fogg was a free Negro and taxpayer, and had been denied the right to vote by Hobbs and others, the judges and inspectors of election in Luzerne County. He brought action and was sustained in the Court of Common Pleas, but the Supreme Court under Judge Gibson reversed this judgment. The decision rendered was an evident straining of law and sense. The judge sought to refer to the decision of 1795, but could cite no written record; he explained the striking out of the word "white" in the constitutional convention as done to prevent insult to "dark colored white men," and held that a Negro, though free, could never be a freeman.[7]

All doubt was finally removed by the reform constitutional convention of 1837–38. The article on suffrage as reported to the convention May 17, 1837, was practically the same as in the Constitution of 1790.[8] This article was taken up June 19, 1837. There was an attempt to amend the report and to restrict the suffrage to "free white male" citizens. The attempt was defended as being in consonance with the regulations of other States, and with the real facts in Pennsylvania, since "In the county of Philadelphia the colored man could not with safety appear at the polls."[9] The amendment, however, met opposition and was withdrawn. The matter arose again a few days later but was voted down by a vote of 61 to 49.[10]

The friends of exclusion now began systematic efforts to stir up public opinion. No less than forty-five petitions against Negro suffrage were handed in, especially from Bucks County, where a Negro had once nearly succeeded in being elected to the legislature. Many petitions too in favor of retaining the old provisions came in, but it was charged that the convention would not print petitions in favor of Negro suffrage, and some members did not wish even to receive petitions from Negroes.[11]

The discussion of the Third Article recurred January 17, 1838, and a long argument ensued. Finally the word "white" was inserted in the qualifications of voters by a vote of 77 to 45. A protracted struggle took place to soften this regulation in various ways, but all efforts failed and the final draft, which was eventually adopted by popular vote, had the following provisions:[12]

"Article III, Section I. In elections by the citizens, every white freeman of the age of twenty-one years, having resided in this State one year, and in the electoral district where he offers to vote ten days immediately preceding such election, and within two years paid a State or county tax, which shall have been assessed at least ten days before the election, shall enjoy the rights of an elector."[13] This disfranchisement lasted thirty-two years, until the passage of the Fifteenth Amendment. The Constitution of 1874 formally adopted this change.[14] Since 1870 the experiment of untrammeled Negro suffrage has been made throughout the State.

52. City Politics—About 5,500 Negroes were eligible to vote in the city of Philadelphia, in 1870. The question first arises, Into what sort of a political atmosphere were they introduced, and what training did they receive for their new responsibilities?

Few large cities have such a disreputable record for misgovernment as Philadelphia. In the period before the war the city was ruled by the Democratic party, which retained its power by the manipulation of a mass of ignorant and turbulent foreign voters, chiefly Irish. Riots, disorder, and crime were the rule in the city proper and especially in the surrounding districts. About the time of the breaking out of the war, the city was consolidated and made coterminous with the county. The social upheaval after the Civil War gave the political power to the Republicans and a new era of misrule commenced. Open disorder and crime were repressed, but in its place came the rule of the boss, with its quiet manipulation and calculating embezzlement of public funds. To-day the government of both city and State is unparalleled in the history of republican government for brazen dishonesty and bare-faced defiance of public opinion. The supporters of this government have been, by a vast majority, white men and native Americans; the Negro vote has never exceeded 4 per cent of the total registration.

Manifestly such a political atmosphere was the worst possible for the new untutored voter. Starting himself without political ideals, he was put under the tutelage of unscrupulous and dishonest men whose ideal of government was to prostitute it to their own private ends. As the Irishman had been the tool of the Democrats, so the Negro became the tool of the Republicans. It was natural that the freedman should vote for the party that emancipated him, and perhaps, too, it was natural that a party with so sure a following, should use it unscrupulously. The result to be expected from such a situation was that the Negro should learn from his surroundings a low ideal of political morality and no conception of the real end of party loyalty. At the same time we ought to expect individual exceptions to this general level, and some evidences of growth.

53. Some Bad Results of Negro Suffrage—The experiment of Negro suffrage in Philadelphia has developed three classes of Negro voters: a large majority of voters who vote blindly at the dictates of the party and, while not open to direct bribery, accept the indirect emoluments of office or influence in return for party loyalty; a considerable group, centering in the slum districts, which casts a corrupt purchasable vote for the highest bidder; lastly, a very small group of independent voters who seek to use their vote to better present conditions of municipal life.

The political morality of the first group of voters, that is to say, of the great mass of Negro voters, corresponds roughly to that of the mass of white voters, but with this difference: the ignorance of the Negro in matters of government is greater and his devotion to party blinder and more unreasoning. Add to this the mass of recent immigrants from the South, with the political training of reconstruction and post-bellum days, and one can easily see how poorly trained this body of electors has been.

Under such circumstances it is but natural that political morality and knowledge should be even slower in spreading among Negroes than wealth and general intelligence. One consequently finds among those of considerable intelligence and of upright lives such curious misapprehension of political duties as is illustrated by the address of the Afro-American League to the mayor of the city, February 8, 1897:

"MR. MAYOR:—We desire first and foremost, to tender you our profound thanks for the honor of this cordial reception. We regard it, sir, as proof of the recognition on your part of that just and most admirable custom of our country's government, which permits the subjects, however humble may be their condition in life, to see their ruler as well as feel the workings of his power.

"We are here to state to your excellency that the colored citizens of Philadelphia are penetrated with feelings of inexpressible grief at the manner in which they have thus far been overlooked and ignored by the Republican party in this city, in giving out work and otherwise distributing the enormous patronage in the gift of the party. We are therefore here, sir, to earnestly beseech of you as a faithful Republican and our worthy chief executive, to use your potent influence as well as the good offices of your municipal government, if not inconsistent with the public weal, to procure for the colored people of this city a share at least, of the public work and the recognition which they now ask for and feel to be justly due to them, no less as citizens and taxpayers, than on a basis of their voting strength of something over 14,000 in the Republican party here in Philadelphia.

"As the chosen organ of this body of men I am actuated by a due sense of their earnestness of purpose in this matter and I regret to be inadequate to the task of convincing you, Mr. Mayor, of the deep interest which is being universally manifested by the colored element in Philadelphia in this somewhat important question. The colored people neither ask for nor expect extremes; we only claim that our loyal fidelity to the Republican party should count, at some time, for some benefits to at least a reasonable number of the colored race when our friends are installed into place and power; and, cherishing as we do, sir, the most implicit confidence in your justice as the chief executive of this great city, we firmly believe that this most unfair treatment of which our people now complain, would not fail, when brought thus to your attention, in moving you in our humble behalf. We, therefore, have here to present for your candid consideration a paper containing the names of some worthy and reliable men of our race and they are respectfully urged for appointment as indicated on the face of that paper, and out of a desire, Mr. Mayor, to facilitate your efforts should you take favorable action upon this matter, these men, as we will state, have been selected as near as possible from every section of the city, as well as upon the proof of their fitness for the places named."

The organization which here speaks is not large or nearly as representative as it claims to be; it is simply a small faction of "outs" who are striving to get "in." The significant thing about the address is the fact that a considerable number of fairly respectable and ordinarily intelligent citizens should think this a perfectly legitimate and laudable demand. This represents the political morality of the great mass of ordinary Negro voters. And what more does it argue than that they have learned their lesson well and recited it bluntly but honestly? What more do the majority of American politicians and voters to-day say in action if not in word than: "Here is my vote, now where is my pay in office or favor or influence?" What thousands are acting, this delegation had the charming simplicity to say plainly and then to print.

Moreover one circumstance makes this attitude of mind more dangerous among Negroes than among whites; Negroes as a class are poor and as laborers are restricted to few and unremunerative occupations; consequently the bribe of office is to them a far larger and alluring temptation than to the mass of whites. In other words here are a people more ignorant than their fellows, with stronger tendencies to dishonesty and crime, who are offered a far larger bribe than ordinary men to enter politics for personal gain. The result is obvious: "Of course I'm in politics," said a Negro city watchman, "it's the only way a colored man can get a position where he can earn a decent living." He was a fireman by trade, but Philadelphia engineers object to working with "Niggers."

If this is the result in the case of an honest man, how great is the temptation to the vicious and lazy. This brings us to the second class of voters—the corrupt class, which sells its votes more or less openly.

The able-bodied, well-dressed loafers and criminals who infest the sidewalks of parts of the Fifth, Seventh and other wards are supported partly by crime and gambling, partly by the prostitution of their female paramours, but mainly from the vast corruption fund gathered from office-holders and others, and distributed according to the will of the party Boss. The *Public Ledger* said in 1896:

> "It is estimated that the Republican City Committee realized nearly if not all of $100,000 from the 1½ per cent assessment levied upon municipal officeholders for this campaign. Of this sum $40,000 has been paid for the eighty thousand tax receipts to qualify Republican voters. This leaves $60,000 at the disposal of David Martin, the Combine leader."[15]

How is this corruption fund used? Without doubt a large part of it is spent in the purchase of votes. It is of course difficult to estimate the directly purchasable vote among the whites or among the Negroes. Once in a while when "thieves fall out" some idea of the bribery may be obtained; for instance in a hearing relative to a Third Ward election:

> William Reed, of Catharine street, below Thirteenth, was first on the stand. He was watcher in the Fifteenth Division on election day.
>
> "Did you make up any election papers for voters?" asked Mr. Ingham.
>
> "I marked up about seventy or eighty ballots; I got $20 off of Roberts' brother, and used $100 altogether, paying the rest out of my own pocket."

"How did you spend the money?"

"Oh, well, there were some few objectionable characters there to make trouble. We'd give 'em a few dollars to go away and attend to their business." Then he addressed Mr. Ingham directly, "You know how it works."

"I'd give 'em a dollar to buy a cigar. And if they didn't want to pay $1 for a cigar, why, they could put it in the contribution box at church."

"Was this election conducted in the usual way?" inquired Mr. Sterr.

"Oh, yes, the way they're conducted in the Third Ward—with vote buying, and all the rest of it."

"Did the other side have any money to spend?"

"Saunders had $16 to the division."

"What did your side have?"

"Oh, we had about $60; there was money to burn. But our money went to three people. The other fellows saved theirs. I spent mine—like a sucker."

James Brown, a McKinley-Citizen worker, began his testimony indignantly.

"Election? Why Reed and Morrow, the judges of the election, run the whole shootin' match," he declared. "It was all a farce. I brought voters up; and Reed would take 'em away from me. When we challenged anybody, Reed and the others would have vouchers ready."

"Did they use money?"

"There was a good deal of money through the division. We wasn't even allowed to mark ballots for our own people who asked for help. The judge would ask 'em if they could read and write. When they said 'yes,' he'd tell 'em they were able to mark their own ballot. There were even some people who wanted to mark their own ballots. Reed would simply grab 'em and mark their ballots, whether they liked it or not."

Lavinia Brown, colored, of the rear of 1306 Kater street, said that Mr. Bradford was judge on election day, of the Sixteenth Division, and that on the morning of the election she cooked his breakfast. She said that I. Newton Roberts came to the house, and in her presence gave Bradford a roll of notes, at the same time throwing her $2, but she did not know for what purpose he gave it.

George W. Green, colored, of 1224 Catharine street, said he was a watcher at the polls of the Sixteenth Division. He told of fraud and how the voters were treated.

"Were you offered any money?"

"Yes, sir. Lincoln Roberts came over to me and shoved $50 at me, but I turned him down and would not take it, because I didn't belong to that crowd." Continuing, he said: "Seven or eight men were challenged, but it did not amount to anything, because Lincoln Roberts would tell the police to eject them. He also vouched for men who did not live in the ward. This condition of affairs continued all day."

Several other witnesses followed, whose testimony was similar to Green's, and who declared that money was distributed freely by the Roberts faction to buy over voters. They said that challenges were disregarded, and that the election was a farce. Voters were kept out, and when it was known that any of Saunders' adherents were coming a rush would be made, making it impossible for that side to enter the booth.

Philip Brown, a McKinley-Citizen watcher, said that the election was a fraud. He saw Mr. Roberts with a pile of money, going around shouting, "That's the stuff that wins!" When asked what the judge was doing all this time he said:

"Why, the judge belonged to Mr. Roberts, who had full control of the polling place all day."

William Hare, of 1346 Kater street, proved an interesting witness. His story is as follows:

"Mr. Lincoln Roberts brought my tax receipt and told me to come around to the club. I went and was given a bundle of tax receipts, marked for other men, and told to deliver them. The next day being election day I made it a point to watch, and saw that every man to whom I gave a receipt came to the polls and voted for Mr. Roberts. I saw Mr. Newton Roberts mark the ballots over six times myself."

Many of the men mentioned here are white, and this happened in a ward where there are more white than Negro voters, but the same open bribery goes on at every election in the slum districts of the Fourth, Fifth, Seventh and Eighth Wards, where a large Negro vote is cast. In a meeting of Negroes held in 1896 one politician calmly announced that "through money from my white friends I control the colored vote in my precinct." Another man arose and denounced the speaker pretty plainly as a trickster although his allegation was not denied. This brought on general discussion in which there were uncontradicted statements that in certain sections votes were bought for "fifty cents and a drink of whisky" and men "driven in droves to the polls." There was some exaggeration here and yet without doubt many Negroes sell their votes directly for a money consideration. This sort of thing is confined to the lowest classes, but there it is widespread. Such bribery, however, is the least harmful kind because it is so direct and shameless that only men of no character would accept it.

Next to this direct purchase of votes, one of the chief and most pernicious forms of bribery among the lowest classes is through the establishment of political clubs, which abound in the Fourth, Fifth, Seventh and Eighth Wards, and are not uncommon elsewhere. A political club is a band of eight or twelve men who rent a club house with money furnished them by the boss, and support themselves partially in the same way. The club is often named after some politician—one of the most notorious gambling hells of the Seventh Ward is named after a United States Senator—and the business of the club is to see that its precinct is carried for the proper candidate, to get "jobs" for some of its "boys," to keep others from arrest and to secure bail and discharge for those arrested. Such clubs become the centre of gambling, drunkenness, prostitution and crime. Every night there are no less than fifteen of these clubs in the Seventh Ward where open gambling goes on, to which almost any one can gain admittance if properly introduced; nearly every day some redhanded criminal finds refuge here from the law. Prostitutes are in easy reach of these places and sometimes enter them. Liquor is furnished to "members" at all times and the restrictions on membership are slight. The leader of each club is boss of his district; he knows the people, knows the ward boss, knows the police; so long as the loafers and gamblers under him do not arouse the public too much he sees that they are not molested. If they are arrested it does not mean much save in grave cases. Men openly boast on the streets that they can get bail for any amount. And certainly they appear to have powerful friends at the Public Buildings. There is of course a difference in the various clubs; some are of higher class than others and receive offices as bribes; others are openly devoted to gambling and receive protection as a bribe; one of the most notorious gambling houses of the Seventh Ward was recently raided, and although every school boy knows the character of the proprietor he was released for "lack of evidence." Still other clubs are simply winter quarters for thieves, loafers and criminals well known to the police. There are of course one or two clubs, mainly social and only partially political, to which the foregoing statements do not apply—as for instance the Citizens' Club on Broad street, which has the best Negroes of the city in its membership, allows no gambling and pays its own expenses. This club, however, stands almost alone and the other twelve or fifteen political clubs of the Seventh Ward represent a form of political corruption which is a disgrace to a civilized city. In the Fourth, Fifth and Eighth Wards there are ten or twelve more clubs, and probably in the whole city the Negroes have forty such places with a possible membership of five or six hundred. The influence of these clubs on the young immigrants, on growing boys, on the surrounding working people is most deplorable. At the polls they carry the day with high-handed and often riotous proceedings, voting "repeaters" and "colonists" often with impunity.

Among the great mass of Negro voters, whose votes cannot be directly purchased, a less direct but, in the long run, more demoralizing bribery is common. It is the same sort of bribery as that which is to-day corrupting the white voters of the land, viz:

(*a*) Contributions to various objects in which voters are interested.

(*b*) Appointment to public office or to work of any kind for the city.

Men accept from political organizations, contributions to charitable and other objects which they would not think of accepting for themselves. Others less scrupulous get contributions or favors for enterprises in which they are directly interested. Fairs, societies, clubs and even churches have profited by this sort of political corruption, and the custom is by no means confined to Negroes.

A better known method of political bribery among the mass of Negroes is through apportionment of the public work or appointment to public office. The work open to Negroes throughout the city is greatly restricted as has been pointed out. One class of well-paid positions, the city civil service, was once closed to them, and only one road was open to them to secure these positions and that was unquestioning obedience to the "machine." The emoluments of office are a temptation to most men, but how much greater they are for Negroes can only be realized on reflection: Here is a well-educated young man, who despite all efforts can get no work above that of porter at $6 or $8 a week. If he goes into "politics," blindly votes for the candidate of the party boss, and by hard, steady and astute work persuades most of the colored voters in his precinct to do the same, he has the chance of being rewarded by a city clerkship, the social prestige of being in a position above menial labor, and an income of $60 or $75 a month. Such is the character of the grasp which the "machine" has on even intelligent Negro voters.

How far this sort of bribery goes is illustrated by the fact that 170 city employes are from the Fifth Ward and probably forty of these are Negroes. The three Negro members of the machine in this ward are all office-holders. About one-fourth of the fifty-two members of the Seventh Ward machine are Negroes, and one-half of these are office-holders. The Negro's record as an office-seeker is, it is needless to say, far surpassed by his white brother and it is only in the last two decades that Negroes have appeared as members of councils and clerks.[16]

In spite of the methods employed to secure these offices it cannot as yet justly be charged that many of the Negro office-holders are unfitted for their duty. There is always the possibility however that incompetent Negro officers may increase in number; and there can be no doubt but that corrupt and dishonest white politicians have been kept in power by the influence thus obtained to sway the Negro vote of the Seventh and Eighth and other wards. The problem of the Negro voter then is one of the many problems that baffle all efforts at political reform in Philadelphia: the small corrupt vote of the slums which disgraces republican government; the large vote of the masses which mistaken political ideals, blind party loyalty and economic stress now holds imprisoned and shackled to the service of dishonest political leaders.

54. Some Good Results of Negro Suffrage—It is wrong to suppose that all the results of this hazardous experiment in widening the franchise have been evil. First the ballot has without doubt been a means of protection in the hands of a people peculiarly liable to oppression. Its first bestowal gained Negroes admittance to street-cars after a struggle of a quarter century; and frequently since private and public oppression has been lightened by the knowledge of the power of the black vote. This fact has greatly increased the civic patriotism of the Negro, made him strive more eagerly to adapt himself to the spirit of the city life, and has kept him from becoming a socially dangerous class.

At the same time the Negro has never sought to use his ballot to menace civilization or even the established principles of this government. This fact has been noticed by many students but it deserves emphasis. Instead of being radical light-headed followers of every new political panacea, the freedmen of Philadelphia and of the nation have always formed the most conservative element in our political life and have steadfastly opposed the schemes of inflationists, socialists and dreamers. Part of this conservatism may to be sure be the inertia of ignorance, but even such inertia must anchor to some well-defined notions as to what the present situation is; and no element of our political life seems better to comprehend the main lines of our social organization than the Negro. In Philadelphia he has usually been allied with the better elements although too often that "better" was far from the best. And never has the Negro been to any extent the ally of the worst elements.

In spite of the fact that unworthy officials could easily get into office by the political methods pursued by the Negroes, the average of those who have obtained office has been good. Of the three colored councilmen one has received the endorsement of the Municipal League, while the others seem to be up to the average of the councilmen. One Negro has been clerk in the tax office for twenty years or more and has an enviable record. The colored policemen as a class are declared by their superiors to be capable, neat and efficient. There are some cases of inefficiency— one clerk who used to be drunk most of his time, another who devotes his time to work outside his office, and many cases of inefficient watchmen and laborers.

The average of efficiency among colored officeholders however is good and much higher than one might naturally expect.

Finally, the training in citizenship which the exercise of the right of suffrage entails has not been lost on the Philadelphia Negro. Any worthy cause of municipal reform can secure a respectable Negro vote in the city, showing that there is the germ of an intelligent independent vote which rises above even the blandishments of decent remunerative employment. This class is small but seems to be growing.

55. The Paradox of Reform—The growth of a higher political morality among Negroes is to-day hindered by their paradoxical position. Suppose the Municipal League or the Woman's School-board movement, or some other reform is brought before the better class of Negroes to-day; they will nearly all agree that city politics are notoriously corrupt, that honest women should replace ward heelers on school-boards, and the like. But can they vote for such movements? Most of them will say No; for to do so will throw many worthy Negroes out of employment: these very reformers who want votes for specific reforms, will not themselves work beside Negroes, or admit them to positions in their stores or offices, or lend them friendly aid in trouble. Moreover Negroes are proud of their councilmen and policemen. What if some of these positions of honor and respectability have been gained by shady "politics"—shall they be nicer in these matters than the mass of the whites? Shall they surrender these tangible evidences of the rise of their race to forward the good-hearted but hardly imperative demands of a crowd of women? Especially, too, of women who did not apparently know there were any Negroes on earth until they wanted their votes? Such logic may be faulty, but it is convincing to the mass of Negro voters. And cause after cause may gain their respectful attention and even applause, but when election-day comes, the "machine" gets their votes.

Thus the growth of broader political sentiment is hindered and will be until some change comes. When industrial exclusion is so broken down that no class will be unduly tempted by the bribe of office; when the apostles of civil reform compete within the ward Boss in friendliness and kindly consideration for the unfortunate; when the league between gambling and crime and the city authorities is less close, then we can expect the more rapid development of civic virtue in the Negro and indeed in the whole city. As it is to-day the experiment of Negro suffrage with all its glaring shortcomings cannot justly be called a failure, but rather in view of all circumstances a partial success. Whatever it lacks can justly be charged to those Philadelphians who for thirty years have surrendered their right of political leadership to thieves and tricksters, and allowed such teachers to instruct this untutored race in whose hand lay an unfamiliar instrument of civilization.

NOTES

1. "Minutes of the Conventions of 1776 and 1790," (Ed. 1825) pp. 32–33; Cf. p. 26.
2. *Ibid.*, pp. 38–39.
3. *Ibid.*, p. 57.

4. *Ibid.*, p. 300. Cf. "Purdon's Digest," sixth edition.
5. "Proceedings and Debates of the Convention of 1837," X, 45. Cf. Purvis in "Appeal of 40,000 Citizens." The printed minutes give only the main results with few details.
6. 6 Watts, 553–560, "Pennsylvania Reports." "Proceedings, etc., Convention 1837–8, II, 476.
7. 6 Watts, 553–60, "Pennsylvania Reports."
8. "Proceedings and Debates," I, 233.
9. "Proceedings and Debates," II, 478.
10. *Ibid.*, III, 82–92.
11. *Ibid.*, Volumes IV–IX.
12. *Ibid.*, IX, 320–397, X, 1–134.
13. "Purdon," sixth edition.
14. The Constitution of 1874 gave the right of suffrage to "Every male citizen of the United States of the age of twenty-one years. . . ."—"Debates," etc., I, 503, etc. See Index "Constitution of Pennsylvania," Article VIII; and also the Act of 6 April, 1870.
15. October 5, 1896.
16. Cf. "A Woman's Municipal Campaign." Publications of Amer. Acad. of Pol. and Soc. Science.

CHAPTER XVIII

◆

A Final Word

56. The Meaning of All This—Two sorts of answers are usually returned to the bewildered American who asks seriously: What is the Negro problem? The one is straightforward and clear: it is simply this, or simply that, and one simple remedy long enough applied will in time cause it to disappear. The other answer is apt to be hopelessly involved and complex—to indicate no simple panacea, and to end in a somewhat hopeless—There it is; what can we do? Both of these sorts of answers have something of truth in them: the Negro problem looked at in one way is but the old world questions of ignorance, poverty, crime, and the dislike of the stranger. On the other hand it is a mistake to think that attacking each of these questions single-handed without reference to the others will settle the matter: a combination of social problems is far more than a matter of mere addition,—the combination itself is a problem. Nevertheless the Negro problems are not more hopelessly complex than many others have been. Their elements despite their bewildering complication can be kept clearly in view: they are after all the same difficulties over which the world has grown gray: the question as to how far human intelligence can be trusted and trained; as to whether we must always have the poor with us; as to whether it is possible for the mass of men to attain righteousness on earth; and then to this is added that question of questions: after all who are Men? Is every feather-less biped to be counted a man and brother? Are all races and types to be joint heirs of the new earth that men have striven to raise in thirty centuries and more? Shall we not swamp civilization in barbarism and drown genius in indulgence if we seek a mythical Humanity which shall shadow all men? The answer of the early centuries to this puzzle was clear: those of any nation who can be called Men and endowed with rights are few: they are the privileged classes—the well-born and the accidents of low birth called up by the King. The rest, the mass of the nation, the *pöbel*, the mob, are fit to follow, to obey, to dig and delve, but not to think or rule or play the gentleman. We who were born to another philosophy hardly realize how deep-seated and plausible this view of human capabilities and powers once was; how utterly incomprehensible this republic would have been to Charlemagne or Charles V or Charles I. We rather hasten to forget that once the courtiers of English kings looked upon the ancestors of most Americans with far greater contempt than these Americans look upon Negroes—and perhaps, indeed, had more cause.

We forget that once French peasants were the "Niggers" of France, and that German princelings once discussed with doubt the brains and humanity of the *bauer*.

Much of this—or at least some of it—has passed and the world has glided by blood and iron into a wider humanity, a wider respect for simple manhood unadorned by ancestors or privilege. Not that we have discovered, as some hoped and some feared, that all men were created free and equal, but rather that the differences in men are not so vast as we had assumed. We still yield the well-born the advantages of birth, we still see that each nation has its dangerous flock of fools and rascals; but we also find most men have brains to be cultivated and souls to be saved.

And still this widening of the idea of common Humanity is of slow growth and to-day but dimly realized. We grant full citizenship in the World Commonwealth to the "Anglo-Saxon" (whatever that may mean), the Teuton and the Latin; then with just a shade of reluctance we extend it to the Celt and Slav. We half deny it to the yellow races of Asia, admit the brown Indians to an ante-room only on the strength of an undeniable past; but with the Negroes of Africa we come to a full stop, and in its heart the civilized world with one accord denies that these come within the pale of nineteenth-century Humanity. This feeling, widespread and deep-seated, is, in America, the vastest of the Negro problems; we have, to be sure, a threatening problem of ignorance but the ancestors of most Americans were far more ignorant than the freedmen's sons; these ex-slaves are poor but not as poor as the Irish peasants used to be; crime is rampant but not more so, if as much, as in Italy; but the difference is that the ancestors of the English and the Irish and the Italians were felt to be worth educating, helping and guiding because they were men and brothers, while in America a census which gives a slight indication of the utter disappearance of the American Negro from the earth is greeted with ill-concealed delight.

Other centuries looking back upon the culture of the nineteenth would have a right to suppose that if, in a land of freemen, eight millions of human beings were found to be dying of disease, the nation would cry with one voice, "Heal them!" If they were staggering on in ignorance, it would cry, "Train them!" If they were harming themselves and others by crime, it would cry, "Guide them!" And such cries are heard and have been heard in the land; but it was not one voice and its volume has been ever broken by counter-cries and echoes, "Let them die!" "Train them like slaves!" "Let them stagger downward!"

This is the spirit that enters in and complicates all Negro social problems and this is a problem which only civilization and humanity can successfully solve. Meantime we have the other problems before us—we have the problems arising from the uniting of so many social questions about one centre. In such a situation we need only to avoid underestimating the difficulties on the one hand and over-estimating them on the other. The problems are difficult, extremely difficult, but they are such as the world has conquered before and can conquer again. Moreover the battle involves more than a mere altruistic interest in an alien people. It is a battle for humanity and human culture. If in the hey-dey of the greatest of the world's civilizations, it is possible for one people ruthlessly to steal another, drag them helpless across the water, enslave them, debauch them, and then slowly murder them by economic and social exclusion until they disappear from the face of the earth—if the consummation of such a crime be possible in the twentieth century, then our civilization is vain and the republic is a mockery and a farce.

But this will not be; first, even with the terribly adverse circumstances under which Negroes live, there is not the slightest likelihood of their dying out; a nation that has endured the slave-trade, slavery, reconstruction, and present prejudice three hundred years, and under it increased in numbers and efficiency, is not in any immediate danger of extinction. Nor is the thought of voluntary or involuntary emigration more than a dream of men who forget that there are half as many Negroes in the United States as Spaniards in Spain. If this be so then a few plain propositions may be laid down as axiomatic:

1. The Negro is here to stay.
2. It is to the advantage of all, both black and white, that every Negro should make the best of himself.
3. It is the duty of the Negro to raise himself by every effort to the standards of modern civilization and not to lower those standards in any degree.
4. It is the duty of the white people to guard their civilization against debauchment by themselves or others; but in order to do this it is not necessary to hinder and retard the efforts of an earnest people to rise, simply because they lack faith in the ability of that people.
5. With these duties in mind and with a spirit of self-help, mutual aid and co-operation, the two races should strive side by side to realize the ideals of the republic and make this truly a land of equal opportunity for all men.

57. The Duty of the Negroes—That the Negro race has an appalling work of social reform before it need hardly be said. Simply because the ancestors of the present white inhabitants of America went out of their way barbarously to mistreat and enslave the ancestors of the present black inhabitants gives those blacks no right to ask that the civilization and morality of the land be seriously menaced for their benefit. Men have a right to demand that the members of a civilized community be civilized; that the fabric of human culture, so laboriously woven, be not wantonly or ignorantly destroyed. Consequently a nation may rightly demand, even of a people it has consciously and intentionally wronged, not indeed complete civilization in thirty or one hundred years, but at least every effort and sacrifice possible on their part toward making themselves fit members of the community within a reasonable length of time; that thus they may early become a source of strength and help instead of a national burden. Modern society has too many problems of its own, too much proper anxiety as to its own ability to survive under its present organization, for it lightly to shoulder all the burdens of a less advanced people, and it can rightly demand that as far as possible and as rapidly as possible the Negro bend his energy to the solving of his own social problems—contributing to his poor, paying his share of the taxes and supporting the schools and public administration. For the accomplishment of this the Negro has a right to demand freedom for self-development, and no more aid from without than is really helpful for furthering that development. Such aid must of necessity be considerable: it must furnish schools and reformatories, and relief and preventive agencies; but the bulk of the work of raising the Negro must be done by the Negro himself, and the greatest help for him will be not to hinder and curtail and discourage his efforts. Against prejudice, injustice and wrong the Negro ought to protest energetically and continuously, but he must never forget that he protests because those things hinder his own efforts, and that those efforts are the key to his future.

And those efforts must be mighty and comprehensive, persistent, well-aimed and tireless; satisfied with no partial success, lulled to sleep by no colorless victories; and, above all, guided by no low selfish ideals; at the same time they must be tempered by common sense and rational expectation. In Philadelphia those efforts should first be directed toward a lessening of Negro crime; no doubt the amount of crime imputed to the race is exaggerated, no doubt features of the Negro's environment over which he has no control, excuse much that is committed; but beyond all this the amount of crime that can without doubt rightly be laid at the door of the Philadelphia Negro is large and is a menace to a civilized people. Efforts to stop this crime must commence in the Negro homes; they must cease to be, as they often are, breeders of idleness and extravagance and complaint. Work, continuous and intensive; work, although it be menial and poorly rewarded; work, though done in travail of soul and sweat of brow, must be so impressed upon Negro children as the road to salvation, that a child would feel it a greater disgrace to be idle than to do the humblest labor. The homely virtues of honesty, truth and chastity must be instilled in the cradle, and although it is hard to teach self-respect to a people whose million fellow-citizens half-despise them, yet it must be taught as the surest road to gain the respect of others.

It is right and proper that Negro boys and girls should desire to rise as high in the world as their ability and just desert entitle them. They should be ever encouraged and urged to do so, although they should be taught also that idleness and crime are beneath and not above the lowest work. It should be the continual object of Negroes to open up better industrial chances for their sons and daughters. Their success here must of course rest largely with the white people, but not entirely. Proper co-operation among forty or fifty thousand colored people ought to open many chances of employment for their sons and daughters in trades, stores and shops, associations and industrial enterprises.

Further, some rational means of amusement should be furnished young folks. Prayer meetings and church socials have their place, but they cannot compete in attractiveness with the dance halls and gambling dens of the city. There is a legitimate demand for amusement on the part of the young which may be made a means of education, improvement and recreation. A harmless and beautiful amusement like dancing might with proper effort be rescued from its low and unhealthful associations and made a means of health and recreation. The billiard table is no more wedded to the saloon than to the church if good people did not drive it there. If the Negro homes and churches cannot amuse their young people, and if no other efforts are made to satisfy this want, then we cannot complain if the saloons and clubs and bawdy houses send these children to crime, disease and death.

There is a vast amount of preventive and rescue work which the Negroes themselves might do: keeping little girls off the street at night, stopping the escorting of unchaperoned young ladies to church and elsewhere, showing the dangers of the lodging system, urging the buying of homes and removal from crowded and tainted neighborhoods, giving lectures and tracts on health and habits, exposing the dangers of gambling and policy-playing, and inculcating respect for women. Day-nurseries and sewing-schools, mothers' meetings, the parks and airing places, all these things are little known or appreciated among the masses of Negroes, and their attention should be directed to them.

The spending of money is a matter to which Negroes need to give especial attention. Money is wasted to-day in dress, furniture, elaborate entertainments, costly church edifices, and "insurance" schemes, which ought to go toward buying homes, educating children, giving simple healthful amusement to the young, and accumulating something in the savings bank against a "rainy day." A crusade for the savings bank as against the "insurance" society ought to be started in the Seventh Ward without delay.

Although directly after the war there was great and remarkable enthusiasm for education, there is no doubt but that this enthusiasm has fallen off, and there is to-day much neglect of children among the Negroes, and failure to send them regularly to school. This should be looked into by the Negroes themselves and every effort made to induce full regular attendance.

Above all, the better classes of the Negroes should recognize their duty toward the masses. They should not forget that the spirit of the twentieth century is to be the turning of the high toward the lowly, the bending of Humanity to all that is human; the recognition that in the slums of modern society lie the answers to most of our puzzling problems of organization and life, and that only as we solve those problems is our culture assured and our progress certain. This the Negro is far from recognizing for himself; his social evolution in cities like Philadelphia is approaching a mediæval stage when the centrifugal forces of repulsion between social classes are becoming more powerful than those of attraction. So hard has been the rise of the better class of Negroes that they fear to fall if now they stoop to lend a hand to their fellows. This feeling is intensified by the blindness of those outsiders who persist even now in confounding the good and bad, the risen and fallen in one mass. Nevertheless the Negro must learn the lesson that other nations learned so laboriously and imperfectly, that his better classes have their chief excuse for being in the work they may do toward lifting the rabble. This is especially true in a city like Philadelphia which has so distinct and creditable a Negro aristocracy; that they do something already to grapple with these social problems of their race is true, but they do not yet do nearly as much as they must, nor do they clearly recognize their responsibility.

Finally, the Negroes must cultivate a spirit of calm, patient persistence in their attitude toward their fellow citizens rather than of loud and intemperate complaint. A man may be wrong, and know he is wrong, and yet some finesse must be used in telling him of it. The white people of Philadelphia are perfectly conscious that their Negro citizens are not treated fairly in all respects, but it will not improve matters to call names or impute unworthy motives to all men.

Social reforms move slowly and yet when Right is reinforced by calm but persistent Progress we somehow all feel that in the end it must triumph.

58. The Duty of the Whites—There is a tendency on the part of many white people to approach the Negro question from the side which just now is of least pressing importance, namely, that of the social intermingling of races. The old query: Would you want your sister to marry a Nigger? still stands as a grim sentinel to stop much rational discussion. And yet few white women have been pained by the addresses of black suitors, and those who have easily got rid of them. The whole discussion is little less than foolish; perhaps a century from to-day we may find ourselves seriously discussing such questions of social policy, but it is certain that just as long as one group deems it a serious *mésalliance* to marry with another just so long few marriages will take place, and it will need neither law nor argument to guide human choice in such a matter. Certainly the masses of whites would hardly acknowledge that an active propaganda of repression was necessary to ward off intermarriage. Natural pride of race, strong on one side and growing on the other, may be trusted to ward off such mingling as might in this stage of development prove disastrous to both races. All this therefore is a question of the far-off future.

To-day, however, we must face the fact that a natural repugnance to close intermingling with unfortunate ex-slaves has descended to a discrimination that very seriously hinders them from being anything better. It is right and proper to object to ignorance and consequently to ignorant men; but if by our actions we have been responsible for their ignorance and are still actively engaged in keeping them ignorant, the argument loses its moral force. So with the Negroes: men have a right to object to a race so poor and ignorant and inefficient as the mass of the Negroes; but if their policy in the past is parent of much of this condition, and if to-day by shutting black boys and girls out of most avenues of decent employment they are increasing pauperism and vice, then they must hold themselves largely responsible for the deplorable results.

There is no doubt that in Philadelphia the centre and kernel of the Negro problem so far as the white people are concerned is the narrow opportunities afforded Negroes for earning a decent living. Such discrimination is morally wrong, politically dangerous, industrially wasteful, and socially silly. It is the duty of the whites to stop it, and to do so primarily for their own sakes. Industrial freedom of opportunity has by long experience been proven to be generally best for all. Moreover the cost of crime and pauperism, the growth of slums, and the pernicious influences of idleness and lewdness, cost the public far more than would the hurt to the feelings of a carpenter to work beside a black man, or a shop girl to stand beside a darker mate. This does not contemplate the wholesale replacing of white workmen for Negroes out of sympathy or philanthropy; it does mean that talent should be rewarded, and aptness used in commerce and industry whether its owner be black or white; that the same incentive to good, honest, effective work be placed before a black office boy as before a white one—before a black porter as before a white one; and that unless this is done the city has no right to complain that black boys lose interest in work and drift into idleness and crime. Probably a change in public opinion on this point to-morrow would not make very much difference in the positions occupied by Negroes in the city: some few would be promoted, some few would get new places—the mass would remain as they are; but it would make one vast difference: it would inspire the young to try harder, it would stimulate the idle and discouraged and it would take away from this race the omnipresent excuse for failure: prejudice. Such a moral change would work a revolution in the criminal rate during the next ten years. Even a Negro bootblack could black boots better if he knew he was a menial not because he was a Negro but because he was best fitted for that work.

We need then a radical change in public opinion on this point; it will not and ought not to come suddenly, but instead of thoughtless acquiescence in the continual and steadily encroaching exclusion of Negroes from work in the city, the leaders of industry and opinion ought to be trying here and there to open up new opportunities and give new chances to bright colored boys. The policy of the city to-day simply drives out the best class of young people whom its schools have educated and social opportunities trained, and fills their places with idle and vicious immigrants. It is a paradox of the times that young men and women from some of the best Negro families of the city—families born and reared here and schooled in the best traditions of this municipality have actually had to go to the South to get work, if they wished to be aught but chambermaids and bootblacks. Not that such work may not be honorable and useful, but that it is as wrong to make scullions of engineers as it is to make engineers of scullions. Such a situation is a disgrace to the city—a disgrace to its Christianity, to its spirit of justice, to its common sense; what can be the end of such a policy but increased crime and increased excuse for crime? Increased poverty and more reason to be poor? Increased political serfdom of the mass of black voters to the bosses and rascals who divide the spoils? Surely here lies the first duty of a civilized city.

Secondly, in their efforts for the uplifting of the Negro the people of Philadelphia must recognize the existence of the better class of Negroes and must gain their active aid and co-operation by generous and polite conduct. Social sympathy must exist between what is best in both races and there must no longer be the feeling that the Negro who makes the best of himself is of least account to the city of Philadelphia, while the vagabond is to be helped and pitied. This better class of Negro does not want help or pity, but it does want a generous recognition of its difficulties, and a broad sympathy with the problem of life as it presents itself to them. It is composed of men and women educated and in many cases cultured; with proper co-operation they could be a vast power in the city, and the only power that could successfully cope with many phases of the Negro problems. But their active aid cannot be gained for purely selfish motives, or kept by churlish and ungentle manners; and above all they object to being patronized.

Again, the white people of the city must remember that much of the sorrow and bitterness that surrounds the life of the American Negro comes from the unconscious prejudice and half-conscious actions of men and women who do not intend to wound or annoy. One is not compelled to discuss the Negro question with every Negro one meets or to tell him of a father who was connected with the Underground Railroad; one is not compelled to stare at the solitary black face in the audience as though it were not human; it is not necessary to sneer, or be unkind or boorish, if the Negroes in the room or on the street are not all the best behaved or have not the most elegant manners; it is hardly necessary to strike from the dwindling list of one's boyhood and girlhood acquaintances or school-day friends all those who happen to have Negro blood, simply because one has not the courage now to greet them on the street. The little decencies of daily intercourse can go on, the courtesies of life be exchanged even across the color line without any danger to the supremacy of the Anglo-Saxon or the social ambition of the Negro. Without doubt social differences are facts not fancies and cannot lightly be swept aside; but they hardly need to be looked upon as excuses for downright meanness and incivility.

A polite and sympathetic attitude toward these striving thousands; a delicate avoidance of that which wounds and embitters them; a generous granting of opportunity to them; a seconding of their efforts, and a desire to reward honest success—all this, added to proper striving on their part, will go far even in our day toward making all men, white and black, realize what the great founder of the city meant when he named it the City of Brotherly Love.

APPENDIX A

◆

Schedules used in the House-to-House Inquiry

UNIVERSITY OF PENNSYLVANIA

CONDITION OF THE NEGROES OF PHILADELPHIA, WARD SEVEN—*Family Schedule, 1*

DECEMBER 1, 1896   No. _____

1.   NUMBER OF PERSONS IN THIS FAMILY _____

INQUIRIES	1	2	3	4	5
2 Relationship to head of family?					
3 Sex?					
4 Age at nearest birthday?					
5 Conjugal condition?					
6 Place of birth?					
7 Length of residence in Philadelphia?					
8 Length of residence in this house?					
9 Able to read?					
10 Able to write?					
11 Months in school during last school year?					
12 Graduate or attendant at any time of any higher school?					
13 Attendant of any industrial school?					
14 Occupations since December 1, 1891?					
15 Present occupation?					
16 Place of work?					

INVESTIGATOR

17   Average income from present occupation { weekly? . . . .
                                                                    { monthly? . . . .
                                                                     { yearly? . . . .

18   Weeks unemployed at above occupation during last twelve months? . . . .
19   Weeks employed at any other occupation during last twelve months? . . . .
20   Name of such other occupation? . . . .
21   Average weekly earnings at such other occupation? . . . .
22   Number of days sick during last twelve months? . . . .
23   Nature of illness? . . . .
24   Sound and healthy in mind, sight, hearing, speech, limbs and body? . . . .
25   When and where have attempts been made to find other employment? . . . .
26   Why was application refused? . . . .
27   Amount of real estate owned? . . . .
28   Situation of such real estate? . . . .
29   Amount of other property? . . . .
30   Member of what building, secret, beneficial or insurance societies, or labor union? . . . .
31   Average monthly dues to such societies? . . . .

32   Budget:
      Total income of family from all sources for one year?
      Expenditure for one year?

EXPENDITURE FOR	WEEKLY	MONTHLY	YEARLY
Rent			
Food			
Fuel			
Clothing			

EXPENDITURE FOR	WEEKLY	MONTHLY	YEARLY
Amusements			
Tobacco			
Alcoholic drinks			
Sickness and Death			
All other Purposes .			

Total expenditure for one year?
Total savings for one year?

33   Chief form of amusement?
34   Member or attendant of what church?
35   Non-resident members of family?
36   Occupation and address of same?
37   Remarks

UNIVERSITY OF PENNSYLVANIA

INVESTIGATION INTO THE CONDITION OF THE NEGROES OF
PHILADELPHIA

Instructions for Family Schedule

A family schedule must be made out for every group of two or more related persons living under conditions of family life. Boarders, lodgers and servants, are to be entered on separate individual schedules. Hotels, etc., should be entered on an institution schedule, and the inmates on family and individual schedules.

Question 1. Enter here the number of persons in the family, exclusive of lodgers, boarders, visitors or servants.

Question 2. Facts for the head of the family should be entered in the first column, and he or she should be designated as *Head*, whether man, woman, married or single. Give the other members the term which will indicate their relation to the head; as wife, son, daughter, sister, etc, or mother (*i. e.* mother of head of family), etc.

Question 3. Abbreviate to M. (male), or F. (female).

Question 4. Give exact years, as, 17, 29, 31, 43, etc., and do not say "about" 25, 30, 35, 40. Enter children less than one year old on the 1st of December, in twelfths of a month, as 6–12, 3–12, etc.; or if not one month old, as 0–12.

Question 5. Enter as married (mar.), single (sing.), widowed (wid.), and separated (sep.).

Question 6. Give State and town.

Question 7 and 8. Give approximate number of years.

Question 11. This refers to the children of the family.

Question 12 and 13. Write "Graduate—Girls' High, '96"; or "Attendant Institute for Colored Youth, 3 yrs.," etc. Schools higher than common schools are here referred to. Answer this for all members of the family.

Questions 14 and 15. This is an important inquiry. Simple as it appears, it is always difficult in census work to get satisfactory replies to this question. Inaccuracy and insufficiency of statement are the most prominent evils to be avoided:

For instance, *remember:* we want to know not what a man "works in," but just what he does.

We want to *distinguish between:* the owner or director of a business and one who works at it; between waiters and head-waiters; between cooks in private families and in hotels; between coachmen, hackmen, and draymen; between merchants and pedlars, and those who keep stands.

Do not say:

"Printer," but "compositor," or "pressman;" not "mechanic," but "carpenter" or "plumber;" not "agent," but "real-estate agent;" not "merchant" or "pedlar," but "dry-goods merchant" or "pedlar—tinware"; not "clerk" but "salesman in hardware-store," "stenographer," "bookkeeper," etc.

Describe women who keep house at home as "housewives;" those who keep house for others as "housekeepers." If the woman does her own housework, and in addition pursues a gainful occupation, as dressmaking, enter: "housewife—dressmaker," or "housewife—day's-work-out."

Daughters, etc., who help with housework, should be entered: "housework—no pay." Those who do nothing should be entered as "no occupation." Children, too young to have an occupation, should be entered "at home," or "at school."

Question 17. Answer only one of these—preferably one of the first two. Seek to approximate the truth as nearly as possible.

Question 22. This refers to sickness that was severe enough to interfere seriously with daily work.

Question 23. Give the name of the disease or ailment.

Question 25. Give dates as nearly as possible, and addresses.

Question 26. Enter either the reason given or the reason surmised, or both.

Question 28. Give street and number.

Question 30. Give names of societies.

Question 32. This question is optional, and is only for those who are able to give their expenditure in some detail. Fill only *one* of the three columns for each particular item (*e.g.* rent *yearly*, food *weekly*, etc.) and seek by reference to written accounts to make this report accurate. Remember that *income, expenditure* and *savings* must *balance.*

Question 33. Enter this under one of the following heads: A. Athletics (bicycling, baseball, etc.). B. Music. C. Church entertainments. D. Indoor games (cards, billiards, etc.). E. Balls. F. House-parties. G. Picnics and excursions. H. Theatres.
Remember to enter here the actual chief amusement, not merely the one the person likes best, but does not often enjoy.

Question 35. Give relationship to head of family.

Where the question only applies to certain members of the family, put a cross in the spaces where there are no answers expected. Where no information is given, put "unknown," or "unanswered."

Finally, remember that the information given is confidential; the University of Pennsylvania will strictly guard it as such, and allow no one to have access to the schedules for other than scientific purposes. We ask, under these conditions, careful, accurate, and truthful answers.

UNIVERSITY OF PENNSYLVANIA
CONDITION OF THE NEGROES OF PHILADELPHIA, WARD SEVEN
Individual Schedule, 2

DECEMBER, 1, 1896　　　　　No._____　　　　　INVESTIGATOR

1　Relationship to head of family? . . . .
2　Sex? . . . .
3　Age at nearest birthday? . . . .
4　Conjugal condition? . . . .
5　Place of birth? . . . .
6　Length of residence in Philadelphia? . . . .
7　Length of residence in this house? . . . .
8　Able to read? . . . .
9　Able to write? . . . .
10　Months in school during last school year? . . . .
11　Graduate or attendant at any time of any higher school? . . . .
12　Attendant of any industrial school? . . . .
13　Occupations since November 1, 1891? . . . .
14　Present occupation? . . . .
15　Place of work? . . . .
16　Average income from present occupation ⎰ weekly?
　　　　　　　　　　　　　　　　　　　　⎱ monthly?
　　　　　　　　　　　　　　　　　　　　　 yearly?
17　Weeks unemployed at above occupation during last
　　　　twelve months? . . . .
18　Weeks employed at any other occupation during last twelve months?
19　Name of such other occupation? . . . .
20　Average weekly earnings at such other occupation? . . . .
21　Number of days sick during last twelve months? . . . .
22　Nature of illness? . . . .
23　Sound and healthy in mind, sight, hearing, speech, limbs
　　　　and body? . . . .
24　When and where have attempts been made to find other employment?
25　Why was application refused? . . . .
26　Amount of real estate owned? . . . .
27　Situation of such real estate? . . . .
28　Amount of other property? . . . .
29　Member of what building, secret, beneficial or insurance
　　　　societies, or labor union? . . . .
30　Average monthly dues to such societies? . . . .

31　Budget:
　　Total income for one year?
　　Expenditure for one year?

EXPENDITURE FOR	W'KLY	MONTHLY	YEARLY	EXPENDITURE FOR	W'KLY	MONTHLY	YEARLY
Rent				Amusements			
Food				Tobacco			
Fuel				Alcoholic drinks . . .			
Clothing				Sickness and Death .			
				All other purposes .			

　　Total expenditure for one year?
　　Total savings for one year?

32　Chief form of amusement?
33　Member or attendant of what church?
34　Remarks.

See Instructions for Family Schedule, 1.

UNIVERSITY OF PENNSYLVANIA

CONDITION OF THE NEGROES OF PHILADELPHIA, WARD SEVEN

Home Schedule, 3

DECEMBER 1, 1896	No. _____		INVESTIGATOR

1 Material of house? . . . .
2 Stories in house above basement? . . . .
3 Number of homes in house? . . . .
4 In which story is this home? . . . .
5 Number of rooms in this home? . . . .
6 Is this home rented directly of the landlord? . . . .
7 Number of boarders in this home? . . . .
8 Number of lodgers in this home? . . . .
9 Number of servants kept? . . . .
10 Total number of persons in this home? . . . .
11 House owned by . . . .
12 Rent paid monthly? . . . .
13 Rent received from sub-letting? . . . .
14 Bath-room? . . . .
15 Water-closet? . . . .
16 Privy? . . . .
17 Yard, and size? . . . .
18 Where is washing hung to dry? . . . .
19 Light? . . . .
20 Ventilation and air? . . . .
21 Cleanliness? . . . .
22 Outside sanitary conditions? . . . .

THE HOME

	ROOM No. 1	ROOM No. 2	ROOM No. 3	ROOM No. 4	ROOM No. 5	ROOM No. 6
23 Use?						
24 Dimensions?						
25 Outside windows?						
26 Furniture?						
27 Occupants at night?						
28 Additional rooms?						

29 When and where have you had difficulty in renting houses?

INSTRUCTIONS FOR HOME SCHEDULE

Every structure in which persons live is a dwelling for the purposes of this investigation, whether wholly so occupied or not. In each dwelling there will be one or more homes; for each such home a Home Schedule must be made out, and at its top the schedule number of the corresponding family or individual inserted.

Question 4. If it occupies the house, put "whole house."
Questions 14, 15, 16, 17. Answer *Yes* or *No*. Note whether these facilities are used by one
    or more homes?
Questions 19, 20, 21, 22. Answer *excellent, good, fair* or *bad*.
Question 26. This refers primarily to the living room. Note the presence of the following
    articles: piano, organ, parlor-suit, sewing-machine, bookshelves, couch, centre-
    table, rocking-chair, etc.

UNIVERSITY OF PENNSYLVANIA

CONDITION OF THE NEGROES OF PHILADELPHIA, WARD SEVEN

House Servant Schedule, 4

DECEMBER 1, 1896   No. _____   INVESTIGATOR

1   Street and number? . . . .
2   Occupation of employer? . . . .
3   Sex? . . . .
4   Age at nearest birthday? . . . .
5   Conjugal condition? . . . .
6   Any home in the city? . . . .
7   Address of same? . . . .
8   Place of birth? . . . .
9   Number of days sick in last twelve months? . . . .
10 Nature of illness? . . . .
11 Able to read? . . . .
12 Able to write? . . . .
13 Graduate or attendant at any time of any higher
        school? . . . .
14 Occupations since November 1, 1891? . . . .
15 Present occupation? . . . .
16 Length of service here? . . . .
17 Weekly earnings? . . . .
18 Is board given in addition to this? . . . .
19 Is lodging given in addition to this? . . . .
20 Number of hours free each month? . . . .
21 Who besides yourself is supported by your wages? . . . .
22 How much is given for this purpose weekly? . . . .
23 Member or attendant of what church? . . . .
24 When and where have you attempted to get other
        employment? . . . .
25 Why was application refused? . . . .
26 What is your chief amusement? . . . .
27 Budget:
    Total income for one year:

EXPENDITURE FOR	W'KLY	MONTHLY	YEARLY	EXPENDITURE FOR	W'KLY	MONTHLY	YEARLY
Clothing				Sickness			
Amusement . . .				Dues to Societies . .			
Lodging				All other purposes .			

Total expense for one year?
Total savings?

28   Amount of property owned?

For Instructions, see Family Schedule, 1.

UNIVERSITY OF PENNSYLVANIA

CONDITION OF THE NEGROES OF PHILADELPHIA, WARD SEVEN

Street Schedule, 5. _____ *Street, between*_____ *Streets*

DECEMBER 1, 1896   No. _____   INVESTIGATOR

1 General Character? . . . .
2 Width? . . . .
3 Paved with? . . . .
4 Street-car line? . . . .
5 Character of houses? . . . .
6 Stories in houses? . . . .
7 Material of houses? . . . .
8 Proportion occupied as dwellings? . . . .
9 Proportion of Whites to Blacks? . . . .
10 Nationality of Whites? . . . .
11 Cleanliness of street? . . . .
12 Width of sidewalks? . . . .
13 Lighted by? . . . .
14 Hydrants? . . . .
15 Schools? . . . .
16 Churches? . . . .
17 Saloons? . . . .
18 Pool-rooms? . . . .
19 Public institutions? . . . .
20 Public conveniences? . . . .
21 Shops? . . . .
22 Remarks? . . . .

INSTRUCTIONS FOR STREET SCHEDULE

A "street" in this Schedule is meant to designate not necessarily the whole street which bears one name—as Lombard from river to river—but rather such parts of streets as have a common character; thus four or five Schedules would be necessary for the distinctive parts of Lombard Street, two for Juniper, several for Pine, one for Wetherill.

1. Characterize the street concisely; as, "respectable residence street," or "blind alley with tumble-down brick houses."
4. Answer by *Yes* or *No*.
5. Note whether the houses are dwellings, stables, etc., respectable, suspicious, etc.
8. Estimate carefully; as one-third dwellings, or one-half back yards, etc.
9 and 10. Ask a policeman, or one or two of the persons dwelling there. Do not depend on your own observation, unless it extends over some time.
11. Answer by *excellent, good, fair,* or *bad.*
14. Give number.
15. Give names.
16. Give number, names and denomination.
17 and 18. Give number.
19. This includes hospitals, clubs, missions, manufactories. Note clubs of all sorts carefully, and ascertain their character if possible. Enter all these institutions by name.
20. This refers to public water-closets, baths, urinals, and lavatories.
21. Give approximate distribution and character of shops.
22. Make here any concise statement that will throw light on the street and its inhabitants.

UNIVERSITY OF PENNSYLVANIA

CONDITION OF THE NEGROES OF PHILADELPHIA, WARD SEVEN

Institution Schedule, 6

DECEMBER 1, 1896	NO._____	INVESTIGATOR

1 Name? . . . .
2 Street and number? . . . .
3 Character? . . . .
4 Proprietors? . . . .
5 Number of members or partners? . . . .
6 Amount of capital invested? . . . .
7 Real estate owned? . . . .
8 Value of same? . . . .
9 Taxes paid last year on same? . . . .
10 Value of other property? . . . .
11 Income last twelve months? . . . .
12 Source of said income? . . . .
13 Expenditures last twelve months? . . . .
14 Objects of expenditures? . . . .
15 History? . . . .
16 Description and remarks . . . .

INSTRUCTIONS FOR INSTITUTION SCHEDULE

This includes all institutions conducted by Negroes wholly or partially, or wholly or partially in the interest of the Negroes; as, *e.g.*, churches, missions, clubs, shops, stands, stores, agencies, societies, associations, halls, newspapers, etc.

Find out the object of the enterprise (philanthropic, social, business, etc.), the capital invested, the property owned, taxes paid, income for past twelve months, character and amount of expenditure, sort of quarters occupied, and persons connected, etc., aiming, in all cases, to collect essential facts.

Especially try and find out whether the enterprise is that of one person, of a partnership, or is a co-operative enterprise among a large number. If in any degree co-operative, bring out the extent, character and objects of the co-operation.

APPENDIX B

◆

Legislation, etc., of Pennsylvania in Regard to the Negro

1682. *Negro Serfdom Recognized.* The charter of the Free Society of Traders of Pennsylvania recognizes the slavery of Blacks. Slaves were to be freed after fourteen years of service, upon condition that they cultivate land allotted to them, and surrender two-thirds of the produce annually.—Hazard's "Annals" (Ed. 1850), 553.

1693, July 11. *Tumults of Slaves.* Action of City Council of Philadelphia against tumults by slaves.—Penna. Col. Rec., I, 380—81.

1700. *Slave Marriages.* Penn proposes a bill regulating slave marriages; bill is lost in Council.—Bettle, 368; Thomas, 266.

1700, November 27. *Trial of Slaves.* "An Act for the Trial of Negroes." Introduced by Penn. This act provided that Negroes accused of high crime should be tried by two justices of the peace and six freeholders; rape of white women to be punished by death, and attempts by castration; Negroes were not to carry arms without special license; over four Negroes meeting together on Sundays or other days "upon no lawful business of their masters or owners" were to be whipped.—Statutes-at-Large, ch. 56. (Disallowed January 7, 1706.)

1700, November 27. *Traffic with Slaves.* "An Act for the Better Regulation of Servants in this Province and Territories." Traffic with slaves forbidden, among other things.—Statutes-at-Large, ch. 49.

1700, November 27. *Duty on Slaves.* "An Act for Granting an Impost upon Wines, Rum, Beer, Ale, Cider, etc., Imported, Retorted and Sold in this Province and Territories." §2. . . . "for every Negro, male or female, imported, if above sixteen years of age, twenty shillings; for every Negro under the age of sixteen, six shillings.—Statutes-at-Large, ch. 85.

1706, January 12. *Duty on Slaves.* "An Act for Raising a Supply. . . ." Imported Negroes, except those who lived at least two years in Jersey, 40s. (or 10s.?) per head.—Statutes-at-Large, ch. 164.

1706, January 12. *Trial of Negroes.* "An Act for the Trial of Negroes." Practically the same as the Act of 1700; attempt to rape and robbery of £5 or more, punished by branding and exportation.—Statutes-at-Large, ch. 143. (Repealed by Act of 1780, q. v.)

1708. *Protest to Legislature.* Protest of Mechanics against hiring out of Negroes.—Scharf-Wescott: "History of Philadelphia," I, 200.

1710, December 28. *Duty Act.* "An Impost Act, laying a Duty on Negroes. . . ."—40s. on Negroes imported.—Carey and Bioren, 1, 82.

1711, February 28. *Duty Act.* "An Impost Act, laying a Duty on Negroes. . . ." 40s. on Negroes not imported for importers own use.—Statutes-at-Large, ch. 181. (Disallowed 20 February, 1714.)

1712. *Petition for Emancipation.* Petition of Southeby for Abolition of Slavery.—DuBois' "Slave Trade," p. 22.

1712. *Negro Plot.* Negro plot in New York.—*Ibid.*

1712, June 11. *Duty Act.* "A Supplementary Act to. . ." the Act of 1710.—Carey and Bioren, I, 87–88. (Disallowed in 1713.)

1712, June 7. *Prohibitory Duty Act.* "An Act to Prevent the Importation of Negroes and Indians into this Province." £20 prohibitory duty laid on slaves imported, because of their plots and insurrections.—Statutes-at-Large, ch. 192. Cf. DuBois' "Slave Trade," p. 22. (Disallowed 1713.)

1713. *Assiento Treaty.* Contract for importing slaves into Spanish West Indies signed by Great Britain.—DuBois' "Slave Trade," pp. 207–9.

1715, May 28. *Duty Act.* "An Act for Laying a Duty on Negroes Imported into this Province." £5 duty; slaves of immigrants not to be sold for a year.—Statutes-at-Large, III, 121. (Disallowed 21 July, 1719.)

1718, February 22. *Duty Act.* "An Act for Continuing a Duty on Negroes. . . ." £5 duty; slaves of immigrants not to be sold for 16 months.—Statutes-at-Large, III, 164.

1721, February 24. *Duty Act.* "An Act for Continuing several Acts. . . ." Act of 1718 continued.—Statutes-at-Large, III, 238.

1721, August 21. *Traffic with Negroes.* "A Supplementary Act to a Law. . . ." On Public Houses. No liquors to be sold Negroes or Indians without leave.—Statutes-at-Large, III, 250.

1721, August 26. *Police Regulation.* "An Act for Preventing Accidents that May Happen by Fire." Slaves shooting squibs or guns in Philadelphia without license to be whipped.—Statutes-at-Large, III, 254.

1722, May 12. *Duty Act.* "An Act for Laying a Duty on Negroes. . . ." £5 duty, as in 1718.—Statutes-at-Large, III, 275.

1722. *Petition of White Laborers.* Laborers petition General Assembly against employment of Blacks. Assembly resolves: That the principle is dangerous and injurious to the republic and not to be sanctioned.—"Watson's Annals," I, 98.

1726, March 5. *Duty Act.* "An Act for Laying a Duty on Negroes. . . ." Act of 1722 continued from 1726 to 1729.—Statutes-at-Large, IV, 52.

1726, March 26. *Status of Negroes Defined.* "An Act for the Better Regulation of Negroes in this Province."

"Whereas, it often happens that Negroes commit felonies and other heinous crimes, which by the laws of this Province are punishable by death, but the loss of such cases falling wholly on the owner, is so great a hardship that sometimes may induce him to conceal such crimes, or convey his Negro to some other place and so suffer him to escape justice to the ill example of others to commit like offences.

"Be it resolved, etc., That Negroes convicted of capital crime be valued and paid for out of money collected as duty on their importation.". . .

§ III. "Whereas, free Negroes are an idle and slothful people and often prove burdensome to the neighborhood and afford ill examples to other Negroes. Therefore, Be it enacted that if any master or mistress shall discharge or set free any Negro, he or she shall enter into recognizance with sufficient securities in the sum of £30 to indemnify the county for any charge or incumbrance they may bring upon the same in case such Negro, through sickness or otherwise, be rendered incapable of self-support."

In case of freedom by will, the executor or administrator was required to give the bond, or such slaves should not be regarded as free.

Any Negro becoming free under age 21 might be bound to service until of age.

The Act further provided penalties for the harboring of Negroes by each other; for trading or dealing with each other without license—all on pain of being sold into slavery if unable to pay fine; also provided penalty of £100 for anybody who should marry a Negro and white person; £30 for Negro caught living in marriage relation with white person, in such cases Negro to be sold into slavery for life.

§ XI of Act prohibited masters, etc., from allowing Negro slaves to hire their own time.

One section also imposed a duty of £10 on imported slaves.—Statutes-at-Large, IV, 59.

1729, May 10. *Duty Act.* "An Act for Laying a Duty on Negroes Imported into this Province." £2 duty.—Statutes-at-Large, IV, 128.

1732, April 17. *Slave Tumults.* Philadelphia Council order Ordinance drawn to prevent tumults of slaves on Sundays.—"Watson's Annals," I, 62.

1738, July 3. *Slave Tumults.* Draft of Ordinance to suppress tumults of slaves considered in Philadelphia City Council.—*Ibid.,* I, 62.

1741, August 17. *Tumults of Negroes.* Order made by Philadelphia City Councils to suppress disorders of Negroes and others on court house square at night.— "Watson's Annals," I, 62–63.

1761, March 14. *Duty Act.* "An Act for Laying a Duty on Negro and Mulatto Slaves imported into this province." £10 duty? Continued in 1768; repealed in 1780.—Carey and Bioren, I, 371, 451.

1761, April 22. *Duty Act.* "A Supplement to. . . ." the Act of 1761.—*Ibid.,* 371, 451.

1768, February 20. *Duty Act.* Acts of 1761 re-enacted.—Dallas, I, 490.

1773, February 26. *Duty Act.* "An Act for Making Perpetual the Act. . . ." of 1761. Additional £10 duty provided for.—Dallas, I, 671.

1775. *Bill on Importation.* Bill to prohibit importation or slaves vetoed by Governor.—Bettle.

1778, September 7. *Recovery of Duties.* "An Act for the Recovery of the Duties on Negro and Mulatto Slaves. . . ."—Dallas, I, 782.

1779, February 5. *Plan of Emancipation.* Supreme Executive Council recommends a plan of gradual emancipation to Assembly.

1780, March 1. *Slavery Abolished.* "An Act for the Gradual Abolition of Slavery."
  § 1, 2. General condemnation of slavery.
  § 3. No child born hereafter in Pennsylvania to be a slave.
  § 4. Children of slaves born hereafter to be bound to service until twenty-eight years of age.
  § 5. All slaves to be registered.
  § 7. Negroes to be tried for crime like other inhabitants.
  § 10. None to be slaves except those registered.
  § 14. Acts of 1725, 1761 and 1773 repealed.—Carey and Bioren, ch. 881.
1786. *Petition for Potter's Field.* Petition of Philadelphia Negroes to Council for leave to enclose Potter's Field as a Negro burial ground.—Penna. Col. Rec., XIV, 637.
1788, March 29. *Act of 1780 Amended.* "An Act to Explain and Amend an Act Entitled 'An Act for the Gradual Abolition of Slavery.'"
  § 2. Slaves of immigrants to be free.
  § 3. Slaves not to be removed from without their consent given before two justices.
  § 4. Persons possessed of children liable to serve till twenty-eight years old must register them.
  § 5. Slave trading forbidden under penalty and forfeiture.
  § 6. Slaves serving for a term of years not to be separated from parents.—Carey and Bioren, ch. 394.
1790, September 2. *Negro Suffrage.* Constitution of Pennsylvania. Art. III, Sec. 1. In elections by the citizens, every freeman of the age of twenty-one years, having resided in the State two years next before the election, and within that time paid a State or county tax, which shall have been assessed at least six months before the election, shall enjoy the rights of an elector.—Purdon's "Digest," 6th ed.
1793, April 11. *Duty on Slaves.* "An Act to Establish a Board of Wardens for the Port of Philadelphia. . . ."
  § 22. Of passengers entering port only slaves to pay head money.—Carey and Bioren, ch. 178.
1800. *Petition to Congress.* Petition of Negroes to Legislature and Congress against slave-trade.—DuBois' "Slave Trade," p. 81–83.
1821, April. *Act vs. Pauperism.* "An Act to Prevent the Increase of Pauperism in the Commonwealth."
  § 1. If any black indentured servant over twenty-eight years of age is brought into the State, his master is liable for his charge if he becomes a pauper.—Laws of Penna., 1821.
1826, March 25. *Act vs. Kidnapping.* "An Act to Give Effect to the Provisions of the Constitution of the United States, Relative to Fugitives from Labor, for the Protection of the Free People of Color, and to prevent Kidnapping."
  § 1. Fine of $500–$2,000 and imprisonment seven to twenty-one years for kidnapping.
  § 2. Aiding and abetting punished.

§§ 3–6. Claimed fugitives to be arrested on warrant and taken before a judge. Oath of alleged owner or of interested persons not received as evidence.—Laws of Penna., 1826. Cf. Prigg *vs.* Penna., 16 Peters, 500, U. S. Reports.

1827, April 17. *Sales of Fugitives.* "An Act to Prevent Certain Abuses of the Laws Relative to Fugitives from Labor." No sales of fugitive slaves to be made in the State of Pennsylvania.—Laws of Penna., 1827.

1832. *Restriction on Immigration.* Bill in Legislature to make free Negroes carry passes. Cf., p. 27.

1837, July. *Negro Suffrage.* Pennsylvania Supreme Court at Sunbury; case of Hobbs *et al. vs.* Fogg. Judgment of Common Pleas Court reversed and Negro declared not a "freeman" in the meaning of Constitution.—Penna. Reports, 6 Watts, 553–60.

1838. *Negro Suffrage.* Revised Constitution of Pennsylvania, Art. III, Sec. 1. "In elections by the citizens, every white freeman of the age of twenty-one years, having resided in this State one year, and in the election district where he offers to vote ten days immediately preceding such election, and within two years paid a State or county tax, which shall have been assessed at least ten days before the election, shall enjoy the right of an elector."— Purdon's "Digest," Sixth Ed.

1854, May 8. "An Act for the Regulation and Continuance of a System of Education by Common Schools."

The Controllers and Directors of the several school districts of the State are hereby authorized and required to establish within their respective districts separate schools for Negro and Mulatto children wherever such schools can be located so as to accommodate twenty or more pupils; and wherever such schools shall be established and kept open four months in every year the Directors and Controllers shall not be compelled to admit such pupils into any other schools of the district.—Laws of Penna., 1854.

1863, March 6. *Immigration.* Petition against immigration of freedmen to Pennsylvania denied by Senate committee of Legislature.—Pamphlet, Phila. Library.

1867. *Separate Seats in Cars.* Pennsylvania Supreme Court; case of West Chester and Philadelphia Co. *vs.* Miles. Held that separation of Negroes to assigned seats for good order is not illegal on railways, etc.—Penna. Reports, 5 Smith, 209.

1867, March 22. *Civil Rights.* Negroes to have same rights on railway cars as white citizens.—Brightley's Purdon, Eleventh Ed., 1436.

1870, April 6. *Negro Suffrage.* § 10 of Act says: "That so much of every Act of Assembly as provides that only white freemen shall be entitled to vote or to register as voters, or as claiming to vote, at any general or special election in this Commonwealth, be and the same is hereby repealed; and that hereafter all freemen, without distinction of color, shall be enrolled and registered according to the provisions of the act approved April 17, 1869."—Laws of Penna., 1870.

1874. *Negro Suffrage.* New Constitution removes restrictions as to color.

1874, April 10. *Civil Rights.* Pennsylvania Supreme Court; case of Drew *vs.* Peer. Damages given Negroes for ejectment from a theatre.—12 Norris, 234.

1878, March 15. *Civil Rights.* Pennsylvania Supreme Court; case of Central Railroad of New Jersey *vs.* Green and wife. Damages granted for compelling Negroes to go from one car to another on railway.—Penna. Reports, 5 Norris, 421, 427.

1881, June 8. *Mixed Schools.* § 1. It shall be unlawful for any school director, superintendent, or teacher to make any distinction whatever on account of, or by reason of, the race or color of any pupil or scholar who may be in attendance upon or seeking admission to any public or common school maintained wholly or in part under the school laws of the commonwealth.—Brightley's Purdon, Eleventh ed., p. 292.

1887, May 19. *Civil Rights.* "An Act to Provide Civil Rights for all People, Regardless of Race or Color." "§ 1. *Be it enacted, etc.,* that any person, company, corporation, being owner, lessee or manager of any restaurant, hotel, railroad, street railway, omnibus line, theatre, concert hall or place of entertainment or amusement, who shall refuse to accommodate, convey or admit any person or persons on account of race or color over their lines or into their hotel or restaurant, theatre, concert hall or place of amusement, shall upon conviction thereof be guilty of a misdemeanor and be punished by a fine of not less than fifty or more than one hundred dollars."—Laws of Penna., 1887, pp. 130–31.

1895, July 2. *Life Insurance.* Life insurance companies are not allowed to make any discriminations as to premiums, dividends, or otherwise, between insured of the same class and expectation of life.—Penna. Laws, 1895, p. 432.

APPENDIX C

$\blacklozenge$

Bibliography

I. GENERAL WORKS

Publications of Atlanta University:
  No. 1. Mortality Among Negroes in Cities.
  No. 2. Social and Physical Condition of Negroes.
  No. 3. Efforts of Negroes for Social Betterment.
                          —Atlanta, Ga., 1896–98.

Edward Bettle. Notices of Negro Slavery as Connected with Pennsylvania. In Mem. Hist. Soc. of Pennsylvania, I.

Charles Booth. Life and Labour of the People. London, 1892.

M. Carey and J. Bioren. Laws of Pennsylvania, 1700–1802. Philadelphia, 1803.

A. J. Dallas. Laws of Pennsylvania, 1700–1781. Philadelphia, 1797.

W. E. Burghardt DuBois. Suppression of the Slave Trade. New York, 1896.

—— —— The Study of the Negro Problems. Annals of the Amer. Acad. of Pol. and Soc. Science. Philadelphia, 1898.

—— —— The Negroes of Farmville, Va. (U. S. Bureau of Labor *Bulletin*, January, 1898.)

[Benjamin Franklin.] An Essay on the African Slave Trade. Philadelphia, 1790.

[Friends.] Germantown Friends' Protest Against Slavery, 1688. (Facsimile copy) Philadelphia, 1880.

[Friends.] The Appeal of the Religious Society of Friends in Pennsylvania, New Jersey, etc. . . . on behalf of the Colored Races. Philadelphia, 1858.

[Friends.] A Brief Statement of the Rise and Progress of the Testimony of the Religious Society of Friends against Slavery and the Slave Trade. Philadelphia, 1843.

Samuel Hazard. The Register of Pennsylvania. Philadelphia, 1828–36.

Hull House Maps and Papers. New York, 1895.

Samuel M. Janney. History of the Religious Society of Friends. Philadelphia, 1859–67.

Walter Laidlaw, Editor. The Federation of Churches and Christian Workers in New York City. First and Second Sociological Canvasses. New York, 1896–1897.

Marion J. McDougal. Fugitive Slaves. Boston, 1891.

Edward Needles. An Historical Memoir of the Pennsylvania Society for Promoting the Abolition of Slavery. Philadelphia, 1848.

William C. Nell. Services of Colored Americans in the Wars of 1776 and 1812. Reprinted, Philadelphia, 1894.

Statutes-at-Large of the State of Pennsylvania. Philadelphia.

Pennsylvania Colonial Records. Philadelphia.

Robert Proud. History of Pennsylvania. Philadelphia, 1797–98.

R. Mayo-Smith. Statistics and Sociology. New York, 1896.

Allen Clapp Thomas. The Attitude of the Society of Friends toward Slavery, etc. (Reprinted from Vol. VIII, American Society of Church History.) New York, 1897.

Census of the United States, First to the Eleventh. Washington, 1790–1898.

George W. Williams. History of the Negro Race in America from 1619 to 1880. New York, 1883.

Joseph T. Willson. The Black Phalanx. Hartford, 1889.

Carroll D. Wright. Slums of Great Cities. Seventh Special Report of the United States Department of Labor. Washington, 1894.

✦ ✦ ✦

II. BOOKS AND PAMPHLETS RELATING TO PHILADELPHIA NEGROES

Benjamin C. Bacon. Statistics of the Colored People of Philadelphia. Philadelphia, 1856.

—— —— Ibid., Second Edition, with Statistics of Crime. Philadelphia, 1859.

A Brief History of the Movement to Abolish the Slums of Philadelphia. Philadelphia. (Pam.)

Collection of Reports of Charitable Institutions for Colored Persons. Philadelphia. (Ridgeway Library.)

Colored Enlistments. Philadelphia. (Pam. Philadelphia Library Co.)

Colored People in Philadelphia. Philadelphia. (Pam. Philadelphia Library Co.)

Colored Regiments. Philadelphia. (Pam. Philadelphia Library Co.)

Education and Employment Statistics of the Colored People of Philadelphia. (MS. in Library of Historical Association.)

Dr. E. O. Emerson. Vital Statistics of Philadelphia (in American Journal of Medical Sciences, July, 1848.)

[Friends.] A Brief Sketch of the Schools for Black People and Their Descendants Established by the Religious Society of Friends, in 1770. Philadelphia, 1867.

A. Mott. Biography of Colored People. Philadelphia. (Pam. Philadelphia Library Co.)

Edward Needles. Ten Years' Progress, or a Comparison of the State and Condition of the Colored People in the City and County of Philadelphia from 1837 to 1847. Philadelphia, 1849.

Daniel A. Payne. History of the A. M. E. Church. Nashville, 1891.

Report of the Committee Appointed for the Purpose of Securing to Colored People in Philadelphia the Right to the use of the Street Cars. Philadelphia, 1865. (Pam.)

Report of the Committee on the Comparative Health, Mortality, Length of Sentences, etc., of White and Colored Convicts. Philadelphia, 1849.

Frederick W. Spiers. The Street Railway System of Philadelphia, etc. Johns Hopkins University Studies. Ser. 15, Nos. 3–5. Baltimore, 1897.

The Present State and Condition of the Free People of Colour of the City of Philadelphia and Adjoining Districts, etc. Philadelphia, 1838.

A Statistical Inquiry into the Condition of the People of Color of the City and Districts of Philadelphia. Philadelphia, 1849.

Trades of the Colored People. Philadelphia, 1838.

John F. Watson. Annals of Philadelphia. Philadelphia, 1830.

A. W. Wayman. My Recollections of A. M. E. Ministers. Philadelphia, 1882.

Why Colored People in Philadelphia Are Excluded from the Street Cars. Philadelphia, 1866. (Pam., Two Editions.)

[John Woolman.] Considerations on Keeping Negroes. Philadelphia, 1784.

◆ ◆ ◆

III. BOOKS AND PAMPHLETS WRITTEN BY PHILADELPHIA NEGROES

Act of Incorporation, Causes and Motives of the African Episcopal Church of Philadelphia. Philadelphia, 1810.

Richard Allen. (First Bishop of A. M. E. Church.) The Life, Experience and Gospel Labours of the Rt. Rev. Richard Allen, etc. Written by himself. Philadelphia, 1833.

Richard Allen and Jacob Tapsico. The Doctrine and Discipline of the A. M. E. Church. Philadelphia, 1819.

Matthew Anderson. Presbyterianism and Its Relation to the Negro, Philadelphia, 1897.

Appeal of Forty Thousand Colored Citizens, Threatened with Disfranchisement, to the People of Pennsylvania. Philadelphia, 1838. (Pam.)

Jeremiah Asher. Autobiography. Philadelphia, 1862.

E. D. Bassett. Handbook on Hayti. Philadelphia.

J. J. G. Bias. Synopsis of Phrenology. Philadelphia, 1859.

Lorenzo Blackson. Autobiography. Philadelphia, 1861.

C. H. Brooks. Manual and History of the Grand United Order of Odd Fellows. 360 pp. Philadelphia, 1864.

Robert Campbell. A Pilgrimage to My Motherland; an Account of a Journey among the Egbas and Yorubas of Central Africa. Philadelphia, 1861.

W. Y. Catto. History of the Presbyterian Movement. Philadelphia, 1858.

Levi J. Coffin. The Relation of Baptized Children to the Church. Philadelphia, 1890. 106 pp.

Martin Robinson Delaney. Condition, Elevation, Emigration and Destiny of the Colored People of the United States, etc. Philadelphia, 1852.

William Douglass. Sermons Preached in the African Protestant Episcopal Church of St. Thomas', Philadelphia. Philadelphia, 1854.

William Douglass. Annals of St. Thomas' Church. Philadelphia, 1862.

John S. Durham. To Teach the Negro History. Philadelphia, 1898.

Frances E. W. Harper. Miscellaneous Poems. Boston, 1854.

—— ——. Forest Leaves. Baltimore, 1855.

—— ——. Iola Leroy: A Novel. Third Edition. Philadelphia, 1892. 280 pp.

Absalom Jones. A Thanksgiving Sermon. . . . On Account of the Abolition of the African Slave Trade, etc. Philadelphia, 1808. (Pam.)

Robert Jones. Fifty Years in the Lombard Street Central Presbyterian Church. Philadelphia, 1894. 170 pp.

H. T. Johnson. The Divine Logos. Philadelphia, 1890.

Jarena Lee. Journal. Philadelphia, 1849.

—— ——. The Color of Solomon. Philadelphia, 1895. 93 pp.

Minutes of the First Annual Convention of the People of Colour. Philadelphia, 1831. (Pam.)

Minutes of Third Annual Convention of Free Negroes. Philadelphia, 1833. (Pam.)

Mrs. N. T. Mossell. The Work of Afro-American Women. Philadelphia, 1894. 178 pp.

Proceedings of Convention of Colored Freemen of Pennsylvania. Philadelphia. (Pam.)

Robert Purvis. Remarks on the Life and Character of James Forten. (Pam.)

William Still. The Underground Railroad. Philadelphia, 1872. 780 pp.

Benjamin T. Tanner. An Apology for African Methodism. Baltimore, 1867. 468 pp.

—— ——. Theological Lectures. Nashville, 1894. 185 pp.

—— ——. An Outline of History and Government for A. M. E. Churchmen. Philadelphia, 1884. 206 pp.

[Joseph Willson.] Sketches of the Higher Classes of Colored Society in Philadelphia. Philadelphia, 1841.

Index

Note: Page numbers within braces denotes Endnote.

William Edward Burghardt Du Bois:
A Chronology

Compiled by Henry Louis Gates, Jr. and Terri Hume Oliver

1868	Born William Edward Burghardt Du Bois, 23 February, in Great Barrington, Massachusetts—the only child of Alfred Du Bois and Mary Silvina Burghardt. Mother and child move to family farm owned by Othello Burghardt, Mary Silvina's father, in South Egremont Plain.
1872	Othello Burghardt dies 19 September and family moves back to Great Barrington, where Mary Sylvina finds work as a domestic servant.
1879	Moves with mother to rooms on Railroad Street. Mother suffers stroke, which partially paralyzes her; she continues to work despite her disability.
1883–1885	Writes occasionally for *Springfield Republican*, the most influential newspaper in the region. Reports on local events for the *New York Globe*, a black weekly, and its successor, the *Freeman*.
1884	Graduates from Great Barrington High School. Works as time-keeper on a construction site.
1885	Mother dies 23 March at age 54. A scholarship is arranged by local Congregational churches so Du Bois can attend Fisk University in Nashville. Enters Fisk with sophomore standing. Contracts typhoid and is seriously ill in October; after recovering, resumes studies and becomes editor of the school newspaper, the *Fisk Herald*.
1886–1887	Teaches at a black school near Alexandria, Tennessee, for two summers. Begins singing with the Mozart Society at Fisk.
1888	Receives BA from Fisk. Enters Harvard College as a junior after receiving a Price-Greenleaf grant.
1890	Awarded second prize in Boylston oratorical competition. Receives BA *cum laude* in philosophy on 25 June. Delivers commencement oration on Jefferson Davis, which receives national press attention. Enters Harvard Graduate School in social science.

1891	Awarded MA in history from Harvard. Begins work on doctorate. Presents paper on the suppression of the African slave trade at meeting of American Historical Association in Washington, D.C.
1892	Awarded a Slater Fund grant to study in Germany at Friedrich Wilhelm University in Berlin.
1893	Grant is extended for an additional year.
1894	Denied doctoral degree at Friedrich Wilhelm University due to residency requirements. Denied further aid from Slater Fund; returns to Great Barrington. Receives teaching chair in classics at Wilberforce University in Xenia, Ohio.
1895	Awarded a PhD in history; he is the first black to receive a PhD from Harvard.
1896	Marries Nina Gomer, a student at Wilberforce. His doctoral thesis, *The Suppression of the African Slave-Trade to United States of America, 1638–1870,* is published as the first volume of Harvard's Historical Monograph Series. Hired by the University of Pennsylvania to conduct a sociological study on the black population of Philadelphia's Seventh Ward.
1897	Joins Alexander Crummell and other black intellectuals to found the American Negro Academy, an association dedicated to black scholarly achievement. Appointed professor of history and economics at Atlanta University. Begins editing a series of sociological studies on black life, the *Atlanta University Studies* (1898–1914). First child, Burghardt Comer Du Bois, is born in Great Barrington on 2 October.
1899	*The Philadelphia Negro* is published by the University of Pennsylvania. Burghardt Gomer Du Bois dies on 24 May in Atlanta and is buried in Great Barrington. Publishes articles in *Atlantic Monthly* and *The Independent.*
1900	In July attends first Pan-African Congress in London and is elected secretary. In an address to the congress, he declares that "the problem of the twentieth century is the problem of the color line." Enters an exhibit at Paris Exposition and wins grand prize for his display on black economic development. Daughter Nina Yolande born 21 October in Great Barrington.
1901	Publishes "The Freedman's Bureau" in *Atlantic Monthly.*
1902	Booker T. Washington offers Du Bois a teaching position at Tuskegee Institute, but Du Bois declines.
1903	*The Souls of Black Folk* is published in April. Publishes the essay "The Talented Tenth" in *The Negro Problem.*
1904	Resigns from Washington's Committee of Twelve for the Advancement of the Negro Race due to ideological differences. Publishes "Credo" in *The Independent.*
1905	Holds the first conference of the Niagara Movement and is named general secretary. Founds and edits *The Moon Illustrated Weekly.*

1906   Second meeting of the Niagara Movement. *The Moon* ceases publication. The Atlanta riots, in which white mobs target blacks, occur in September; Du Bois responds by writing his most famous poem, *A Litany of Atlanta*. After the riots Du Bois's wife and daughter move to Great Barrington.

1907   Niagara Movement in disarray due to debt and dissension. Founds and edits *Horizon*, a monthly paper that folds in 1910.

1908   Fourth conference of Niagara Movement; few attend.

1909   The National Negro Committee, an organization dominated by white liberals, is formed (it will later be renamed the National Association for the Advancement of Colored People [NAACP]); Du Bois joins. The fifth and last Niagara Conference is held. *John Brown*, a biography, is published.

1910   Appointed director of publications and research for the NAACP; becomes the only black member of the board of directors. Moves to New York City to found and edit *The Crisis*, the official publication of the NAACP.

1911   Attends Universal Races Conference in London. Publishes his first novel, *The Quest of the Silver Fleece*. Joins the Socialist Party.

1912   Endorses Woodrow Wilson in *The Crisis*. Resigns from Socialist Party.

1913   Writes and presents *The Star of Ethiopia*, a pageant staged to commemorate the fiftieth anniversary of emancipation.

1914   Supports women's suffrage in *The Crisis*. Supports the Allied effort in World War I despite declaring that imperialist rivalries are a cause of the war.

1915   Booker T. Washington dies on 14 November. *The Negro* is published. Protests D. W. Griffith's racist film *The Birth of a Nation*.

1917   Undergoes kidney operations early in the year. Supports the establishment of separate training camps for black officers as the only way to insure black participation in combat.

1918   In his July editorial for *The Crisis*, he publishes "Close Ranks," urging cooperation with white citizens. The War Department offers Du Bois a commission as a captain in the army in an effort to address racial issues, but the offer is withdrawn after controversy. Goes to Europe in December to evaluate the conditions of black troops for the NAACP.

1919   Organizes the first Pan-African Conference in Paris, and is elected executive secretary. Returns to the U.S. in April and writes the editorial "Returning Soldiers," which the U.S. postmaster Albert Burleson tries to suppress; the issue sells 106,000 copies, the most ever for *The Crisis*.

1920   Founds and edits *The Brownies' Book*, a monthly magazine for children. Publishes *Darkwater: Voices from within the Veil*, a collection of essays.

1921	The second Pan-African Conference is held in London, Brussels, and Paris. Du Bois signs group protest against Henry Ford's support of the anti-Semitic forgery, *Protocols of the Elders of Zion*.
1922	Works for passage of the Dyer Anti-Lynching Bill, which is blocked by Senate.
1923	Writes "Back to Africa," an article attacking Garvey for encouraging racial division. Organizes the third Pan-African Conference in London, Paris, and Lisbon; declines to attend Paris session due to disproval of French assimilationists. Receives the Spingarn Medal from the NAACP. Travels to Liberia to represent the United States at the Liberian presidential inauguration.
1924	Publishes *The Gift of Black Folk: The Negroes in the Making of America*.
1925	Contributes "The Negro Mind Reaches Out" to Alain Locke's *The New Negro: An Interpretation*, one of the most influential works of the Harlem Renaissance.
1926	Founds the Krigwa Players, a Harlem theater group. Travels to the Soviet Union to examine life after the Bolshevik Revolution. Praises Soviet achievements in *The Crisis*.
1927	The fourth and last Pan-African Conference is held in New York City.
1928	Daughter Yolande weds the poet Countee Cullen in Harlem; the marriage ends within a year. Du Bois's novel, *Dark Princess, A Romance*, is published.
1929	*The Crisis* faces financial collapse.
1930	Awarded honorary Doctor of Laws degree from Howard University.
1932	Du Bois's daughter Yolande and her second husband, Arnett Williams, have a daughter, Du Bois Williams.
1933	Losing faith in the possibilities of integration, Du Bois begins to publicly examine his position on segregation. Accepts a one-year visiting professorship at Atlanta University. Relinquishes the editorship of *The Crisis* but retains general control of the magazine.
1934	Writes editorials encouraging voluntary segregation and criticizing the integrationist policies of the NAACP. Resigns as editor of *The Crisis* and from the NAACP. Accepts the chairmanship in sociology at Atlanta University. Named the editor in chief of the *Encyclopedia of the Negro*, which is never completed or published.
1935	Publishes the revolutionary historical study, *Black Reconstruction*.
1936	Spends five months in Germany on a grant to study industrial education. Travels through Poland, the Soviet Union, Manchuria, China, and Japan.
1938	Receives honorary Doctor of Laws degree from Atlanta University and honorary Doctor of Letters degree from Fisk.
1939	*Black Folk, Then and Now*, a revised edition of *The Negro* is published.

1940   Publishes his first autobiography, *Dusk of Dawn*. Founds and edits *Phylon*, a quarterly magazine examining black issues. Awarded honorary Doctorate of Humane Letters at Wilberforce.

1941–1942   Proposes and then coordinates the study of southern blacks for black land-grant colleges.

1943   Organizes the First Conference of Negro Land-Grant Colleges at Atlanta University. Informed by Atlanta University that he must retire by 1944, he attempts to have the policy reversed.

1944   Named first black member of the National Institute of Arts and Letters. Despite his protests, he is retired by Atlanta University. Although hesitant to work with Walter White, he rejoins the NAACP as director of special research and moves back to New York. Publishes the essay "My Evolving Program for Negro Freedom" in Rayford Logan's collection *What the Negro Wants*.

1945   Writes a weekly column for the *Chicago Defender*. Serves as consultant, with Mary McLeod Bethune and Walter White, at the San Francisco conference that drafts the United Nations charter; criticizes the charter for failing to oppose colonialism. In October he presides at the Fifth Pan-African Conference in Manchester, England. Nina Du Bois suffers a stroke, which paralyzes her left side. Publishes the first volume of *Encyclopedia of the Negro: Preparatory Volume* with coauthor Guy B. Johnson. Publishes an anti-imperialist analysis of the postwar era, *Color and Democracy: Colonies and Peace*. Resigns from the American Association of University Professors in protest of conferences held in segregated hotels.

1946   Invites leaders of twenty organizations to New York to draft a petition to the United Nations on behalf of African Americans; the appeal becomes an NAACP project.

1947   Edits and writes the introduction to *An Appeal to the World*, a collection of essays sponsored by the NAACP to enlist international support for the fight against racial discrimination in America. At the United Nations, the appeal is supported by the Soviet Union but opposed by the United States. Publishes *The World and Africa*.

1948   Fired from the NAACP after his memorandum critical of Walter White and the NAACP board of directors appears in the *New York Times*. Supports Henry Wallace, the Progressive Party candidate for president. Takes unpaid position as vice chairman (with Paul Robeson) of the Council of African Affairs, an organization listed as "subversive" by the U.S. attorney general. Begins writing for the *National Guardian*.

1949   Helps sponsor and addresses the Cultural and Scientific Conference for World Peace in New York City. Attends the First World Congress of the Defenders of Peace in Paris. Travels to the All-Union Conference of Peace Proponents in Moscow.

1950   Nina Gomer Du Bois dies in Baltimore in July; she is buried in Great Barrington. Elected chairman of the Peace Information

Center, an organization dedicated to the international peace movement and the banning of nuclear weapons. Organization disbands under pressure from the Department of Justice. Du Bois is nominated by the American Labor Party for U.S. senator from New York. Receives 4 percent of the vote statewide, 15 percent in Harlem.

1951   Secretly marries Shirley Graham, aged 45, a writer, teacher, and civil rights activist, on Valentine's Day. Indicted earlier that month as an "unregistered foreign agent" under the McCormick Act: Du Bois, along with four other officers of the Peace Information Center, is alleged to be agents of foreign interests. He suffers the indignity of being handcuffed, searched, and fingerprinted before being released on bail in Washington, D.C. National lecture tours and a fundraising campaign for his defense expenses raise over $35,000. The five-day trial in Washington ends in acquittal.

1952   Publishes *In Battle for Peace*, an account of the trial. The State Department refuses Du Bois a passport on grounds that his foreign travel is not in the national interest. Later, the State Department demands a statement declaring that he is not a Communist Party member; Du Bois refuses. Advocacy of leftwing political positions widens the distance between Du Bois and the black mainstream.

1953   Prints a eulogy for Stalin in *National Guardian*. Reads 23rd Psalm at the funeral of Julius and Ethel Rosenberg, executed as Soviet spies. Awarded International Peace Prize by the World Peace Council.

1954   Surprised by the Supreme Court decision in *Brown v. Topeka Board of Education*, which outlaws public school segregation, Du Bois declares "I have seen the impossible happen."

1955   Refused a U.S. passport to attend the World Youth Festival in Warsaw, Poland.

1956   Supports Reverend Martin Luther King Jr. during the Montgomery bus boycott. Refused a passport in order to lecture in the People's Republic of China.

1957   Publishes *The Ordeal of Mansart*, the first volume of the *Black Flame*, a trilogy of historical novels chronicling black life from Reconstruction to the mid-twentieth century. A bust of Du Bois is unveiled at the Schomburg Collection of the New York Public Library. Refused a passport to attend independence ceremonies in Ghana. His great-grandson Arthur Edward McFarlane II is born.

1958   A celebration for Du Bois's ninetieth birthday is held at the Roosevelt Hotel in New York City; 2,000 people attend. Begins writing *The Autobiography of W. E. B. Du Bois*, drawing largely from earlier work. A Supreme Court ruling allows Du Bois to obtain a passport. His subsequent world tour includes England, France, Belgium, Holland, Czechoslovakia, East Germany, and the Soviet Union. He receives an honorary doctorate from Humbolt University in East Berlin, known as Friedrich Wilhelm University when Du Bois attended in 1892–1894.

1959   Meets with Nikita Khrushchev. In Beijing, makes broadcast to Africa over Radio Beijing and meets with Mao Zedong and Zhou Enlai. Awarded the International Lenin Prize. Publishes the second volume of the *Black Flame* trilogy, *Mansart Builds a School.*

1960   Participates in the celebration of Ghana's establishment as a republic. Travels to Nigeria for the inauguration of its first African governor-general.

1961   Du Bois's daughter Yolande dies of a heart attack in March. *Worlds of Color*, the final book in the *Black Flame* trilogy, is published. Du Bois accepts the invitation of Kwame Nkrumah to move to Ghana and direct a revival of the *Encyclopedia Africana* project. Before leaving for Africa, Du Bois applies for membership in the Communist Party.

1962   Travels to China. His autobiography is published in the Soviet Union.

1963   Becomes a citizen of Ghana. Turns ninety-five in February. Dies in Accra, Ghana, on 27 August, on the eve of the civil rights march on Washington. W. E. B. Du Bois is buried in a state funeral in Accra on the 29th.

1968   *The Autobiography of W. E. B. Du Bois* is published in the United States.

1992   Honored by the United States Postal Service with a 29-cent commemorative stamp as part of the Black Heritage Series, and again in 1998, with a 32-cent commemorative stamp.

1999   Du Bois's efforts to produce alternately an encyclopedia of the Negro and of Africa and Africans are realized when *Encarta Africana* is published by Microsoft, and *Africana: The Encyclopedia of the African and African American Experience*, edited by Kwame Anthony Appiah and Henry Louis Gates Jr. is published by Basic Civitas Books. In 2005 a second much-expanded edition of *Africana* is published by Oxford University Press.

Selected Bibliography

WORKS OF W. E. B. DU BOIS

The Suppression of the African Slave-Trade to the United States of America, 1638–1870. New York: Longmans, Green, 1896.

Atlanta University Publications on the Study of Negro Problems. Publications of the Atlanta University Conferences, ed. Du Bois (1898–1913).

The Philadelphia Negro: A Social Study. Boston: Ginn and Company, 1899.

The Souls of Black Folk: Essays and Sketches. Chicago: A. C. McClurg, 1911.

John Brown. Philadelphia: George W. Jacobs, 1909.

The Quest of the Silver Fleece: A Novel. Chicago: A. C. McClurg, 1911.

The Negro. New York: Harcourt, Brace, 1928.

Darkwater: Voices from within the Veil. New York: Harcourt, Brace and Howe, 1920.

The Gift of Black Folk: Negroes in the Making of America. Boston: Stratford, 1924.

Dark Princess: A Romance. New York: Harcourt, Brace, 1928.

Africa—Its Place in Modern History. Girard, Kansas: Haldeman-Julius, 1930.

Africa, Its Geography, People, and Products. Girard, Kansas: Haldeman-Julius, 1930.

Black Reconstruction: An Essay toward a History of the Part Which Black Folk Played in the Attempt to Reconstruct Democracy in America, 1860–1880. New York: Harcourt, Brace, 1935.

Black Folk Then and Now: An Essay in the History and Sociology of the Negro Race. New York: Henry Holt, 1939.

Dusk of Dawn: An Essay toward an Autobiography of a Race Concept. New York: Harcourt, Brace, 1940.

Color and Democracy: Colonies and Peace. New York: Harcourt, Brace, 1945.

Du Bois, W. E. B., and Guy B. Johnson. *Encyclopedia of the Negro, Preparatory Volume with Reference Lists and Reports.* New York: Phelps-Stokes Fund, 1946.

The World and Africa: An Inquiry into the Part Which Africa Has Played in World History. New York: Masses & Mainstream, 1947.

I Take My Stand for Peace. New York: Masses & Mainstream, 1951.

The Ordeal of Mansart. New York: Mainstream, 1957.

In Battle for Peace: The Story of My 83rd Birthday. With Comment by Shirley Graham. New York: Masses & Mainstream, 1952.

Fourty-Two Years of the USSR [sic]. Chicago: Baan Books, 1959.

Worlds of Color. New York: Mainstream, 1961.

An ABC of Color: Selections from over a Half Century of the Writings of W. E. B. Du Bois. Berlin: Seven Seas, 1963.

The Autobiography of W. E. B. Du Bois: A Soliloquy on Viewing My Life from the Last Decade of Its First Century, ed. Herbert Aptheker. New York: International Publishers, 1968.

COLLECTIONS

Aptheker, Herbert, ed. *Creative Writings by W. E. B. Du Bois: A Pageant, Poems, Short Stories, and Playlets.* New York: Kraus-Thomson Organization, 1985.

Aptheker, Herbert, ed. *The Complete Published Works of W. E. B. Du Bois.* 35 vols. Millwood, NY: Kraus-Thomson, 1973.

Aptheker, Herbert, ed. *The Correspondence of W. E. B. Du Bois.* 3 vols. Amherst: University of Massachusetts Press, 1973–1978.

Aptheker, Herbert, ed. *Writings by W. E. B. Du Bois in periodicals Edited by Others.* 4 vols. Millwood, NY: Kraus-Thomson, 1982.

Foner, Philip S., ed. *W. E. B. Du Bois Speaks: Speeches and Addresses 1890–1919.* New York: Pathfinder, 1970.

Huggins, Nathan I., ed. *W. E. B. Du Bois: Writings.* New York: Library of America, 1986.

Lewis, David Levering, ed. *W. E. B. Du Bois: A Reader.* New York: Henry Holt, 1985.

Sundquist, Eric J., ed. *The Oxford W. E. B. Du Bois Reader.* New York: Oxford University Press, 1996.

BIBLIOGRAPHIES

Aphtheker, Herbert. *Annotated Bibliography of the Published Writings of W. E. B. Du Bois.* Millwood, NY: Kraus-Thomson, 1973.

McDonnell, Robert W., and Paul C. Partington. *W. E. B. Du Bois: A Bibliography of Writings About Him.* Whittier, CA: Paul C. Partington Book Publisher, 1989.

Partington, Paul C. *W. E. B. Du Bois: A Bibliography of His Published Writings.* Whittier, CA: Paul C. Partington Book Publisher, 1977.

BIOGRAPHIES

Broderick, Francis L. *W. E. B. Du Bois: A Negro Leader in Time of Crisis.* Stanford: Stanford University Press, 1959.

Du Bois, Shirley Graham. *His Day is Marching On: A Memoir of W. E. B. Du Bois.* Philadelphia: Lippincott, 1971.

Lewis, David Levering. *W. E. B. Du Bois: The Fight for Equality and the American Century, 1919–1963.* New York: Henry Holt, 2000.

Marable, Manning. *W. E. B. Du Bois: Black Radical Democrat.* Boston: Twayne, 1986.

Rudwick, Elliot M. *W. E. B. Du Bois: Propagandist of the Negro Protest.* 1960; reprint. New York: Atheneum, 1968.

CRITICAL WORKS

Appiah, Anthony. "The Uncompleted Argument: Du Bois and the Illusion of Race." *Critical Inquiry* 12 (Autumn 1985): 21–37.

Aptheker, Herbert. *The Literary Legacy of W. E. B. Du Bois.* Whit Plains, NY: Kraus International, 1989.

Ashton, Susanna. "Du Bois's 'Horizon': Documenting Movements of the Color Line." *MELUS* 26.4 (2001): 3–23.

Baker, Houston A., Jr. "The Black Man of Culture: W. E. B. Du bois and *The Souls of Black Folk*." In *Long Black Song.* Charlottesville: University of Virginia Press, 1972.

Balfour, Lawrie. "Representative Women: Slavery, Citizenship, and Feminist Theory in Du Bois's 'Damnation of Women.'" *Hypatia: A Journal of Feminist Philosophy* 20.3 (2005): 127–148.

Bauerlein, Mark. "Booker T. Washington and W. E. B. Du Bois: The Origins of a Bitter Intellectual Battle." *Journal of Blacks in Higher Education* 46 (Winter 2004–2005): 106–114.

Bell, Bernard, Emily Grosholz, and James Stewart, eds. *W. E. B. Du Bois on Race and Culture: Philosophy, Politics, and Poetics.* New York: Routledge, Chapman, and Hall, 1996.

Bhabha, Homi K. "The Black Savant and the *Dark Princess.*" *ESQ: A Journal of the American Renaissance* 50.1–3 (2004): 137–155.

Blight, David W. "W. E. B. Du Bois and the Struggle for American Historical Memory." In *History and Memory in African-American Culture*, ed. Genevieve Fabre and Robert O'Meally. New York: Oxford University Press, 1994.

Bremen, Brian A. "Du Bois, Emerson, and the 'Fate' of Black Folk." *American Literary Realism* 24 (Spring 1992): 80–88.

Bruce, Dickson D., Jr. "W. E. B. Du Bois and the Idea of Double Consciousness." *American Literature: A Journal of Literary History, Criticism, and Bibliography* 64.2 (June 1992): 299–309.

Byerman, Keith. *Seizing the Word: History, Art, and the Self in the Work of W. E. B. Du Bois.* Athens: University of Georgia Press, 1994.

Castronovo, Russ. "Beauty along the Color Line: Lynching, Aesthetics and the *Crisis*." *PMLA: Publications of the Modern Language Association of America* 36.2 (2006): 1443–1159.

Crouch, Stanley, and Playthell Benjamin. *Reconsidering the Souls of Black Folk: Thoughts on the Groundbreaking Classic Work of W. E. B. Du Bois.* Philadelphia: Running Press, 2002.

Early, Gerald, ed. *Lure and Loathing: Essays on Race, Identity, and the Ambivalence of Assimilation.* New York: Allen Lane, 1993.

Fisher, Rebecka Rutledge. "Cultural Artifacts and the Narrative of History: W. E. B. Du Bois and the Exhibiting of Culture at the 1900 Paris Exposition Universelle." *MFS: Modern Fiction Studies* 51.4 (2005): 741–774.

Fontenot, Chester J., Mary Alice Morgan, and Sarah Gardner, eds. *W. E. B. Du Bois and Race.* Macon, Georgia: Mercer University Press, 2001.

Frederickson, George. "The Double Life of W. E. B. Du Bois." *New York Review of Books* 48.2 (February 8, 2001): 34–36.

Frederickson, George. *The Black Image in the White Mind: The Debate on Afro-American Character and Destiny, 1817–1914*. New York: Harper and Row, 1971.

Gabiddon, Shaun L. "W. E. B. Du Bois: Pioneering American Criminologist." *Journal of Black Studies* 31.5 (2001): 581–599.

Gooding-Williams, Robert. "Du Bois's Counter-Sublime." *The Massachusetts Review: A Quarterly of Literature, the Arts and Public Affairs* 35.2 (Summer 1994): 202–224.

Herring, Scott. "Du Bois and the Minstrels." *MELUS* 22 (Summer 1997): 3–18.

Hubbard, Dolan, ed. *The Souls of Black Folk One Hundred Years Later*. Columbia, Missouri: University of Missouri Press, 2003.

Jones, Gavin. "'Whose Line Is It Anyway?' W. E. B. Du Bois and the Language of the Color-Line." In *Race Consciousness: African-American Studies for the New Century*, ed. Judith Jackson Fossett and Jeffrey A. Tucker. New York: New York University Press, 1997.

Judy, Ronald A. T., ed. "Sociology Hesitant: Thinking with W. E. B. Du Bois." Special Issue: *Boundary 2: An International Journal of Literature and Culture* 27.3 (2000).

Juguo, Zhang. *W. E. B. Du Bois and the Quest for the Abolition of the Color Line*. New York: Routledge, 2001.

Kirschke, Amy. "Du Bois, *The Crisis*, and Images of Africa and the Diaspora." In *African Diasporas in the New and Old Worlds: Consciousness and Imagination*, ed. Geneviève Fabre and Benesch Klaus. Amsterdam: Rodopi, 2004. 239–262.

Lemke, Sieglinde. "Transatlantic Relations: The German Du Bois." In *German? American? Literature? New Directions in German-American Studies*, ed. Winfried Fluck and Werner Sollors. New York: Peter Lang, 2002. 207–215.

McCaskill, Barbara, and Caroline Gebhard, eds. and introd. *Post-Bellum, Pre-Harlem: African American Literature and Culture*. New York: New York University Press, 2006.

McKay, Nellie. "W. E. B. Du Bois: The Black Women in His Writings—Selected Fictional and Autobiographical Portraits." In *Critical Essays on W. E. B. Du Bois*, ed. William L. Andrews. Boston: G. K. Hall, 1985.

Meier, August. "The Paradox of W. E. B. Du Bois." In *Negro Thought in America, 1880–1915; Radical Ideologies in the Age of Booker T. Washington*. Ann Arbor: University of Michigan Press, 1963.

Miller, Monica. "W. E. B. Du Bois and the Dandy as Diasporic Race Man." *Callaloo* 26.3 (2003): 738–765.

Mizrunchi, Susan. "Neighbors, Strangers, Corpses: Death and Sympathy in the Early Writings of W. E. B. Du Bois." In *Centuries' Ends, Narrative Means*, ed. Robert Newman. Stanford, CA: Stanford University Press, 1996.

Moses, Wilson Jeremiah. *Creative Conflict in African American Thought: Frederick Douglass, Alexander Crummell, Booker T. Washington, W. E. B. Du Bois, and Marcus Garvey*. Cambridge, England: Cambridge University Press, 2004.

Pauley, Garth E. "W. E. B. Du Bois on Woman Suffrage: A Critical Analysis of His *Crisis* Writings." *Journal of Black Studies* 30.3 (2000): 383–410.

Peterson, Dale. "Notes from the Underworld: Dostoyevsky, Du Bois, and the Discovery of the Ethnic Soul." *Massachusetts Review* 35 (Summer 1994): 225–247.

Posnock, Ross. "The Distinction of Du Bois: Aesthetics, Pragmatism, Politics." *American Literary History* 7 (Fall 1995): 500–524.

Rampersad, Arnold. *The Art and Imagination of W. E. B. Du Bois*. Cambridge, MA: Harvard University Press, 1976.

Rampersad, Arnold, and Deborah E. McDowell, eds. *Slavery and the Literary Imagination: Du Bois's* The Souls of Black Folk. Baltimore: Johns Hopkins University Press, 1989.

Rothberg, Michael. "W. E. B. Du Bois in Warsaw: Holocaust Memory and the Color Line, 1949–1952." *Yale Journal of Criticism* 14.1 (2001): 169–189.

Schneider, Ryan. "Sex and the Race Man: Imagining Interracial Relationships in W. E. B. Du Bois's *Darkwater*." *Arizona Quarterly: A Journal of American Literature, Culture, and Theory* 59.2 (2003): 59–80.

Schrager, Cynthia D. "Both Sides of the Veil: Race, Science, and Mysticism in W. E. B. Du Bois." *American Quarterly* 48 (December 1996): 551–587.

Siemerling, Winfried. "W. E. B. Du Bois, Hegel, and the Staging of Alterity." *Callaloo* 24.1 (2001): 325–333.

Smith, Shawn Michelle. *Photography on the Color Line: W. E. B. Du Bois, Race, and Visual Culture*. Durham: Duke University Press, 2004.

Sundquist, Eric J. "Swing Low: *The Souls of Black Folk*." In *To Wake the Nations*. Cambridge, MA: Harvard University Press, 1993.

Temperley, Howard, Michael B. Katz, and Thomas J. Sugrue. "W. E. B. Du Bois, Race, and the City." *The Times Literary Supplement*. No. 4996 (1999).

"The Study of African American Problems: W. E. B. Du Bois's Agenda, Then and Now." *Annals of the American Academy of Political and Social Science* 568 (March 2000): 1–313.

Warren, Kenneth W. "Troubled Black Humanity in *The Souls of Black Folk* and *The Autobiography of an Ex-Colored Man*." In *The Cambridge Companion to American Realism and Naturalism: Howells to London*, ed. Donald Pizer. Cambridge: Cambridge University Press, 1995.

West, Cornel. "W. E. B. Du Bois: The Jamesian Organic Intellectual." In *The American Evasion of Philosophy: A Genealogy of Pragmatism*. Madison: University of Wisconsin Press, 1989.

Williamson, Joel. *The Crucible of Race: Black-White Relations in the American South Since Emancipation*. New York: Oxford University Press, 1984.

Wolters, Raymond. *Du Bois and His Rivals*. Columbia, Missouri: University of Missouri Press, 2002.

Zamir, Shamoon. *Dark Voices: W. E. B. Du Bois and American Thought, 1888–1903*. Chicago: University of Chicago Press, 1995.

Zamir, Shamoon. "'The Sorrow Songs'/'Song of Myself': Du Bois, the Crisis of Leadership, and Prophetic Imagination." In *The Black Columbiad: Defining Moments in African American Literature and Culture*. Cambridge, MA: Harvard University Press, 1994.

Zwarg, Christina. "Du Bois on Trauma: Psychoanalysis and the Would-Be Black Savant." *Cultural Critique* 51 (2002): 1–39.

Printed and bound by CPI Group (UK) Ltd, Croydon, CR0 4YY